SAVING
JAHAN

HANS JOSEPH FELLMANN

A Russian Hill Press Book
United States • United Kingdom • Australia

Russian Hill Press

The publisher is not responsible for websites or their content that are not owned by the publisher.

ISBN: 9781734122046
Library of Congress Control Number: 2020901941

Cover Design by Ghislain Viau

For Tommy

Author's Note

This adventure is based on actual events that occurred during my Peace Corps service in the Central Asian republic of Turkmenistan from the fall of 2006 to the winter of 2008. Some names, locations, descriptions, and scenes have been altered or changed completely to protect the identities of those involved and to suit the flow of the story.

A note on foreign terms: Turkmen and other foreign language terms appear in italics at first mention, roman thereafter. In cases where it might be helpful to the reader, explanatory footnotes have been added; otherwise, Turkmen and other terms are listed in a glossary at the back of the book.

JAHAN (Persian: جهان)——A Persian word meaning world or universe.

1

IT WAS A SATURDAY morning. I crawled out of bed, scratched myself, and plopped in front of the computer. After clicking through a few sites, I came to it: an ad for a Peace Corps Cultural Festival at Peacock Meadow in San Francisco. I scrolled down and checked the date. September 17, 2005.

"That's today," I mumbled. I got on the horn and called my buddy Bert. He answered with a mouth full of cereal.

"Chuuuuuuup?" he said.

"Hey man, there's a Cultural Festival for the Peace Corps in SF today. Wanna roll?"

"I guess."

I threw on some clothes and hopped in my Toyota. There was fuel in my guts because something finally seemed to be happening. A month prior, I had finished the grueling two-week process of filling out my online application for the Peace Corps. They hadn't responded. Since finishing at UCSD[1] in June of that year, I'd only come up with two other options for what to do with myself. The first was sailing away to the Adriatic to start a travel company. The second was to continue living with my parents in Livermore and open a hookah lounge with Bert. My folks were less than thrilled about either option. This Peace Corps thing had to work.

---

[1] University of California San Diego.

I picked up Bert and we drove to the nearest BART.[2] We took the train into the city. We got off at Civic Center and walked the mile to Peacock Meadow. The whole way I acted like a moron.

"This shit's gonna be fuckin' baumish."[3] I said, spinning circles around Bert.

He yawned and plucked the underwear from his ass crack.

"We'll see."

The guy was playing it cool, but he was curious too. Same as me, his options after having graduated with a BA in dingleberry farming were severely limited.

We showed up at around 4:00 p.m. The festival was already dying down. A few toddlers were up front pushing an inflatable globe around. Behind them were a dozen tented "tribal villages" representing every region of the world. A handful of people wandered between each tent. One guy caught my eye. He was dressed in a puffy black two-piece with silver trimming. He wore swirled eyeliner and purple shoes that curled up at the toe. Bert looked at him and scoffed.

"Check out Mr. Faggot-Ass Arabian Nights," he said.

I chuckled. I told Bert I was going in for a closer look.

He collapsed on a bench. "You go right ahead," he said. "I'ma sit here n' watch these kids dick around with the globe."

"Suit yourself."

I walked toward the villages. I wanted to find one that represented a part of the world I'd never seen. I'd already been to most of Europe, Latin America, and Asia. I'd even dipped into North Africa and the Caribbean. None of the villages representing these places piqued my interest. I wandered through them—past tiny Asian girls waving their long fingernails in circles, and leathery dickheads in ponchos serving beef cubes on skewers—till I came to a tent that read "Central Asia." The woman running it was tall and wiry. An

---

[2] Bay Area Rapid Transit.

[3] Great; awesome; excellent; delicious (when referring to food). See Hans Joseph Fellmann, *Chuck Life's a Trip*, Russian Hill Press, 2019.

anemic blond ponytail ran down her back. She stood sorting stacks of paper. I approached her with a smile.

"Hey, my name's Johann," I said. "And I'm interested in joining the Peace Corps. Were you a volunteer?"

She winced and sat down. Then she looked up at me with eyes like two ping pong balls floating on still water.

"Yes, I was a volunteer," she said. "Name's Trish. How can I help you?"

"Well," I said, blinking, "I'm interested in maybe going to Central Asia. You served there, right?"

She cocked a half-smile and laced her fingers across her chest.

"Yeah, I served there," she said. "Twenty-seven months of teaching English in the desert of Uzbekistan. Now I'm here doing this. Any more questions?"

"Um, did you like it?"

She spiked an eyebrow. "It was hell on Earth," she said.

At this point, any normal person woulda vanished. I pulled up a chair and pressed her for details. She gave them like she was handing me a loaded pistol.

"I served in a tiny village about a hundred miles from the capital, Tashkent," she said. "In the summer, it was hot enough to melt plastic, and in the winter, it was so cold the water froze in our family well. Electricity was sporadic year-round. I tried to teach the local kids English, but they weren't having it. This pissed me off at the time, but it makes sense now. Most of my students would never make it out of that village. So, what use did they have for English when adult life for them would consist of herding goats or picking cotton?"

Despite my travels, I could scarcely fathom this. And while it did seem like hell, there had to have been a bit of good sprinkled in. I asked Trish for some positives.

"Well, Uzbekistan is a Muslim country," she said. "So, if you're a Western chick, you're kinda screwed. Most days, when I wasn't teaching, I had to sit at home with my host family and cook or clean. For the guys, it was a little better. They could at least go out with the local men, drink shitty vodka, and bang Russian prostitutes."

"God, that sounds awful. Why the hell did you stay?"

She zeroed in on me again with her big scary eyeballs.

"Because," she said, "when you make a commitment, you stick with it."

I gulped. The biggest commitment I'd ever made was saving tips I'd earned delivering pizzas, so I could go on summer trips with my childhood buddies. I needed something more than just stick with it. I asked Trish for anything at all. She gave me a little yellow smile.

"Don't go out there trying to save the world," she said. "Just find one *real* reason to stay. The rest will fall into place."

A WEEK LATER, Peace Corps contacted me regarding my application. They invited me for a personal interview the following Monday. I celebrated by raiding my dad's wine rack. On Monday morning I took BART into the city. I looked like a Mormon missionary who'd fallen off the wagon. I had on a wrinkled white collared, black slacks, scuffed shoes, and a blue tie that poked sideways. My hair stuck up in gelled knots. My eyes were patches of cranberry worms. I arrived at the SF branch of Peace Corps five minutes before my interview. I hit the john for my wake-me-up ritual—three splashes of cold water and a slap to the face, followed by a "Get it together, shithead," in the mirror. I cursed my way back to the waiting room. The receptionist looked at me and smirked.

"Ms. Alva will see you now," she said.

"Okay."

I walked down the corridor toward her office. Ms. Alva came out big as a dugong at a Sunday brunch and greeted me at the door.

"Well, you must be Mr. Felmanstien," she said.

"The one and only," I replied.

We shook hands and went in. I sat in the chair in front of her desk and looked around. Her walls were plastered with photos of her stuck between rows of gangly African tribesmen. I asked her where she'd served, and she grinned.

"I was in Ethiopia," she said, easing into her hissing chair. "Three wonderful years."

"Really? That's pretty cool."

I knew dick about Ethiopia, except it was at the rear end of nowhere and had good food and hot women. The same was true of Georgia, which made it and Ethiopia my top two picks. I mentioned my desire to serve in these countries. Ms. Alva clasped her hands together.

"That's excellent," she said. "I'll definitely keep it in mind."

After a bit more chitchat, Ms. Alva picked the smile from her lips and placed it neatly in her pencil tray. She then proceeded to peel me back like a yogurt lid to ascertain why I wanted to be a volunteer. Canned phrases like "cultural enlightenment," "community development," and "global awareness" fell from my lips like crap-drops. By the end of it, we were staring at each other over a heaping pile of bullshit. Ms. Alva furrowed her brow and breathed in through her nose.

"Soooo" she said, "you wouldn't be just another one of those middle-class, post-university travel addicts looking for a free ticket to anywhere and a chance to avoid adulthood for another two-and-a-half years, now would you?"

I nearly choked. My mind raced back and forth behind my skull. Bells were ringing and devils were singing. It took me three deep breaths, ten cracked knuckles, and a furtive ball-pinch to compose myself.

"Absolutely not," I said. "I wanna do some good and change lives. And hey, if I change my own life in the process, all the better."

Ms. Alva squinted at me. I tried to smile but opened my mouth like I might for a dentist. The scene hung that way for an eternal minute. Ms. Alva plucked that wedge of sunshine from her pencil tray and spread it back across her lips.

"In that case," she said, "I'd be honored to nominate you as a volunteer, Johann."

THE FOLLOWING WEEK I received a letter from the Peace Corps. It congratulated me for having been nominated a volunteer then unfurled into a spiraling staircase of steps I had to take to ensure that I was legally, mentally, and physically fit to serve. I kicked myself for having been so honest about my past during the online application process. I knew it would take months to finish what Peace Corps was asking of me.

I tackled the legal and head checks first. They were a bitch, but I completed them inside two weeks. The final hurdle was being medically cleared. I'd had many injuries as an adolescent and split a pretty heap of asses as a young adult, which meant the number of tests and checkups I had to undergo was staggering. The doctors tested my blood, spit, and urine for every kind of drug, disease, chemical, and congenital defect in the book. Then they examined a "bone deformity" in my left foot, an atrophied muscle in my left calf, four damaged bones in my left hand, one damaged bone in my right hand, three suspicious freckles on my nutsack, and finally, a "right bundle branch block," which is basically a heart defect that inhibits the right ventricle from opening correctly. Since cardiac problems run in my family, this last bodily fuck-up of mine scared me the most. I nearly fainted with relief when the doctors told me that it was no big deal.

When March of '06 rolled around, it seemed I was in the clear. I'd mailed my shit to Peace Corps and gotten a thumbs up on all of it. The only things left to do were stack cash and pack for an 85-day trip around the world I had planned with my buddies. I'd talk about it at length, but that's another book. While on a supply run to REI one day,[4] I got a call. It was a lady from Peace Corps.

"There's an issue with your medical file," she said.

"An issue?"

"Yes. We've just done a final review and it says here you passed a small kidney stone back in 2000."

"Yeah, so?"

---

[4] A retail chain selling outdoor and fitness gear.

"*Sooo*, we're gonna need to have you get your bladder checked before we can give you final clearance."

I about chucked my phone through the windshield. I took a deep breath and straightened my neck. I thanked the lady for the heads-up. The next day I called our family urologist, Dr. Nguyen. The receptionist who answered told me the guy had changed offices.

"But his replacement, Dr. Hong, would be happy to see you," she said.

I came in the following Monday for my appointment. I was hungover and grouchy. The receptionist greeted me with a smile.

"The doctor will see you now," she said.

I nodded and walked to the back. Dr. Hong was standing in the hall waiting. He was a pudgy little smurf with black hair and shiny cheekbones. I shook his hand and it wilted like steamed cabbage. We exchanged pleasantries, and he took me to the examination room. He asked me some questions about my kidney stone. I gave him half-answers and eyed my surroundings. Everything seemed pretty standard except for the seat behind me. It was raised and reclined with two big leg braces, bent at the knee and spread apart. I asked Dr. Hong what that was all about, and he blinked once behind his specs.

"That's where I'll be conducting your bladder exam," he said.

I didn't like it but figured what the hell. I dropped my pants, whipped it out, and got in the seat. I assumed Dr. Hong would do some kinda touchy-feely crap followed by a few X-rays. You can imagine my surprise when he pulled out a digital TV screen with side-handles and a twelve-inch black proboscis hanging off the front.

"What the fuck are you gonna do with that?" I yelled.

A bead of sweat trickled down Dr. Hong's cheek.

"Don't be alarmed," he said. "I'm going to insert this tube camera gently into your urethra."

"Like hell you are."

I cupped my junk and scrambled myself up. Then I remembered all the shit I'd been through to get to this point. Reason told me one more turd on the pile wouldn't matter. I shrunk back down, un-cupped myself, and frowned.

"Have at it," I said.

Dr. Hong nodded and swabbed my dick tip with a numbing agent. Once it kicked in, he squared his glasses, fired up the probe, and stuck it hole-side. I grabbed his hand.

"Is this gonna hurt?" I asked.

He raised a corner of his mouth. "Not so much. Just maybe a small sting."

I exhaled and let go of his hand.

"Okay," I said. "Proceed."

Dr. Hong inched his way in. At first, I felt little: a slight swelling at most. When he reached my bladder, I felt a burn. It ran hot, hot, hotter up the wire till my entire penis was exploding with fire. I screamed in agony and almost made him drop the camera. He jiggled it back in place, looked deep into the screen, then drew out the probe. I was panting and sweating. I locked eyes with him and snarled.

"Have you ever had that done to *you*?" I said.

He shrugged and shook his head. "No."

"Well, try it on yourself sometime. Then you'll know not to tell your next patient it only causes 'a small sting.'"

The bladder exam turned up nothing. And though it may have been an excruciating ordeal, it did lead to my obtaining full medical clearance. Now all I had to do was wait for placement. Peace Corps said they'd get back to me on that "sometime during the summer." I put the finishing touches on our big trip. On April 9, 2006, my buddies and I boarded a plane for Bangkok and took off.

ON JULY 3, 2006, our plane from Frankfurt touched down in SF. I'd been gone for so long and drunk, fucked, tripped, and exploded so much, the thought of volunteering was nothing more than a hangnail on the thumb of a guy balls-deep in a thousand-person orgy. All our families picked us up at the airport. The pampering and the camera flashes lasted for three days. Then one afternoon the phone rang. I answered it with a cheekful of homemade enchiladas.

"Hellowb," I said from the corner of my mouth.

"Hello Mr. Felmanstien, this is Nancy from Peace Corps Headquarters in San Francisco."

"Ugh, yeah?"

"I'm calling to inform you that you've been invited to serve."

"What, like at a dinner party?"

"No, like on assignment. You selected Eastern Europe/Central Asia as one of your preferred regions, correct?"

"Yeah?"

"Then we've got just the country for you."

Nancy went on to tell me I'd need thirty hours of English teaching experience by the end of September. She also said I'd be receiving a blue folder in the mail shortly.

"It'll inform you of where you'll be serving and the steps you'll need to get there."

The guessing game began. My entire family wanted to throw a question mark on the frying pan. My dad said "Azerbaijan?" and my mom said "Kyrgyzstan?"; my gramps Papito said "Mongolia?" and my sister Hannah said, "The Ukraine?" I was still rooting for my original picks. However, since headquarters had emailed during the trip saying the leave dates for Africa were all back in May, I knew Ethiopia was probably out the window.

With Georgia on my earlobe, I got to teaching. My buddy Mason's mom, who worked at a school that taught English for foreigners, got me the gig. I put in my hours with a headful of images—scaling the snowy peaks of Ushguli[5], or lounging on the beaches of Batumi,[6] guzzling sweet reds in Kakheti,[7] or munching on *khachapuri* in Kazbegi.[8]

---

[5] Ushguli is a community of four villages located in the Svaneti region of northeastern Georgia.

[6] Batumi is a resort town on Georgia's Black Sea coast.

[7] Kakheti is a region of eastern Georgia famous for wine production.

[8] Kazbegi is a small town in the mountains of northeastern Georgia, famous for its nature reserve, Mount Kazbegi, and the Gergeti Trinity Church.

When Friday the fourteenth rolled around, I was halfway to Tbilisi in my head. I had fifteen hours left of teaching and a guidebook on the Caucasus. I came home that afternoon ready to crack it and start planning. I found my family in the kitchen. They were sitting around the table with hands folded and mouths grinning. I asked them what was up, and they pointed. Next to the saltshaker was my fate. My dad picked it up and handed it to me.

"So where do you think they're gonna send ya?" he asked.

"I'm thinkin' Georgia. I really connected with my interviewer and told her it was the place for me."

He nodded. My mom chimed in.

"Hey guys," she said. "Let's finalize our guesses."

Everyone said the same as before except Hannah. She just sat there thinking.

"I know my guess was the Ukraine, but I'm feeling something different now," she said. "I can't put my finger on it, but it seems another place is calling you, Johann."

"Damn right."

I popped open the blue folder. I pulled out a white page with black lettering. I scanned down till I saw "Country of Service." My brain twitched.

"Is it Turkmenistan?" Hannah said.

"How the fuck did you know that?"

The room flew into an uproar. Everyone kept asking, "Where the hell is that?" I looked at my giant hairy father. He was shaking his giant bearded head.

"Are you sure you still wanna do this?" he said.

I glanced back down at the page. The letters T.U.R.K.M.E.N.I.S.T.A.N. threaded through my pupils and into my brain. They spun into a little tornado of razorblades. I'd say it felt bad, but *man* it felt good. I looked up at my dad with red glints in my eyes. His face dropped onto his lap.

THE NEXT TWO months were crucial. I spent them crunching numbers, mailing papers, doing research, and stacking cash. I even went out and bought myself a video camera. I figured I'd make a little documentary of my whole experience. Come mid-September I was pretty much set. All that remained was the big going away party. We had it on a Saturday. It was a good time to deflower my camera. I brought it out after the booze had been flowing for a few hours. People saw it and got candid. Some said things like "Have fun in that third-world shithole" or "Say hello to the Taliban for me." Others attempted to wish me bon voyage but kept butchering the place name. Among their screw-ups were "Termeccastan," "Turministan," and "Turduckistan." The best came from a buddy wearing a "Got Tequila?" shirt. He tried his hardest to say "Turkmenistan." After five attempts, he threw his hand up.

"Aw hell," he said. "Live it up in Jerk-a-man-named-Stan or whatever."

I laughed and went to the backyard. Between the patio, lawn, and garden there must have been fifty people. Everyone was drunk and chatty. I noticed my father, in the middle of it all, standing still. He was like a sequoia among partying ants. He looked at me with one eye and motioned me over. A green sickness coated my stomach. I stood next to him and kept my head down. He raised his glass and clinked it with a fork. The whole mob hushed. He put his big arm around my little shoulder. Then he lifted his chin.

"Friends and family," he said. "Johann is going to Turk-menistan . . ."

Leaves rustled. A cricket burped.

"And though a lot of you may not know where that is, you can tell by the name it's in a tough part of the world. So, we are doubly proud of him for making this sacrifice."

Sacrifice? I thought.

"Furthermore, it's not just a sacrifice he's making for himself or us, it's a sacrifice he's making . . . for his country."

His voice cracked. I looked over at him and saw his eyes jiggling with tears. This made me wanna cry. Not out of pride or bonding, but out of guilt. I knew damn well I wasn't going to Turkmenistan for patriotic reasons. Nor did I see myself as making any kind of "sacrifice." I was running, plain and simple; running from responsibility, running from home, and running from myself. All I could think about was what Trish had said to me at the festival a year prior: "Find one *real* reason to stay." With this ringing in my ears, I raised my glass. People cheered but I heard zilch.

SEPTEMBER 29, 2006, was my last day in California. I woke up that morning feeling groggy and sick. The night before had been big. It had started with my buddies drunkenly shaving my head and ended with us pounding Taco Bell and whiskeys at 4:00 a.m. Luckily, I was already packed. I dragged my mountain of shit downstairs and chilled with my family. We all sat around the kitchen table and ate breakfast. My mom had made my favorite—*huevos con chorizo y chili verde picante*— eggs with Mexican sausage and hot green chile. I hardly touched my food. I just sat there with my jowls swaying above my plate.

After breakfast, I dumped my bags in the trunk and said goodbye. Papito gave me a rickety hug and Nina, my grandmother, gave me fat red kisses. Our dog Buffster ran her smelly tongue all the way up my cheek. Hannah gave me a gift. It was three books on Buddhism and a card.

"Read them when you get there," she said.

I told her I would. I hugged her and got in the car with my folks. We drove off honking and waving. We arrived at SFO an hour later.[9] Check-in was a bastard with his fly open. We got through it and walked to security. We stood in line and things got low. I can remember my feet and hands, then my father's face. It was shaking like a dam with a crack down the middle. I reached out and hugged him tight.

"You're the best, Dad," I said.

He inhaled a mountain of air.

---

[9] San Francisco International Airport.

"I love you, son," he said, sighing. "Please be careful out there."

I promised I would. We unhooked and I went to my mom. I took her in my arms, and she shook like a frightened dove. I told her I'd be safe and not to worry. She nodded against my armpit then pulled away.

"You know what I'm going to give you," she said, reaching into her purse.

I smiled and held out my hand. As always, she placed in it the little amethyst egg meant to remind me that wherever I go in this world, I'm still her baby boy. I thanked her and gave her a kiss. I threw on my pack, tipped my hat, and went through security. Once out, I waved to my folks. Then I ran to the bathroom and vomited. As I was wiping my face, I heard the boarding call for my flight to Arlington, Virginia.

At least I'll have a few days of orientation before I parachute down the devil's asshole, I thought.

THE TRIP WAS a drag. Not only did I have to change planes unexpectedly in Dallas, I suffered through two rotgut meals and a spell of ball-crushing turbulence over Kansas. I arrived in Arlington looking like a sizzled shit nugget. Thankfully, my only task was to make it to the hotel. I checked my orientation pack for the name. I was hoping for the Marriot.

"The DoubleTree, huh," I mumbled.

I took a cab. I lugged my crap into the lobby and up to the front desk. The receptionist raised her chin and simpered.

"How may I help you?" she asked.

"Yeah, I'm with the Peace Corps. I'm here for orientation. Name's Johann Felmanstien."

"Uhhh," she said, pointing to her list. "We have a Mr. Johann Felmanstein. E.I.N. Might that be you?"

"Yeah, the 'e' and the 'i' are switched."

She curled her lip and penned the correction.

"Okay, Mr. Felmanstien. You're in room 222. Here's your card."

I grabbed it and took the elevator. All I wanted to do was get in my room, drop my bags, hit the shower, bust a load, and crash. I arrived at my door and slipped the card in. The light beeped green and I pushed it open. I was expecting darkness, but I saw light. There was also a smell I couldn't place. It was something between Roquefort cheese and dirty jockstrap. This further soured my mood. I waltzed past the threshold and around the corner. On the bed near the window was a 220-pound cherub of a man with toilet cleaner eyes and greasy red curls. He was piled up against his pillows in a wife-beater and shorts. His fat fingers were gripping a book and his big feet—crooked toes, yellow nails and all—were out fuming the walls. I thinned my eyes and sneered.

"Who are you?" I said.

"The Corps has us shackin' up together. I'm Hal."

I exhaled and extended my hand. Hal paused for a moment then did the same. We shook and started talking. I told Hal my name and story then asked him his deal. He told me that a few months prior, he'd been an English teacher in Seoul. I asked him what that was like.

"Crazy," he said, chuckling. "I taught mostly businessmen, and they all wanted to party. We'd go to these wild bars and order a bunch of drinks. It was always fun to watch those guys get wasted."

I laughed. A seagull flew by and crapped in my brainpan.

"Watch?"

"Yeah. I'd just order cherry juice. I'm Mormon."

"Wow," I said. "That's, um, a really interesting thing there."

Leave it to Peace Corps to shack me up with a Mormon. It was like sticking Satan in a room with Snoopy.

"So, before Seoul, what was it?" I asked.

Hal looked down at his fungus-covered toes.

"I was home for a bit but that's not a good place. Dad's a major jerk and most of my family is estranged. Before that, I was in Afghanistan. I saw a lotta bad things and did a few too. Guess that's why I'm here doin' the Turkmen thing."

"Damn."

We clicked out the lights. I hoped the morrow would bring some cooler volunteers. I bunched my pillow and closed my eyes. Sleep came on a cloud of Hal's footrot.

ORIENTATION WAS NOT the volunteer bonding experience I'd hoped for. I met volunteers, yes. I even made a few acquaintances. But no real friendships were forged because, at the end of the day, we were just a bunch of jetlagged Americans, snoring our way through seminars before drinking our way through bars.

After three days of this, I was left with one semi-clear memory. It happened on the second day of orientation. PC staff herded us into the hotel meeting room. They sat us down in chairs and rolled a TV up front. Some guy with two anchovies for a mustache popped in a video. He joined the points of his fingers and addressed the room.

"This is a short documentary on your country of service," he said. "You'd do well to pay attention."

I'd done my research, so I knew what to expect. I leaned back, kicked my feet up, and switched my brain off. The video started rolling. As my eyes clicked open and shut, I heard scattered fragments . . .

"Turkmenistan is a landlocked, Central Asian country that is slightly bigger than California. It is bordered counterclockwise from the top by Kazakhstan, Uzbekistan, Afghanistan, and Iran. Its western and longest border is shared with the Caspian Sea. Despite a few hills and mountains, the country is teeth to asshole desert . . ."

Click.

"Fewer than five million people live in Turkmenistan. The ethnic make-up is 85% Turkmen, 5% Uzbek, 4% Russian, and 6% other. Together, the Turkmen and the Uzbeks compose the Sunni Muslim population, while the Russians and the 'others' compose the Eastern Orthodox and otherly religious populations . . ."

Click.

"Turkmen is a Southwestern common Turkic language of the

Turkic branch of the greater Altaic language family. It is closely related to Turkish and Azeri. And more distantly to Kazakh and Uzbek . . ."

Scratch balls.

"As the Turkmen were originally horse-breeding nomads, they have, at the center of their state emblem, what is known as an Ahal-Teke horse. The Ahal-Teke has been prized by the Turkmen for centuries for its graceful stride and shiny gold coat. 'Ahal' refers to the province, or *welaýat*, it is from, and 'Teke' to the nomadic tribe that first bred it. Around the Ahal-Teke are five motifs, each of which represents one of the following major Turkmen tribes: Teke, Yomut, Ersari, Chowdur, and Saryk . . ."

Sniff fingers.

"Turkmenistan's economy rests largely on the shoulders of natural gas and cotton production. It has the fourth-largest quantity of natural gas reserves and frequently ranks among the top ten cotton producers in the world. Recent crop failures brought about by irrigation problems have meant a sharp decline in cotton production. As a result, the Turkmen manat[10] has nose-dived into the shitter . . ."

I wonder if Mr. Anchovy-stache diddles little boys.

"The area of land that constitutes modern Turkmenistan has been invaded or settled by many groups. Among them, in chronological order, are the Scythians,[11] the Macedonians,[12] the

---

[10] The manat is the currency of Turkmenistan.

[11] The Scythians were a nomadic Eastern Iranian people who inhabited portions of the Eurasian Steppe from the ninth century BC to the fourth century AD.

[12] The Macedonians were an ancient tribe who inhabited the northeastern part of mainland Greece. Their empire extended from Greece to India and lasted from the ninth to the second century BC. Alexander the Great was the most famous of the Macedonian kings. There is a village in southwestern Turkmenistan called Nokhur, whose inhabitants believe they descend from Alexander the Great and his troops.

Parthians,[13] the Arabs,[14] the Oghuz Turks,[15] the Seljuk Turks,[16] the Mongols,[17] the Timurids,[18] the Khivans,[19] and finally, the Russians . . ."

Lift cheek and let out an extremely quiet but extremely smelly fart.

"On October 27, 1991, Saparmurat Atayevich Niyazov—former Chairman of the Supreme Soviet of the Turkmen USSR—was appointed president of Turkmenistan. To exert his dominance, he declared himself Türkmenbaşy, or Supreme Leader of the Turkmen, and President for Life. Thereafter, he crushed all political opposition, closely monitored or shut down all internet cafes, closed all libraries and hospitals outside Aşgabat,[20] fired many public health workers, revoked the pensions of one third of the elderly population, and

---

[13] The Parthians were an ancient Iranian people, descended from the Parni tribe, who controlled an empire extending from eastern Turkey to eastern Iran and parts of modern Turkmenistan from 247 to 224 AD.

[14] Arabs, in this context, refers to a largely nomadic group of Semitic people from the Arabian Peninsula and surrounding areas, who conquered what is now known as Turkmenistan during the early Muslim conquests of the seventh and eighth centuries.

[15] The Oghuz Turks were a western Turkic people who formed the Oghuz Yabgu State (750–1155), which included most of modern-day Turkmenistan. The descendants of the Oghuz later founded the Ottoman Empire.

[16] The Seljuk Turks were a group of Turks who broke away from the Oghuz and converted to Islam in the tenth century. The Seljuks later went on to establish the Seljuk Empire (1037–1194), which incorporated almost all of modern-day Turkmenistan.

[17] The Mongols were a group of Mongolic peoples native to Mongolia and parts of China and Russia. Perhaps the most famous Mongol in history was Genghis Khan, who in 1206 was proclaimed ruler of all Mongols. He and his invading armies began a campaign of expansion which soon created an empire stretching from Eastern Europe to the Sea of Japan, making it the largest contiguous land empire in history. The borders of modern Turkmenistan were swallowed by this empire.

[18] Timurids: those of the Sunni Muslim Turco-Mongol dynasty descended from the warlord Timur (a.k.a. Tamerlane), who was an in-law of Genghis Khan. The Timurids were strongly influenced by Persian culture and created two significant empires, the Mughal Empire (1526–1857), which occupied the Indian subcontinent, and the Timurid Empire (1370–1507), which occupied Persia and Central Asia, including the lands of modern Turkmenistan.

[19] The Khanate of Khiva was an Uzbek state which almost continuously occupied the historical region of Khwarezm (covering much of Turkmenistan) from 1511 to 1920, and whose Khans (rulers) were descended from Jochi, a grandson of Genghis Khan.

[20] Aşgabat is the capital city of Turkmenistan.

created a cult of personality, the more peculiar aspects of which included thousands of statues and photos of him around the country; his own book of Turkmen history called the *Ruhnama*, or *The Book of the Soul*, which was compulsory at every grade level; and days, months, schools, airports, cities, towns, villages, and even a meteorite named after family members, famous Turkmen, and in many cases, himself—"

I was three tweaks from dreamland. Then I heard the words "assassination attempt." I choked on my spit and cricked awake. Mr. Anchovy-stache gave me a dirty look. I shrugged it off and tuned in. There wasn't much info, but it was enough to pique my interest.

"On November 25, 2002," the narrator said, "Former minister Boris Shikhmuradov allegedly staged an assassination attempt on President Niyazov. In the days following, a brutal police crackdown led to dozens of arrests and disappearances. Among those arrested was Shikhmuradov. He was tried and sentenced to life in prison. As an added measure, he was forced to give a taped confession stating that he was a drug addict and that he had hired mercenaries to carry out the assassination. Despite this, many believe that the attempt on Niyazov's life was staged by the Turkmen government itself to justify a blanket stomp-out campaign against the growing dissent in the country."

How could I have missed this vital piece of information? I was certain I'd done a thorough job of Wikipediaing the Christ outta Türkmenbaşy. I contemplated digging deeper. In the end, I decided the hell with it. In forty-eight hours I'd be stepping on a plane headed straight for the fucker. Why spoil two perfectly good nights of drinking?

2

OUR PLANE TOUCHED down in Aşgabat on the night of October 3. The atmosphere inside the cabin was tense. We rolled along the tarmac then slowed to a stop. The lights clicked on overhead and we grabbed our bags. The door opened and we shuffled off. We walked through a steel tube then into a long glass corridor. This led us to a room with yellow walls. There was a metal detector and two customs control booths. Three armed guards were posted up front. They were dressed in creased green suits and black police caps. They glared at us through paper-cut eyes. Their veiny brown arms hung ominously at their sides. We tiptoed by and went to customs. Fat-necked bureaucrats with sweaty foreheads demanded our passports from behind plate glass. We handed them off and smiled awkwardly. They stamped us up and moved us through. We formed a group and hit the baggage claim. It took an hour for our crap to arrive. We grabbed it and went to security. After two hours of checks and posturing, we were allowed through the gates. A woman was waiting for us outside. She was wide as a fence with buck teeth and curly black hair. She threw open her flabby arms and smiled like a scarecrow.

"*Türkmenistana hoş geldiñiz,*" she cried. "Welcome to Turkmenistan."

She told us her name was Mahym and that she was from Peace Corps. As she blabbed, a bus pulled up. It was dirty yellow with green trim. It jittered like a dying meth addict. Mahym peeled open the doors and ushered us in. We went up the steps, poured into our seats, and froze. Once the doors were closed, our bus coughed back to life. We pulled away from the curb in a cloud of fumes and onto the open road. I pressed my face against the window. I saw a paved highway lined with trees like mangled skeletons. Beyond them was an immense darkness. It looked like space with its stars plucked out. A series of street lights came into view. They hung above us like plesiosaur necks, screaming their light down on us. We drove and drove and drove. Little nubs of white began popping up from the black landscape. They grew bigger and taller and whiter. Soon we were moving through an organized jungle of marble. It was steep and jagged and gleaming. There were towering fountains and grand plazas, ministries, mega-malls, and mile-long promenades. On every corner, a bearded Turkmen hero was raising his bronze hands to the sky and giving thanks. Not to Allah, mind you, but to the man in the blue suit with the twinkling pinky ring, smiling benevolently from the placard over every threshold. I thought of the people he'd erased from this planet. I wondered if their ghosts gave Aşgabat its eerie glow.

At 3:00 a.m. our bus pulled up at a hotel. It was tall and square and ivory with flags of every sort hanging in a circle above its entrance. At its head were the words *Ak Altyn*. I asked Mahym what they meant, and she smiled.

"It means 'White Gold,'" she said. "This referring to our wonderful Turkmen cotton."

We parked and grabbed our bags. Mahym led us into the lobby where blond women in knee-high boots sat cross-legged and puffed thin cigarettes. I glanced at them and grinned. They looked right past me, their red mouths issuing smoke rings. We got our room keys and went upstairs. The Peace Corps had us boarding in pairs and there was no co-ed. My roomie was a dude named Mick. He had curly white locks, green eyes, and skin like a tomato. From the few words we exchanged, he seemed chill. I'd have taken the time to chop it up with him, but I was dead to the wind.

THE NEXT FOUR days were a blur. When we weren't snoring through some "safety and security" meeting, we were visiting "sites of interest", learning Turkmen phrases, or pounding shots of *arak* (Turkmen rotgut) in our rooms. A couple of the nights some T-14s— the fourteenth group of Peace Corps volunteers in Turkmenistan— came to party with us T-15s. They dropped a bit of knowledge on us like where the best bazaars and discos were and where we could get decent Turkish and American food. They also told us about the meeting point for every volunteer worth a damn. It was called the Zip Bar and it was *the* place to pre-game.

We never got a chance to hit the Zip. We were on hotel lockdown after-hours, plus time was tight. Come October 7th, we were readied to be shipped off to our training sites. Peace Corps divided us into groups, told us which village we'd be trained in, gave us the addresses of our host families for the next ten weeks, then bid us a hearty "*Sag aman bar.*" We were out the door by noon. A half dozen vans waited for us curbside. I say vans, but they were *marşrutkas*—Soviet-style wagons made of sheet metal you could punch your finger through. Nine of us climbed abroad one bound for Annau—a town of 10,000 some twenty minutes from Aşgabat. As Annau is the capital of Ahal province, I figured it might be nice. Images of marble-hewn tearooms and gold-leaf minarets waltzed through my mind.

After a stretch of highway, we turned off onto a paved road. It fed onto a tree-lined boulevard that curved and dispersed into dirt trails. Our driver picked one and we clunked onto it. The potholes were so deep I thought we'd blow our tires. With each neck-snapping bounce, a little piece of the pretty Annau I'd imagined came tumbling out my ears. When we came to a stop, all that was left of the image was what I was actually seeing. Just beyond our windshield lay a sprawling trash dump. Piles of every godawful thing imaginable were heaped on top of one another in crooked Dr. Seuss towers. At their center was one lone crane. It was bent and rusted, its long metal tongue swaying lifelessly in the desert wind.

We putted down another dirt road. To our left was the dumping ground in all its hideous glory. To our right was a row of homes made of dusty bricks and tins roofs. At the fifth house, our driver stopped and looked back.

"*Siz şu taýda ýaşaýañyz,*" he said to me. "You sir, live here."

I glanced around the marşrutka. Eight pairs of American eyes were staring at me. I could feel them all saying, "Glad you're first and not us." I nodded resolutely and grabbed my shit.

THE MARŞRUTKA CLUNKED away, and I was left staring at my new home. It was a one-story, yellow-brick L with an outhouse in back and a gravel lot up front. I breathed in deep and stepped past the threshold of the open metal gate. A screen door slammed, and a man came out. He was tall and hunched with long arms and legs. A crop of gray hair rested on his head like an upturned milkweed. He sloth-walked up to me and extended a hand. Its fingers were gnarled, and its palm was calloused and greasy. I bit my lip and shook it. The man unzipped his jaws and revealed a mouthful of gold teeth. They hung from his addled gums like tiny kitchen knives. I'd have been frightened, but the milky brown eyes above were so kind.

"Hoş geldiñiz," he said. "I'm Maksat. You must be Johann."

His Turkmen was quick but clear. I understood him fully and nodded my head. He grabbed my rolly-bag and led me to a concrete slab in back. On top was a red Turkmen rug ringed with pillows. In its center was a circle of porcelain teacups hugging the base of a kettle that was steaming at the snout. He jabbed a finger at the pillows and smiled. I dropped my backpack and hopped up. He turned and sliced off a whistle. I heard a rustling inside, then the screen door flung open. The first to come out was a boy my age. He was thin as a toothpick with big ears, dark skin, and glasses. He grinned the whole way with his one gold tooth. I held out a hand, and he sandwiched it with two.

"Welcome," he said. "I'm Rahym."

Next out was a taller boy with more meat. He had Asian eyes and black hair and smiled with bunched lips. He shook my hand and said his name was Mekan. I grinned and told him I was Johann. The door swung open again. This time a girl walked out. She was frail and tan with long fingers and brown hair in a bun. She flowed up to me in her green dress.

"I'm Çynar," she said. "Hoş geldiňiz."

The four of us drank tea in silence. We tried to make conversation, but my host family's three words of English and my five words of Turkmen had been used up with the introductions. When the silence became unbearable, Maksat stood and reached in his pocket. He pulled out a skeleton key and handed it to me. I looked down at it and shrugged.

"*Bu näme?*" I asked. "What's this?"

"Your room," he replied in Turkmen. "Open."

He stepped down from the concrete slab and pulled me with him. We walked across the backyard and over toward the outhouse. To the right of it was a small barn with two chickens and a black sheep. To the left was a walled extension of the barn with a blue door and a single window. I made a valley with one eyebrow and a peak with the other. Maksat chuckled and pointed to the door.

"This is your room," he said.

I laughed like, "Okay let's see where I'm really staying." Maksat grabbed the key from me and opened the door. I scrunched my face and stepped inside. The place was no bigger than a midget's shitter. There was a tiny wardrobe at one end and a tiny desk at the other. In the middle were a couple of wool rugs that smelled of sheep sweat. Above everything hung a single lightbulb with a fly burnt into the glass. I stared at it for a moment then cocked my head. Maksat took this as a sign that I was cool with the place. He snapped his fingers and his kids brought my bags. Once they'd piled everything in the center of my room, he looked at me and smiled.

"Three hours," he said. "Then dinner."

He walked out with his kids and closed the door. It shut with a click, then I heard silence. I looked around my room and it slowly dawned on me: for the first time in almost a week, I was alone.

For the next three hours, I busied myself. I unpacked my bags, put away clothes, stacked books, and straightened my room. Then I set up my laptop. There was no internet, of course, but there was one outlet, which at least meant I could type out poems and short stories. I planned on writing as much as possible during my free time. Along with my crummy documentary, writing was the closest thing I had to a real reason for being in Turkmenistan.

After a bit of writing and filming, I checked my watch. There was an hour till dinner. My walls were closing in on me like a ring of tarantulas on a mouse. I went outside to explore my surroundings. My first order of business was that outhouse. Upon inspection, I realized that it was both a washing and a squatting room. The two areas were separated by a wall of gapped wooden planks. The former area contained a rusty tub and a flaming water heater, and the latter, two bricks, a hole, and a mound of shit underneath. Flies and feculent odors comingled through the gaps. I left them in each other's dirty company and moved on.

Next, I had a look at the barn. It was dinky as a pinched dickhole, but there were a few stacks of hay in the back where the chickens could play. The black sheep chilled up front all by his lonely. When he saw me, he lifted himself on his scrawny legs and walked over. I thought he'd beg for food. Instead, he put his little head through a gap in the fence and waited for a pet. I smiled and scratched him behind the ears. He flopped his head from side to side and baaed. This put a tickle in my chest. My little homie had just nicknamed himself.

TIME WENT AND dinner came. I washed up, changed, and walked into the house. Laid across the main rug was a plastic table cover. It was lined with porcelain cups and wooden spoons and bottles of fluorescent soda. Set in the middle was a big bowl of beat-up fruit.

This was accompanied on either side by a plate of dry cookies. My host family were seated around the eating area. They were all smiling at me as was their benevolent leader from the calendar on the wall. I took my place and introduced myself to mommy—a manatee of a woman with a bulbous nose, four gold teeth, and cinnamon eyes. She greeted me and said her name was Jennet. Then she got up and waddled outside. She came back in carrying a steaming black pot. It smelled of cottonseed oil and over-boiled meat. She ladled me a bowl. Out of politeness, I ate the first spoonful. It tasted like suede drenched in scrotal sweat.

"This is delicious," I said, smiling.

Jennet slurped down a spoonful herself.

"It's *çorba*," she said. "Our traditional Turkmen soup."

Dinner carried on much like the tea ceremony. We all tried to break the language barrier but ended up butting foreheads. When it ended, I went to my room to study Turkmen. I grabbed the grammar books Peace Corps had given me, splayed them out on the floor, and got to it. I've always had a penchant for languages, so my brain soaked up most of what I read. After a few hours, I was stringing together simple sentences and speaking in past and future tenses. Once my eyes started to sag, I called it quits. I set up my *düşek*, clicked off the lights, and passed out.

THE NEXT MORNING, my room was like an infant's coffin. I rolled at its base and pressed at its sides and tried to forget the hideous dreams I'd had during the night. The sunshine coming through my window helped. I stood and cracked my whole spine. This loosened my guts. I felt a massive crap coming on. I left my room and went to the outhouse. I opened the wooden door and stepped inside. The stench of a thousand bowel movements filled my nostrils. I cupped my nose, turned around, and placed a foot over each brick. I steadied myself and dropped my drawers. A gust of wind blew up against my balls. They spun up into a knot then back down into a dangle. I looked at them in disgust and popped a squat. I pancaked my insides and let 'er rip. The shit sailed out of me like piss through a whistle. It splattered to specks down below then slowed to a drip. I sat for a moment, musing at a fly that was crawling over my big toe. It buzzed away and I went to wipe. I reached for TP, but my fingers hit cardboard. I picked up a slice and dragged it across my anus. It stung like lemon juice on an open wound. I scraped three more times to little effect.

Fuck it, I thought. Gonna shower anyways.

I grabbed my pants and went to the *banýa*. It was hot inside and choked with steam. The furnace was blazing, and the tub was full. There was a stool with a cup on top. I undressed completely and stood in the center. The concrete felt slimy under my feet. I grabbed the cup and dunked it in the tub. I lifted it over my head and tilted it. The hot water poured its fingers over my scalp. They braided down my back and legs and melted into the concrete. I repeated this process half a dozen times. By the end, I felt clean. I stood for a moment, dick, balls and all. It was liberating to be that alone and that naked.

THAT MONDAY WAS the first day of training. I woke up in a foul mood. The parameters of my shitbox were starting to wear on me. Plus, I'd spent half the night smashing flies. I crawled outta my düşek and did my banýa routine. I petted Baa and had some breakfast. By 8:00 a.m. I was okay to go. Rahym gave me a little map he'd scratched out to guide me to *Birinji Mekdep*—School #1. I thanked him and cut. As I stepped out the gate, I heard an awful noise. It was like a troupe of ogres trying to out-belch each other in an elevator. I looked to my right and saw a herd of camels. They were bobbing their heads and batting their eyelashes. Every few seconds, one swung its long neck around and belted its neighbor in the throat. On impact, the two exploded with burps. It was a dance only aliens could have created. The camels trotted past me. A dude in back whacked one on the ass with a stick. This dislodged a turd from its swishing butt cheeks. It hit the ground rolling and stopped at my feet. I looked down at it and scowled.

"Fuck this place," I muttered.

I tightened my straps and got moving. I walked past the trashyard and through the rusty pipe field, over the gravelly avenue and into a thicket of houses. Twenty minutes later, I was at Birinji Mekdep. I stood at the gate and looked on. There was an E-shaped building on the right and an L-shaped building on the left. Fly-ridden outhouses and dirt-patches with dying trees were off to the sides. At the center of it all was an altar bearing a gold bust of Türkmenbaşy. Underneath it, a crowd of pupils stood silently. The boys were in one group and the girls in another. Each had on their own little uniforms. The boys wore slacks, collared shirts, and oversized ties. Their feet were wrapped in pointy shoes, and their heads topped with red *tahýas*. The girls had on deep green *köýneks* down to their ankles. They wore heeled shoes and flowered tahýas and braids the length of jump ropes. Both groups stood facing The Great Leader with their hands on their hearts. They remained this way while the adults behind them got in position. Once everyone was in a layered circle, the ceremony began. It started with one adult—a tall man with a round belly and a hooked nose, whom I gathered was the *müdir*—leading them in the national anthem. My Turkmen wasn't good enough to grasp everything he and the children were singing. I did, however, catch the bit at the end. It was loud enough to shake the flies from the air: "*Halk. Watan. Türkmenbaşy.*" "People. Nation. You know who."

The ceremony ended and people dispersed. I crossed the quad and headed to the E-building. I found the other volunteers out front. Mick, my hotel roomie, was among them. I said hey and asked him what was up.

"We're waiting on our LCFs,"[21] he said.

A few minutes later, two ladies came out. I was shocked by the dichotomy in their appearances. One was round as a grapefruit with big fat boobs. She had skin the color of root beer and eyes the color

---

[21] Language and cross-culture facilitators.

of coal. The other was thin as a coatrack with doorknob tits. She had skin the color of buttermilk and eyes the color of crickets. The former was named Hurma and the latter, Arzygül. They greeted us and divided us into groups. We were split five to four. Mick and I were in the group of five with Hurma. This made me happy till I saw our classroom. It was the size of a truck bed with peeling walls and one window. Hurma walked up front and clicked on the light. It showered down like dust over our crummy table and chairs. We took our seats and pulled out our notebooks. For the next four hours, we did nothing but learn Turkmen.

After a shit lunch of çorba and three more hours of Turkmen, Hurma and Arzy took us on a little tour of Annau. We went to the local bazaar and post office. Then we saw people's guest homes. I was appalled at how good the other volunteers had it. Not only were all their rooms bigger than mine, most of them had loads of furniture, TVs, and, in some cases, flush toilets. I felt like a three-eyed freak who'd been tossed in a snake cage. I vowed to tell Peace Corps the first chance I got.

The tour ended at 7:30 p.m. Everyone was fried by the October sun, but Mick and I still had it in us to throw down a few cold ones. We spotted an outdoor bar on the main avenue. We said we were going to hit it up and our LCFs flipped.

"You can't go," Arzy said.

"Why not?" I asked.

"Because, um, the dogs will bite you."

"I'm sure the dogs don't give a damn if we have a few beers," Mick said.

"No, it's right," Hurma added. "Also, you can attack of Turkmen men."

"That barely makes sense," I said.

"Hurma is trying to say that Turkmen men can attack you," Arzy said. "They are very aggressive. And police can get you after dark because of curfew. Also, drinking is taboo in our country. You can get bad reputation and bring shame to your family."

Mick and I looked at each other. We knew our LCFs couldn't stop us, and that they were most likely using scare tactics taught to them by Peace Corps. We decided to chance it and check the place out. We said goodbye, crossed the street, and took a seat. A skinny guy with a black crew cut and horrible breath took our orders. We got a couple of beers and a plate of *shashlik* each.[22] The food and drinks came out *tout de suite*. The beer tasted like piss and the meat like feet, but the feeling of freedom was oh, so sweet.

I WOKE UP with a hangover. It was my first day of teacher training. Luckily, I only had to observe. I spent three long hours snoring at the back of my counterpart's[23] classroom with my index finger lodged in my left nostril. I crawled my way through Turkmen under Hurma's devil-eyed admonishments. Then I hobbled home, slurped down dinner, and went to bed.

The next day was a Wednesday. This meant it was a hub day when all the trainees got together at PCHQ in Aşgabat.[24] I was mildly excited about this. Sure, I'd have to sit through a bunch of boring meetings, but at least I'd get to use the internet, eat some real food, and tell Peace Corps what a turd-cabinet I was living in.

We made it to our first hub day on time. All the T-15s were there, as were a number of 14s. We piled into the conference room upstairs. A muskrat of a man with a tiny head and ripped arms was standing there waiting. He introduced himself as Batyr, our "safety and security officer." Then he began his speech. It was on the dangers of Turkmen *alabais*—the ginormous white and brown mastiffs that roam the streets of every village in the country.

"Alabai proud animal," Batyr began. "Dangerous. He volking

---

[22] A dish of meat cubes which are seasoned, skewered, and grilled.

[23] A counterpart is a country national who is assigned by Peace Corps to work with a trainee or sworn-in volunteer so that they may better perform their job (i.e., teaching English as a second language, implementing community development, improving healthcare, etcetera.).

[24] Peace Corps Headquarters.

strit. He bitting you. Be careful. Turkmen history say alabai half-tiger, half shipdog. Now he guard dog and fighting dog. Only to finding you alabai in Tuuuuurkmenistan."

Mick looked over at me.

"The guy really has a way with words," he muttered.

We suffered through a few more speeches. Then we got a lunch break. Before hitting the buffet, I went down to our Country Director Bob's office. I knocked twice on his door. He was sitting at his desk, thumbing through a stack of papers. His silver hair sparkled with sweat. His long, dumb face swayed this way and that. He looked up at me with the blue eyes of a dog.

"Yes, Johann?" he asked. "What can I do for you?"

"I don't mean to be crass," I said. "But my new room is a total dump. Any chance you could ask my host family to put me in a better spot?"

He eyed me up. A bead of sweat slid down his jowl and into the dimple on his chin. He wiped it away with his pudgy fingers.

"I'll see what I can do," he said.

"Thanks."

I left and went to lunch. I piled my plate with lamb, squash, *palow*, *manty*, and salad. When it was ready to tip over, I looked for a seat. I found one next to a cute T-14. Her name was Fernanda. We got to talking about my training site. I mentioned my host family. As I reeled their names off, Fernanda chuckled.

"You mean you're in Paul Newbury's old house?" she said.

I bit a cucumber in half and chewed it against my cheek.

"Who the hell is that?"

"Haha, I guess they wouldn't tell you."

"Tell me what?"

"Well, Paul was this huge hippie with long scraggly hair and a beard. He used to constantly piss Peace Corps off. Somehow, he always got away with it. Then one time we had an English camp in Çüli—this cool place in the mountains. Paul was there, but instead of teaching the kids English, he told them that if the boys didn't want to grow up to be drunks and the women didn't want to grow up to be housewives or whores, they had to rise up and fight for their rights. Then he started bashing Türkmenbaşy on his blog and in letters to students and other volunteers. Peace Corps was afraid he'd get us kicked out of Turkmenistan or start a mini-revolution so they admin sep'd him."

"Admin sep'd?"

"Administratively separated."

"Jesus. So, do you think they put me with Paul's old family for a reason?"

"Prolly not," she said, smiling. "It is kinda funny though."

When hub day ended, we took a marşrutka. It dropped me off in front of my house. Hurma and Arzy were there talking with my host family. I could tell it was about my room. I walked up and asked what was going on. Jennet gave me a funny look and told me to come with her. I followed her to a room in back. She opened the door and let me scope the place. There were two big windows, a desk, a wardrobe, and a heater. On the floor was a beautiful red carpet and on the walls were a few pictures. One of them was of a teenage boy in army fatigues. I asked Jennet who this was, and she stared at the ground.

"My dead son," she said. "This was his room."

She closed the door and left. It felt weird being in the room of a deceased soldier, but hey, he wasn't gonna use the place anymore, plus I was tired of living in a converted barn next to a shitter and a sheep called Baa. I unpacked my things and set up shop. Come midnight, I was in dreamland, catching hot little fairies with a net.

3

FOR THE NEXT six weeks, my life as a volunteer in training became a cycle that revolved around four main things: host family, hub days, language studies, and Mick.

I DIDN'T SEE my host family much. If I wasn't locked in my room, loading my journals with ink or studying Turkmen, I was at school, in Aşgabat, or over at Mick's. Dinner was the only time I really saw my host family. I figured this was enough. During my personal interview, Mahym mentioned they had expressed a desire to be closer with me. I felt like a miserable old hermit. I asked her if she had any suggestions on how to approach this problem.

"Actually, I have, Johann," she said. "End of Ramadan will be in three days. It would be nice if you helped them prepare for celebration and did fasting for last day."

I mulled the idea over for a minute.

"Sounds like a plan," I said.

That night I told my host family. They informed me that the preparations would begin the next day. We finished eating and parted on a good note. I went straight to my room to figure out exactly what Ramadan was. Before leaving, I'd bought a few books on Islam. I cracked them across my pillows and gleaned the following:

In the Islamic calendar, Ramadan is the ninth month. It lasts 29 – 30 days and is a time during which all Muslims who are not sick, traveling, pregnant, menstruating, or breastfeeding must refrain from eating, drinking, smoking, cursing, and having sex, from sunup to sundown. There are three crucial points during Ramadan. *Hilal* (The Crescent) is the day (or days) during which the crescent moon first reveals itself and marks the beginning of the lunar month. *Laylat al-Qadr* (The Night of Power) occurs on an odd-numbered night during the last ten days of Ramadan; Muslims believe that it was on this night that God breathed the first words of the Qur'an to Mohammed, stating that this night alone was "better than a thousand months of proper worship." *Eid al-Fitr* (Festivity of Breaking the Fast) signals the end of Ramadan and the beginning of *Shawwal*, the next lunar month.

Muslims are allowed two meals per day during Ramadan. The first of these meals is *suhoor*, which is eaten before dawn. The second is *iftar*, which is eaten after dusk.

A higher level of *zakat* or alms-giving and Qur'an recitations is practiced by Muslims during Ramadan. It is said that doing these things will be looked upon favorably by Allah during the "Last Judgment."

The following night, Çynar invited me to walk around Annau and give zakat. Since there are almost no homeless among the Turkmen, giving alms just means taking food to your neighbors, friends, and family members. The food we took was simple: mutton palow and eggplants stuffed with pickled vegetables. We piled each item in a big bowl. We covered them with a towel and cut.

The sky was a gorgeous mess. It looked like a Greek god's bratty kid had tossed giant cans of pink, orange, red, and yellow paint way up in the air, then just as all the colored tentacles were bending down back to earth, they froze. We went from house to house under this sky. While Çynar did the giving, I poked my eyes through the windows. Some Turkmen families were huddled around crackling old radios or gossiping over steaming pots of *çay*. Others were splayed out on their prayer rugs or reading thoughtfully from the Qur'an. When Çynar knocked, they all stopped what they were doing and answered their door with a smile. Our gift of food was accepted with grace and was always followed by an offer to come in and eat. Since Çynar and I had a route to maintain, we had to decline. This was understood, and we were sent off with the same warmth with which we were received.

Before stopping at Çynar's sister Läle's—our final destination—we visited an old widow. She lived in a lopsided shack at the edge of the garbage dump. As it was now night, the dump was a bog of darkness. I walked up to it and stared deep into its tarry womb. Its sticky black fingers reached out and peeled the skin from my chest. I felt my spirit being drawn from between my ribs. It shone beautifully in the emptiness. I had the sudden desire to take my host family to America and show them my way of life as they had done for me.

I glued myself back together and joined Çynar. We said goodbye to the old widow and hit the road. It curved like a rattlesnake's spine up a small hill. We followed it to a lone brick home soaked in moonlight. Çynar knocked and we held out our goods. A young woman answered the door. She was thin as a stork's leg with big hands. When she saw we'd brought food, she grinned. Her teeth spread like organ keys under her tiny nose and eyes.

"Hello, I'm Läle," she said. "And you must be Johann. Please come in."

We followed her into a warm den with a woodburning stove. Her husband and two boys sat on the floor. They immediately rose to greet us. We shook their hands and Läle offered us dinner. I was keen to accept but Çynar declined.

"We've got dinner waiting for us at home," she said.

Läle nodded and thanked us for the food. We said our so-longs and cut back toward home. On the way, Çynar turned to me and smiled. Flakes of paper light filtered down through the clouds. I asked her what was up. She cocked her head.

"Thanks for doing this," she said.

I told her no problem. She bit the happiness from her lips in contemplation.

"You need a Turkmen name," she said.

I was flattered but at a loss for words. My knowledge of Turkmen names was minimal. I told her this and she thought for a moment. The gears in her brain clicked.

"I know," she said. "We'll call you *Han-Guly*."

I crinkled my eyebrows.

"Han-Guly? What the hell does that mean?"

She pointed to something on the ground next to me. I squinted my eyes and focused in on it. When I realized what it was, I scowled.

"Dog shit?" I said. "What kinda nickname is that?"

Çynar pitched forward and laughed with her buck teeth out. I stood with my hands on my hips. She straightened her *ýaglyk* and looked at me.

"I'm just kidding," she said. "The name Han-Guly means . . ." She knelt down and pressed her hands together. Her thin eyebrows glistened like silverfish. I watched hard, trying to decipher her pantomime.

"Does it mean Servant of God?" I said in English.

Çynar shrugged. I checked my dictionary later that night. The name Han-Guly literally translated to "The Ruler's Slave." I liked my translation better.

The next day my entire host family were calling me Han-Guly. As Laylat al-Qadr was at hand, the nickname seemed appropriate. There was a ton of crap to do before the extended family arrived. Rahym and I were given the tasks of clearing out my new room for the *myhmanlar* (guests) and beating all the rugs to a shine. Afterwards, we were herded into my old room. A group of older men was there. They sat around a tablecloth piled high with breadcrumbs. I sat next to Maksat and asked him what the deal was. He told me we'd be making Turkmenistan's national dish, *dograma*.

"What's that?" I asked.

Before he could answer, a pear-shaped man ducked into the

room. His hairy arms were cradling a giant aluminum bowl that was steaming at the mouth. He placed it in front of me and flashed his gold nuggets. I smiled back at him and looked down. Inside was a Picasso-face of boiled lamb parts. Everything but the hooves and head were present. Maksat grabbed the bowl and tipped it over. Its contents tumbled out with a sickening "schflop." Hands flew at the pile like starved rats. They ripped and tore and slashed and beat. Maksat handed me a dull knife. I grabbed it and hacked at a gristly thigh. The runny grease burnt my hands pink. It took me a few tries, but I got the thing clean. Within twenty minutes the entire lamb was in little pieces. Maksat said it was time to mix it with the breadcrumbs. We lifted both ends of the tablecloth and swamped everything together. We rolled back our sleeves and dug our forearms in. We squished and mashed and smeared and pressed until every last piece of fat, muscle, organ, and cartilage was glued to the breadcrumbs. Then we stuck the gelatinous hump in the bowl and washed up.

The family arrived at eight. Mick and some other volunteers came as well. We were given a room in back. This gave us a chance to let our hair down and be stupid Americans. We gossiped and joked and drank and laughed. My host sisters brought in the dograma. It was just all those lamb parts and stale breadcrumbs floating in a thin broth. I choked down my disappointment and accepted a bowl of it. Mick dared me to take the first bite. Feeling confident in my abilities as a chef, I dipped in. I raised the *çemçe* (spoon) to my lips and sipped. The taste of gutter water and boiled dog hair slid across my tongue. I swallowed the mouthful and went for another. Mick raised his eyebrows.

"That good, huh?" he asked.

"Oh, yeah."

Dinner ended and the volunteers left. I followed them out to the *waratan* (gate) and said goodbye. When I came back in, a brigade of men in tahýas grabbed my arm and ran me up to the attic. There were a dozen bright red prayer rugs in neat rows of four across the floor. The men took their places and waited with their hands folded. I retired to the back corner to watch. At first, there was no movement. Then a man came creaking up the steps. He was short and round with a beard of lightning wires. He wore a green cape that swished from side to side and a high sheepskin hat that made him look like Frankenstein with a Jheri curl. He padded up to his prostrated flock. A second later, he let off a beam-rattling *Allaaaaaah hoo Akbaaar*. The men bowed their heads and touched behind their ears. With robotic motion, they folded to their knees and kissed their foreheads to the ground. A chorus of whispered prayers rose from their rugs like steam. I felt like I was alone in my tent at a campground full of schizophrenics at night. The men bathed their faces with their hands. Then they fell silent and stood. The *imam* looked them over and breathed in deep. He belted out another, Allaaaaaah hoo Akbaaar, and the cycle repeated.

At four-thirty the next morning, I awoke to a flickering in the dark. The power had been blown out by a sandstorm, so suhoor was being served by candlelight. I followed Çynar to the living room and took a seat at the *klionka* (tablecloth). Spread across it, were a few big plates of palow and some pickled veggies. I filled my stomach to the breaking point then guzzled a liter of soda. I knew I wouldn't be eating or drinking for the whole day, so I had to get my fix. After a mumbled prayer, I retired to my room and crashed. I didn't wake up until noon.

Fasting for the rest of the day was tough. I'm a huge foodie so keeping myself away from the fridge, even for a few hours, is cuticle-chewing agony. I managed to distract myself by writing in my journal and studying Turkmen. Come evening, I was so starved, I could have eaten the week-old contents of an obese cripple's bedpan and been perfectly happy.

Before sitting down for iftar, I went out to the banýa and cleaned up. On my way back, I took a little detour over to Baa's pen. I expected to see him rolled into a little black ball on his bed of hay. Instead, I saw those two dickhead chickens spearing their beaks at an apple core. I was too tired and hungry to think much of it. I went into the house and sat at the klionka. Jennet appeared at the doorway. She was carrying a wide plate with a big upturned bowl on it. She bent down gingerly and placed it in front of me. Then she plopped in her spot and motioned for me to do the honors. I nodded and slid my fingers around the lips of the bowl. I looked up at her and raised an eyebrow.

"What is it?" I asked.

She clasped her pudgy hands together.

"It's a surprise," she said.

I chuckled and lifted the bowl. A billow of steam rose like a trapped ghost from under an uprooted gravestone. When it cleared, I got a look at dinner. It was a phantasmagoria of gore. Around the sides were four severed hooves. The skin on them had been boiled so thin that the fat underneath was bursting through in greasy little daisies. At the center of this bone and gelatin mess was the mantelpiece—a charred and grinning sheep's head with its skullcap removed. I stared at the frightening white teeth for a second. Suddenly my asshole puckered. The suck was so hard it pulled my mouth to a dot. Maksat pitched his chin back and howled. He grabbed a knife and jabbed it at Baa's face. With a twist of his wrist, he scooped out Baa's left eyeball. He skewered it and held it up for me. My composure crumbled like so many Jenga blocks from a tipping tower. I took the knife from him with a quivering hand.

"What am I supposed to do with it?" I asked.

Maksat smiled.

"You're our guest and it is Eid al-Fitr," he said. "You must eat it."

My heart melted into threads. Not two days prior, I was petting Baa behind the ears and telling him what a good boy he was. Now I was supposed to eat his fucking eyeball? What kind of people were these? I glared at them from behind the knife. I wanted to tell them to shove it up their asses. Then I thought of all the hungry family members Baa had fed. I thought of the desert, its unyielding soil and terrible heat. I lifted the knife and cracked my teeth. I bit down over

Baa's eyeball and slid it from the tip. It rolled over my tongue and lodged against my cheek. I looked around the room and chewed. The eyeball instantly burst into slime. I swallowed it quickly and forced a smile. The whole room erupted with laughter. I wiped my face and joined in.

BEFORE VISITING OUR permanent sites, we had four hub days. The third of these is most salient in my mind. It began like any other. I came to headquarters by taxi and sat in the meeting room with the trainees. Peace Corps did their thing: safety and security, cross-cultural training, blah fuckin' blah. By hour two, I was ready to slump over and die with boredom. I had to pinch my scrotum through my pocket to stay awake. The teacher training presentation began. It was conducted by a T-14 who reminded me of a casino pit-boss. He had broad shoulders, thick arms, and tan skin. His hair was like black curly fries and his eyes like balls of gray marble. He wore a white collared shirt and navy slacks. He walked back and forth in a straight line. He told us his name was Ken and that he was stationed in Mary City. This caught my attention as Mary welaýat was where I was hoping I'd be stationed. The place had a bit of everything; the cities were big but not too big, the other volunteers were close by, the primary language was pure Teke-Turkmen and not Russian or Uzbek, and it was supposedly very pretty.

When Ken finished, I asked what his primary project was. He cracked his mouth and made half-circles with his hands.

"You've brought me to my next point," he said. "I work at the American Corner which is a place where local kids can come to practice their English, use the internet, attend cross-cultural interest groups, and apply for ESL programs to the US. We've helped a lot of Turkmen youths achieve their dreams. If any of you think you've got what it takes to aid us, we'd be glad to put you to the test."

Here was an opportunity to let my shit shine. If I were serving at the American Corner, I could use my knack for languages and knowledge of world cultures to really help people. I told Ken I wanted to know more.

"We can discuss it more in-depth later," he said.

After training, I approached him. He greeted me with the stern discomfort of a politician who'd just farted silently at a White House banquet. I ignored this and quizzed him about the American Corner. He listened patiently then pursed his lips into a little O.

"To be honest," he said. "I'm tired of talking about the place. I do need a beer though. Why don't you grab your green friends and come with me to the Zip."

He could have invited me to an upturned latrine; anything was better than hanging out at PCHQ. Plus, none of us T-15s had actually seen the Zip yet. I grabbed Mick, hooked up with Ken, and we split.

The Zip was spitting distance from headquarters. We walked there in under three minutes. From the outside, it didn't look like much; just a flickering red sign above a dirty white door. Ken led us in. The place opened into a wide lounge area with triangular orange ceiling lamps and a mirrored bar. Bruised Russian waitresses flitted back and forth with plates of food and bottles of booze. The air was blue with smoke and reeked of mackerel and bad breath. Ken wove his way through the tumult. We followed him into an outdoor seating area. There were a dozen tables ringed with plastic chairs, a small bandstand, and a series of grills. A few bamboo dining huts were in back next to the crumbling shitters. A large oak tree grew in the center of everything like the gnarled hands of a forest god. We took a seat in its shade and ordered a round of beers. They came quick and we clinked glasses. Ken congratulated us on breaking our Zip-cherries. We thank him and chugged. The beer tasted like anus juice, but what the hey; it was beer and we were out on the town.

Other volunteers soon arrived. Ken leaned in and spoke in a low voice.

"I know you're interested in the American Corner and that's terrific," he said. "But there's another more important thing I should cover first."

"What's that?" I asked.

"Pussy."

The word unfurled from his tongue like a yawning panther. Mick and I leaned in closer.

"Continue," Mick said.

"Well, as I'm sure you've both gathered, village Turkmen chicks are off-limits. Even holding hands in public will signal that you intend to marry. So, unless you guys want to father children in this place and spend your lives eating dograma and picking cotton, hands off the locals. But that doesn't mean you won't get laid. In fact, I can guarantee that with a little effort you guys can fuck every chick in your welaýat within six months."

"Jesus," I said.

"But this comes with a price. PC is one big rumor mill. So expect that if you nail a volunteer, she's gonna tell her friends everything from the way you fuck to the size and shape of your cock, and that shit will get around fast. No secrets in Peace Corps, my friend."

The thought of this was unsettling. Heaven forbid I crapped myself during a drunken blowjob one night only to awake the next morning to 80+ volunteers around the country laughing their asses off at me. I asked Ken if he had any advice on how to maintain dignity in the face of embarrassment.

"I got nuthin'," he said. "But what I can say is that we're all in the same boat. Anyways, after the first few rumors about you get out, you'll be used to it. My advice is, if the opportunity to get laid comes, take it and forget the consequences. 'Cuz once training ends and you're stuck out there in the great lunar wasteland, it can get pretty damn lonely."

LEARNING TURKMEN FLUENTLY was a goal of mine. The minute I got myself situated, I began crunching at its nouns, verbs, and adjectives like they were rocks hiding specks of gold. My efforts caught Hurma's attention. She challenged me by giving me harder assignments. Often, she'd tell me to write short stories or study more advanced grammar. She even gave me my own corner of our tiny classroom so I could complete my work undisturbed. To thank her, I burnt through my lessons then horned in on hers. It's not that I was trying to be a dickhead, I just was. Hurma and the other volunteers went batshit over this. I was routinely scolded or thrown out of class.

One such incident occurred the day before Zoya, the boss LCF at Peace Corps, performed our preliminary Turkmen oral exams. Hurma was teaching the days and months à la Türkmenbaşy while I was piddling with one grammatical anomaly or another. When I finished, I handed in my assignment and sat next to Mick. Poor bastard was trying his damnedest to learn how to ask what the date was in Turkmen. Hurma repeated, "*Şu gün aýyň näçesi?*" a half-dozen times. Mick tried to mouth the words but only looked like he was blowing a ghost. He threw up his hands in defeat.

"I can't fuckin' say 'Shoo Nancy Reagan outta the room' or whatever," he said. "It's all just in one ear and out the other."

I giggled into my fist. Hurma hissed at me then turned to Mick.

"You tell after me," she said in her bar hag's voice. "*Şuuuuu . . . güüüüün . . .aýýýýýýň . . . näääääçesi?*"

Mick's eyes were wide blue ponds behind his specs. He raised his hands and illustrated his confusion. With his right, he made a pointer and stabbed the foreign words into his ear. With his left, he made a fist and pulled them unlearned like a washcloth from his other ear. Then he dusted his palms and turned them upwards for her to see.

"*Men bilemok,*" he shouted. "I don't know."

I shot my skull back and roared. Hurma slammed both fists on the desk and speared her arm at the door.

"Get out, Johann," she screamed.

I made puppy dog eyes and shrugged.

"Maybe you could teach us something we actually *wanna* learn," I suggested.

Hurma closed one eye and bunched her lips. Her face grew fatter and her hips grew wider. She looked like a mutant purple tomato. She folded her arms over her belly and lasered her open eye at me.

"Like what?" she snarled.

"Cuss words?" I said.

I thought she was gonna blow. I walled my hands out to protect myself from flying limbs. Hurma inflated with air. Before her köýnek split, she let it all out.

"Why *nohhh?*" she said.

The next hour was a blast. Hurma taught us all the basics—*sik* (cock), *um* (pussy), *bok* (shit), *ýumurtgalar* (balls), *göt* (ass). Then she opened the floor to suggestions. People went for the standards: fuck you (*Sikdir*), and whatnot. I wanted something more.

"How 'bout 'Go fuck your grandmother's mouth'?" I asked.

The class unhinged with laughter. Hurma shook her head and grinned. She taught us everything we asked, even my *"Eneniň agyzyny siksene."* We walked home that evening speaking Turkmen like *gurluşykçylar* (construction workers). It was the perfect training for our coming oral exams.

The next day at 9:00 a.m. sharp, Zoya arrived. Though I'd seen the woman before, her presence still amazed me. She stood six foot three with linebacker shoulders. She had the face of an embittered ostrich and the swag of a Sicilian mob boss. She came lumbering into our classroom clucking orders. After she tested a few volunteers, she barged up to me.

"Hello Johann," she chomped. "Let's have our exam."

I was nervous but prepared. I followed her into the classroom and took my seat. She started things off simple.

"Hello, how are you?"

Then she fired into heavier questioning. At first, it was like an ice pick to my forehead. I found myself slipping in and out of the realm of understanding. Suddenly, everything clicked. I caught eighty percent of what she spit, and I held it tight. From then on, we blew through topics like family, travel, culture, and teaching. We even talked about booze and blowing up. This naturally led to food. She asked me what I thought of the stuff here and I smirked.

"No offense," I said in Turkmen. "But I think it tastes like monkey shit."

Zoya craned her neck and clucked a "Wha-what?"

I chuckled.

"Well maybe not like monkey shit," I said. "But certainly like monkey crap. I mean, it's always the same four godawful dishes— palow, manty, dograma, and çorba. And when it's not these things, it's either sheep hooves or cow guts or goat eyeballs. It's worse than *The Temple of Doom*, for Christ's sake."

Zoya glared at me with her big veiny vulture eyes. I could feel my heart start to sizzle. I held my mouth closed and looked straight ahead. Zoya frowned and nodded.

"I understand you don't like our food *now*," she said. "But after a while, you will."

I folded my arms and gave her the yeah, right sniff. The language exam continued. We talked about my living situation and my host family. Then we discussed my aspirations for a permanent site. I told her I was hoping to get sent to a town or city in Mary welaýat. I said I thought I had a chance. Zoya gave me a look like maybe.

"In my opinion, though," she said. "You should be sent to a village because you're so *interesting (gyzykly)*."

I couldn't tell if she was being facetious. I decided to poke her back anyway. I hit her with the only word I knew in Turkmen that rhymes with gyzykly.

"Well you're a *gurlusykçy*," I said.

She raised an eyebrow.

"What does that word mean?" she asked.

"You mean, you don't know?"

"No, I was raised in Aşgabat, so I use many Russian words."

"I see."

That concluded my language exam. Zoya gave me a damn fine score, but I took it with a grain of salt.

MICK WAS THE buddy I'd been hoping for; dude was my motherfuckin' homeboy. We did everything together. In the mornings, we snored through Hurma's lessons and screwed around. At break, we hit the bazaar and grabbed lamb pies. At lunch, we cracked jokes about the miserable food and the lame Turkmen music videos our host families threw on the tube. In the evenings, we hung out at each other's places, worked on Peace Corps projects, and shot the breeze. We even made up nicknames for the staff at Birinji Mekdep. Our mammoth librarian with the hideous purple dresses and sweaty pits was Barney. Our gangly vice-principal with the gold teeth and pointy shoulders was Skeletor. Our goofy müdir with the glossy lips and cheap suits was Bubbles (after Michael Jackson's pet chimp). Our skinny janitor with the shit-caked heels and long dick nose was Andy Griffith. And our LCFs, Hurma and Arzygül, were Sponge and Spiker—the evil aunts from *James and the Giant Peach*. Our nicknaming didn't stop at School #1. It reached all the way up to the big man himself. Instead of calling him Türkmenbaşy (Great Leader of the Turkmen), we went with T-Money, T-Bag, T-Diddy, T-Pain, and even T-eez Nuts.

Besides the same scathing sense of humor, Mick and I had other things in common. We both had undivorced folks and close families. We both had a core group of childhood friends that we did everything with. We both drank heavily and blew up huge. And we both came from small towns where everyone knew everyone else.

During our three months of training, Mick and I got into a lot of shit. I got stories up the wazoo, but only one is worth telling. It happened one night around Halloween, in the year of our Lord, 2006.

I LEFT MY house at seven. The moon hung in the sky like a sweaty pair of gym shorts. Mick met me on the road with his fro out. The two of us were headed to a party. The thing was being thrown for the host grandfather of another Annau trainee. The guy was turning sixty-three—a special birthday for Muslim males as that's the age when Muhammad is believed to have died.

We stopped at a *dükan* and grabbed a bottle of *Ak Bürgüt* (White Eagle), the finest vodka Turkmenistan had to offer at three bucks a liter. We turned a corner and dipped downhill. This brought us to a fenced-off mansion. Behind the wires, the scene was pumping. Three hundred-plus people were dancing and eating and singing and drinking. We pushed open the gate and entered the spill. We stepped and clawed past tables of gold-grilled fat ladies slurping çorba, rows of ancient dudes with wispy white beards and Mongolian eyes pounding shots, troupes of crew-cut punks in tight suits and oversized ties dancing circles, and in the middle, a bud of pretty young girls in daisy köýneks unfurling their hands like flower petals.

Presiding over everything was the man of the hour. He was short, fat and bald with a ten-dollar grin on his cheeks and a bright red tahýa gripping his scalp. As the DJ ripped odd beats like octopi on bongos, homeboy graced the stage with his hands fanned and yodeled through his nose.

Mick and I knew we'd need a few to get into the spirit of this shindig. We hiked upstairs to the guestroom. The other trainees were in there, listening to American tunes and sucking the necks of vodka bottles. We sat down and joined in. The hands spun cartoon-like around the nose of the clock.

When the night was thick, we stumbled downstairs. We sat at a table in the middle of the crowd and hung our tongues out. The food was being served and we were starved. We gorged ourselves on palow, çorba, shashlik, *burç dolamasy* (stuffed peppers), and manty. By the end of it, we were popping buttons. A few of the trainees peeled off to go sleep. Then we were three: me, Mick, and one lone chick. Her name was Abby. She was so shitfaced she could barely keep her blond locks from flopping into her shot glass. I grabbed her by the hand and shook her awake. She lifted her head and grinned like a crushed tomato. I told Mick we'd better take her home. He gulped down a penny's worth of rotgut and nodded. Just as we were leaving, we heard a sharp whistle. We looked across the crowd and saw a dude we knew holding up a bottle. It was the guy with the black crew cut and smelly breath who owned the restaurant we'd escaped to on our third night in Annau. He'd served us up fat many a time, so it'd have been rude to refuse him. We staggered over there with Abby between us. Her head pitched back and forth, and her legs curled like worms. We got to the table and plopped her down. She threw her red face back and laughed.

"Let's have sum shoddy woddy wooohooo," she shouted

By some grand miracle of Allah, our friend understood her. He uncapped the bottle and tipped it around. The vodka flowed like rainwater from the gutters into all our open mouths. We drank and we laughed, and we poured, and we drank. I looked over at Abby to see how she was faring. Mr. Candy Breath had his arm around her shoulder and was grinning up at her sagging lips like a deranged fox. I glanced at Mick to see what the haps were in his world. Homefry had ditched his glass and was now chugging from the neck. Through a haze of bad alcohol and worse music, I was able to hatch a single good thought.

"Why don't we get the hell outta here?" I said.

Mick slapped his palms down and shot up.

"Sprew dat," he croaked. "Ah frunna gro out ona dance foor n'see whud ah kin fruck."

I should have stopped him. I knew it was the right thing to do. I didn't stop him. Instead, I took out my camera and taped him.

The video rolled and so did ol' Mick . . . right into the midst of the dancing ladies. They moved like enchanted roses in a fever dream. He moved like a crippled zombie in a vodka nightmare. He bumped and tumbled and crashed through them, all the way till he hit the main stage. Then he looked for a partner. The girlies had scattered, leaving only one choice. Mick smiled and locked arms with the birthday boy. The man's eyes lit up with shock and he stomped his feet. Mick got about two good spins in before he slipped and fell on his ass. Birthday Boy lifted him up and shoved him toward the gate. I couldn't let the horror show go on any longer. I grabbed my two friends, bowed to the crowd, and split.

The walk to Abby's was a disaster. I thought we were doomed for the bushes more than once. Miraculously, we arrived unscathed. We staggered through her waratan and to her front door. The plan was to get her to her room without waking her host family. It seemed to be working just fine. Then Mick shrugged his shoulders and unzipped his pants.

"I thrilly gotta fluckin' friss," he said.

Abby offered to show him to the outhouse. She roped her arms around his shoulders and aimed him away from the porch. This must have dislodged something in his bladder. Piss came spraying out of his bent pecker like foam from a fire extinguisher. It ripped against the open door and showered the floor below. Every one of Abby's host family's shoes got soaked. Mick made a goofy face and continued pissing with his pants around his ankles. Abby and I cracked apart laughing.

When the show ended, I grabbed Mick. We said our guh'byes to Abby and left her there cackling. On our way home, we took a wrong turn. We ended up in a dirt lot on the fringes of the trash dump. Mick could no longer walk. He collapsed to the ground with a thud. I pulled out my camera again. While he rambled on about how we were such good bros, I videoed. I let the camera run for a few minutes. I started feeling bad. The second I switched it off, Mick went into a choking fit. He kicked himself to a seated position then vomited all over his crotch.

"Jesus," I cried.

I picked the poor bastard up by his arm and walked him toward the road. He was wobbly at the knees and dripping with puke. I couldn't say how, but we found our street. Mick saw his house and shot a finger at it.

"Der ah am," he said.

He broke into a sprint and crashed against the gate. He tried to yank it open, but it was locked. He stuck his hands and feet in the slots and started climbing. He reached the top and a light clicked on. His host sister opened the front door. This spooked him, and he lost his balance. He pitched forward with his hands out and tumbled to the ground. The noise made all the lights in the house click on. His host family came running outside. Mick just sat there, chuckling in a cloud of dust. His host mom grabbed him by the arm. I offered to help but she spat at me.

The next day, Mick got a visit from Mahym. She slapped him with a contract that was pretty harsh. From then until swearing-in, he was to be home every night by six. He wasn't allowed any weekend jaunts to Aşgabat, nor was he allowed to hit the Zip with us after hub days. This was a blow but not a deadly one; we could still party indoors.

One night a week before site visit,[25] we shared a bottle of Ak Bürgüt in Mick's room. We got on the topic of permanent sites, and I asked Mick where he thought his would be. He put his fist to his cheek and stared at the ground.

"Well, I got my passport taken today at lunch," he said.

"What does that mean?"

"It means Peace Corps is prolly gonna send me to Daşoguz."

Daşoguz is the welaýat farthest to the north. It's also the hardest to access due to a dozen roadblocks along the way and a series of permits one must carry just to make it through them. Being sent there meant you were a ghost to the other volunteers. The fact that my passport hadn't been taken and his had, presumably to fit it with all the necessary permits to enter Daşoguz, meant the chances of me and Mick serving near one another were slim to none.

The next day Zoya came by and joined us at lunch. She just sat there like a big green witch pouring tea into her wicked grin. Mick and I couldn't take it. We asked her if she knew anything about our permanent sites and she clucked.

"Yes, I do," she said.

"Well then tell us," Mick said.

She raised a long eyebrow and stirred her çaý.

"Mr. Carvey," she said. "You'll be going to Daşoguz. And Mr.

---

[25] A site visit is when a PCV visits their permanent site for the first time.

Felmanstien. . . you'll be staying here in Annau."

"Aw fuck," we both said.

4

THE NEXT MORNING, I woke up sad but chill; sad because Mick might as well have been slingshot to the moon, but chill because at least I'd be living in a part of the country I knew. I'd also be staying with a host family I liked. I'd told them the news the night before and they'd flipped.

After breakfast, I showered and hit the *poçta* (Post Office). The Annau crew was already there waiting. We caught cabs to headquarters. We found the T-15s standing around a crude map of Turkmenistan drawn on the pavement. Zoya was up front. She had a wide smile on her face. I thinned my eyes at her and smirked. She gazed back at me tenderly. I sidestepped her and went to the map. Ata, our site coordinator, started calling off names. People scrambled to their sites. Mick was already in Daşoguz. When Ata got to F I stepped forward.

"Mr. Felmanstien," he said. "Please go to . . ."

I walked over to Annau. I didn't see my name. I crinkled my brow. Ata let it fly.

"Gurbagahowda," he said.

I looked at him like he'd snubbed a lit cigarette on my nipple.

"What the fuck?"

The trainees broke into laughter. Zoya looked at me and grinned.

"I only joke with you coz' I *looove* you, Johann," she said.

I felt like spitting in her stupid face. I balled my fists and walked over to my site. It was smack dab in the middle of the Ahal desert. Nothing was around it for miles. I asked if anyone else would be with me. Ata puffed through his nose.

"You will enjoy your service alone in Gurbagahowda."

I sucked my teeth at him.

"Yeah, I bet."

THAT NIGHT WAS tough. Mick and I spent it draining vodka bottles in our room at the Ak Altyn and reminiscing about "the good old days." Though we had another month left in Annau together, it was still sad knowing we'd barely see each other over the next two years. We promised to visit and write as much as possible.

At five-thirty, we were cracked awake by Mick's nasty alarm. The guy had to catch an early morning flight to Daşoguz for his site visit. He grabbed his bags and gave me a tight hug. Then he slipped out the door. I'd have gone back to sleep but my marşrutka was leaving at seven. I went to the bathroom and rotted in the shower. I toweled off and assembled my shit. At six-thirty, I staggered down to the lobby in dirty jeans and a wrinkled coat. I looked like a mustard packet some furious soldier had crushed with his boot heel. The vols accompanying me were in a similar state. Our chariot arrived an hour later. We got in without saying a word.

The driver twisted the key and we clunked off. I pasted my eyes to the window and watched the scene unfold. Aşgabat was a shroud of fog. Its marble towers loomed in the mist like giants in hibernation. We drove past them and out onto the desert. Its infinite canvas was brown and brown and brown. The peaks of the Kopet-Dag[26] rippled along our window. Soon even they were sucked to the

---

[26] The Kopet-Dag is a mountain range running along the border between Turkmenistan and Iran.

ground by the pull of the Garagum.[27] I counted tiny villages for a time. They popped up like tufts of dusty hair then disappeared into the sandscape. I looked around the marşrutka. Four others were in the same boat as me. I knew all of them from hub days. There were Dick and Dora, a married couple from Milwaukee. Fletcher, an Ivy League prick from Yonkers. And Brooke, a kicking horse of a woman from Jasper, Indiana. I knew her best. We'd hung out a couple times at the Zip and gotten trashed, even shared a rare moment or two. I preferred her to the other three. We chatted as taxis, tractors, and vans whipped past us on the one-lane highway. Much of what we said was lost to me. We were just killing time till our chauffeur dropped us off.

The first to go was Fletcher. We left him at a village called Kaka. Next to go were Dick and Dora. Their site was a town named Tejen, which at least had a few restaurants and a bank. We then went to Brooke's site. The place was called *Bitaraplyk* (Neutrality), which, along with *garaşsyzlyk*, or independence, were virtues T-Bag felt his country eternally embodied. We dropped her off at a white school with light blue doors. Its walls were feathered with cracks and its sidewalks were riddled with potholes. She got out of the van and grabbed her shit. Before she split, I had her turn around for a pic. She stood with a hand on her bag and another on her hip. The freckles on her cheeks glinted angrily and her mane of red hair burned like a flag at war. I told her, "Say Cheese," and she said, "Screw you." I snapped the photo and bid her adieu.

Now it was just me. All I knew was the name of my site. Despite my good Turkmen, the meaning of Gurbagahowda was a mystery to me. I busted out my dictionary and tried to find it. Just then we pulled up at a crappy restaurant on the outskirts of Tejen. The driver parked and told me to get out. I asked him "What the fuck?" and he shrugged.

"Peace Corps told me to drop you off here," he said.

---

[27] The Garagum is a desert in Central Asia that covers 70% of Turkmenistan. The name translates as "Black Sand" in many Turkic languages.

I curled a lip and grabbed my shit. The driver sped off and I heard a shout. I turned around and saw a dude. He was six foot two and skinny as a snorkeling tube. His eyes were wide and his glasses, wider. He had scruffy brown hair and wore a peacoat and bowtie. He raised a hand and waved me hi. I waved him back and walked on up. I told him my name and he huffed.

"I know that," he said. "I'm Cyrus, the T-13 handing your site over."

Cyrus was an odd bloke. He carried an air of constant pondering and irritation. Even small movements he found bothersome. It was almost as if an unexpected brush against the shoulder would send him squealing up the neck of his peacoat like a newly castrated cat. Despite all that, he seemed like a nice enough guy. I shook his hand carefully and followed him into the restaurant. We took our seats amidst the flies and gold-toothed yokels munching *gutap* (fried lamb pockets) and sipping çaý. We ordered a big plate of manty. It came out hot and steaming and smothered in *gatyk* (yogurt). We dug in deep and stuffed our faces. In between chews, Cyrus gave me the lowdown.

"I brought you here today because you're my successor. I wanted to do something nice for you that nobody did for me when I first arrived."

"Thanks."

"I also wanted to give you some advice. Now, I know you're probably worried about having a more difficult site, but don't be. You're going to get a real understanding of this culture out here, plus you'll earn your stripes and bragging rights. Isn't that better than partying at a bunch of shitty bars back in Aşgabat?"

The man had a point. I was feeling better already. I envisioned my site as somewhere tough but cool; a cross between Mickey Rourke and the Pink Panther, if the two were spliced together and made a Turkmen village. Even the name Gurbagahowda took on a rogue-like hue. In my swelling imagination, it now meant things like "Sand-Blown Badass," or "Lion of the Black Desert."

We finished our meals and got in a taxi. As we blasted toward the unknown, I asked Cyrus what Gurbagahowda meant. He turned around with a blank face.

"Bullfrog Pond," he said.

The name hit me like a greased dick to the lips.

"You mean to tell me I'm gonna spend two years of my life in a fucking village named after a place where oversized amphibians go to fornicate?"

Cyrus huffed in consideration.

"I hadn't thought of it that way before. But yes, Johann, you are."

THE DESERT BLED by in many streaks of brown. Bent telephone poles lined the road. The sky was a measureless inhalation of gray. I sat in the back seat thumbing my nails. I was nervous but excited just the same. Cyrus was in the front seat snoring. Braving Hitler's sandbox was like going to Denny's for him. I must admit I was jealous.

We came upon a checkpoint manned by guards. They were dark and portly with cleft chins and hats that shined like new nickels. When they saw who we were, they waved us through. We blew past two gold pillars and a sign that read Gurbagahowda. The place crawled up on us like ticks. There were haystacks, barns, and houses, livestock, cars, and buildings. We veered to the right and up a mud hill. We stopped in a parking lot with other taxis. We got out of the cab and told the dude to wait. He said he would, and we split. I followed Cyrus around the bend. He led me to a courtyard made of dirt. It was littered with bricks and hollowed by puddles. A lone crib of branches rustled in the wind. A few old buildings sagged up ahead. They were white and peeling with windows ready to slip from their frames like sucker-punched teeth. I looked at them with mild interest.

"What is this place?" I said.

Cyrus exhaled.

"It's your school."

I soaked the joint in. A man in a tattered black coat walked up. He had frizzy hair and red skin. His eyes were black marbles, and his cheekbones glistened. He shook my hand with both of his. Then he cracked his jaws and showed me his carousel of gapped teeth.

"Ehh, I am Azat," he said in jagged English. "And I will to be your counterpart."

I nodded and told him how great that was. He grinned at me again.

"Come," he said. "I will take you to Islam."

I shrugged and followed him. We walked to a building at the far end of the school and went in. The floors were made of ancient wood planks. We creaked up to a blue door and opened it. The room beyond was long and narrow. Its walls were lined with paintings of T-Bag in various suggestive poses. At the back was a big desk with a tiny man at it. He was browner than fudge with knife-slit eyes. He waved us forward with a microscopic hand. We creaked up to him and took our seats. At first, the man was silent. Then he cracked up laughing. His laughter filled the room like drunken warlocks. As suddenly as it had started, it stopped. The little man patted his tie back down and offered me a hand.

"I'm Islam," he said. "The müdir of zis school."

"Umm, nice to meet you. I'm Johann, your new volunteer."

"Ahh, I sought zis."

He leaned forward and raised his eyebrows to the coves of his widow's peak.

"Soooo," he said, making a tiny O with his mouth. "*Sen schoolda worklejekmi?*"

I retracted my face.

"Huh?"

"*Sen Iňglis dili teachmeli*," he said, slapping his desk.

Somewhere some poor clown slit his own throat. I breathed out through my nose and forced a smile.

"*Oh*, I get it," I said. "You're mixing Turkmen with English. That's extremely hilarious. Yeah, I'll be working here."

"*Tüweleme*," he shouted. "We will give you tour tomorrow. Now, let's see your Turkmen family."

WE ALL SQUEEZED in the cab and bumbled down the unpaved artery. My host-family-to-be lived on the other side of town. I got a good look at the guts of Gurbagahowda. There were a few white buildings speckled with mud, a shabby bazaar, a couple of dükans. A park of dead trees made it official. The place was a dump. I was still at a loss as to why it was called Bullfrog Pond. I asked Cyrus and he clenched his teeth.

"You'll see in the spring," he said.

We pulled up to a light blue waratan. We parked and got out. As we were unloading my bags, a boy walked up. He was tall and skinny with a bowl cut and big hands. His eyes were the color of snail shells. His ears were chimp-like, and his cheeks and nose drooped. He greeted me and said his name was Merdan. I greeted him back and he grabbed my crap. We followed him through the gate and into the courtyard. To the right was a dilapidated bath/kitchen area, and to the left, an L-shaped brick house with two wings. The bottom was the bigger wing where the family lived. The top was the smaller wing where I'd be. We hiked up the outside steps and across the balcony. Merdan opened the door and we went in. The place wasn't half bad. Its floors were covered with clean brown rugs, and there was a tiny desk and a bed. At the back was a mural of some Turkmen hunter capping a wild boar. The creature was in mid-pounce as the bullet ripped through its head. Merdan set my stuff down and left. A few moments later, he came up with food. It was bowls of watery çorba, but what the hey? The four of us were starving.

Throughout the entire meal, Islam cracked his jokes. At first, they were mildly funny. They soon flagged. I decided to call it a night. Islam told me to be at school the next day at eight. I nodded and said late. Azat and Islam walked off. Cyrus stopped. His eyes were weird blue orbs behind his glasses. I asked him what the deal was.

"Careful if you go to the outhouse in back later," he said. "Your host brother warned me that a very aggressive alabai lurks around there, especially at night."

I told him not to worry. I was too exhausted even to shit. He left and I closed the door. I schlepped to my bed and crashed.

At 6:00 a.m. there was an itch in my belly. It crawled through my intestines like a hairy earthworm. When it reached my anus, I snapped awake. My butt cheeks broke into a painful jitter. I gripped my stomach and propped myself up. The whole load in me almost exploded against the sheets. I clenched my rear and bolted to the door. Dog or no, I had to make it to that outhouse. I pounded across the balcony and down the stairs. I raced across the courtyard and made a sharp left. The outhouse was right in front of me. It was tall and peeling and crooked with a door that dissolved into dirt. I opened it and looked down. There were two bricks on either side of a hole in the concrete floor. Below was a mountain of feces. I could smell its presence like a demon at my toes. I knew the routine from Annau. I dropped my drawers, popped a squat and let 'er rip. It sounded like a bunch of sweaty midgets having an orgy on a bed of wet balloons. I laughed at the sickening ridiculousness of it all. I finished and wiped my ass with some old newspaper. I stood, pulled my pants up, and buckled them. I opened the door and jumped back. A girl was standing there with her arms folded. She was wrapped in teal köýnek. She had a slender frame and a long neck like a lily. Her face was a perfect oval. It would have been pretty were it not twisted into angry splinters. I tiptoed to her sandals and extended a hand.

"Nice to meet you," I said. "I'm Johann."

She scowled at my mitt with her furious green eyes like it was the shred of newspaper I'd just wiped my ass with.

"I know who you are," she spat.

She turned and walked off. Her shapely rear end jiggled and swayed. Merdan jogged up to me, giggling.

"That was my older sister Aziza," he said. "She's just shy."

"Shy?"

I shrugged it off and got ready. I had to layer it on thick as it was chilly out. Merdan walked me to school. On the way, I asked him where the rest of his family was. He told me his father was working construction in Aşgabat and his mother and four other siblings were visiting family.

"You'll meet them all when you come back for New Year's," he said.

THE REST OF the day was a whirlwind. After watching the students sing the national anthem like a clan of screaming baby Klingons, Cyrus and Azat took me all around Gurbagahowda for a meet-and-greet. First, we did the school. Cyrus warned me to say hello to each teacher individually lest they all get jealous and turn against me. Next, we hit the police station. The cops were disgusting fat blobs, but they registered me without incident. Finally, we went to Azat's house. His sweet wife cooked a gang of manty and we chomped it down over bottles of Bulgarian wine. Afterwards, Azat busted out the arak. We drained shots till we were good and plastered, then Cyrus walked me home.

Back at my place, we ate pumpkin çorba and gossiped up in my bedroom. Cyrus told me I should teach my host sister Aziza English because he found her cute. I agreed that she was a looker but figured I should wait on the teaching part.

"I tried to shake her hand after taking a massive shit this morning," I said. "She wasn't too thrilled with that."

He snickered. We gossiped a bit more, then he gathered his stuff. As he walked out, he told me to be at school at eight the next morning. I said I would. I closed my door and did some reading. Sleep slowly crept up on me. I clicked off the light and slipped under my covers. I was just at the point of passing out when I heard a knock. I shuffled up and answered the door. It was my school director, Islam. His hands were shaking, and his eyes were pinched. A cloud of arak stalked him from behind like a garlic fart. I asked what he wanted. He grinned at me with rotted teeth.

69

"Preeze kung to my hoang," he said.

I was inclined to tell him to piss off. He looked so desperate standing there drunk. I dropped my shoulders and rolled my eyes.

"Why not?" I said.

I grabbed my coat and slippers. I followed him out the waratan and across the road to his house. It was a dinky little joint that glowed orange against the night. We went inside and sat by the electric heater. Homeboy's wife served us tea and cookies. Then out came the arak. We poured a couple of shots. We clinked glasses and clicked on the tube. Lurid images oozed from the screen. Barrel-chested Turkish dudes with beards and gold chains ass-pounded pretty young blondes. Islam looked at the TV then back at me.

"You like zis?" he asked.

"Hell, yeah."

He smiled and poured two more shots. Then he pulled out a box. He opened it and there were pictures. He picked up a handful and thumbed through them.

"Zis pictures are from 2000 camp in Çüli," he said. "We do zis wiz first Gurbagahowda volunteer, Lenny Dunst."

He showed me Lenny's photo. The guy was tall and skinny with glasses like two bike wheels. Next to him was a much younger, much less wrinkly, Islam. He was mid-jump, with a big-ass smile on his face.

"It was so much party," he said. "We sing, we dance, we laugh, we play game. Zen when kids go to sleeping, we drink and have fire. It was best time in my life. And you know, Johann . . .?"

He put his arm around my shoulder and squeezed me in close. He breathed in my face, and my nose hairs detached from their follicles and sprinkled out my nostrils. I raised my eyebrows at him and he smiled.

"We are going to make even better Çüli camp, yust me and you," he said.

Something warm unfurled inside me. I felt strangely at home. I looked at the photos then at my müdir.

"Let's do it," I said.

WE SPENT THE rest of the night cracking jokes, downing arak, and watching Turkish porn. At around one, I got up to leave. Islam tried to stop me.

"I have to be at school by eight tomorrow," I said.

He grunted and walked me out. On the way to the road, he seemed nervous. I asked him what was up.

"Preeze to be carefoo," he said.

I figured he was just drunk. I told him okay and walked to my house. I opened the waratan door and stepped inside. I closed it behind me and the metal latch slipped in place without a sound. I turned around and saw a movement in the shadows. It streaked past the goat den and around the chicken coop. It came closer and closer and closer. It popped from the darkness and into the light. With paws slapping against the concrete, it ran up snarling and barking and snapping and drooling. Its eyes were red with menace, and its teeth were pink with blood. I kipped backwards and fell against the waratan. My heart pounded against my ribcage like a thundercloud. I screamed for Merdan. He came stumbling out the front door. He saw what was going on and freaked.

"Laika," he shouted. "Bsss."

In a snap, the hound in front of me went from big white badass to little beige beagle. I was shocked at how much smaller he seemed now that he was under control. Merdan grabbed him by the neck fat and yanked him back. I sidestepped them both and hopped up to my room. As I opened the door, I looked down at my host brother.

"Is that mutt gonna kill me if I take a shit later?" I asked him.

He belted Laika in the ribs and sent him whimpering to a corner.

"Hiç zat diýmez," he said. "He won't do nuthin'."

I ARRIVED AT school at eight the next morning. Before we started class observation, I told Cyrus what had happened with Laika. He could have given a rat's ass. I changed subjects and told him about my visit to Islam's. I asked him if he too had done some camps. He shook his head.

"Camps are tough these days," he said. "The Turkmen KGB or KNB has been really strict about that stuff since nine-eleven. I doubt you'll get permission. Islam tried to get me to do the same thing, but it was pretty much impossible. After many attempts, I gave up."

My heart flopped into my stomach. It stayed there till I left site.

5

THE NEXT THREE weeks were a rush to get things done. After a mediocre Thanksgiving with the volunteers in Aşgabat, we were shipped back to our respective training sites and inculcated with as much Turkmen as our brains could fit. Soon after that, we were given our language proficiency tests. My examiner gave me an intermediate high but Zoya bumped that down to intermediate mid because she felt my accent was muddled. Still, mine was one of the three highest scores among the T-15s. This meant I'd have to give a speech entirely in Turkmen during our swearing-in ceremony. I spent a good week scribbling that bitch out. When it was near perfect, I brought it to Hurma. She and I carved it a new asshole. Come mid-December we had it shining. I knew I was looking nice in the eyes of Peace Corps. At least I had that much.

One Sunday shortly before swearing-in, I hit PCHQ. I took a shower then went up to the lounge. Brooke was posted at a computer with her eyebrow cocked. Code was streaming down her screen like molten wax. Besides being a sav, the girl was also a computer whizz. None of what she was doing I could comprehend. I made some comment about it all being geek shit. She chuckled and fluttered her fingers over the keyboard. I sat down across from her and punched out some emails to family and friends. Then I felt a dryness coil up in my throat. I turned to Brooke and shrugged.

"Wanna grab a beer at the Zip?" I asked.

She pressed Enter and spun around in her chair.

"You read my mind."

We got to the place at five. It was packed, loud, and smoky. Cute Russian waitresses were threading up and down the aisles serving dried mackerel and shots of vodka. Brooke and I grabbed the only free booth. We ordered a couple Zips and sipped them. As we gossiped and laughed, three T-15s walked in the door. The first was a guy named Hal. Not Mormon Hal, my roomie in Arlington with the smelly feet, but Texas Hal on account of he was from Austin. Tex was as thin as a panhandle with a bent neck. He walked like a lazy day, showing his big white teeth to everyone. He had square glasses, licorice hair, and brown eyes. I'd also heard through the PC grapevine that his cock was the size of a country gourd.

Next in was a dude named Truman. He'd already garnered the nickname "Cluster Fuck" because he was a walking disaster. Besides just being a chunky klutz with scruffy hair and perpetually bloodshot eyes, the guy couldn't hold his liquor. I remember one night in particular where he'd gotten so smashed, he'd tripped on a sidewalk crack and shattered his nose and glasses. Even still, he was smart as fuck. Dude could blow through a tome on quantum physics and still have time at the end of the hour for lunch.

Last to come in was Brooke's bestie Dimuira. She was tall and slim with ivory skin and hair like threads of night. Her eyes were eerie blue, and her lips were pretty red slugs. She'd have been my perfect woman, except the gods had taken an ice cream scoop to her brain. Regardless, she had my little man's attention. I slid away from Brooke, so homegirl could sit next to me.

The conversation roared and the drinks poured. We went from beer to wine to shots. I suggested we go dance. Everyone agreed. We left and went to a dükan for road beers. Then we got a joint room at a smelly little piss-hole called the Daýhan where anyone with three bucks could grab four walls and a stained mattress. We called our host folks and told them the news. They weren't thrilled but hey, what could they do?

We went to a place called the English Pub. It had a bar upstairs and a club down below. We opted for the latter and drank. Then Dimuira and I hit the dance floor and shamelessly grabbed each other's asses. I went in for the kiss, but she pulled away.

"You should dance a little with Brooke," she said.

I said okay and grabbed Brooke. We did a quick two-step, then I went and licked my wounds at the bar. The arak flowed down my gullet. Things got hazy from then on. I remember holding Dimuira's hand. I also recall shooing away some dude that was hitting on her. We left the bar and stumbled back to the hotel. More drinking ensued and Tex and Truman gave Dimuira a massage. Brooke sat back and guzzled beer. I'd have joined her, but I could barely lift myself from the bed. Before too long my eyes slid over. I was out in seconds.

I WOKE UP drooling. An orchestra of pain was playing drearily in my skull. I winged my eyes over and saw Truman slumped across his sheets. His ass was in the air and his face was smashed into a pillow. I chuckled at him. He flattened out and groaned.

"How do you feel?" I asked.

"Not great. What time is it?"

I looked at my watch.

"Holy Christ, it's noon. We're late for everything."

I looked around the room. The others had gone.

"We should go back to site," Truman said.

"Yeah, no shit."

We cleaned up and went our separate ways. I got back to Annau at 1:00 p.m. I went straight to the lunch place. Everyone was eating manty and watching TV. I sat in with them and grabbed a spoon. I was hoping my prior absence had gone unnoticed. For a few minutes, things were cool. I started to relax and crack jokes. Then Hurma's phone rang.

"*Alew?*" she said. "Hello?"

Her conversation was muffled. I figured she was talking to her husband. Mick grilled me about the previous night. Before I could tell him the dirty details, Hurma elbowed me.

"*Mahym jañ etdi,*" she said. "Mahym's on the phone."

My stomach folded in on itself. I took the phone and put it to my ear.

"Hello?"

"Johann, where's Truman?" Mahym said.

I played dumb.

"Ummm, he should be at his site, I guess."

"He's the only one of you I can't account for."

"Oh, okay. Well, ah, try his site."

She thanked me and hung up. I knew we were fucked. Mick told me it was a stupid thing for Peace Corps to be pissed about. Rules are rules, though, and we weren't to be spending the night in Aşgabat until *after* swearing-in. Three minutes later, Mahym called back. She told me the situation was serious and that Bob wanted to speak to everyone involved.

"We're sending Jeeps to get the four of you now," she said.

Four?

THE JEEP CAME and took me to headquarters. Mahym was the first one I talked to. She was calm but firm.

"What happened last night?" she asked.

"Well . . ."

I told her the extent of our criminal actions in full detail. The only part I left out was how many of us there were. She tried to fish that info from me. I stonewalled her. She switched to scolding.

"Your host families were extremely worried," she said. "If you hadn't come by lunch, we'd have called to your parents in US to say you were missing."

I slouched accordingly. Mahym continued.

"I don't understand you, Johann. You're like man with two sides. One side is Big Johann who is responsible, hard-working leader. Other side is Little Johann who is troublemaker and brat. Most time you are good, but sometimes you let Little Johann have control. Why do you do this?"

The bitch had stuck her fingers in dark water. I wanted to introduce Little Johann to her fat ass. Before I did anything stupid, the phone rang. Mahym picked it up and nodded.

"Bob will see you now," she said.

I WENT INTO Bob's office. He was seated at the meeting table with his hands folded over his belly. He looked up at me plainly. Then he broke into shakes.

"What the hell's goin' on, Johann?" he said. "I thought things were straight with you."

I apologized profusely and offered to castrate myself. He ignored me and continued.

"You have so much potential, and you're throwing it away, man. And now here I am wondering if I should order your plane ticket home."

This last bit shook me up. I assured him I'd behave and that sending me home wasn't necessary.

"Well, you'd better be sure," he said. "'Cuz two years in the Turkmen desert ain't no cakewalk."

Bob calmed down a bit. He said I'd have to sign a performance contract but I could stay. I wiped my brow and shook his hand. Then I went upstairs. Though I wasn't going home, I still felt like shit. I hadn't even been sworn in and already I was screwing up. I entered the lounge with my head down. I saw a big box on the table. It was from my folks. I ripped it open and looked inside. There were candies, food, and school supplies, a big blue jacket, and woolen gloves. I felt a little better. As I fiddled with my new stuff, Tex, Truman, and Dimuira rolled up. They were paranoid as all hell. I told them what the deal was, and they chilled.

"What about Brooke?" Truman asked.

"Bob didn't mention anything."

We all looked at each other. Tex shrugged.

"Looks like she got away with it."

"Let's keep it that way," I said.

I LIVED ON lockdown for the next bit. My performance contract stipulated that I couldn't leave site until after I was sworn in and I had to be home every night before eight. I was still allowed to see Mick. The two of us hung out after school and talked endlessly about our week-long ceremony at the Ak. We agreed we'd get a room together and throw wild Christmas parties. We also talked about the girls we liked. Mick said he'd shoot for a cutie from Fargo named Clarissa. I had my sights on Dimuira. Come December 18th, we were chewing our fingers to bits. We packed our shit, bid our families a heartfelt adieu, and split.

We arrived at headquarters at noon. The place was swarming like someone had touchdown-smashed a beehive of embassy goons. We skirted them and went up to the lounge. It was buzzing at the teeth with volunteers. Mick went to the pisser. I skipped into the tiny movie room. I was hoping to get some shuteye before heading to the Ak. I walked in on a bombscape. The floor was littered with shoes, clothes, and books. A backpack was in the center of everything. It was sliced across the stomach and bleeding dirty underwear. Over it stood one very red and agitated Cyrus. He saw me and jumped back into his skin. I greeted him kindly.

"Knock before you enter," he barked.

"Okay. Jesus. Are you flying home today?"

"Yes."

I could see he didn't wanna be bothered. I tipped him two and said, "So long." His face softened. He looked me in the eyes and exhaled.

"Good luck in Gurbagahowda," he said.

"Thanks, man. I'll need it."

I turned and walked out. A strange feeling hit me. It was almost as if Cyrus was handing over his deformed but beloved child to me. I could sense his conflicted relief in the air. I wondered if this was just the by-product of his stay in a wild place like Gurbagahowda. I wondered if there wasn't something more.

An hour rolled by. Brooke and the rest of our demented little crew arrived. We greeted each other with hugs. Then Brooke made an announcement.

"I turned myself in."

"Really?" we all said.

"Yup, I couldn't let you guys take the fall while I got off scot-free. I came and told staff my involvement the day after you guys got busted."

"So, what happened?" I asked.

"Oh, Bob put me on the same lame performance contract. It sucked for a while, but it's over now. I vote since we're all free birds, we tie one on hard tonight. Whaddaya say?"

We looked at each other and laughed. There was no question.

WE SNORED THROUGH our welcome ceremony. By eight, we were ready to explode. Mick and I set up our room. We got a bunch of arak and fluorescent soda and brought it back. The hours flowed by with the drinks. By midnight, we were hammered. Mick went to find Clarissa. The Dayhan crew and I went down to the Ak disco. It was a sight for sloshed eyes. Scumbags with gold teeth and chains were kicking around its flickering blue womb with drinks in their hands and cigs in their lips. The moat of black sofas surrounding the dance floor was riddled with seedy figures in white suits. Blond hookers in fishnets and pumps tick-tocked up to them. We swerved around the tumult and to the back bar. We ordered sambucas and cheers'd.

Brooke, Truman, and Tex started chatting. Dimuira sat next to me in silence. She looked like a china doll with electric blue eyes. The hair on my body rose. I reached around her waist and pulled her to me. Before she could react, I kissed her. It lasted for a soft minute. Then we broke apart laughing. The others were watching with mixed expressions. Tex was smiling, Truman was frowning, and Brooke was straight up scowling. I ignored them all and pulled Dimuira out on to the dance floor. We started spinning and she whispered in my ear.

"There goes the promise I made to myself."

"Which promise was that?"

"Two years of celibacy."

I smiled and gave her another kiss. I had it in the bag.

THE NEXT TWO days were a similar mix of boredom, booze, and high school romance. We sat through dozens of meetings with bleeding hangovers, then retired to our rooms to get trashed. I tried to take things further with Dimuira, but she wouldn't let me. It was mostly just dancing and the occasional kiss. Poor Mick was having zero luck with Clarissa. She seemed to want to be his friend but nothing more.

On the night before swearing-in, Mick and I walked to Teke Bazaar to get arak. The avenues of Aşgabat were lit up like funeral pyres and its buildings stood like white moon-crafts. On every corner was the smiling face of Türkmenbaşy. The glare of his teeth dug into my skin. I chatted with Mick to ignore the creepiness. I told him to not worry about Clarissa.

"Just play it cool tonight," I said. "Who knows. Maybe you'll get lucky."

He thanked me for the advice, and we bought some arak. The night slunk away on the tail of an alley cat.

MORNING ENTERED OUR room like a fat ballerina. It wobbled in through the windows and planted its giant sweaty ass right on my face. I spit it from my mouth and scratched it from my eyes. I looked over to see how Mick was faring. He was nowhere in sight. I said a silent prayer that he'd gotten laid. I took a shit and washed my balls. Then I looked at my watch. It was 7:30 a.m. I had an hour to get dressed, practice my Turkmen speech, and head downstairs. As I was forcing a foot through my pant leg, Mick burst in the door. He was bouncing up and down in his Spiderman boxers with a blank expression on his face. I asked him if he'd nailed Clarissa. He shook his head.

"Even better," he cried. "Türkmenbaşy just died."

A crack split my toe. It crawled over my nail and along my instep. It coiled up my calf and around my thigh like ivy. Soon my whole body was a punched-in mirror. For a second, everything held its place. In a finger-snap, it shattered from my skin in a trillion pieces. I felt my heart shake and my mind unfurl. The clouds above me poofed and the sun poured into the void like cosmic orange juice. I felt happy for the first time in months. The man who'd hung like a sledgehammer over everyone's head was now dead. I revealed in my morbid joy for a bit. Then a troubling question crept into my conscience. It wasn't "Who?" or "Why?" or "How?" or "When?" but "What the fuck is gonna happen next?"

Visions of tribal warfare filled my head. I saw Tekes strangling Yomuts and Ersaris stabbing Saryks. I ran to the window. I saw empty streets and two dudes in the parking lot lowering the flag. I took out my camera. I wanted to have some record of this moment in history. I filmed the flag men for a bit. Then I hit up the T-15s. They were scattered up and down the halls, chattering. I went around to each of their little cadres and had them comment. Their main concern was "Would we be sent home?" Some said yes, and others said no. In the latter group, were those who felt we'd be shipped to another country. If such were the case, most were praying for Thailand. I myself was hoping for Georgia. We argued about the pros and cons of each place, then we clicked on the TV. We wanted to see what the world thought of T-Bag's death. Some of us were convinced it would make us famous. We flipped through the channels. BBC came up third. There was something about the weather in Britain.

Then came the hot report. A blonde in red told us T-Bag had bit it. She mentioned his personality cult and heart problems. She said he'd died sometime during the night. Then she moved on to EU fish quotas. We all stood in silence. Truman busted up laughing.

"The world doesn't give a shit about this place," he said.

An hour later, Peace Corps called us downstairs. They told us not to be alarmed and that our swearing-in ceremony would be postponed until the morrow. They also told us that for our safety, we'd be staying at the hotel for the next five days.

"If on day six, things are looking good," Bob said, "we'll ship you off to your permanent sites."

SWEARING-IN WENT as well as could be expected. It started with a dry but not entirely insincere speech by Bob during which he reminded us that, "When you lose the celebration of accomplishment, you don't lose the accomplishments themselves." Afterwards, he swore us in. To do this, he told us, "Raise your right hands and lie through your teeth after me." Then came the speeches. I nailed mine but was shaking throughout. When all was said and done, we got our diplomas. They read, "In recognition of so-and-so's completion of Peace Corps training in Turkmenistan."

Later that day we were given our start-up funds. It was only four hundred bucks, but since the highest denomination of manat at that time was 10,000 (roughly sixty cents), every one of us walked away with a bag full of cash. Most people saved their wads. I opted to blow mine on booze and discos, but not before stacking it ceiling-high and posing in front of it in a black beanie and shades with bottles of arak all around.

That night we had a bumpin' party. It ended at three-thirty, but Truman stayed behind and drank. Mick whipped out his penis again. He drenched his clothes in smelly gold, then smacked his lips and collapsed on his bed. Truman and I grabbed the camera. We filmed poor Mick lying there in a suit of his own urine, mumbling oddly and scratching himself. When it became too shameful, we clicked the camera off. After that, I have no memory.

I WOKE UP to Mick washing his yellow clothes in the shower. I congratulated him on a job well done and got ready. The next few hours were meetings. I didn't listen to a one. My head was filled with other thoughts. Mostly they were about Dimuira. I figured it was a good time to tell her how I felt. If she rejected me, I'd have a few days to nurse my wounded heart before going to site. I approached her after the meetings and asked her if we could talk. She seemed confused but said okay. I went to my room and grabbed a bottle of arak. Then I knocked on her door. She opened it and stood there.

"Rrroom serveez," I said.

She laughed and let me in. We sat on the bed and drank and chatted. It soon got quiet. I looked her in the eyes.

"There's something I've been meaning to tell you," I said.

She bent her neck and dimpled her cheek. My tongue dried up and my throat tightened.

"What is it?" she said.

"Well . . . I . . . um . . . think you're cool."

The second the words left my mouth I wanted to retract them. Never in all my years as a self-proclaimed cocksman had I started the Let's-date speech with something as fucking stupid as "I think you're cool." Dimuira stared at me with her vibrating blue eyes. Then she blinked.

"I'm sorry, Johann. I'm not looking for a boyfriend," she said.

Her words burned. I tried to play it off like *I* was the one who was cool, but I ended up wiggling around on the bed as if someone was trying to force a rusty nail through my pee-hole. I knew I was done. I thanked Dimuira for her honesty and left.

That night I got indecently drunk. I wandered the halls of the Ak muttering nonsense with a bottle of arak hanging from my wrist. I was just about to crash. A sweet voice entered my ears. It asked me if

I'd like to have a drink with it. I told it I would and followed. We went to its room and sat down. I started coming to. I saw two built legs and a pair of tits, long brown hair, and hazel eyes. All of it was smiling and leaning in at me. When I realized it was Clarissa, it was too late.

THE NEXT MORNING, one horrible realization was followed by another. Not only had I fooled around with Mick's crush, I'd done so in *our* room, not hers, and in front of the man himself. I looked over and saw Mick listening to his iPod and staring at the ceiling. I knew he was fuming inside. I had to get Clarissa out. I told her she'd better go, and she nodded. She got up silently and walked toward the door. She got to the corner and paused. I asked her what was wrong, and her cheeks turned green.

"I'm gonna be sick," she said.

She ran in the bathroom and puked. It sounded like someone dumped a school of live sardines in the toilet. I bolted in to hold her hair. Mick just lay there listening to his tunes. The whole ordeal lasted an hour. When Clarissa left, Mick and I got ready. As we dressed for meetings, we said very little. It was the day before Christmas and my gift to my best friend in Peace Corps was a punch to the gut.

Meetings were tough. I tried to get through them without thinking about what I'd done to Mick, but I couldn't. I felt too terrible. When everything was over, I approached him. He wasn't in bad spirits but there was a noticeable tweak in his aura.

"Can we talk?" I said.

"Sure."

We went up to our room and sat on the bed. I took a deep breath.

"I'm so fucking sorry, Mick," I said.

He tensed up. I could tell he expected more of an explanation.

"It's just that . . . " I continued, " . . . with all the stress, alcohol, miscommunication, sexual repression, and insanity of the past few days, I didn't know what I was doing. I wasn't trying to hurt you or be devious. Dimuira rejected me and I was crushed. Then outta nowhere, Clarissa took an interest in me. Under normal circumstances, I'd never have made a move. But in this jam, I just couldn't help myself."

Mick nodded. I took this as a conciliatory sign. I opened my arms and went in for the hug. He broke and we came together.

That night, we drank and snorted Xannies[28] and painted each other's nails. Five of us—me, Mick, Brooke, Clarissa, and Truman—passed out in our room. We woke up at 7:00 a.m. with a call from Peace Corps. They told us to meet in the conference room in an hour for a briefing on the state of things in Turkmenistan. We all got up except Truman. He was zonked out between the beds, drooling with his head to one side. Mick and I tried to wake him. Three times he lifted himself, and three times he lay back down. On the fourth time, we screamed at him that we had an obligatory briefing. He twitched into a little ball and snored. My face turned red. I grabbed him by the shoulders and yanked him up.

"You gotta get the fuck up, Truman," I yelled.

He looked at me from behind his crooked glasses.

"For?" he said.

"Ahhhh."

I let go of him and marched off. I went downstairs and into the conference room. There was a podium set up and a dozen rows of chairs. I took my place among the volunteers and waited. A few minutes later, the embassy rep arrived. He was short as a barstool and had neatly parted hair. He got behind the podium and greeted us. Truman came stumbling in. He was half-conscious and half-dressed. His nails were still painted pink from the night before. He took a seat next to Clarissa. She giggled.

"Okay," the rep said. "Now I know you're all anxious to hear about what's going to happen. We've discussed it with the Turkmen government, and they feel it's safe for you to stay. Since it's Türkmenbaşy's funeral today, we're gonna hold off and let the nation

---

[28] Xanax pills.

mourn. You'll be shipped to your sites in two days."

This was hardly the news we'd been hoping for. Most of us wanted to be sent to Thailand or to another country in Central Asia. Underneath that desire, however, was a modicum of satisfaction. We'd just spent three months preparing to live in Turkmenistan. Why let all that training go to waste?

THAT NIGHT I decided to throw a big Christmas party. I wanted to make up for my indiscretion with Mick, plus, in a small way, to celebrate the continuation of our service in Turkmenistan. I went to Teke Bazaar and bought a fuckload of arak, juice, and soda. I returned to the Ak and brainstormed with Brooke. She and I designed the party. We invented two seasonal drinks—The Secret Santa and The Grinch—drew decorations for my room, set up a bar and seating area, and hung a sign that read GUTLY FUCKIN' BOLSUN (Merry Fuckin' Christmas) outside my door.

At eight, people started showing up. By ten, the place was packed. We had music blaring and drinks flowing. Everyone was dancing in the middle of the room or jumping up and down on the beds. I took this as evidence that I'd done my job. Without saying anything, I exited the room. As I shut the door, Clarissa walked up.

"We should talk," she said.

"Okay."

We went to her room and closed the door. She poured us some drinks.

"I want you to know," she said, "that I'm aware you have a thing for Dimuira. I also want you to know that I don't have a thing for Mick."

It felt good to have the air cleared. I told her things were done with Dimuira. I also told her Mick and I had patched things up, hence the Christmas party I'd paid for. She smiled and put her hand on my knee.

"I commend you, Johann," she said. "You took a hairy situation and made it better."

"I guess."

"Anyways, we'll just be friends for now, okay?"

"Sure."

I WOKE UP in my room to a huge mess. It was a bit irritating, but a sign nonetheless that the party had been a success. Mick and I spent an hour cleaning. We got dressed, snored through a few meetings, then retired to Truman's room where a little party was happening. The whole crew was listening to Tropicália[29] and drinking arak. I took a seat next to Brooke on the bed and she smiled.

"I made you this card," she said.

It was an odd card. A drawing of a man in uniform reaching for a screaming woman was on the front. I opened it up. It bore one line:

To the coolest guy I know.

My heart melted. I thanked Brooke and gave her a hug. She squeezed me tighter than was comfortable. I pulled away and started jabbering. A moment later, I heard a noise. It sounded like wild laughter. I got up and opened the door. I saw Mick standing at the end of the hall. He spotted me and waved me over. I went and grabbed my camera. I clicked it on and raced up there. A crowd of people was in the lounge. They were seated in a ring around the elevators. I wondered why they had formed. I squeezed in amongst them and saw my answer. It was Fletcher and he was bombed out of his gourd.

"Yeah, yeah," he said. "A kid's fuckin' mentally retarded and he's takin' a shit and I'm deliverin' it for him. You fuckers shoulda heard me. I was just like, 'Keep givin' it, buddy. Push a lil' harder. We all want it to come out.'"

Before Peace Corps, Fletcher had been a camp counselor for disabled children. I assumed this was one of his experiences. I started

---

[29] A style of music that arose in the late 60s in the southeast region of Brazil. Tropicália combined psychedelic rock, pop, samba, bossa nova, and others.

filming him. All was fine until he caught me.

"Oh, fuck you, Johann," he said.

People cracked up. I zoomed in on his face. It turned redder and darker and more angular. He glared at me with smoldering black dots from behind his glasses.

"What's wrong?" I asked. "Don't you wanna tell us more about the turd you delivered?"

"No, I don't. Why don't you bring that camera a little closer?"

I took a few steps forward and zoomed in deep. His evil face filled my viewfinder. The laughter dissipated.

"C'mon Johann," Mick said. "It ain't worth it."

I knew the man was right. Fletcher was practically my site mate. And Dick and Dora, my other near site mates, were buddies of his. Even still, I winked at Fletcher and shot him a little kiss. He did nothing.

I WOKE UP in a panic. The Ak was hemorrhaging volunteers and I was late for my marşrutka. I splashed water on my face and grabbed my shit. I raced downstairs and found my group. They were sitting on the lobby couches waiting for me. Mick was there with them. I gave him a hug and told him, "Be safe." He told me the same and left for his site. It was time to brave the lava pit. I laced my shoes, donned my pack, and joined my crew. In single file, we exited the hotel. With our sagging faces and slumped shoulders, I couldn't help but imagine us like a row of criminals being readied for transport. When we hit curbside, our paddy wagon arrived. We flung open the door and crawled inside. The air was heavy and acrid. Our driver was a troll with hotdog neck. We took our seats and slid the door shut. It clapped against the frame like jail bars. I looked around the cabin. There my ass was with no one to keep it company but an unrequited crush and three pricks who hated me. The silence among us was tight enough to stab. As we rolled past towers of marble and statues of a corpse, I could feel the walls of the marşrutka breathing at my neck.

I wanted to fling my window back and jump out onto the freeway. I hugged my knees instead. A few others did the same. This caught Fletcher's attention. He went from dead-eyed zombie to wide-eyed freak. He looked around the cabin and flared his nostrils. Our collective misery had reached its zenith. He drew back his arms, scooped it forward with both hands and clapped it together.

"Look good, feel good, people," he cried.

6

I WAS A mummy at site. I sealed myself in my room and hardly came out for twelve days. I masturbated dozens of times. I looked at pictures of previous trips with the Chucks[30] and cried my eyes red. I drank to excess. When I had to vomit or shit, I went to the rancid porthole to Duat[31] that was our outhouse, but that was it. I didn't even piss outside. Instead, I pissed in old soda bottles and hid them behind my bed. The smell of urine filled my room. It got so bad that one night, when my host brother Ali brought up my scalding bowl of guts for dinner, he said something about it.

"What is that?" he groaned, setting my bowl on the klionka.

"What's what?"

"That smell. It's worse than the goat pen."

I contemplated telling him that it was a leaking pipe. I remembered how he'd thrown firecrackers at my crotch when I'd gone to take a shit on New Year's Eve. I grabbed his little hand and pulled him over to my treasure trove. My nine bottles of urine were glowing under the lightbulb like cones of prehistoric amber. His eyes widened.

"Oh my god," he said. "I'm telling my mom."

I dug my nails into his wrist.

---

[30] The name that I and a group of adventurous and travel-loving friends gave ourselves. See Hans Joseph Fellmann, *Chuck Life's a Trip*, Russian Hill Press, 2019.

[31] The underworld or realm of the dead in ancient Egyptian mythology.

"You do that, and I'll pour one of these in your mouth while you sleep."

He chuckled nervously and ripped his hand away. He ran out of the room and slammed the door. That night I emptied all nine bottles in the shitter along with my dinner. I slept like a corpse.

THE FOLLOWING MONDAY, school started. I'd done little to prepare and had agreed to only twelve hours of teaching per week instead of the twenty required by Peace Corps. I gathered my materials—a sheet of He-Man stickers and a ruler—and stuffed them in my backpack. I threw my wrinkled work attire on my unwashed body and left for school. It was freezing outside. The puddles of water on our driveway looked like pools of congealed semen. I almost slipped on one while walking through the waratan. I heard Ali snicker at me from behind the window of his heated family room.

"Little prick," I muttered.

The walk to School #17 was thirty minutes through ice and snow and frozen animal dung. Twice I was almost hit by a moving object: the first a Lada and the second, a camel. The whole way I was gawked at by rings of Turkmen squatting under the limbs of frozen trees and chewing *çigits* (dried sunflower seeds). As they feasted their dark, stupid eyes on my pathetic image, the thought of decking their teeth out crossed my mind. The only thing that stopped me was the knowledge that after the last gold tooth hit the dirt, I'd be on the first plane back to unemployment and eternal shame. Plus, I'd prolly have my ass riotously kicked by a dozen pointy black shoes.

I made it to school without incident. My counterpart Azat greeted me at the doors. He was wrapped in his black wool coat. His near toothless grin looked like a few chicklets threaded together by a loose string. He reached out and clamped my gloved hand with both of his.

"*Geldiňmi?*"[32] he said. "Did you come?"

"Not since last night," I replied.

"What?"

"Never mind."

I followed him inside. The school smelled of lead paint, mold, and burning fat. We passed a few classrooms of blank-faced Turkmen children being screamed at by their teachers under photos of the late Türkmenbaşy. I felt sick to my stomach. We arrived at our classroom. The children sat with their hands folded, staring at the chalkboard. Azat walked in front of them and said a few sentences in machine-gunned Turkmen. Then he turned to me with sadness in his eyes.

"Johann, I am so sorry but, please to help me wiz class today," he said.

"What do you mean?"

"My friend's dad's cousin's son just died, and I must make *sadaka*." Sadaka refers to any act of love, compassion, or friendship. In this case, I took it to mean attending a funeral.

"*O-kaaay* . . ."

"So please, you will take my classes today and tomorrow."

"Are you kidding?"

"No kidding. I must make funeral. Children are will behave."

He shook my hand and walked off. The children remained silent and still. When their teacher was out of earshot, they broke into madness. They screamed at the top of their lungs and threw pencils and rulers and books at me. One boy climbed on his desk and jumped up and down. Another boy grabbed the braids of a little girl and dragged her around the classroom. I have a naturally loud voice. I tried using it to boom the little fuckers into silence. Every time I shouted, the lot of them combined their shrills into one ear-splitting roar. It drowned me out completely. After an hour of this, I gave up. I let the next three classes act like shit while I read *Crime and Punishment*.

---

[32] This is the Turkmen way of asking if one arrived safely and in good health.

AT 3:00 P.M. my day of teaching ended. I was exhausted down to my toenails and craving a hot meal. There was no way in hell I was gonna go home and let my host mom serve me a boiled version of whatever she'd shoveled off the floor of the goat den. I spotted what looked like a restaurant and went in. The place was more of a vacant warehouse. There was a small bar at the far-right corner and a few metal benches. I picked one and had a seat. A little boy with grimy hands and a paper chef's hat sauntered up and asked me what I'd have. I ordered a bowl of manty, a pair of *lüle kebap,* and a beer. He nodded and walked off. Someone tapped me on the shoulder. I turned around and saw a young man, maybe twenty-one. He was tall and thin with big ears and dark eyes. He was wearing an ironed dress shirt, and slacks. An oversized tie was fastened just below his Adam's apple. He extended his big hand.

"My name is Öwez," he said. "And I just wanted to welcome you personally to Gurbagahowda."

I nearly farted the bench out from under my legs. Not only did this dude have perfect English grammar but a perfect English accent to boot.

"Thank you Öwez," I said, shaking his hand. "I'm Johann. And if you don't mind me asking, where did you learn to speak English like that?"

"Well, I studied every English book I could find. And when I ran out of books here, I took trips to classrooms and libraries in Aşgabat for new books. Eventually, I felt my English became good enough to take the FLEX test.[33] So last year I took it—"

"And?"

His face melted to a dark point.

"I failed."

"How is that possible?"

"I do not know. Maybe it was because there were too many applicants, or because I did not pay any bribe. Whatever is the case, I am out of luck now because each Turkmen student has one chance

---

[33] Foreign language exploratory course test.

to take the test and if he fails, he will never have a chance again to go to America through this program."

I didn't know what to say. I just sat there staring at his sad, hanging face. The little server with the grubby hands picked that moment to serve me my beer and plates of food. I was starving and impatient and this made me feel even guiltier. Öwez softened his expression and waved goodbye.

"Enjoy your meal, Johann," he said.

THAT NIGHT I hardly slept. I woke up the next morning with rings under my eyes. I took a lukewarm bucket shower and dressed in the same clothes from the day before. I did my thirty-minute walk to School #17 with little strength to scowl at the eyeballing Turkmen along the way. When I got to my classroom, the kids were already there. They were seated silently with their eyes all pointed at the same spot on the blackboard. The instant I walked in, they threw up their hands and started screaming and fighting and tossing things around. I picked up a piece of chalk and went to the blackboard. I wrote down a single word. I stood back and folded my arms. A few kids noticed and stopped acting like shit. Soon others fell in line. The whole class became silent. I smiled and pointed to the blackboard.

"Does anyone know how to pronounce this word?" I asked.

Half the class wrinkled their eyebrows. The other half stared dumbly ahead. One little girl raised her hand.

"Zar-ks?" she said.

"Close, but it's 'Zrrr-ks.'"

"What is a Zrks?" a boy said.

"Well, in America they're our pets."

"Really?" another boy said. "Do you have one?"

"Of course."

"Wow. What does it look like?"

"Well, it's about twenty feet tall with ten fire-breathing heads and long black claws that it uses to pluck little children from their beds at night and rip them apart."

The air in the classroom froze. Dozens of tiny brown eyes sparkled with fear. I smiled and picked up my book. I read in silence for the next four hours.

AT THE END of my fourth class, a woman entered the room. She was pudgy but cute, like a little girl who ate too much ice cream. Her soft body was wrapped in a red köýnek with white polka dots. Her auburn hair was twisted up in a tight bun. Her cheeks were puffed with pink splotches. Her chin had a deep round dimple. Her eyes were the color of freshly cut hay. I recognized a playfulness in them. She stood in front of me and folded her arms limply.

"Öwrenişýäňmi, Han-Guly?" she asked. "Are you adjusting?"

I hadn't heard the name Han-Guly since training. It jarred me a little.

"I guess," I said. "How did you know my Turkmen name?"

Her moon face bent into a frown.

"You told me when you visited in November," she said. "Don't you remember? My name is Jahan. I said, hello to you in the hall and we chatted."

I vaguely recalled the encounter. Plus, I found it odd that our names were so damn similar. I surmised that Jahan chose to call me Han-Guly because of this fact. I looked her over and shrugged.

"Oh yeah. Well, what do you want?"

"I want you to teach me French."

"French? How did you know I spoke French?"

Her cheeks reddened.

"We are a small village, Han-Guly. Everyone knows everything."

I thought about the empty piss bottles behind my bed. I wondered how thin the curtains over my windows were.

"Why do you wanna learn French anyways?"

"Because it's such a romantic language," she said "I've heard it on old tapes and soap operas. It's my dream to learn this language and go to Paris. I want to see the Eifel Tower and drink espresso at a café on the Champs-Elysées."[34]

I almost screamed out loud, "Ha. You really think you'll ever make it outta this fucking shithole? Much less to Paris, so you can speak French and sip coffee and people-watch on the boulevard? You're fucking crazy lady."

I swallowed these words. In their place, I offered a curt "Maybe."

Jahan chewed her lips and looked at the floor.

"Okay," she muttered. "*Au revoir.*"

She turned and walked out the door. The dirty winter sunlight filtered through the window. I looked at my schedule and smirked. Three days later, I agreed to teach Jahan French.

OUR FIRST LESSON was the following Tuesday. I walked to her classroom after finishing with my silent and well-behaved students. I found her at her desk, staring out the window. Her classroom was full. One little girl was at the front holding what looked like a science book. She was reading from it like a robot with a crushed head whose damaged chips were sparking a dead string of words out its mouth. I stood at the doorway and watched. A little boy in back giggled. A tiny ape of a man wearing a humongous blue tie blew past me. He marched right up to the little boy, drew back his hand and slapped him across the cheek. It sounded like a firecracker. The little boy's head jerked and wobbled. Before he could catch his breath, Ape-Fuck drew his hand back and belted him again. The little boy exploded into tears. Ape-Fuck stared down at him with roots of cruelty growing up the sides of his nose. I wanted to rain bows on the guy's face. It took an act of sheer will to keep me contained. When the little boy was thoroughly degraded and weeping, Ape-Fuck puffed his chest and marched toward the door. As he passed under my armpit, I muttered, "Why don't you try that shit on me you little fuck?"

---

[34] A boulevard in Paris famous for its cafés, theatres, and luxury shops.

"*Näme?*" he barked. "What?"

"Oh, just wishing you the best of luck."

He scowled and walked away. The bell rang and the kids left. I sat down next to Jahan. She had a puzzled look in her eyes.

"I can see you don't like that man," she said.

"You're damn right. What kind of teacher leaves a little girl to teach his class and only comes in to beat the shit out of students who aren't paying full attention to his non-lesson?"

"You can't blame him, Han-Guly. He is Soviet teacher."

"I don't give a shit if he's a syphilitic teacher. He has no right to beat children like that. I should merk his ass."

Jahan's hazel eyes widened with fear. I took in a sack of air and blew it out. This made me feel a damn sight better. I grabbed my dogeared French book and laid it on the desk.

"Whaddaya say we do a little'a this?" I said.

Jahan grinned so hard I thought her cheeks might freeze. I grinned back and we started with the basics: *Bonjour, ça va?, très bien, la la.* Jahan was an attentive pupil but had trouble with the throaty French Rs and the kissy Us. We worked on it.

After an hour, we got to chatting. The topic of my staying in Gurbagahowda came up. Jahan cracked her knuckles.

"What is it?" I asked.

"Well, I was talking with one of teachers here, and he said you are crazy party man who likes to get girls and drink and that soon you be will be tired of our village and go because it is too quiet here."

I grunted.

"Who told you that?"

"Baýram teacher. You remember him?"

Baýram was one of our LCFs during training. My only memory of the guy was him coming up to me while on a PC trip to some mosque and asking me excitedly if we were going to get whores together once I moved to Gurbagahowda. I told Jahan that I did indeed remember him. Then I assured her of my intention to stay.

"This is a tough place," I said. "But I like it here. The silence helps me think. Anyways, Aşgabat's only a few hours away. If I need to be party man, I can go there."

Jahan laughed and said, "Okay."

We went back to the French.

THE WEEK ROLLED by. I got permission to pick up a package from my folks in Aşgabat, then was sent directly back to site. I was on a three-month no-leave policy; all the volunteers were. I was in desperate need of some sort of explosion. I drank cheap vodka in my room for three nights straight. A week later, I got a call from Baýram the LCF. He invited me for dinner that evening, and I accepted. I did my shitty day of teaching and came home. After a short nap, Ali tried to hand me a bowl of guts.

"I'm going to Baýram teacher's house for dinner," I said.

He clucked and went back in the house. I contemplated saying goodbye to my host family but said "Fuck it" instead. I walked out the waratan and onto the long dirt road. The sky was frighteningly blue and the phone poles, with their moth-speckled lights, hummed menacingly at me. I turned a corner and came to another long dirt road. At the end of it were two little girls in green dresses that I recognized from my school. They were Baýram's daughters, Bibi and Gülbahar. They greeted me kindly and led me to their house around back.

It was warm inside. The lights were soft and the stove was burning and the smells coming from the kitchen were actually good. Baýram's wife, Gözel, greeted me with a smile. She took my coat and led me to the living room. She closed the door behind me. Baýram's skinny ass was stretched across the floor with one leg over the other and a pillow under his elbow. His rich black hair was parted down the side. His square jaws were shadowed with stubble and his thick eyebrows were plucked into arrows. His dark, close-set eyes smiled when they saw me. He reached out a veiny pianist's hand. I shook it and sat down in front of him. A klionka between us was covered with bowls of palow, boiled beets, pickled tomatoes, carrot salad, apple marmalade, and fresh honey. We exchanged pleasantries and dug at everything with hunks of *çörek*. Once our guts were stuffed, Baýram grinned.

"It is possible that I may go to America in April," he said.

"Really?"

"Yes. IREX[35] will take one hundred and thirty-six teachers from Turkmenistan for six weeks training. I may be one from them."

"That's awesome."

"Yeah, I am very excited. It will be first time I am student again and not teacher for long time."

"Yeah, I hear ya. Where did you go to school?"

The corners of his mouth touched his earlobes.

"I studied in Ukraine for five years in a city called Chirnihiv. The university I attend have ninety percent women, most of them beautiful blondes. My friends and I called this place *Zhensky Monistyar*, which is Russian for Monastery of Women."

"Sounds like the place to be."

"It was. This was good time in my life. I had many parties, loved many women. In summer, we would go to Dnieper River[36] and all guys would have two girls each in small bikinis. Things were so free during Soviet Union. We didn't need to leave. Yes, it was hard to get visa to another country, especially America, because our government considered this imperialist country, but we didn't care because Soviet Union was so big. If I wanted to see Moscow, St. Petersburg, no problem. I don't even need passport."

Baýram narrowed his eyes. The smile on his face warped and fell.

"But now everything change."

"How do you mean?"

"Because of Türkmenbaşy, we cannot leave Turkmenistan

---

[35] International Research & Exchanges Board, a nonprofit organization.

[36] The Dnieper is the fourth-longest river in Europe. It begins in the Valdai Hills near Smolensk, Russia, and runs through Belarus and the Ukraine, where it flows into the Black Sea.

almost never. Also, I must show my passport just to go to Aşgabat. Why though? I am citizen of Turkmenistan. And if I say to police, 'Hey, I want to travel to Moscow to see friends,' they will absolutely say no."

Baýram bit into a tomato and chewed it angrily. He swallowed the bite and continued.

"Türkmenbaşy always speak about how he give us our independence, but he didn't. It was given to us by Russia as gift after break-up of Soviet Union. Then Türkmenbaşy came with his 'democracy' and he write Ruhnama and force us to learn it in school. This is so stupid book. All it tells me about is old Turkmen history, the epics, and Magtymguly.[37] How does this help me in the new world? If I want to learn these things, I can take history course. I don't need fifty percent of classes and hundred percent of TV dedicated to this. It is ridiculous. Turkmen school and TV just control your mind. All they say is good things about Turkmenistan: free oil, free water, free gas, free salt. Then people in Turkmenistan only see few good things and their mind is blind to bad. And those who are smart enough to see, do nothing because they are afraid of KNB. They can take your job, your house, your family. This country is in so bad condition . . ."

I was shocked at Baýram's honesty. He didn't know me from dick, and here he was bashing the dictatorship in front of me over tea and cookies. I didn't know what to say. I just sat there and stared. He went on about how the government under the newly 'elected' president Gurbanguly Berdimuhamedow promised internet, educational reforms, foreign investment, and new business. He said he was hopeful that Turkmenistan would soon be opening up, and that he desperately needed to feel free again. I noticed a sizable shelf of old books behind him. I asked if he'd read them all and he laughed.

"Of course," he said. "Books are my escape from this shit place. I also watch MTV. I know that sounds stupid, but in both, I don't

---

[37] Magtymguly Pyragy (1724–c.1807) was a Turkmen poet and spiritual leader who fought for his people's independence and autonomy in the eighteenth century.

have to hear about Türkmenbaşy or Ruhnama. Without books or satellite, I would be prisoner."

I thought of Jahan and her situation. My cheeks sagged. Baýram's youngest daughter walked in. She was wearing an oversized white T-shirt and no bottoms. She padded up to her father and plopped in his lap. He lifted her arms in the air, and she laughed.

"You want to know something special about Yasmin?" he said.

"Okay."

"One time she watching MTV with me and she love it so much that when I put her to bed this night, she whisper to me that her name is not Yasmin, but new. And I ask, 'What is your new name?' And she say, 'American.'"

I WAS IN a funk after Baýram's. I felt like a giant American flag with ears, lips, arms, and eyeballs floating around my village while people gawked at my colors and prayed they had the power to lift them from the hell they were in. I went about my tasks perfunctorily. I woke up, taught, came home, jacked off, slept, and repeated.

One day at school, I was meandering the halls in a daze. A little kid jumped in front of me and screamed, "Stupid." I snapped out of it. I looked down and saw Ali. His face was bubbled around a smirk. His eyes were giggling slits. He was tap dancing in circles and twirling his finger in the air. The kids around him were pointing up at me and laughing. Rage boiled in my throat. I grabbed Ali by the shirt collar and slammed him against the wall. The kids around him scattered. I pressed my big chest up to Ali's little chest and drilled my eyes into his. The fear swirled in them like two mini vortexes. I was so close I could have taken a bite out of his cheek. He whimpered pitifully. I clenched my teeth.

"Don't you ever insult me in front of the students like that again," I screamed.

I let go of his collar. He collapsed to the floor like he was made of Slinkys. His brown eyes turned milky. He circled at them with his fists. I felt disgusted with myself. I skulked away before anyone else saw me. I went to Jahan's classroom hoping for a peaceful French lesson. I found her staring at the plants along the windowsill. I sat down next to her and asked her what was up. She crunched a piece of paper into a ball.

"I've been trying for past six weeks to train my students in English so I could get special diploma from the Board of Education," she said. "This diploma would mean more respect from other teachers and less work. My students took the test yesterday, and the Board said almost certainly I would get the diploma. Then they called me today and told me no without any reason."

I looked over at her students. They were all staring at their Ruhnamas. I looked back at Jahan.

"Jesus, I'm sorry," I said.

"I feel so angry, Han-Guly," she cried. "I am losing hope that things will ever change."

I thought of the similar things Baýram had said. It crushed me like a slab of concrete. I looked around the room for something to take the load off. I noticed how well-behaved Jahan's students were. I mentioned this to her. She sneered.

"Yes, they are well-behaved," she said. "This is because they are afraid of how badly I will punish them if they don't behave."

I didn't know what else to say. The bell rang, and the students left. We started in on the French. I gave Jahan a quiz and she got a B minus.

THE FOLLOWING WEEK was more of the same; more depressing stories from Jahan, more ridicule from Ali, more cold winter, more horrendous food, more of Azat having deaths in his extended family and dumping his classes on me. By Valentine's Day, I was so beat up and angry I could have sawed my own head off. For whatever reason, this made me wanna call Brooke. I asked her if she wanted to do lunch in Tejen the following day. She happily agreed.

I went to school the next morning with a slightly renewed sense of purpose. I arrived at my first class expecting to find a room full of bored, albeit well-behaved students. What I got instead was a mound of screaming brats the devil would have kicked out of hell. I marched to the front of the classroom and asked what the fuck was going on. A little boy laughed.

"Last night I talked to my sister," he said. "She studies in Aşgabat and she knows Americans and I asked her about the Zrks monster and she said it wasn't true that Americans have them as pets, so you're a liar."

The whole class pointed at me with their wicked little fingers. With their wicked little mouths, they called me a *ýalançy* over and over and over again. The blood drained from my cheeks and out my toes. My heart dangled behind my ribs like a sad bird in its cage. I dropped my book on the desk and pulled out my headphones. For the next four hours, I listened to Elliott Smith while the children screamed and threw erasers at me.

When my day ended, I was a wreck. I got a cab to Tejen and hung my head out the window the whole way. I had the cabbie drop me off in front of the crappy restaurant Cyrus had taken me to. I waited for Brooke inside. She walked in a few minutes later. She had her blanket of red hair pulled back in a ponytail and a smile on her freckled face. I prayed it was an ironic smile that would soon dissolve. She sat down in front of me, threw her tiny hands up and said, "I just had the best week ever."

My jaw unhinged. You could have wheeled a dumpster into my open mouth. I tried to play it off cheerful. I asked her the news and she ran with it.

"On Monday I introduced Valentine's Day to my fourth formers. I told them it was the American holiday for love and they ate it up. I had them draw pictures of hearts and cupids and roses. They decorated the class with this stuff, which caught the eye of the other teachers and got them doing it with their kids. The next day we all had our big Valentine's Day bash. The kids got together and gave me this huge box of candy and told me I was their favorite teacher. Then the guys in my village heard about what was going on. I guess they liked the idea, so they went out and bought their wives fake flowers and cookies and chocolates from the dükan. My host mom even wrote me a little card in English that said, 'I love you.' I swear to God, Valentine's Day is taking my village by storm."

Brooke finished her reverie and looked over at me. I imagined she saw a black beanie resting neatly on a pair of snow boots. She grabbed my shoulder and shook me out of it.

"What's going on with you?" she asked.

"It's nothing."

"No, tell me."

"Well, it's just that, you seem to be making a difference at your site, and all I seem to be doing is getting furious at helpless children before playing with my balls in dark corners."

She raised her fingers to her widening lips. I beat her to the punch. We laughed out loud together. It was the best I'd felt all winter.

AFTER A FUCKLOAD of beer and greasy food and good old-fashioned gossip, Brooke and I called it a night. I went back to my site feeling nicely buzzed. I went up to my room and changed into my jammies. Then I heard Ali call me from the house door.

"*Parahatçylyk Korpusy telefon edýä*," he yelled. "Peace Corps is on the phone."

I groaned and plodded downstairs. Ali was still at the door, grinning with his booger-flecked teeth. I brushed past him and grabbed the phone.

"Hello?" I said, cringing.

"Johann, it's Mahym from Peace Corps."

"Oh, hiiiii. How are you?"

"Fine. Listen, I'm calling to inform you of All-Vol[38] at Merv Hotel in Aşgabat. It will be twenty-sixth of this month."

I almost leaped outta my boxers. A smile shattered my cheeks.

---

[38] Peace Corps All Volunteer Conference.

It took me a second to compose myself. I squared my shoulders and breathed in deep. "Thank you for informing me. I will see you then." I hung up the phone. I ran upstairs, buried my face in my pillow and screamed.

ON THE MORNING of the twenty-sixth, I was beaming. I slung my neatly packed bag over my shoulder, donned my winter jacket and cap, and hit the road. I got a cab to Tejen and met Brooke at the *awtostanzia*. She was as pumped as I was. She got in the back seat with me. We gathered two more fares and drove off. It was a steely winter day. Inside the cab, it was warm. I'm not sure how we got on the topic. Maybe it was the bleak majesty of the Kopet-Dag to our left, or the deadening expanse of desert to our right, or the humongous gray sky above us, or the Turkmen in our cab buzzing with prayer and splashing invisible water on their faces every time we passed a sacred ruin, but whatever it was, we started talking about God. I'd been reading the Buddhist literature my sister had given me before I left.

"The way I figure it," I said, "the whole God thing goes something like this. People must do three things in life and then they can take a leap of faith. First, they must accept whatever befalls them. Then they must seek to understand the roots of their circumstances, be they negative or positive. And finally, if their circumstances are indeed negative, and furthermore, the result of another's ill intentions or actions, they must reach deep within their hearts and forgive that person unconditionally. If they make a habit of these things and perfect them, they'll be able to take a leap of faith and believe in God."

I raised my chin and put a hand on my heart. Brooke lifted an eyebrow and curled the opposite lip corner.

"That's all fine and dandy," she said. "But I'm an empiricist, so unless God comes walking outta the clouds in his long white robe, stroking his long white beard and smiling at me, no amount of acceptance or forgiveness or whatever is gonna make me jump with all the lemmings off the faith cliff."

"Just what the hell are you saying?"

"I'm saying that I've never seen any evidence of his existence, so why should I believe in him?"

"Hence the leap of faith."

"Not in my nature. I need something more concrete."

"Okay, well what about all those strange simultaneous happenings in life that are just too damn crazy to be coincidences? I know you've experienced these."

"I guess I have. But I think they're just coincidences. The universe is vast and wild. There's bound to be a few of these in everyone's life. It doesn't mean they mean anything."

Our car slowed to a stop. I asked our driver what was going on and he clucked. I poked my head out the window. I saw a line of cars that ended in what looked like a pile of trash. As we crept closer things came into focus. I saw the top of a tall vehicle and the capped heads of policemen working furiously around it. We pulled alongside the scene and I gasped. A gray Lada carrying an entire family had slammed head-on into the spinning blades of a combine harvester. The car was a hideously twisted mess. The family was equally twisted and bleeding. The policemen were doing all they could to save them. They were yanking and pulling at the knots of metal and limbs while onlookers watched in horror. As we got up close, I saw an officer reach into a car window with both arms and grab something. He emerged carrying a dead boy in his arms. The boy's broken legs swung lifelessly, and his mouth popped open like a black dot. I had to look away. The Turkmen in our cab clucked and prayed. I prayed with them, then looked over at Brooke. She was curled into a ball against her seatback. Tears were streaming down her cheeks.

DESPITE A LINGERING feeling of death, All-Vol was simply All-Vol. It was a lot of volunteers, booze, sex, gossip, hangovers, boring meetings, and a lot of people getting into a lot of shit.

The only thing that juts out in my mind happened on the next-to-last morning after a night of binge drinking and blowjobs. As per usual, I missed the first meeting of the day. I wandered into the conference room at 10:00 a.m. with my tie loosened and the lower facing of my Mervyn's collared hanging out over my unironed slacks. I took a seat with my crew at the back. PC staff sneered at me like sewer rats. I blew them off and focused my attention forward. Some Turkmen bigwig in a green suit and tie gave an unintelligible speech. Then he put his hand on his heart. People rose from their seats. I did the same. Mr. Bigwig announced the start of the Turkmen national anthem. I'd never heard the thing before, so I was curious. I listened closely. I'll be damned if the first few notes weren't dead-on-balls the same as those at the start of "Frosty the Snowman." I whispered this to Brooke. She squealed at her fingertips as the music played. When it finally ended, we were hyperventilating. A presence at the center of the room shut us up. It was big and busty and nasty. It wore a three-piece suit that was pinned to its body by a single button under its enormous tits. I thought it might explode. It stepped forward, wrenched its squiggly red lips, and spoke.

"My name is Bartha and I am your new associate director."

Everyone rolled their eyes. Bartha waited.

"I know you guys loved your last AD," she continued, "and that I've got some big shoes to fill, so here's what I'm gonna do. I'm not gonna start by reading you the riot act. Nor am I gonna talk about safety or security. I'm just gonna tell you this story from my service in Morocco that happened not too long ago."

"This aughta be ripe," Brooke said.

"I had just arrived at my training site," Bartha continued. "It was a small village outside of the capital, Rabat. I didn't know anyone, and I didn't speak any Arabic. I was desperate for some volunteer contact. One weekend, I was able to travel to Rabat with some other volunteers for a visit. We went out to dinner at this little restaurant which was mostly filled with locals. We were five girls and three guys. We sat at a big round table, and when the waiter came to take our orders, he approached the men first. As Morocco is a male-dominated society, we figured this was custom, but when the waiter left without taking any of our—the women's—orders, we became quite angry. I, being a woman and having the temper that I have, marched right up to the waiter and asked him what his deal was. He didn't speak any English, but his boss, who spoke some English, came over to our table later and explained to us that the reason our waiter hadn't taken the women's orders was not because he saw us as inferior and wanted to disrespect us. On the contrary, he was afraid that if he'd spoken to us, the men at our table would have assumed he was flirting with us, so as a sign of respect to both the men and the women, he spoke to only the men."

When Bartha finished her story, I yawned. I declined to participate in the stupid get-to-know-your-neighbor games that staff had us play afterwards. That night I drank to excess. I passed out in a haze of sweat and vodka.

THE NEXT MORNING, we had our shitty hotel breakfast and split. Brooke and I went to the Aşgabat awtostanzia with Dick and Dora and got a marşrutka to Tejen. Two minutes in, I passed out. I was jostled awake an hour later by our wheel going over a bump. I heard the sad clucking of our driver and his wife. I looked to my left and saw a white Lada with its teeth bashed in. The passenger—a skinny old man in a cheap suit—was splayed out on the concrete with his head in bloody chunks at his shoulders. The driver—a skinny old woman in a purple dress—was bent forward with her face melded into the steering wheel. Neither party had been wearing their seatbelt. Dick looked at the accident and sneered.

"These fucking people never learn."

His wife Dora shushed him. He brushed her off.

"Nah, I'm serious," he went on. "I don't even give a fuck if there's kids in the back seat. All I wanna do is get around this mess and get to site."

I looked over at him in astonishment. I was expecting to see his face pinched with anger. His mouth was a little teardrop. His eyes were wobbling strangely. Dora curled an arm around his head and pulled it into her breast. I turned and looked at Brooke. She was sitting silently. None of us said a word the rest of the way.

7

AT SITE, I was a mummy again. I locked myself in my room for a week and went to it. I filled a dozen *baklaşkas* with my smelly urine and stored them behind my bed. I didn't shave my head or face, nor did I shower, change clothes, or even brush. My facial hair started to look like unkempt pubes. My pubes started to look like a forest of tangled wires. My body and teeth stunk of cheese, booze, and animal fat. I was drinking every day—all day—in my room, looking at pictures of family and trips with the Chucks, and crying till my eyes were crushed ladybugs and my throat was a corn husk. I only left to shit and dump my piss bottles in the outhouse pit. On rare occasions, I crept outside at night to stand on the *tapçan* and look at the stars. They were clear as little bells against the frosted black canyon of space. If I waited long enough, the moon came lumbering down like a happy sphere of glow-putty and joined them. They were my only friends in this state—them, and maybe Laika the dog, who growled every time I approached his haystack.

Monday came in a hearse. I knew I had to make an appearance at School #17. I scraped myself outta bed and dug through my laundry box. I grabbed a wad of wrinkled clothes and unpeeled them down my body. I still hadn't brushed, bathed, or shaved. I pulled my beanie around my patchy scalp and muttered, "Fuck it." I walked downstairs and into the courtyard. My host mom and her six kids were boiling water, cracking sticks, lighting fires, and feeding animals. They leered at me as if I were a giant funky toenail walking by. I ignored them and cut.

Forty minutes later, I arrived at school. I went straight to Azat's classroom. He had his finger raised and was shouting in broken English to a group of bored students. He saw me and dropped his finger.

"*Baaaay*,[39] where you was?" he asked.

I walked over and shook his hand. The kids' eyes were glued to me like flies.

"All-Vol went on longer than expected," I said. "But hey, I'm here now."

Azat scanned me over. I could tell by the curl on his lip that he thought I looked less like a teacher and more like a vagrant that had just been pitched headfirst into a log shredder. I asked him if he wanted me to teach. He politely declined and told me to plan lessons. I obliged him for two hours, mostly by reading. When the lunch bell rang, I walked with him outside. I was hoping he'd accompany me for at least a measly *fitçi*. He didn't say anything. I took the initiative and asked. He swung his eyes to the side and scratched his spine.

"I must to speak wiz my *çopan* now about somesing," he said.

Ahhh, I thought. The old speaking-wiz-za-çopan excuse.

I told him okay and went to the *uly çaýhana*[40], where I'd eaten on my first day of class. I ordered a plate of lüle and took it to the street. As I sat on a lump of mud, devouring my meal and grunting, I had a moment of clarity. My whole messy being came into focus and, my god, like a scene out of some silly 80s movie about ending poverty in Africa, "Man in the Mirror" went reeling through my head, especially that ridiculous line: "I'm gonna make a change . . ." etcetera, etcetera. I still finished my meal and belched afterwards. But I did go to the bazaar to see what I could scare up in terms of new work clothes and shoes. I walked away with three collareds, two slacks, and a pair of

---

[39] An expression of disbelief, frustration, or dismay.
[40] *Uly çaýhana* means big teahouse.

black pointys. I took them home, proud as can be, and after a hot bucket shower and a shave, set to trying everything on. The first pair of pants fit swimmingly. The second pair, not so swimmingly, but they'd do. The shoes were too big but could be filled out with enough socks. And the shirts, well, they blew ass all over the room.

I accepted that all I had was a single pair of pants. I went downstairs to see if my host family could help me with the rest. I knocked on the door and my host mother answered. She didn't look happy to see me. I asked her if she could work the sewing machine on my clothes. The first words outta her fetid gold mouth were, "I want you to teach Ali and Aziza one hour of English a day."

I felt like slapping the bling from her gums. I said I'd think about it and she scoffed and walked off. From inside the TV room, I could see Ali wiggling a finger at me and Aziza sneering. I was just about to leave when Merdan put his lobster claw on my shoulder.

"How 'bout I go with you to the bazaar tomorrow and help you get your money back," he said.

My heart leaped in the air and clicked its heels.

"Deal," I said.

THE NEXT MORNING, Merdan met me in the courtyard. He was dressed in clean slacks, a blue collared, and a faux-leather jacket that glinted like silver in the cold sun. I was in my dirty old jeans and jacket. I could tell Merdan was embarrassed to be seen with me. We walked to the bazaar and hit all the spots where I'd bought my stuff. We returned the shoes and slacks, but the toothless old fucker at the shirt shop wouldn't budge. Merdan tried reasoning with him in Turkmen. That didn't work, so I threw my arms in the old man's face and lit him up in Spanish.

"*Hijo de puta. Dame el pinche dinero o te mato.*" "Son of a bitch. Give me the fuckin' money or I'll kill you."

The old man shrieked and fell off his perch. Merdan's eyes widened with shock. I wrung my fists and shouted. A crowd started forming. Merdan slung his arm around my shoulder and pulled me away. Outside the bazaar, I calmed down. Merdan looked at me. His lips were smeared with pity.

"You know, Johann," he said. "I think you're alright . . ."

My eyes went gooey.

"Really?" I said.

"Yes," he said, smirking. "But you're kind of a fucking idiot."

The comment reached through my shame and jangled my bones. I wrapped my arms around my gut and blasted the most horrendous laughter out my mouth. Merdan caught my bug and did the very damn same. For a good half hour, we fried the worms in their dirt and shook the crows from their trees.

THE NEXT MORNING, I was still sans clothing. Merdan had a friend who was looking for some shirts like the ones I'd bought. The guy came and paid me full price for them. I took the money and went back to the bazaar. I bought myself three shirts, some slacks, and a pair of pointys that fit. I even coughed up a coin for a clean new beret. I took everything back to my little room. I got dressed for school in front of the mirror. I was a regular thirties mobster in my outfit. All I was missing was a Tommy Gun and a bouquet of red roses. I strolled to school with my hat cocked like a champ. The squatters still stared but not quite as hard. When I arrived at Azat's, I could tell he was impressed. He gave me the go-ahead to teach some classes. I did so with relish. The final bell rang and I announced to my fourth formers that I'd be starting clubs that week. The coot little things were overjoyed.

"Where you will go now?" Azat said as the kids bounced out.

"To Jahan's class. It's time for our French lesson."

"Ah."

"What do you mean, Ah? Do you not like Jahan?"

"No, no. She is wery *interesting* girl. She just always want somesing from someone."

"I see."

I said goodbye to Azat and went to Jahan's classroom. I found her sitting at her desk, thumbing through her students' notebooks. She jerked a little when she noticed me. Then her eyes swelled.

"You look a bit like Turkmen," she said.

"Thanks, I guess."

"And how was your trip?"

"Good. Too much drinking but good, haha."

She smirked.

"*Et comment-allez vous?*" I said. "And how are you?"

"*Bien*," she said, blushing. "Well."

I smiled and sat down next to her. I continued speaking to her in French. She froze up. The words wouldn't leave her mouth. She pouted and crumpled a piece of paper into a ball.

"My French isn't getting any better," she said, lobbing the ball onto her desk.

"Nonsense. You can't expect to learn it overnight."

"I know, but we only have lessons once or twice per week and lately you are gone. I want you to teach me French like you teach your students English."

"That's ridiculous. For starters, I don't speak French that well. And to teach you as often as I teach the kids would be way too time-consuming. I'm willing to do three times a week for an hour, with lessons on the board, but you're gonna hafta recruit some other teachers."

"Okay," she said.

The next day Jahan approached me after class. She was smiling.

"I've found four teachers who want to join our French class," she said.

"Jesus. That fast?"

"Yes."

"Well, okay then. Do they wanna start today?"

"No, but definitely this week. Today we can just have normal French lesson."

"Alright."

We went to her class. I taught her a few complex conjugational forms, then we reviewed some vocab. She seemed satisfied. I felt satisfied too.

"I hope you don't mind me asking," I said. "But did Cyrus ever do anything like this for you?"

She frowned.

"He did some adult classes, but he was very nervous and rude teacher. And one time he got so angry at us, he throw all his books to the floor and leave classroom."

"Wow," I said, trying not to smile.

"He was also very *boring* teacher," she continued. "For lesson, he would ask us to respond to silly American proverbs like 'Rome wasn't built today,' or 'Pot calling coffee black.' Also, he change his behavior a lot. For example, with happy talking people, especially girls, he was a bit more open. But I am quiet girl, so he was very quiet around me. This is why I am happy you are here, Han-Guly. You are open, talking boy and this makes me to open."

Jahan looked at me sideways. I could feel a spot of heat on my chest. I quickly changed the subject. We parted shortly thereafter.

THE FOLLOWING DAY, I didn't see Jahan. This was fine because I wanted to start my clubs. I had my fourth formers meet me after class. We played Pictionary and romped around outside. Azat came by and told us to go inside for some strange reason. This pissed the kids off something fierce. They started acting like shit. I dismissed them and cut home. I fiddled around in my room and ate a bowl of guts for dinner. Then I heard a knock at my door. I went over and opened it. Baýram was standing there, thin as a broom handle.

"Hello, Johann," he said.

"Hey man, how you been?"

"Not so good. I was at health spa for many days."

"What for?"

"My liver. The doctor says it is very bad."

"I'm sorry."

"It is okay. Listen, I want to invite you to dinner tomorrow night. Will you come?"

"Of course."

"Good. My wife will cook something delicious. No guts soup."

I laughed and walked Baýram to the waratan. As I walked back toward my room, I saw a dark figure near the *tamdyr*. It was crouched like a mushroom over the slow-burning fire. The flames were licking and reflecting off its gold teeth.

"What did Baýram teacher want?" the figure creaked.

"To invite me to dinner," I said.

There was silence. Then my host mom creaked again.

"You had better not drink."

I felt that hot rage stew inside me. I walked up to my room and shut the door.

THE NEXT EVENING, I walked over to Baýram's. Like before, his two eldest daughters, Bibi and Gülbahar, were waiting for me in their flowered köýneks at the little dirt turn-off. I said "Hello" and followed them to the house. It was warm as a baked apple and smelled of spices and meats and kindness. Gözel greeted me with a smile and a handshake. She took my coat, then introduced me to two new members of the family. The first was Baýram's mother. She was like an ancient hollowed-out oak tree in the snow. Her hair, skin, and eyes were neon white. I shook her frail hand. She smiled at me with her one yellow tooth. Then she stepped aside so I could meet Baýram's baby boy, Kakajan. The little guy was resting in his crib. He was wrapped tightly in a blue blanket with his big brown eyes and wispy hair popping out the top. I leaned in a patted him on his forehead. It was as smooth as a wave-tumbled seashell.

Gözel led me into the living room. The klionka was already spread out on the floor and covered with bowls of pickled tomatoes, sweet preserves, cookies, candies, fruit, and fresh honey. Gözel told me to have a seat and help myself.

"Baýram will be home shortly," she said in Turkmen.

I nodded and grabbed a plum. Baýram walked in. He looked thin but happy. He sat down in front of me and we started chatting.

"You will not believe what I saw today," he said.

"Oh yeah, what's that?"

"Well, like I told you I have a satellite dish and it is very good. I was surfing channels at lunchtime and I saw one of your volunteer boys talking about Peace Corps in Turkmen."

"Really? What was he saying?"

"Just telling about his site in Mary welaýat and how he is teaching English. Of course, this isn't so crazy news, but I teach for Peace Corps many years and never see such thing on television. Only Türkmenbaşy this, and Ruhnama that. But now they are interview American volunteer and show it on television? It is sign things are finally changing."

"Damn. I'm glad to hear it."

Baýram cut into his usual spiel about his hopes for Turkmenistan to open up. I was with him on it, but somewhere in me, I hoped that it wouldn't open up *too* much. Part of what made the place cool was that it was isolated and rare. It was like the gods had thrown a hundred Turkmen tribes, some Arabs, some Persians, and some Mongols, in a big black pot and let them simmer for a thousand years. Then, when everything was good and braised, they took the lid off, shook in a bunch of Russians for structure, stirred the mix with the stem of a magic mushroom, then let the pot sit out in the desert to bake and freeze, bake and freeze, bake and freeze for another grip of years. The end result was that whack-yer-brains-outta-yer-skull çorba we call Turkmenistan. And yeah, real health care, education, and freedom of speech would be nice. Just hold the Mickey Ds and the Starbucks, please.

In the middle of our talk, Gözel brought in dinner. And wouldn't ya know it, it was in a big black pot, but instead of çorba, there was *greçka* (boiled buckwheat) with lamb and carrots. She served us two big steaming bowls. Before she could make it out the door, we were already wolfing our food down. When we finished, Baýram got a twinkle in his eye. He held up a finger and slipped off to the back room.

"What are you doing?" I asked.

"You will see."

He came out with a bottle of clear liquid. It had a bright silvery cap and matching decorations. He was cradling it with both hands and smiling down at it tenderly like it was his baby son Kakajan. I popped a grape in my mouth.

"What's that?" I asked.

He lifted his head and grinned.

"This is excellent Ukrainian vodka. I bought it while studying in Chernihiv and have saved it many years. I want to open it with you. Will you have some?"

I leaned forward and nodded out each word slowly.

"Are . . . you . . . fucking . . . kidding . . . me?"

"I guess this is yes?"

"Yes."

Baýram laughed and busted out the shot glasses. He poured us two full ones, and we clinked and threw 'em back. After that, we switched on the tube. Baýram fired up some titty vids and we drooled and drank and lay on our sacks. At some point, I remember Baýram telling me to take it easy on the vod. I brushed him off like a slow fly and kept at it. The bottle up and vanished. But that was okay 'cuz the two of us were elbows-deep in a clip from "Russia's Funniest Home Videos," where some poor fuck was trying desperately to extricate his head from an elephant's ass.

Once midnight rolled around, it was time to split. I was clocks-to-the-ceiling drunk and could barely make it out the door. Baýram was nice enough to help me to the main road. I slurred him a "Fanks fur evey'thring" then staggered off into the wild blue night with rabid dogs snarling and howling at me from the dark. When I got home, I nearly broke the waratan door. I followed this up by crashing to the concrete several times on my way across the courtyard. I banged up my metal stairs with Laika the dog barking at my every step. Then I completed the whole act with one *Finito* slam of my door.

THE NEXT MORNING was brutal. I was riddled outta my sheets by a cacophony of bleating goats, crowing roosters, screaming children, barking Laika, and my crazy, alien-nest queen of a host mother, screeching at everyone to "Do this. Do that. Do this. Do that." My head felt like a watermelon in a microwave on high. My breath reeked of vodka, and my whole body ached. I knew I couldn't go out in this state. I waited till it got quiet then I slipped my clothes on, slipped out the door, and slipped to school.

The children elected today to act like shit. I guess they knew my guard was down, and boy did they take advantage. Their shitty behaviour even extended to the clubs. I tried to solve the issue by throwing some kid's tahýa out the window. This only made him cry and the rest of the kids laugh. By the end of the day, I was zonked. My one wish was to go home and melt into my covers for eternity. As I was hobbling out the door, I saw Jahan. She ran up to me in a flurry.

"Han-Guly, we will have our first group French class today," she said.

My shoulders sank. I rolled my eyes and threw up a hand.

"Allllriiiight."

I followed Jahan to her class. The only person there was the stubby dickhead teacher I'd caught beating his student a few weeks back. He introduced himself as Meret. Not "Ape-fuck" as it turns out. I shook his hand and gave him an iron glare. I set up and did the lesson. It was long and stuffy and filled with off remarks, dumb questions, and awkward silences. When it finally ended, I was ready to die. I said goodbye to my *deux étudiants* and hit the road.

I schlepped through my waratan forty minutes later. I found the courtyard silent and empty. I mustered a ragged smile. I rounded the corner and, my god, there was my host mom at the foot of the stairs, arms folded, teeth gleaming, eyes burning like two molten embers under the shadow of her ýaglyk. I strummed up a tiny "Hi." She flicked it away with her gnarled finger.

"You were drunk last night," she screamed.

"I know."

"And you were extremely loud and woke us all up."

"Sorry."

"Don't you have anything to say for yourself?"

"No."

"It figures, you poorly raised brat."

Now the bitch had gone too far. You can insult me, but when you take a stab at my family, it's eye-gouging time. I knew I couldn't pull anything physical on the ho. But I could do the next best thing.

8

FOR THE NEXT month, I was a phantom. I floated around from site to site without giving a shit about my host family or anyone else in the swill pit that was Gurbagahowda. I ignored the three-month site restriction that was still in effect. I failed to inform Peace Corps of my whereabouts on every occasion, and instead told Merdan and Azat to lie for me and say I was busy in the event Big Brother called. Most of the trips I took were to see other volunteers and get hammered. But on one occasion, I did take a trip that had a real purpose. I was avoiding Aşgabat for obvious reasons and Mary was the closest city with an American Corner. I wanted to go there so I could use the internet and find out what kinda shit-hoops I'd hafta leap through to get visas for my folks to come visit me in the summer.

I took two cabs to get to Mary proper. I had to get another cab to the American Corner. It was a massive bitch to find. This wasn't entirely annoying because Mary was a pretty city with wide green parks, colorful spice bazaars, and a big blue-domed mosque. After two or three loops, we finally found the American Corner. It was in a ratty brown apartment block with cracks for ivy and a dead lawn. I paid the cabbie and went inside. I followed the sign to the second floor and opened the door. The atmosphere was cheerful and bright. There were shelves of books everywhere and well-watered plants on the windowsills. To the right was a sizable computer room. It had eight relatively new computers, all equipped with speakers and some form of internet. To the left was a lounge area. There was a big comfy couch piled with students, plus bookshelves and a stereo. Beyond that was the conference room. It had an oblong table with ten black leather chairs around it and a beautifully painted world map on the back wall.

I asked the smiling Turkmen lady at the front desk if I could use the internet. She told me, "Oh, go ahead," with an almost perfect American accent. I thanked her and got on the newest-looking computer. The internet was slow, but it worked. I spent an hour dicking around on various Turkmen visa websites. I found out that for my folks to visit me they'd need a notarized letter of invitation from the government, which would be a serious pain in the ass to get. As I searched for more info, I heard a ruckus in the entry room. I heard children laughing and then a deep, chocolaty American voice. I recognized it as belonging to Ken, the T-14 and casino-pit-boss-looking motherfucker who'd schooled us one hub day, then after-wards had shown a select few of us the Zip for the first time. I went in and shook the guy's hand. He was shocked to see me, and from what I could tell, a little uncomfortable. We hadn't gotten along so great at the swearing-in ceremony over Christmas. Something to do with too much vodka and one of us making an offhand comment about the other's reputed lack of sexual prowess, but that's beside the point.

I asked Ken the haps. He said things were fine, but that he had a lot of work. We agreed to do lunch. He told me to wait in the lounge while he finished up. I said okay and chilled on the couch. I started chatting with a FLEX student who'd studied English in Arizona for a year. I asked him about his experience. He told me he'd done a lot of partying, but in the end had gotten decent grades. He said he'd even learned some Spanish. I told him I was half Mexican and that I spoke the language. His eyes widened.

"You should teach Spanish here," he said.

I told him that would be tough as I lived three hours away. He laughed.

"So, you can move," he said. "I'm sure it will be possible. Just ask Ken."

Ken walked in. He told me he was ready. I thanked the kid for his stories and encouragement. I followed Ken out and we got a cab. On the way to the restaurant, I felt good. For the first time since arriving at site, I had actually felt wanted by a student.

The cabbie dropped us off at the restaurant. It was a nice place with bright wood booths and glass tables. We grabbed a spot in back. Ken ordered pork shashlik for both of us. While we waited for our food, we sipped urine-flavored beer and chatted. I asked Ken what he thought of me changing sites to Mary and working at the American Corner. He nearly spit his beer out.

"No chance," he said.

"Whaddaya mean, 'no chance'?"

"I mean, no chance."

"Why?"

"First off, to even be considered for a site change, you have to prove to Peace Corps that it's physically *impossible* for you to work at your current site. And from what I've heard, our new associate director, Bartha, is a real hard ass, and she's the one you've gotta run all this by."

"Well, what if I *can* prove it? What if I tell them how long of a walk I have to school and how the kids I teach don't give one single fuck about my lessons and how my host family hates me, especially my bitch host mom, and how my counterpart is a total flake, and how the only person that gives any sort of a shit that I'm there is this pathetic, whiny little English teacher who only wants me around so I can teach her French."

Ken took a gulp of his beer and chuckled.

"Bartha would probably tell you to quit bitching and do your job."

"Oh well, that's great," I said. "Everyone else gets a site they love and can make a difference at and I get stuck in a dump that's so isolated and miserable it makes Fargo look like Rio de Janeiro."

Ken lit a cigarette. He took a long drag then hissed a line of smoke at his beer. He scratched his temple with his thumb.

"What is it?" I asked.

"Well, there's a reason you are where you are."

"What do you mean?"

"I'm pretty tight with Peace Corps, and I gotta tell you that the shenanigans you pulled during training didn't go over so well with them."

"Yeah, I know. But I thought I paid my dues for that shit."

"It's not just about paying your dues. It's about the image they have of you now."

"Which is?"

"That basically you're just a little boy who likes to drink and get loud."

My heart slipped down and plunked against my asshole. My eyes swelled with tears. I chugged my beer and ordered another. Then the food came. It smelled divine and looked the same. I grabbed a glistening hunk of pork and bit into it.

"Gob da's goob," I said, chewing.

Ken nodded with a full mouth. I decided to drop the issue.

I PARTIED THE next few nights with Ken. I arrived in Gurbagahowda on a Tuesday afternoon, hungover and exhausted. I didn't have the strength to teach that day, so I crashed. I woke up relatively fresh the next morning and headed to school. When I got to my classroom, I saw Azat. I could tell he was pissed about my having been gone so much. We taught a few pointless lessons. I said late and went over to Jahan's. I had a grain of excitement about teaching her, and whomever else, French. When I got to her classroom, I found the door closed. I pushed it open and saw her sitting at her desk by herself. She looked like a life-sized porcelain doll that had been locked in a closet for a century. I walked up next to her and sat down. I could tell from the red veins in her eyes she'd been crying.

"What is it, Jahan?" I asked.

She dabbed a napkin at her tear ducts. Then she looked at me sidelong.

"One of our teachers committed suicide yesterday," she said.

"What? Who?"

"Eneş teacher."

"Oh my god, no."

Eneş was the only Russian teacher at our school. I'd seen her every day on my walk to class. She'd always had a pretty smile on her face and asked me "*Kak dyela?*"[41] She was the last person I'd have expected to commit suicide. I wasn't gonna push the issue but my morbid curiosity got the better of me. I comforted Jahan for a minute, then I asked her how Eneş had done it.

"She burnt herself alive in the banýa," she said.

"Jesus Christ, that's horrible."

She crimped her face.

"Are you really so surprised, Han-Guly?"

"Well, yeah. That's so painful. And I don't mean to sound insensitive, but why not use a gun or something?"

She clucked.

"Normal people don't have guns in Turkmenistan. So, when life becomes hard and we want to end it, we either drink lots of vinegar, hang ourselves, or put ourselves on fire."

Jahan and I parted ways. I walked outside and found the skies heavy with clouds and gray. I could smell the dirt and the air and the trees blistering with spring. The ground was still dry, but I knew it might rain. I picked up the pace and headed toward home. A bolt of lightning cracked across the clouds, ripping their giant bellies open. Their clear blue blood bulleted down in hard, grape-sized droplets. They pelted my body and the earth around me hundreds and thousands and millions of times. The unpaved roads quickly turned to rivers of mud. They swallowed my feet with hungry, disgusting mouths of sludge. I took refuge at the uly çaýhana. The little dude with the chef's hat greeted me and gave me a back room. It had a

---

[41] "How are you doing?" (Russian).

heater and a softly flickering lightbulb hanging from its ceiling. I sat down on a stinky sheepskin rug and ordered a beer, some shashlik, and a shot of vodka. Little Chefy brought me everything in a jiff. I took it all down and ordered more. When I was drunk and stuffed, I lay on my back. As I drifted to sleep, the roar of the rain outside filled my head like an angry mob.

I woke up a few hours later. I could hear the rain had stopped. I paid my bill and left. The mud outside was horrendous. I chugged my way through it. I gripped my head and choked back the urge to puke. When I came to the last bend, I heard the strangest noise. It sounded like a whole village of cherubs burping out their assholes at once. It was coming from a newly formed lake just in front of my house. I walked to the edge of the water. As soon as my foot touched down, an giant bullfrog leapt from the mire and landed "Plop" on the nose of my shoe. He shifted his warty gut around and looked up at me. We blinked at one another. I felt something warm and wet seeping into my sock. My eyes widened. I lifted my knee and kicked my fat friend up in the air.

"Piss on you too, you little fucker," I screamed.

The bullfrog tumbled down from the sky with his arms and legs out. He hit the dark water with a splash, sending a dozen other bullfrogs leaping and farting into the gloom. I flipped the whole thing off and went to my room. I fell asleep with visions of Eneş's crispy corpse haunting my brain.

THE FOLLOWING WEEKEND, I went back to Mary. I figured I'd be safe there from the fried ghost of Eneş and all the giant, pissing bullfrogs. I returned to Gurbagahowda in the middle of the week again. I showed up late for class with a hangover and a peppered chin. Azat scowled at me.

"You leave willage too much time," he said.

"Why, does it require less?"

"What?"

"Nothing."

"Hey, not no'sing. I am sorry, but you must to stay here more. Peace Corps calling school all time, and I must to lie for you and say, 'Hey, Johann sick.' Or, 'Hey, Johann sleeping.' Zey sink problem now."

"Alright, man. I won't go anywhere for the next two weeks."

"Okay, sank you."

We finished teaching our classes. I felt bad about having been outta site so much. I asked Azat if I could treat him to lunch at the uly çaýhana. He looked stunned.

"We will go," he said, smiling.

We packed our crap and walked over there. We got a big heated room in back and ordered two double shots of vodka, plus beer, lüle, shaslik, and manty. Little Chefy brought us everything lickety-split. He closed the door behind him quietly. Azat and I clinked our double shots and threw 'em back. Then we dug into our food and beer. As we chomped and guzzled, we started chatting. Azat asked me why I'd been gone so much lately. I had to tell him something he'd understand.

"I met a girl."

He grinned with his four crusty teeth.

"Hey, tell me her about," he said.

I proceeded to tell him about how she was this gorgeous chick I'd meet in Mary some weeks back. I told him we'd gone on a couple dates, but that her mother was making a fuss over things because I was a few years older. Azat asked me her nationality. I told him, "Uzbek."

"Ohhh, be careful wiz Uzbek girl. Zey are wery lying."

"Really?"

"Yes. Only girls more lying zan Uzbek are Tatar girls."

"Why do you say that?"

"Because one time I meet Tatar girl in Moscow and she say, 'Hey, let's we go to my apartment.' And I sink, 'Why she ask me?' But zen I am drunk so I go. And we are inside and kiss, zen I hear door knock and she open and sree boys zey hit to me and take money.

But zen I take knife, yes? And I take one boy and put knife on sroat and say, 'Give me *my* money and give me *your* money.' Zey scared so zey give. Zen I cut zis boy's leg and jump out window."

"Damn."

For some reason, I felt compelled to test the guy. I reached into my pocket and pulled out my own blade. I whipped it open in front of his face and smiled.

"Was your knife anything like this?" I asked.

Azat leaned against his pillow and puffed his cigarette.

"Mine bigger," he said.

I nodded sharply and whistled. Little Chefy came in with the bill and I paid it.

I MADE GOOD on my promise to Azat. For the next two weeks, I didn't leave Gurbagahowda once, not even to have lunch in Tejen with Brooke. It was a mixed two weeks. On one hand, it was nice because the cold was cracking and the sun was coming out. But on the other hand, it was shit because my relationship with my host family, especially with my host mother and host siblings Aziza and Ali, wasn't getting any better, and to top it off, the squatting old fucks in the streets were still staring at me.

I can remember one bullfrog-filled walk to school in particular. The squatters were out in droves because the weather was nice and the flowers—all five of them—were blooming. The assholes just sat there under the green trees, crunching their çigits and greasing my body up and down with their black eyeballs. I wanted to march right up to one of them with a stick, crack him across the jaw, and scream, "I've been here for four months now, you prick. What's the fucking novelty?"

When I got to class, I was fuming. I eked out my four lessons with Azat then went over to Jahan's for French. Luckily it was just her. I taught her the past tense. Then I had to get a load off. I told her I was sick to my bones of being stared at in the streets. She flipped her pencil around and rolled her eyes.

"Han-Guly, you are guest here," she said. "People don't recognize you, and they are curious."

"I understand this," I said, gritting my teeth. "But I find it extremely rude when they do it not once, not twice, but over and over and over again."

Jahan got quiet. She folded her hands on her lap and stared at them.

"I mean, what is it?" I continued. "I've tried to integrate as best I can. I speak Turkmen pretty damn well. Plus, I wear the beret, the sweater, the pointy shoes, the pinstriped pants. Yet they still stare at me."

"You mean you don't dress like this in America?" she asked.

"Absolutely not. In America, I had hair down to my asshole and wore ripped jeans and T-shirts and a silver piercing in my lip."

She crinkled her eyebrows at this last bit. I flipped my lip forward and showed her the hole. There was a pause while she examined it. Then she pitched forward, wrenched her mouth open, and laughed so hard and loud it almost popped the lightbulbs from the ceiling. I'd never heard Jahan do anything more than chuckle. Seeing her with her limbs shaking and her mouth howling with pure laughter made me feel something. Her laugh went on for a few more seconds. Then as quickly as it had come, it vanished. She looked at me with a haze in her eyes. I opened my mouth to say something, but she broke into laughter again.

"I-I-I'm soooooo sorry, H-Han-Guly," she said, panting. "P-P-Please d-don't be offfffense. Bwahahaha."

I wasn't offended. In fact, the whole incident reminded me of a night at the beginning of my stay where I was holed up in my room amongst my piss bottles and my stacks of books and Merdan had come in and seen me like this and said with genuine concern:

"You know why you're bald, Johann? Because you read too much."

I laughed so hard I nearly crapped my boxers.

OUR FRENCH LESSON —and the laughing— ended and I bid Jahan adieu. As I walked home, I tried as best I could to ignore the gawking buttholes along the road. I was able to make it home without incident. I was smiling as I walked through the waratan. I reached into my pocket and found that the skeleton key to my door was missing. I panicked into an explosion of hairless cats. I ran all the way back to school to look for it. I searched both Azat's and Jahan's classroom. Neither they nor the key was anywhere to be found. I decided to ask Islam if he had, by chance, found my key. When I arrived at his office, his secretary—a delicious little thing with a giant ass and bright red hair wrapped in a ýaglyk—informed me that he'd gone home.

"That's too bad," I said.

She crossed her legs and opened her pocket mirror. She fixed her pink lipstick with her fingertip then clasped the mirror shut.

"But I'm still here," she said, grinning with all her gold teeth.

I looked her up and down and grinned back.

"You sure are," I said.

The two of us got to chatting. She told me her name was Gülalik and that she knew a secret about Jahan. She asked me if I wanted to know it. I shrugged.

"She tells everyone in town everything," she said.

To emphasize her point, she formed her hand into a duck's head and went, "Quack, quack, quack." I thanked her for the information and cut back home. I found Ali and my host mom in the courtyard. Ali was swinging a stick around while making fart noises. My host mom was stirring her cauldron. I knew this moment would have to come sooner or later. I walked up and broke her the news. She stopped stirring and looked up at me with her scary white eyes. She went into the house and came back a minute later. She held out her wrinkly palm. A skeleton key was on it. I took it and thanked her. She nodded and walked back to her cauldron.

"Lose this one and you're out," she muttered.

This tickled Ali something fierce. He burst into laughter and swung his stick at me. I parried it with my hand and went upstairs. I didn't leave my room for the rest of the night. At some point, Merdan brought me my çorba. He told me he'd seen what had happened in the courtyard earlier.

"The next time my mom leaves for the dükan, I'll slap Ali in the head for you."

Had this been a few months prior, I'd have been appalled by his offer. But at the current moment, I found it quite nice. I told him I'd even like to watch.

"Preferably this weekend," I said.

Merdan laughed.

"I can't this weekend."

"Why not?"

"'Cuz I'm going to Aşgabat with my friends to fuck prostitutes."

He said it as casually as if he were going to get gas. I asked him if he was serious.

"Of course," he said.

"Well, who are these prostitutes? The ones at the hotels?"

"Sometimes. But me and my friends also fuck the street ones."

"Jesus. Do you guys at least use protection?"

"What do you mean?"

"Like condoms. You know, the rubber things that you put on your dick?"

"Oh no, we never use those, haha."

"Oh my god."

I went over to my backpack and rummaged through it. I pulled out a handful of the free condoms PC had provided me. I handed them to Merdan. He took them from me and laughed.

"It isn't funny," I said. "One of my friends fucked a prostitute without a condom and a week later his dick rotted off."

Merdan slicked his face back poisonously.

"Are you serious?" he asked.

I looked him dead in the eyes.

"Of course."

THE FOLLOWING MORNING, Merdan left for Aşgabat. Seeing him drive off in his fresh clothes with a fresh smile on his face made me wanna cut too. I sublimated this desire and walked to school. I found Azat in our classroom looking sad. After we finished teaching our first lesson, I went outside with him and asked what the problem was. He lit a cigarette and blew streams of smoke through his gapped teeth.

"My granfaza sister die last night," he said.

"Oh."

"So, we will need to make sadaka today."

"I see."

I knew where this was going. I knew that making sadaka meant getting together with family and friends multiple times for the first month or so after a loved one's death. I was certain Azat would try to dump his classes on me on all those occasions. I decided to go to Mary the following day. I informed him of my plans. He looked irritated.

"But you promise you don't go for two weeks," he said.

"Yeah, well those two weeks ended yesterday."

He frowned and tossed his cigarette on the ground. He smooshed it with the tip of his shoe then turned to me with a pathetic look on his face.

"I go now," he said.

"Go ahead, man. I got you."

I LEFT FOR Mary the next morning. It was a rush climbing into that cab and blasting across the desert after more than two weeks of being trapped in Gurbagahowda. I arrived at the American Corner in a fantastic mood. I stepped up in there with long legs, a jazzy smile, and my hat cocked over one eye. Everything looked perfect and bright. I could hear kids laughing in the computer room. I strolled on in. A deep voice yelled, "Speak of the devil."

I darted my eyes around for the source. She was sat on the tallest chair, in the middle of the room, with her black hair down, her brown eyes boppin', and her shoulder tats out fresh. I didn't recognize her at first because she was heavily tanned with longer hair and a few extra pounds. When I got a load of her streak-of-sunshine smile, though, it hit me.

"Holy Jesus, Stella?"

Stella was a T-14 I'd had a fling with back in training. I say fling, but it was just me hitting on her and her laughing away my advances. Under normal circumstances, this would have bruised my fragile male ego beyond repair. But as Stella was so awesome, so much larger than the teeth of life dripping with lightning, I just had to punch my wounded little prick down in its hole and be a bud. I gave her a big hug and told her it was good to see her. Then I asked her where she'd been all these months.

"Thailand," she said. "I had to have surgery on my knee, and they didn't have the equipment to perform it in Aşgabat, so PC sent me to Bangkok. I spent eight weeks recovering, which really meant eating tons of curry, drinking tons of booze, and tanning on the beach for hours on end. It was fucking great. But when I got back at the end of February, PC was like, 'Get to site and get to work.' I've been in Baýramaly ever since, trying to get these damn day camps off the ground. I'm here today getting the last bit of permission for the first of my day camps, which will be on Sunday."

"Wow, really?"

"Yeah. And in fact, the kids here were just telling me how you've been visiting recently and how they want you to be a part of it. Would you be interested?"

"Fuck yeah."

"Great, you can stay at my place with the rest of the volunteers."

THE NEXT TWO days were a blast. We spent them at Stella's big flat in Baýramaly—a town about fifteen minutes from Mary—gossiping, cooking, dancing, singing, and getting trashed. Stella was the queen of the whole show. Not only did she cook a huge dinner both nights, but she busted out the little karaoke machine she'd bought in Thailand and let us all break the fucker in. We made a ruckus to yank the clouds down and send the moon pissing its skirt off into space. It's a wonder we woke up Sunday morning with our eyes, ears, mouths, and throats still intact.

It took me a long hot shower and a shit the size of Gibraltar to get my troops together. I walked out of the bathroom with my knees shaking and my kidneys still aching. Stella looked at me and smiled pityingly.

"Don't worry, Johann. I've got just the thing," she said.

She served me and the rest of the groaning volunteers a big plate of scrambled eggs with sausage and a glass of fresh OJ. It was enough to soak up the booze and bring life back into our veins so we could handle the day ahead of us.

STELLA'S CAMP WAS a bust. I spent most of it being chewed by fire ants, herding bratty, psychotic little boys, and scolding an evil little girl who'd crushed a turtle with a brick. By the end of it, I was done with kids. I was so fucking done with them I could have stood by grinning while God flushed them all down the neck of a black hole. I arrived in Gurbagahowda the following evening. School was already over, so I went home, ate, shat, wanked, and crashed. I woke up the next day feeling strangely refreshed. I walked to school with a smile on my face and a bullfrog in my step. When I got to my classroom, Azat was already teaching. I greeted him and joined in. I could tell the kids were confused by my newfound good mood. I smiled at them and taught alongside Azat without ever raising my voice.

The last class ended. Azat asked me if I would accompany him while he smoked. I nodded and followed him out of the building. He lit up a cigarette and inhaled. He blew smoke through his teeth and picked a fleck of tobacco from his tongue. I folded my arms and waited. He took a few more drags. Then he turned to me.

"Tomorrow we make seven day sadaka for my granfaza sista," he said.

"Mm-hmm."

"Hey, please, can you to teach my lessons?"

"Why, of course I will."

He cocked his head in surprise. He shook my hand, said "Sank you," and walked off. I went home that evening and drafted a plan. I passed out shortly thereafter.

THE NEXT MORNING, I packed my things and cut to school. I arrived at my classroom and found my students waiting silently with their hands folded and their eyes on the blackboard. I walked to the front and greeted them. They greeted me back, then a little boy asked me where Azat *mugallym* was. I told him he was at a sadaka and that he'd be back the following day. The instant I finished my sentence, the kids broke outta their desks and started whistling and screaming and throwing crap all over the room. I watched them for a moment with a smile on my face. Then in one clean movement, I heaved my chest, filled my lungs, opened my mouth, and like a shotgun blast in slow-mo, screamed "*Ýuuuuuuwaaaaaaşşşşş.*"

The word blanketed the room like a wave of death. The kids snapped their little hands against their ears and pinched their faces. I waited till they got back in their seats and put their eyes on me. Then I smiled wickedly.

"You've all just been given your first warning. See that pool of mud outside?" I said, pointing out the window. "If any of you test me again, I'll throw your tahýas out the window for a little swim. Get me?"

They all nodded. Then a little girl raised her hand.

"Yes, Amira?" I said.

"What if we do it again?"

"Funny you should ask. If you do it again, I'll bring you to the front of the class, and depending on my mood, I'll either cover your clothes in chalk, make you stand on one leg, or have you sing embarrassing songs in front of us all for the remainder of the lesson."

Amira closed her mouth. It was quiet for a moment. A little boy who had a penchant for chucking erasers at me raised his hand.

"Yes, Berdi?" I said.

"And what if we do it again?" he asked slyly.

Without saying anything I reached into my back pocket and pulled out a giant, gleaming pair of scissors. I cocked them open, walked over to Berdi and grabbed his oversized tie. I looked down at him and poured my searing anger into both of his little brown eyes. I could see he was on the brink of crying.

"If you test me a fourth time," I said, clipping the scissors shut, "I'll cut something off."

The entire class gasped. The rest of the day was a breeze.

THE NEXT DAY, I was spared the knife. My kids behaved well, partly because Azat was there and partly because they knew if they hadn't, they'd have been walking out of class hatless, braidless, and/or finger-less. After Azat cut, I rewarded the kids with a little club time. It wasn't anything big, just a bit of drawing and looking at photos of America. At 3:00 p.m., I went over to Jahan's for our group French lesson. I found only her, sitting at her desk and staring at her plants. She looked over at me and threw her arms in the air.

"No one came again," she cried.

"Eh, no worries. Just gives us more time to hang out."

I sat down next to her and pulled out the French book. Jahan looked at it like it was a lettuce sandwich left in the rain.

"What is it?" I asked.

She pinched her mouth into a little muffin.

"You've been gone a lot," she said.

I rolled my eyes.

"I know I have. I got the same guilt trip from Azat a few weeks ago. Are you gonna start now too?"

She didn't say anything. I could tell I'd injured her.

"Alright. How 'bout I show you some photos of America?"

Her eyes brightened like two windows blown open with sunlight. She scooted next to me and cracked her knuckles two at a time. I reached into my pack and pulled out the small album my folks had compiled for me. It contained photos of us drinking wine on our porch while the sun set, family trips to Australia and Mexico, the old sycamore grove behind our house, big Mexican cookouts and BBQs, and all us Chucks posing with our backpacks at the airport before blasting off on the World Explosion 2006.[42] Every time I flipped a page, Jahan's expression changed. She went from ecstatic, to happy, to glad, to bland, to sorry, to slumpy, to downright sad. When she got to the point of crying, I closed the album. I gave her a moment to compose herself, then I asked her:

"What's up?"

She picked the tears from her ducts and turned to me.

"You seem to enjoy life," she said.

"Well, I do enjoy life. I mean, not always. But I try."

"But why not always?" she said. "Your family is good, your house is beautiful, you travel, you have good work, good food, good friends. When I look to my life, I feel very alone and scared. My mother is dying in front of my eyes, and my sister is stranger. Also, I see myself getting old very quickly. I'm twenty-six now, but one day I will wake up to be sixty-six. My life will be gone. I won't be married or have kids. My dreams will disappear, and everything will be over."

I felt like a grasshopper under a mountain of feces. I poked my tiny green leg out and hoped it would touch Jahan's shoulder.

"But you're educated and have a job," I said. "Doesn't that count for something?"

Jahan sighed.

"In the end, this doesn't matter. Most women in Turkmen villages have my same future if they have educations or families. It is hopeless."

---

[42] The World Explosion refers to a trip I took around the world with my childhood buddies in 2006. See Hans Joseph Fellmann, *Chuck Life's a Trip*, Russian Hill Press, 2019.

I was scrambling for a response. I fell back on the crap I used to get myself going.

"You gotta get motivated," I said. "Set a goal, set the steps, and one by one, take them all. Before you know it, you'll have reached the stars and beyond."

I felt like a shitty personal trainer. The look on Jahan's face confirmed it.

"You don't understand, Han-Guly," she said. "When a Turkmen woman does not get married by a certain age, she becomes separated from her family. They see her like 'damaged' and don't want a relationship with her. This is slowly coming true for me. My last hope now is to save enough money to build a house. Except when I finally have this money, I will be forty and live alone."

I had a vision. It was of me in a red, white, and blue suit of armor atop a big, white colt that was galloping with flared nostrils straight toward poor little, meek Jahan in a flowered dress. My colt came within inches of running her over. Then just at the final moment, it swerved, and I scooped Jahan up in my gleaming arms and saved her last pointed toe from being snapped off by the humungous, sand-breathing dragon that was charging at her from behind. My vision ended and I looked at Jahan. I noticed her wide freckles like autumn leaves and her slightly crooked nose. Her hazel eyes were on my face. I asked if she had something else to tell me. She looked down at her lap.

"It's nothing," she said.

THAT EVENING I felt like pond scum, which was made worse because somehow Ali had found my club Frisbee and was chucking it on the roof and then pounding up and down my stairs to retrieve it and restart the process. I ignored him and thought about how I was gonna escape again. As I formulated a plan, Ali yelled, "Johaaaaaan, telefon."

I jumped outta my bed and ran downstairs. I slid into the living room and took the phone, panting. The person on the other end was laughing. I could tell by the breadth of the laugh it was Stella.

"What you been up to?" she asked, still laughing.

"Oh, you know, a little private time in the banýa."

"Well, I hope you're not gonna spend tomorrow in there."

"Why's that?"

"Because it's a Cheshire Cat moon. And a bunch of us are camping at Merv."

9

YOU COULD HAVE stuffed popcorn seeds up my asshole and had me burst them into the family bowl, I was so fucking excited when I woke up the next morning. I didn't even eat the stale çörek and *bal* breakfast my host mom had prepared for me. I just scrubbed my balls, grabbed my big backpack of fun, popped my cap on my scalp, and split. As I was two-steppin' down the dirt road, I ran into good ol' Baýram. He had an even bigger smile of escapism on his face than I did.

"Johaan, you won't to guess what I heard today," he said.

"Bullfrogs raping one another?"

"Huh? No, the T-Program.[43] They have selected me, and I will be going to America this summer for six weeks."

"Well, hot diggity dog, Baýram. We'll for sure celebrate when I get back."

"Oh, where you go?"

"To the back side o' the moon, baby."

I bid Baýram adieu and walked to the taxi stand. I picked the biggest, baddest-looking Lada on the lot and got inside. I waited for the thing to fill with ýaglyks and gold teeth and clucking heads and knock-off clothes. When it was all loaded up, I rolled my window

---

[43] A program that sends ESL teachers from other countries to train in various cities around the US.

down, stuck my head out, and let the wind rip my cheeks back so the bugs would have somewhere to splat.

I arrived in Baýramaly a few hours later. I was let off in the courtyard of Stella's apartment block. I met up with her and a group of other volunteers. The first thing we did was hit the dükan. We bought tons of vodka, beer, fruit, sausages, and sandwich supplies. Then we grabbed a marşrutka out to the ruins. They didn't look like much from the window; just dusty rings of earth jutting up from the endless scrubland. I thumbed through my guidebook. I found the following blurb about Merv.

During the first millennium, Merv was an important city for successive Persian empires and was a place of worship for a number of major religions, including Buddhism, Zoroastrianism,[44] Christianity, and Manicheanism.[45] In the seventh century, it was occupied, and its residents were converted to Islam by the Arabs. In 1037 it was peacefully taken over by the Seljuk Turks, whose prowess in trade turned it into what Arab and Persian geographers called, The Mother of the World. Some historians estimate there were as many as 200,000 people living in Merv at the time, which would have made it one of the most populated places on earth. This changed in 1221 when the Mongols, under the leadership of Genghis Kahn's son Tolui, razed the city. Apart from a handful of artisans, they slaughtered every man, woman, and child until 'the mountains became hillocks, and the plains were soaked with the blood of the mighty.' In the 1500s, the Uzbeks came and delivered the final blow. The remaining inhabitants of Merv were deported to other parts of

---

[44] Zoroastrianism is a religion that was started in the Achaemenid Empire (Persia's first empire) in the fifth century BC by an Iranian-speaking spiritual leader called Zoroaster. It is a faith centered on the dualistic cosmology of good and evil. Its major features—heaven and hell, free will and judgment after death—may have influenced other religions such as Christianity, Buddhism, and Islam. It is one of the oldest continuously practiced religions in the world.

[45] Manichaeism is a religion started by the Iranian prophet Mani (216–274 AD), which taught that existence is a struggle between a good, spiritual realm of light and an evil, material realm of darkness.

the Bokhara Oasis[46] and the once majestic city was slowly eaten away by the desert.

Our marşrutka dropped us off near the crumbling back walls. We hiked five minutes in and picked a clearing amidst the shrubs. We gathered a bunch of wood. We had a couple of hatchets, so we were able to make quick sticks of it. The sun set behind the hills. It lit the thin cloud cover with milky pinks and oranges that softened our joints and put us down on the rocks. We busted out our fixings and made sandwiches. While I rigged up a fatboy with *kielbasa*,[47] cheese, lettuce, onions, tomatoes, and whole-seed mustard, I got to talking with a volunteer named Jimmy. He had thick hairy arms and a dimpled chin. His brown mop was thinning in front, and he wore a five o'clock shadow around his jaws. His eyes were wicked sick; they were like two little children's heads, mouths wide open in the throes of laughter. He told me he was from Tennessee and that his daddy was a pastor.

"I woulda followed in his footsteps," he said, "but I like ta' party too much."

"Yeah, I hear ya. What did ya do instead?"

"Well, I was in corporate for a minute. I made some good money and had a lot of real good parties, but all the paperwork and big office bullshit started gettin' to me after a while. Then I went to Nicaragua with my church to build schools. I wanted to make some kinda difference seein' as how my daddy helped our community some and I was just fuckin' off, gettin' drunk with my corporate buddies in Memphis. We got two schools up in a village just outside'a Managua. And that felt real good. Then I heard about Peace Corps through one'a them vegan shindigs they throw in the city. Met some real nice folks there, so I figured, fuggit, why not give it a try? Thought they might send me somewheres tropical like Tonga or somethin'. Never imagined I'd end up in this shit dungeon."

---

[46] The Bokhara Oasis is an area around the city of Bukhara, Uzbekistan, first inhabited by Indo-Aryan tribes in the third millennium BC.

[47] A sausage from Poland that may contain any kind of meat.

I nearly choked on my kielbasa.

"I fuckin' feel ya, man. All that keeps me goin' in this place are the sunsets and this right here."

I lifted my bottle of vodka. Jimmy's laugh-eyes flashed like two gold scarabs.[48] I cracked the top off and poured a couple doubles. Jimmy raised his glass. "To that Cheshire Cat moon."

I looked up in the sky. The moon was grinning down on us like a mouth of white razorblades. Jimmy and I threw back our shots and howled. Then I heard Stella say "Those two are gonna go fuckin' nuts tonight."

Things got slizzy after that. The sun melted into the sand, and the night flew up like a deranged bat and the stars came out shining like the exploded eyes of unicorns across the black face of space. Jimmy and I got real, *real,* busy on the bottle. So busy that our bones saluted and our blood sang and our hearts turned into hungry baby mouths, just begging to suck at the liquor nipple. When we were good and trashed, we went running up the dunes of the ruins like whack jobs. The crescent moon was out so big and bright it looked like the clipped fingernail of God, floating up in the sky, and it put so much juice through us that when we got to the very jagged end of the walls, we sucked our chests in, tipped our heads back, and screamed at that gigantic glowing scythe blade until our throats popped and the stars zigzagged. I can't remember much after that. Maybe just coming back down the mound with Jimmy, shoulder-to-shoulder like big fuckin' heroes, welcoming in all the volunteer applause and laughter, and then joining the others at the foot of the great flaming throne of Satan that was our bonfire to chat and drink and tell tall tales s'more. I can't recall what time we slipped into our bags. Prolly somewhere between the fifteenth shot and five o'clock. Mr. Nighttime stole us from our skulls shortly thereafter. We were out within seconds.

---

[48] Scarabs are a family of beetles consisting of over 30,000 species, most of which have bright metallic colors and stout bodies.

THE SUN CRAWLED over our bags at eight thirty. I opened my eyes and felt the skin around them swollen with mosquito bites. I lifted the lip of my bag carefully so as not to provoke the itchiness of other potential bite areas. A white spider with a butt the size of a grape flew out from underneath my mat and burrowed itself into the sand. I bolted up to avoid any other creepies that might be lurking around. I looked over and saw Jimmy sitting on a rock, swigging rotgut, and watching the embers smoke. He pulled the bottle from his lips with a swishy plunk.

"Wanna sip?" he asked.

"Nah I'm good. Let's get the fuck outta here."

We packed our shit and Stella called the marşrutka guy. He came a half hour later and gave us a ride. Jimmy was still going at the bottle. He looked so happy with his red face and blown-up hair that I just had to grab the booze from him and take a few pulls myself. We got re-drunk and made up songs. We came up with this doozy that set the words, "*Siz boldyňyzmy?*" or "Art thou finished—cumming?" to the tune of "I'm So Excited" by The Pointer Sisters. We sang that baby all the way to Baýramaly. I'm pretty sure our driver would've killed us had we not gotten off when we did.

I was in no state to travel, so Stella offered her flat. I accepted with a smile and said late to the other volunteers, especially Jimmy. Me and the guy gave each other daps and big hugs. When we pulled apart, Jimmy said in his twangiest drawl, "Don't be a stranger ta' Türkmenhalk, now, ya hear?"

I told him I would visit his site hella soon. We said a last goodbye, and I went up to Stella's flat and crashed.

STELLA AND I woke up sometime in the afternoon. I was in agony, not just from my hangover but from my loads of itchy red bites. Four big fat ones were across the top of my right hand. I scratched at them all through the lunch Stella made and into the evening while we watched *Project Runway*. By that time, my hand had swollen to the size of a softball. This didn't alarm me too much at first, as my mosquito bites can get pretty big, but when Stella noticed my hand and shrieked, I got a bit nervous.

"You think I should call Peace Corps?" I asked.

"Fuck yes, I do."

"Shit."

I put some cream on the bites.

"If they don't look better by tomorrow morning, I'll call PC."

The next morning my hand didn't look any better. In fact, it was even stiffer and more swollen. I had trouble just packing my backpack. As I was leaving, Stella looked down at my wretched puff.

"Those are not mosquito bites, Johann. Promise me you'll call PC the minute you get to site."

I promised her I would. I gave her a big hug and thanked her for everything. On my way out of the building, I thought about what my bites might be from. Then it hit me.

"That fucking spider with the grape butt," I muttered.

I hailed a cab and got inside. The whole way to Gurbagahowda, I was in a panic. I kept imagining neon green spider venom creeping up my arm and into my brain and blowing the lights out. I was so red and sweaty when I got home that I could have passed for a barbequed tomato. I staggered through the waratan and found Merdan in the courtyard. He told me Islam had come by and that host mommy had told him I was camping in Merv.

"Islam was pretty pissed," he said.

This threw me into even more of a panic. I went in the house and called Peace Corps. I got permission to come in and see the PCMO.[49] Without showering or saying goodbye, I ran to School #17. My hand was throbbing so hard I thought the skin might split. I went to Islam's office but his bubble-butt secretary, Gülalik, told me he'd already left to give his monthly report to the Department of Education. I knew his review of me wouldn't be stellar. I didn't give a fuck. I ran to Azat's. He looked very concerned when he saw my hand.

---

[49] Peace Corps medical officer.

"You will be okay?" he asked.

"I hope so. I have to go to Aşgabat now, so they can check me out."

"Okay. I will tell to Islam."

I thanked him and got a cab. I popped two Benadryls and passed out. I came to five hours later at the gates of PCHQ. I paid my cabbie and walked straight to the medical office. Thankfully, our PCMO was still on call. I say this, not just because my hand was in a state, but because the woman was so loin-flaringly beautiful I almost prayed for sickness. Her name was Aynabat (Moonlight) and she was tall and slender with an oval face, onyx hair, and green eyes. I found her seated cross-legged in her office, wearing tight jeans and a frilly blouse. She was penning a prescription and softly kicking her top leg out. The point of her stiletto heel was jabbing at my crotch. She noticed me and put her pen down.

"Khello, Jokhaan," she said in her gravelly Russian accent. "Vat for you can I do?"

"Well . . ."

I showed her my swollen hand. She grabbed it and pulled it to her face. I could feel the breath from her nostrils as she looked it over. She nodded and let it go.

"Doz are spider bites," she said.

"Jesus Christ, I knew it."

"Ver you recently in desert?"

"Yeah, I camped at Merv two nights ago."

"Vel, you are wery lucky. From vat I can see, spider took four bites den run out of wenom at vrist. If khee bite past dis, you could be wery sick. But as it is, I can give you shot and you vil be okay."

I breathed a sigh of relief. Aynabat pulled out a big syringe and pumped me full of antihistamines. She told me I could stay a night or two in Aşgabat. I thanked her then cut to the lounge. I got on the computer and checked my email. The tour agency I'd contacted about my folks coming out had messaged me saying that along with visas and a letter of invitation from the Turkmen government, I'd also need to pay a guide to take us around, plus find a national to act as a responsible party for my folks. It all seemed like a giant pain in the ass. I emailed my folks with the news and told them we might have to postpone the trip till the following summer.

I tried booking a room at the Daýhan but it was full. I went downstairs to ask staff what they thought I should do. The only one in was Bartha. She was plopped in her chair and grimacing at an email. I approached her delicately and told her my sitch. She wheeled around and looked at me with her big sow eyes. I thought she was gonna chew my head from my neck.

"I can put you up for the night," she said.

I almost browned the backs of my pant legs. I accepted her offer immediately. We got in her car and split. As we cruised through the labyrinth of marble buildings, we started chatting. Bartha had some disturbing news about the state of PC Turkmenistan.

"I'm sure you've noticed that Bob hasn't been around lately."

"Yeah, why is that?"

"He's got brain cancer."

"Damn, that's terrible."

"Yeah. He just had brain surgery, which left him paralyzed. He's now in a wheelchair and undergoing physical therapy in the US. The docs say his condition is stable but the cancer could easily return. His wife and daughter are a wreck. That poor family."

We arrived at Bartha's apartment building. It was tall, white, and ghostly with black windows. We pulled into the parking garage and got out. We took the elevator to the twelfth floor. We walked all the way down the hall to Bartha's flat. When she opened the door, I was stunned. The entryway and kitchen alone were bigger than my Turkmen host family's entire house. There was a living room off to the side with a big-screen TV, stacks of DVDs, white leather couches, and high-ceilinged walls filled with knock-off Picassos, Rembrandts, and Dalís. Bartha told me I could pick any of the three guestrooms in back. I gulped down my astonishment, walked down the mirrored hall, and selected the room with the biggest, most comfy-looking bed. When I came back in the kitchen Bartha had a slight smile on her cheeks.

"Why don't you check out the pantry and pick what you want to eat," she said.

I nodded and ran to it. I threw open the doors and was blinded by the shine from all the packaged American foods. There were all kinds of chips: Doritos, Tostitos, Fritos, Lay's. There were cases upon cases of Pepsi, Coke, Sprite, Slice, and Mountain Dew. There were Skittles, Snickers, Fruit Roll-ups, gummy bears. There was every type of cereal: Frosted Flakes, Cheerios, Apple Jacks, Joe's O's. There were Cup o' Noodles, cans of chili, canned veggies, chip dips, every type of spice. There were taco and enchilada sauces, TV dinners, pancake mixes, syrups, spreads, jams, jellies, bananas, oranges, plums, pears, smoked clams, oysters, salmon. I looked at all of it with my eyes bulging like road apples. I thought of my host family's food supply, which was a tiny fridge stocked with sheep's milk and a few bits of rotting meat and vegetables, plus a klionka in the back room with a few piles of rice and grain on top. For the blood of me, I couldn't choose what the fuck I wanted. I must've stood there for ten minutes.

"Just pick something," Bartha said.

I was at the point of sweating. Then I blurted out, "I want Speedy Burros."

Bartha looked at me like I'd just asked for deep-fried protozoan nostrils.

"What the heck are those?" she asked.

"You'll see."

I gathered all the ingredients. I cooked my family's take on beef flautas[50] with homemade guacamole and sour cream. It turned out pretty good. I served it up hot, and Bartha broke out the Coke.

"I'd offer you some booze but since 9/11, PC staff isn't allowed

---

[50] A Mexican dish that consists of various rolled-up flour or corn tortillas containing shredded chicken, beef, or cheese. They are either pan-fried or deep-fried and then topped with sour cream, cheese, and guacamole.

to drink with volunteers."

I wasn't quite sure what alcohol consumption among Peace Corps volunteers and staff had to do with airplanes crashing into the Twin Towers. I brushed it off, told her to pour me a glass of Coke, and we dug into our food. I could tell Bartha was enjoying her meal. She took a few hearty bites and said, "It's so nice having you here, Johann."

"Thanks," I said. "It's nice being here. Do you put a lot of volunteers up?"

"A few. Last week your little friend Truman was here, haha."

I hadn't thought much of Cluster Fuck since our overnight fiasco during training. I asked how he was, and she puffed.

"Okay, I guess. He was here getting his back checked so I put him up. Smart guy but not very exciting. All he talked about were his plans to become some famous writer. He reminded me of this guy I served with in Armenia."

"Armenia? I thought you served in Morocco?"

"I did. But before that, I was in Armenia."

"Wow, what was that like?"

"Well, first off, we didn't have the same tough site restrictions you guys have. I would leave my site every week and come into the capital and nobody would say anything. I was also constantly visiting other volunteers and vice versa. I can remember one winter I had fourteen people living in my flat for almost two months."

"Good God. Was the culture really liberal or something?"

"No, it was pretty much like here. The people in the villages spoke more Armenian and wore traditional clothing. But in the cities, they wore Western clothes and spoke more Russian. Like here, everyone drank a ton of vodka. I gotta say, the food was sure better."

"What about the gossiping? It's terrible in my village."

"Yeah, it was the same in Armenia. The villagers were constantly slandering one another. Plus, they were always comparing us to the volunteers that came before. My site mate, who was this crazy, fiery redhead, hated them for this. She picked all sorts of fights, and because of it she got admin sep'd."

"Were any PCVs whack evac'd?"[51]

"Oh, sure. There was this one guy who walked through his village naked in the snow with an orange in his outstretched hand. Then there was this other guy who went native and learned the language perfectly but stopped showering or maintaining his personal hygiene and got involved with some sort of political dissidents. I hate to say it, but the guy kind of reminds me of you, haha."

"Hey."

"Oh, I'm just kidding. But yeah, the former Soviet countries are no joke. We had a volunteer who did six tours in West Africa, and he told us that Armenia was still the toughest by far. Places like Africa have physical challenges and such, but the Bloc countries, with all their secret police forces, bad bureaucracy, extreme weather conditions, and terrible food, really screw with your mind. I learned a saying in Armenia about PC volunteers that went, 'Those who go to Southeast Asia come back laid and happy. Those who go to Latin America come back tan and happy. Those who go to Equatorial Africa come back sick and happy. And those who go to the Soviet Bloc come back downright bitter.'"

"That pretty much sums it up. What about Morocco though? I mean, that's not *real* Africa . . . if such a thing exists."

"Yeah, Morocco was a different story. When I was at my permanent site, I had even less contact with volunteers than you guys do here. In fact, the closest volunteer to me was four hours away, and since he was a man and both of our villages were very traditional, he could never visit me, and I could never visit him."

"Jesus."

"The gender separation was terrible, which was tough for me after having served in Armenia. I can remember one time this guy from staff came to visit me and see how my site was. I didn't even

---

[51] Whack evac'd refers to a volunteer who is evacuated from their country of service for reasons of mental health.

realize it, but I was grabbing his hand the whole time we talked. I swear to God, I wanted him to take me away from that place. And I remember thinking how lucky staff was that they could just pick up and leave in their little white cars and go back to their nice lives in their nice big apartments."

"Yeah, I know the feeling."

"I know you do, Johann. But you have to understand that I'm not coming out of left field. I just finished my service in Morocco six months ago."

"Wow, really?"

"Yes. And the worst thing is, I feel like after two tours in some tough places I have so much to give to the volunteers here. But none of them seem to want to listen to me. I don't know if it's because I served in different countries or because I'm your superior. But it's bothering me a lot, and I don't know what to do."

I pressed my thumb to my teeth and thought for a moment. I looked Bartha up and down and could tell she was being sincere. A bit of something wise came to me. I spit it to her clean.

"If you wanna connect with us, never mention your service in Morocco or Armenia. Instead, provide the sound advice you've gained from your experiences and we'll see that it doesn't matter where you've served, the point is you understand what it's like and you're there to help us. This is how you'll gain our trust, and ultimately our respect."

"That's some good advice. Thank you for that."

"No problem."

"You know, despite your reputation, you seem to have things figured out."

"I wouldn't go that far."

"Oh?"

"Yeah, I'm having a helluva time getting things off the ground at my site."

"How do you mean?"

"Well, I tried to start a French club, but that pretty much failed.

Then I tried to do clubs for my students, but the kids acted like crap. Plus, they act like crap in class. It's like I have no motivation to do anything because nobody wants to learn a damn thing."

Bartha laughed.

"I had the same problems at my sites. Your best bet is to assess your community's needs and go from there. For example, all the kids in my Moroccan village loved soccer but had nowhere to play it. They would get into a lot of trouble after school, so to keep them from doing that, I got permission to build a soccer field. It took a whole year but we got it built. Now they're having tournaments every month."

"That's impressive. I can barely get my host brother to use condoms when he sleeps with prostitutes."

"Haha. Well, every little bit helps."

"Yeah, I don't know. I just wish my students gave more of a crap."

"Don't worry about all your students. Just pick one that wants to learn and run with it. I remember in Armenia there was this one little boy who loved biology. I didn't know much about the subject, but I learned as much as possible so I could teach the little guy. Sure enough, by the time I left, he was a biology whizz. He even had dreams to go to college."

"Damn."

THAT WEDNESDAY, I was back in Gurbagahowda. The swelling in my hand was down, and I had a renewed sense of purpose. I asked Azat if he would be interested in planning some summer camps. He said he would but that we'd have to talk to Islam first. We went over to the guy's office. We found him at his desk, dusting off his golden bust of Türkmenbaşy. He barked at Gülalik to get us some tea. Then he looked at us pointedly.

"What is your business here, Mickey Mouse boys?" he said.

I had forgotten his penchant for nonsensical jokes involving anything American. I tried not to laugh. Azat explained in Turkmen the purpose of our visit. Islam listened to him with a frown.

"It sound good," he said.

"Really?"

"Yes. The first volunteer here make wonderful camp in Çüli. You remember I show you photos, Johann? It was best time in my Santa Claus life. I will get permission, and you and Davey Crockett will get place, activities, supplies, volunteers, teachers, food, and drinks. Okay? Come to my office tomorrow. I will have permission then."

Azat and I thanked him and left. We agreed to meet the following day. I walked over to Jahan's for our French lesson, whistling the whole way. I found her scribbling something in her notebook. Her tongue was poking out the side of her mouth. She noticed me, popped her tongue back in, and smiled.

"Look at this," she said.

I took the notebook from her hands and looked at the open page. On it was a detailed drawing of what looked like a shed, in all its dimensions. I asked what it was.

"It's the house I'm going to build," she said proudly.

"Wow. Did you draw this on your own?"

"Yes. I was tired of waiting for the builders, so I just did it. I calculated the house will cost one thousand five hundred dollars. The rooms will be empty, but I will just keep saving money and buying furniture until I reach my goal. I wanted a house and now I will have it, maybe in five years. I've already saved thirty-five dollars. And next week, I will have seventy. I'm doing just like you said, Han-Guly. I'm getting motivation and I'm not giving up. Thank you for this. I now feel my life has purpose."

I didn't know what to say. I just sat there with every orifice in my face wide open. I became conscious that I probably looked like a fucking moron. I crunched my eyes and mouth back together and looked at Jahan. She was still smiling. I handed back her notebook and nodded.

"You're welcome," I said.

I WALKED HOME fresh as a snapped pickle. I had no conflicts with my host family and slept the whole night through. I came to school the next day, revived and full of guts. I walked into my classroom and Azat was stood there like a fool with a frown on his face. I asked him kindly what the problem was.

"Hey, Johann. I'm soooo sorry, but today I must make sadaka again," he said.

"Are you serious? I thought we were gonna plan our camps."

"We will soon, but hey. I must to go now so, please to teach my classes?"

I held my anger down at the pit of my stomach.

"No problem. I'll talk to Islam myself after class and we'll figure everything out tomorrow."

"Okay."

Azat left me with his band of brats. By the end of fourth period, the mud patch outside was peppered with tahýas. I locked the classroom and walked over to Islam's. I had a few ideas for activities and was eager to share them. I got to his office and found it empty. I asked Gülalik where he was, and she smirked.

"He's on the *Saglyk ýoly*,"[52] she said.

My face expanded into a fire-breathing demon's.

"What the hell is he doing a health walk for? He was supposed to give me permission for my camps today."

She laughed out loud. I flipped her the bird and cut. I walked to Jahan's, steaming mad. I found her at her desk, crunching figures for her new house. I pulled up a chair and folded my arms. She turned to me and asked me what was up.

"Will *you* at least help me with my fucking camps?" I yelled.

She dropped her pencil and widened her eyes. I sucked in my anger and blew it out cool.

"Sorry," I said. "It's just that I'm trying to start these summer

---

[52] The Saglyk ýoly, or Walk of Health, consists of two trails—one 8 km, the other 37 km—in the Kopet-Dag mountains outside the city of Ashgabat. They were created by former president Niyazov to improve the health of Turkmen citizens.

camps, and no one is helping. Islam was supposed to get permission today, but now he's at Saglyk ýoly. And Azat was supposed to help me plan activities, but he's off at another sadaka. I'm not that pissed at Islam because this is the first time he's done this. But Azat is always dumping his classes on me to go to these damn sadakas and it's driving me crazy."

Jahan waited for me to calm down again. Then she spoke.

"Han-Guly, first let me tell you. I will help you with your camps, okay?"

"Okay."

"And second, you must understand that when someone makes sadaka in Turkmenistan it is a very serious thing."

"What, like a funeral?"

"Kind of. Every Thursday for the first forty days after that person dies, all relatives and friends come together at their house because they believe that the spirit of the dead person will visit on these days. It is a very sad event because many people, especially the mother and close family, are crying very loud and screaming, and every time a new person arrives, they start crying and screaming again because they are reminded that their family member is truly dead."

"That's pretty harsh."

"It is. Eneş teacher just had her sadaka, but I couldn't go because I knew I will cry so much. I just stayed at home and prayed for her. That's why you must please respect Azat for going to sadaka all these times. He is brave for this, and many people have been dying in his family."

I felt like the most tremendous bundle of dog shit to ever splat on the face of the earth. I told Jahan I would do my best to be patient with Azat. That night, after mowing through a bowl of my host mother's watery pumpkin soup, those old legs started kicking up in me again. I looked over at my backpack and its zipper winked.

I WENT AWOL for the next two weekends; the first to Aşgabat to plan my summer trip to Vietnam, and the second to Lebap to celebrate

Truman's birthday at some godforsaken mud lake in the desert. I got back to Gurbagahowda and realized I hadn't made much progress on my summer camps. I called Brooke to see if she had anything planned. She told me that her camps were set and that all she needed to do was fill out her grant proposal.

"Actually, I'm meeting Tex tomorrow in Tejen," she said. "He's gonna bring the forms and help me fill them out."

"Mind if I join?"

"Oh, fuck no. We'll make a party of it."

The next afternoon, I took a cab to Tejen. I was curious to see how Tex was doing as last I'd heard he hated his site. My cabbie dropped me off in front of the restaurant where we'd agreed to meet. I went inside and found Tex and Brooke chatting. I sat down with them. Then the waiter came.

"Three beers, to start," I said.

He shook his head.

"No beer," he said.

"What?"

"I will bring you Cokes."

He scuttled off. I turned to my friends and said what the fuck?

"I'm pretty sure this is President Berdimuhamedow's doing," Tex said.

"What makes you say that?"

"Well, the guy is making changes left and right. For example, my site is super close to Aşgabat, and already I'm noticing that around the city he's replacing T-Money's photo with his own. My host family was pretty pissed about this. They said it was way too soon."

"Now that you mention it," Brooke said, "I went to my bazaar the other day to buy my American buddy who may come to visit some photos of both the old guy and the new guy, and strangely, the new guy's pics were more expensive."

"Really?"

"Yeah. I'm not sure what it all means, and I was hopeful at first that this new guy would be different, but now it seems that it's gonna be the same ol' shit all over again."

"At least you guys live far away from Aşgabat," Tex said.

"What's that supposed to mean?"

"It means that you live in a Podunk village, so the new government doesn't give a fuck what you do. I, on the other hand, am in Gök-Depe, which is right next to Aşgabat. Plus, it's where the new guy is from, which means the KNB is constantly on my ass to get things done and present a good image."

"Well, at least that gives you motivation to actually do something. In my village, people care so little I could paint my face white and start miming naked in the park and no one would give a fat dump."

"Come on guys, this isn't a cock-measuring contest," Brooke said.

I chuckled. Tex scowled at his Coke.

"Let's get the fuck outta here and get a bottle of vodka."

"I second the motion," Brooke said.

We paid for our meal and grabbed a bottle of cheap vodka. We took it to the English Center and started slamming shots. When we were nicely buzzed, Tex pulled out the grant proposals. Brooke and I filled ours out with half-truths about how much we'd planned and what state our government-issued permission was in. We handed them to Tex. He said he'd give mine to PC once I got the final go-ahead from my school director.

"Yeah, we'll see how that goes," I said. "The guy spends more time getting smashed off vodka and polishing his golden bust of T-Money than he does doing anything else."

"Haha, my director's the same way," Tex said. "He's always going off in front of people about what an important addition the work 'he and I' are doing to help Turkmenistan's *Altyn Asyr* (Golden Age), then once the doors are closed, he goes back to drinking himself belligerent."

"Hey, I can relate," Brooke said. "My director thinks it's his personal mission to aid me in all my projects. He follows me around like some lost puppy, claiming he's there to help, but in the end, he just makes a nuisance of himself."

"That's kinda weird," I said.

"Maybe he's super eager to get the Golden Age off the ground in your village," Tex said.

"Maybe."

THE NEXT DAY I went to see Islam. I found him in his office, half-drunk and chatting on the phone. He pretended not to notice me. I sat in the chair across from him and waited. Five minutes passed. He hung up the phone with a loud bang. He folded his hands in front of his snarly little face and glared at me.

"What can I do for you, Peter Pan?" he said.

"I'm here about the permission for my camps," I said. "I've already filled out my grant proposal and outlined some activities for the kids."

He made a steeple with his two index fingers and jabbed it against his lips.

"Why don't you come next week," he said.

"Next week? I've already waited two."

"Yes, well I need one more week."

"I see. Well look, I have something you can do right now."

"What is it?"

I reached into my backpack and pulled out the permission slip for my summer trip to Vietnam.

"You can sign this," I said, handing it to him. "I'll be gone for the entire month of July."

He took the slip and read it with a sour face. He signed it because he knew he had to. I collected it and thanked him for his time and effort. He picked up the phone and made another call.

MY WALK HOME was transcendentally hot. The sun was out big as

God's glowing ass cheek and I thought my head might crack and lay an egg. I contemplated buying an air conditioner. I checked out the one shop in town that had a few, but they were way outta my price range. I resolved to ask Peace Corps for half the money. The assholes hadn't even provided me with a fan, and I'd already suffered through enough horseshit, so the least they could do was throw me a couple bones for an AC.

I got to my room and stripped my clothes off. The air was so hot it burnt my skin. I threw back my curtains and opened my windows. I grabbed my laundry tub and filled it with the last of my filtered water. I dunked my bedsheet in and wrapped myself with it. I sprawled out on the floor below the window, hoping the breeze and the dampness would cool me down. After an hour of flopping around, I drifted to sleep. I got to where my big toe was touching the rainbow dream waters, then I heard, "Bang. Bang. Bang." I lurched upwards and farted. My body was drenched in sweat. My genitals were like melting toffee. I heard "Bang. Bang. Bang." again.

"What?" I screamed.

"Johannis," Aziza shouted. "Two girls down here are asking for you."

I could sense jealousy in her voice. I scrambled up and threw on some clothes. I walked out the door, still buttoning my shirt. I was imagining two Russian bikini models waxing their legs on our Lada. I looked down and saw two Turkmen girls. They were in faded köýneks and wore tahýas and braids. One of the girls was bony and tall with bug eyes. The other was short and plump with a pencil-thin mustache. I still found them fairly attractive. I walked up with a smile and an outstretched hand.

"Hey, I'm Johann. What can I do for you?" I said.

Neither girl shook my hand. I caught myself and retracted it. "Sorry."

"It's okay," the plump one said. "My name is Selbi and this is Nyazik. We are wondering if you would teach us advanced English this summer?"

My first instinct was to tell them to pound it down their daddy's sweet ass. But since camps were pretty much in the toilet, and I had only my hand to keep me company through the long broiling nights, I decided to be a gent and let it fly.

"Why not."

"Really? You will teach us?" Nyazik said.

"Yes, I'll teach you. But only through the month of June. In July I will be gone."

"Wonderful. When can we start?" Selbi said.

"After school's out."

10

SCHOOL ENDED TWO weeks later. I went to the crappy ceremony and said goodbye to Jahan. She asked me if I'd teach her French over the summer. I told her it would have to wait until August because of my new "advanced English" classes and my trip to Vietnam. She was pretty bummed. I cheered her up with a big smile and a dirty joke about Islam.

That weekend, I took a much-needed trip to Türkmenhalk to visit Jimmy. We drank Jack Daniels and cooked American food and scratched our balls in front of the TV. I left that Monday with a merciless hangover. For some odd reason, my host mom took pity on me. She gave me a jug of *çal* (camel's milk) and told me to chug it all down. It tasted like curdled bat jizz, but by God, if it didn't have me feeling better within a day.

My first advanced English class was that Wednesday. My plan for it was simple: 40 minutes of grammar, 40 minutes of writing about a topic of my choice, and 40 minutes of discussion about that same topic. I walked to class in the unbearable heat. I found Selbi and Nyazik sitting in the two front desks. A new guy was off to the side. He was tall and skinny with daddy-long legs. He had a pockmarked face and mean little eyes under a faded Ferrari cap. I smiled and asked his name.

"Baýmyrat," he said.

"Well, it's nice to meet you."

I started in on the grammar. I taught the kids the difference between the present perfect and the present perfect continuous. I switched to writing. I gave them their topic: "Five things you would change about Turkmenistan." I sat down and pulled out my horrendous Stan Brown book. I looked over at my students periodically. Selbi and Nyazik were biting their lips and scribbling furiously. Baýmyrat was sat there with his arms folded, staring down at the three sentences he'd written. The forty minutes ended. I got up and walked in front of the blackboard.

"Okay," I said. "Who wants to read theirs first?"

Selbi raised her hand.

"Go ahead," I said.

She squared her shoulders and lifted her notepad.

"Five Things I Would Change about Turkmenistan," she said. "By Selbi Jafarowa."

"Very nice."

"The five things I would change about Turkmenistan would be . . ."

I was imagining her listing things like the shitty food, the access to flowers and dresses, the number of melon patches, etcetera. You can imagine my shock when she said, "Healthcare, education, roads, borders, and hospitals."

"Wow," I said. "Those are good places to start."

"Thank you."

"But I have a question for you."

"Okay."

"How exactly would you change, say, healthcare?"

The room fell silent. Selbi looked over what she had written. Then she looked up at me.

"I would make it better," she said meekly.

"Okay, I understand that. But *how* would you make it better?"

She looked down at her notebook again. I followed her eyes and saw that she'd simply written down five things then switched to a homework assignment for another class. I asked her why she'd written what she had. She grew a sad look.

"Cyrus teacher was always complain about these things and so I wrote them."

I slapped my forehead. Then I turned to Nyazik.

"Did you, by chance, write the same five things?"

She stared at me with her big brown eyes and nodded. I shrugged my shoulders and huffed.

"It's okay. We'll get back to this later. And how 'bout you, Baÿmyrat?" I said, turning to him. "Did you find five things you'd like to change about Turkmenistan?"

He flicked his pencil across his desk.

"No, I just find one," he said.

"And what's that?"

"I would want to see much more sports cars in Gurbagahowda."

"Great."

THAT NIGHT, I realized I'd demanded too much of my students for a first lesson. I decided to put a more exciting and personal spin on the next topic. On Friday, I taught the kids gerunds and infinitives. Then I introduced the topic.

"Today," I said, "I want you guys to write about your dream jobs."

I got a panel of blank stares. I grabbed a piece of chalk and went over to the board.

"For example," I said, writing my words, "when I was a little kid, my dream was to be a genetic engineer. Does everyone know what that is?"

Everyone shook their heads.

"It's a person who uses science to change the genes of a person or an animal so that they can do cool stuff. For example, maybe you want a rabbit to fly. So, you change its genes so that it grows wings and then it can fly."

The girls looked puzzled. Baÿmyrat chuckled.

"What if I change Azat teacher's genes so he turn into piece of shit?" he asked.

The girls giggled. I choked back my laughter.

"That's definitely a feasible option," I said. "Anyways, do you guys get it?"

Everyone nodded.

"Okay, now write me your dream jobs."

They pulled out their notebooks and got to it. I sat at my desk and read my Stan Brown book, the title of which was something like *Assholes and Dildos*. Forty minutes passed and I went to the front of the class. I told my students it was time. I called on Selbi to read first. She squared her pudgy shoulders and looked down at her notebook.

"My Dream Job," she read. "By Selbi Jafarowa."

"Tremendous."

"My dream job would be ambassador to United States for Turkmenistan."

"Wow. That's a huge responsibility."

"Yes, it is."

"And if you were the ambassador, what would be your first mission?"

"My first mission would be to ask the American President all his knowledge about our great Ruhnama."

I swallowed my laughter.

"That might be a pretty short conversation," I said.

"Why do you say this?" she asked.

"Well . . ."

I realized I'd slipped in pig shit.

"Um, because our president likes listening more than talking. Anyways, why did you choose talking about the Ruhnama for your first mission? Surely there are other things you could talk about or do?"

Selbi smiled.

"Ruhnama isn't my *only* topic for conversation. I would also talk about our great first leader Türkmenbaşy, and all the good things he did for Turkmenistan."

"Great. I think you'd make a fine ambassador. And how about you Nyazik? What would your dream job be?"

She stared at me. Her eyes were filled with bleary desperation.

"Please tell me you wrote something other than 'Ambassador to the US,'" I said.

She looked like she was about to wet her dress. I walked over to check her notebook.

"English translator," she shouted.

"Okay," I said. "Not bad. And why do you want to be an English translator?"

"Ummm... b-because I like it?"

"Because you like it. Well, I guess we both have our work cut out for us. On to you Baýmyrat. What would your dream job be?"

He stretched out like a longboard and folded his hands behind his head. Then he cracked his lips into a wide, gray smile.

"Porno star," he said, emphasizing the "P".

I looked over at Selbi and Nyazik. They were both staring at the top of their desk.

"Okay," I said, slapping my hands together. "We're done for today."

THE NEXT LESSON was more of the same. I asked my students which country they would visit besides the US and they all said either England or Turkey. I imagined this was because in England they could practice their English, and in Turkey they could speak Turkmen and be understood. Even though they were learning their grammar well, I didn't feel like I was reaching them. For the next few lessons, I just showed them pictures of California.

One Wednesday toward the end of June, I started feeling a little stir crazy. I had a free-topic lesson that day. Then I went home and called Brooke. I asked her if she wanted to do lunch.

"Hell, yeah," she said.

I blasted off to Tejen. I walked inside the restaurant and found

Brooke. We gave each other a big hug. We ordered beer, vodka, shashlik, fitçis, *somsas*, gatyk, manty, and gutap. We drank and ate and chatted. I asked Brooke how things were going at her site and she grinned.

"Shit's going awesome," she said.

"Wow. That's great. How so?"

"Well, I've already got all the grant money and activities planned for my camps. They're gonna be huge with a bunch of cool games and shows. My director has been helping me out a lot. He's a little creepy but still, I need his help. On top of that, my summer clubs are going really well. All the kids fight over who gets to invite me for dinner afterwards, and sometimes I have to go to two houses in one night."

"Geez, swell for you."

She spiked an eyebrow and took a slug of beer. I just sat there glowering at my fitçi.

"Okay, what is it?" she said. "You got a rash on your balls or something?"

She broke into a furious cackle. Her red hair danced like blood from a knife wound under water. I felt tiny and silly and worthless. She stopped laughing and sliced off a piece of her shashlik.

"No seriously, what's the problem?"

"I don't know. I guess I just feel like everything I do at site is a failure."

"Still?"

"Yeah. I mean, my clubs are down the toilet, and school has ended. And now all I've got going is this advanced English class with three students who are decent at grammar but terrible at writing."

"What kind of topics are you giving them?"

"Lately we've just been looking at pictures of Cali. But before it was things like dream jobs and countries besides the US you would visit, and five things you would change about Turkmenistan."

"Oh my god, Johann."

"What?"

"How old are these kids?"

"I don't know. Thirteen? Fourteen?"

"Well, there you go."

"What do you mean?"

"These kids grew up with zero opportunities in a dictatorship that monitors their phone calls, harasses their families, and snuffs out all opposition. You can't expect them, especially at such a young age, to be able to think critically right off the bat about what's wrong with their situation and how to change it, let alone ask them where they'd travel to *besides* the US and what their dream jobs might be. You gotta start smaller, man."

"Fair enough. What do you suggest?"

"I dunno, just focus on them and what they like about Turkmenistan. Then maybe you can widen the scope."

"Could work. To be honest, though, I'm sick to death of hearing about this place. In fact, I'm getting sick to death of this place in general."

Brooke slugged her beer.

"Yeah, you're not the only one. I was just in Aşgabat to pick up a package and Bartha told me twelve volunteers have ET'd[53] since we were sworn in."

"Jesus. Why?"

"Some were sick and others just sick of it."

"Fuckin' hell."

Brooke and I finished our meals and parted ways. I went home and thought about tomorrow's lesson. I came up with a decent topic. The next morning, I went to class with a thin smile on my face. Selbi, Nyazik, and Baýmyrat were all waiting for me. I said hello and taught them some phrasal verbs. I cleaned the blackboard and told them to take out their writing notebooks. Baýmyrat rolled his eyes. Selbi and

---

[53] ET: Early Terminate. A volunteer may ET at any time during their service in country. Most volunteers ET because of issues with their training or permanent site, problems at home, conflicts with PC staff, or because they're just little bitches who can't handle the heat.

Nyazik smiled and did as they were told. Once everyone was listening, I spoke.

"Today guys," I said. "I want you to tell me about one good experience you've had recently."

When I heard myself say it out loud, it sounded dumb. But the kids seemed happy enough and went to work. I read my new Stan Brown book, *Digital Dingdong*. When time was up, I went to the front and asked who wanted to read first. Selbi and Nyazik both raised their hands. I smiled.

"Would you read first, please, Baýmyrat?" I said.

He popped his cap off and humphed.

"Do I must?"

"You do must."

"Okay. One Good Experience I Khev Recently, by Baýmyrat Mamedow."

"Fantastic."

"Tank you. One good experience I khev recently is dis writing assignment. I like dis assignment because it is good and so is Jokhann teacher. I love Jokhann teacher."

He looked up and gave me a sly smile. I folded my arms and returned the smile.

"You really are a treasure, Baýmyrat," I said.

"I know dis."

I turned to Selbi. She leveled her shoulders and held up her notebook. I asked her to read. She pinched her lips into a little flower. The story she told was of how she'd visited her grandmother the previous weekend. Apparently, they'd eaten palow and boiled various fruits for winter preserves. She finished her story. I thanked her and turned to Nyazik.

"Do you have something for me?" I asked.

She stared at me in horror like a doe might at a giant, sweaty hunter who'd cornered her with a shotgun to the face. I almost let her have a pass. She puffed and dropped her shoulders. Then she lifted her notebook.

"One Good Experience I Have Recently, by Nyazik Hojayewa," she said.

I continued looking at her. She looked up at me then back at her notebook.

"One good experience I have recently," she read, "is visiting of sacred shrine of Paraw Bibi. This shrine is small, white mosque in mountains near willage Paraw where beautiful woman name Bibi live many years before. Bibi was most beautiful and honest woman in Paraw and many women jealous to her. So one day, horrible old woman give information to enemy about Bibi, and when Bibi find out, she use powers and make old woman to become black stone. Then Bibi go to mountains and see enemy coming so she open mountains and go inside so enemy can't to take her beauty and honesty. After willagers see this, Allah tell them build shrine where Bibi open mountains. Today, many Turkmen people come to this place to pray."

Nyazik looked up at me. I was patting the floor for my eyeballs.

"That was awesome, Nyazik," I said.

"Thank you, Johann teacher."

"But I have a question for you. Why did you enjoy visiting the shrine of Paraw Bibi so much?"

She put down her notebook and folded her hands.

"I enjoy it," she said, "because Paraw Bibi is wery brave woman. And she remind me my mother who also died."

I didn't know what else to say. I thanked the class for their hard work and called it a day.

THAT WEEKEND I went to Mary with Brooke. On the way, I told her about my small success with Nyazik. She asked me what topic I'd done.

"I told them to write about one good experience they'd had recently," I said.

She chuckled into her fingers.

"Not exactly the most *original* topic," she said. "But yeah, I can see how that would work."

I rolled my eyes and changed the subject. We arrived in Mary and met up with Stella and Jimmy. We did some crap at the AC.[54] Then we spent the weekend at Stella's cooking, eating, drinking, and listening to tunes. It was a nice respite from my advanced English class. During the car ride back, I thought a lot about what the following day's topic would be. I decided on something educational but fun. I came to class the next day feeling good. I taught the kids some prepositions then introduced the topic.

"Today guys," I said, "I want you to write about one historical figure. It can be Turkmen or foreign, a man or a woman, young or old, whatever you want. Okay?"

The kids nodded and went to work. I reclined in my chair with my good buddy Stan and his latest novel, *The Stinky Pink Chode*. Forty minutes passed. I stood in front of the class and announced that time was up. I pointed to Nyazik.

"Would you mind reading first today?" I asked.

Selbi scowled. Nyazik nodded softly.

"Historical figure I choose," she said, "is Turkmen poet, Magtymguly Pyragy."

"Excellent," I said. "Tell me about him."

"Well firstly, he is very, very big. Almost three meters."

"Wow, that's really tall. Are you sure about that?"

"Oh yes. He is very big, and he have everything gold, even book and clothes."

"That seems like an exaggeration to me."

"It's true," Selbi said. "Why you don't believe us?"

I thought about it for a moment. To their credit, I had recently read on Encarta about a man named Robert Pershing Wadlow, a.k.a. The Giant of Illinois, who, in the 1930s had reached a height of 8 feet 11 inches or 2.72 meters, thus making him the tallest man in recorded history. Based on this fact, and the fact that Magtymguly was from an obscure region of the world and born almost two

---

centuries prior, I surmised it was possible, with the help of legendary aggrandizement, of course, that the man could actually have had a height of somewhere near three meters. As for the all gold thing, well, everybody knows famous historical dudes from the Silk Road liked gold, so there it was.

I finished my thought bubble and smiled.

"I believe you," I said. "Please keep reading, Nyazik."

She nodded and looked down at her notebook.

"Magtymguly," she said, "is very famous. And you can visit him at Aşgabat Fountain where he live today."

"Alright, stop," I said.

"Why, Johann teacher?"

"Because, Nyazik, I'm willing to accept that Magtymguly was almost three meters tall and that he wore gold clothes and carried a gold book. But what I'm not willing to accept is that he's alive and well today at the ripe old age of two hundred and eighty-three, and furthermore, that he hangs out in some scholarly hovel down by the Aşgabat Fountain, spouting his lousy poems at the five stupid tourists who come to visit him each year. I mean, c'mon . . . Do you really expect me to believe all that?"

Nyazik and Selbi were at the point of tears. Baýmyrat laced his arms across his chest and smirked.

"They are talking about statue, dude," he said.

I whipped my face at him and sneered. Suddenly it dawned on me. I dropped my shoulders and hung my head back.

"I didn't mean figure literally, guys," I cried.

I took a deep breath and caught my cool. I looked back at the girls. They were still terrified and confused. I flattened a hand and sliced away my point, layer by layer.

"When I told you to write about a historical figure," I said, slicing, "I meant for you to pick a famous person from history and write about the things they did that made them famous."

I received blank stares.

"For example, Gandhi was famous because he helped the people of India free themselves from British rule."

More blank stares.

"Have you guys ever even heard of Gandhi?"

Everyone shook their head.

"Okay, then we're done for today."

I WALKED HOME in a foul mood. It was still blisteringly hot out, and I was still no closer to teaching my advanced students a damn thing. I thought about my trip to Vietnam. It was ten days away, but it felt like ten decades.

I schlepped through my waratan and rounded the corner. I saw Ali in the courtyard, jabbing a stick at Laika's balls. I grabbed the stick from him and threw it into our desiccated garden. Laika bolted away, barking. Ali stuck his tongue out at me. I flipped him off and walked upstairs. He flipped me off, too, and ran into the house. I stripped down and sprawled across the floor in my wet undies. I heard that infernal "Bang. Bang. Bang." again. I asked what the fuck whoever it was wanted.

"*Parahatçylyk Korpusy jaň edÿä,*" Ali yelled. "Peace Corps is calling."

I shot up and toweled off. I threw my shorts on and ran downstairs. Ali was waiting for me in the common area with the phone in his hand. I ripped it away from him.

"Hello? This is Johann."

I heard what sounded like a hippopotamus farting underwater. Then a garbled voice said, "Hallo, Johann. How are you?"

"Oh *hi*, Mahym, I'm fine. Thanks for asking."

"Look, I am coming to Tejen tomorrow with driver. I would like to meet you at restaurant and talk about your site and plans for your secondary project."

"My secondary project?"

"Yes. You should have one by this time."

"Oh yes, my *secondary* project. Yes, that's coming along

swimmingly. I work on it four times a day now."

"Tüweleme. See you tomorrow at noon."

I hung up and went back upstairs. I stripped down to my skivvies, did the sheet thing, and passed out. I woke up to a dinner of scalding lentils and stale çörek. I sauced it[55] all down then thought about what my actual secondary project might be. I knew it had to involve Jahan as she'd castrate me with her teeth otherwise. I also knew it would have to incorporate the Turkmen language, as this was the sole thing I'd excelled at in this dadgum country. I decided I'd write a Turkmen–English grammar book of some sort. The details of it, I'd work out on the ride to Tejen.

THE NEXT MORNING, I took a cab to Tejen. I mulled over some ideas for a grammar book with my head out the window. I had the driver drop me off in front of the restaurant. I waited in the heat, picking my dirty nails with the tip of my pocketknife. I saw Peace Corps drive up. I knew it was them because they were the only ones in a river of beat-up Ladas pushing a glinting white Jeep. They pulled up in front of the restaurant. The driver, a tall Russian man with blond hair and black shades, got out and went around to the passenger door. He opened it and stood to one side. A bison in a peach two-piece stepped out and waved at me.

"Hello Johann," it said.

"Hello, Mahym," I said, waving back.

She waddled up the steps with her driver at her heels. I opened the door and we all sat down at a plastic table. Flies and specks of dried food were all over the klionka. My guests curled their lips.

"So," I said, startling them. "What'll you both have?"

The driver grimaced and said he wasn't hungry. Mahym simpered and asked for a menu. I whistled the waiter over and he read the thing off. She looked like she was going to blow chunks

---

[55] To eat (especially a lot of delicious food.) See Hans Joseph Fellmann, *Chuck Life's a Trip*, Russian Hill Press, 2019.

into her knock-off Louis.

"I'll just have some çaý and a small bowl of *yagsyz* çorba," she said.

"And for me," I said, "it'll be one fitçi, two somsas, three skewers of shashlik, and a beer."

The waiter nodded and sped away in a cloud of flies. He ran back with our orders. I started in on mine off the bat. Mahym and her driver watched me like two horrified parents watching their cannibal child feed. I finished and burped. Then I guzzled the rest of my beer.

"So anyways, what are you guys here for again?" I asked.

"Well," Mahym said. "*I'm* here to find out first how your site is, and second, to hear about your secondary project."

I picked up a piece of fat and gnawed on it.

"Site's fine," I said. "Couldn't be better."

"Really? I heard you were having troubles with your camps."

"No troubles. They're just not going to happen because my school director is, let's say, unmotivated."

"I see. And what about your classes? Are you teaching any this summer?"

"Well, yeah. But the kids think historical figures refers to statues built by Türkmenbaşy in Aşgabat, so progress is a bit slow."

"Okay. And how about your secondary project?"

"It's still in its elementary stages, but I'm working on a Turkmen verb book where I translate the most common 501 Turkmen verbs into their various meanings in English. Then I give example sentences in both Turkmen and English that clarify these meanings and employ all corresponding prepositions. At the back of the book, I'm going to provide comprehensive conjugation and morphological case tables. I'm also thinking of incorporating a glossary of common idiomatic expressions, but that's still dayz away."

The blood drained from Mahym's face. She looked like she'd just bitten a cyanide capsule. She grabbed her tea and sucked it down.

"Well, okay then," she said.

The meal ended. I let my friends pay the bill. We walked outside and stood in the sun. Mahym told me to be in Aşgabat on the third for the Fourth of July All-Vol. I told her I would. Then I walked toward the awtostanzia.

"Are you sure you'll be safe in taxi?" she asked.

I looked over my shoulder and smirked.

"Don't you worry about me."

MY LAST CLASS was on a Monday. I sauntered to school in a fantastic mood. When I got to my classroom, I was whistling. I saw Selbi and Nyazik, but instead of Baýmyrat, there was Azat. He stood in front of the blackboard talking to the girls in Turkmen. He saw me and grinned.

"Hallo, Johann," he said.

I knitted my brow.

"Hey Azat, are you teaching today?"

"No, but hey, I want ask you somesing."

"Oh?"

"Hey, when you leave Turkmenistan, can you please to give me your camera as gift?"

My toenails almost flew off. I chuckled uncomfortably.

"Okay, okay, don't mind," he said. "When you leave for Wet-Nam?"

"I leave tomorrow for Aşgabat and the eighth for Hanoi. Why?"

"Well, how much is camera zer? Because may be cheaper. Here camera cost sree hundred dollars and zer maybe fifty dollars. Is correct?"

"I don't know. If you want a digital camera, it'll prolly cost a hundred and fifty dollars minimum, wherever you buy it."

"Hundred and fifty? Hmmm, well if you have zis money . . ."

He paused for a moment with a pathetic look in his eyes. I let it swell till it covered his face.

"No, no, don't buy zis for me," he said. "You don't have to."

"Okay."

"But hey, tell me. How much is video camera in States?"

"I don't know—four hundred dollars?"

"Wow, because zey are eight hundred here. Hey, when you go to America?"

"In December."

"Oh. Okay, well, have good trip to Wet-Nam. And bring me back nice present."

He patted my shoulder and walked off. I felt like shitting in a jar and leaving it on his doorstep. I flushed my psyche and turned to the girls. They were staring up at me with big, expectant eyes.

"How would you ladies like to look at photos of a trip I took around the world with my best friends?"

"We would love to," Selbi said.

I took them to the computer room the school had just built. It was hot, windowless, and smelly. Its computers were humming dinosaurs. I picked one in back and plugged in my camera. The girls crowded around me. I opened the files and spun them off. I showed them pictures of crazy, stupid, Chuck shit: drinking cobra blood in Bangkok, climbing the ruins of Angkor Wat, trekking in the mountains of Manali, burning in the gorges of Bled. I kept it PG-13 so as not to rupture their hymens. Everything was going swimmingly then bam. There was the photo of the hotel sink in Tirana, Albania that we all jerked off in with the propped-up porno mag and the photos of hot Czech chicks opening their mouths for flying cumshots. I tried my fastest to click past it. The girls caught it and sat back. I thought they'd run away and tell mommy. To my delight, they giggled. I looked at them and frowned.

"Sorry, girls."

"It's okay Johann teacher," they said.

I breathed a sigh of relief and continued. I finished the photos without incident then said goodbye. I shook the girls' hands and gave them superstar stickers. They blushed and thanked me.

"Tell your friends about us," Selbi said.

I puffed through my nose affectionately.

"I will."

11

I GOT OFF the plane. The sun was a burning vat of gasoline on my shoulders and the sky was a blue vacuum pulling at my bones. I walked down the steps and onto the tarmac. I could feel the asphalt melting the soles of my flip flops. I went into the airport and toward security. The twangy blips and quacks of Vietnamese, which I'd grown so accustomed to over the past three weeks, were replaced with the throaty clicks and guttural U's of Turkmen. *Daýzas* wrapped in paisley cloth stared at me with black eyes over yellow teeth. My hair was growing out in patches, my skin was angry red, my ear was newly pierced, and I was dressed in knee-length shorts and a Vietnamese flag T-shirt with a paddy hat cocked to one side on my head. I walked to customs. The pudgy officers glared at me with criminal suspicion. After a barrage of inane questions, one of the officers stamped my passport and let me through. I gathered my backpack from the conveyer belt and found that none of the bottles of whiskey I'd purchased had broken. I walked to the baggage check smiling. The inspectors rooted through my shit, but I kept my mouth in a crescent.

I got in a rusty Lada outside and told the driver to take me to Teke Bazaar. I looked out the window, and the smile I had pinned to my lips drooped like a tulip in a microwave. Gone were the beaches with crystalline sand and topaz waters, the mountains of cheap, delicious shellfish, the humid jungles, the booze cruises through limestone cliffs dotted with dragon-shaped pagodas, the easy drunken women and jars of fresh fruit juice and alcohol, the lazy nights under fans with the crickets chirping outside and the geckos crawling up the walls, the endless rice paddies and the tall blue mountains, the steam, the sweat, the pretty Asian faces that seemed to greet us around every corner. The cherry red motorbike I road through countless narrow lanes populated by screeching chickens in cages and little ladies boiling up fresh bowls of *pho*[56] was now replaced by the rattling box of tin that was my taxi. And the scenery, the incredible fucking scenery that was once filled with so many trees and colors and waterfalls, was now a sucking brown wasteland that grew bigger and bigger the farther we drove into it.

The desert receded as we touched Aşgabat. Its alien marble ministries and dismal apartment blocks were a strange and unwanted comfort. My cabby dropped me off in front of Teke Bazaar. I walked over the cracked sidewalks and through the dusty heat to Peace Corps Headquarters. The first person I encountered was Bartha. She was standing big as a Norwegian Christmas tree in her doorway and sweating up her purple blouse. When she saw me, her brown eyes popped a shade lighter.

"Hey Johann, how was your trip?" she asked.

I scratched my ear. "It was great. Except for that last part."

"Yeah, I heard. Did you really spend that whole time at the airport?"

My connecting flight from Bangkok to Aşgabat had been delayed four days. I'd spent them drinking Mai Tais, eating curries, and taking hot showers with an old flame—a grand time to be sure—but I wasn't about to get screwed out of precious vacation days for something that hadn't been my fault, thus I'd concocted the airport camp-out story. Peace Corps could do jack to prove me a liar. And the way I figured, they owed me.

---

[56] A Vietnamese rice noodle soup which contains either chicken or beef and is served with bean sprouts and various herbs.

"Sure did," I said frowning. "I'm not gonna get docked vacation time for this, am I?"

"Probably not. But you'll hafta talk to Harry. He's on site visits now, so maybe next time you're in."

Harry was our new country director. He'd replaced Bob after the poor sap's brain had got eaten over with cancer. I'd seen Harry give a little speech during All-Vol before I blasted off to Vietnam. The speech had been so-so; something about having to wait thirty years for a thank-you from one of the locals he'd helped while serving in Afghanistan. I hadn't thought much of the guy after that.

"How's it going with him, by the way?" I asked.

Bartha pinched her lips into a circle.

"Good," she said. "I mean, after Bob, I must admit it was nice being interim director. But it's also nice having another opinion to consider."

I smiled and tipped her my lampshade. "Good luck with that," I said.

I walked up to the lounge and dropped my bags. I got on the internet and checked some emails. I heard footsteps up the stairs. Tex walked into the room with a giant backpack on. His hair was a black mess and his skin was pale. He looked like a man-locust that had just had its guts sucked out through its tail. He waved me a pathetic hand and collapsed onto the couch. He didn't remove his backpack.

"What's up with you?" I asked.

"Oh, nothing. I just think I'm gonna ET."

"Seriously?"

"Yeah, I'm tired of pretending I like this fucking place, always smiling and saying thank you to these people as they serve me shitty food and overwork me. My school sucks and so does my host family. And let's face it, the work we do here means shit."

I got up and sat next to him. Then I grabbed him by the elbow. "You can't leave," I said.

"Why?"

"'Cuz it'll hurt me. And it'll *kill* Brooke."

He looked away. There was something in his eyes I couldn't place.

"Where is Brooke, by the way? She's always in the lounge on weekends."

"The States."

"What? Why?"

"I promised her I wouldn't say."

"You'd better fuckin' tell me," I said, squeezing his elbow. "Is she sick?"

"No."

"Pregnant?"

"No."

"Did she ET?"

"No."

"Well, what the fuck? Did someone in her family die or something?"

"Johann, I promised her I wouldn't say. She just wants to tell you herself."

"Alright man, whatever. At least tell me she's okay though."

"She's okay, man."

"Good."

THE NEXT MORNING, I saw Tex in the lounge again. I was determined to pry Brooke's damn secret outta him. I invited him to lunch at the Zip. The minute we got our beers, I started in.

"I don't understand why she's making me wait so long to find out what happened," I said. "I'm her best fucking friend out here. I deserve to know."

Tex eyed me like a spooked horse.

"Johann, it's really hard for me not to tell you what happened. But if you knew, it would all make sense."

I ran a greasy eyeball over his face. The possibilities fluttered through my head. Tex had already ruled out sickness, pregnancy, ET, and familial death. The only thing left was injury.

"Did she hurt herself?"

Tex remained silent.

"Did someone . . . hurt her?"

His eyes sparkled painfully. A tear wriggled itself free from his duct and slid down the side of his nose. Another one followed, then another and another. My mouth dropped open and my lungs froze.

"No," I whispered.

He nodded softly. A wave of hatred swelled in my guts. I grabbed the steak knife next to me and stabbed it into the tablecloth.

"I'll fucking murder the son of a bitch," I screamed.

Tex reached across the table and grabbed the knife out of my hand.

"*See* Johann," he said. "This is exactly why Brooke was afraid to tell you. She didn't want you doing something stupid."

"Who the fuck was it, Tex?" I yelled.

"I promised her I'd let her tell you."

"Who?"

"God, Brooke's gonna kill me."

"Who?"

"He worked for her school. That's all I'm gonna say."

"Fine. Does Dimuira know?"

"Yes, but Brooke told her herself."

"What's gonna happen now?"

"Peace Corps is pulling Brooke outta Bitaraplyk and may be placing her in Türkmenabat with Dimuira. I can't believe she's coming back after all this. She's so fucking strong. You shoulda seen her, Johann. I stayed with her a few nights at Bartha's before she went back to the States. She didn't cry once. In fact, we had a great time. It was like nothing had happened."

"Do you know when she'll be back?"

"Probably next week. But I'm sure you'll hear from her before then."

"I sure as fuck hope so."

I WOKE UP the next morning in a fatal state. Tex and I had spent the entire night sobbing, swilling whiskey, and listening with our tumblers to the wall as two Russian hookers got fucked by a gang of Iranian businessmen in the next room. I finally made it out of bed at 3:00 p.m. I said late to Tex, ran to Teke Bazaar for a *lavash*,[57] then hopped in a cab for Gurbagahowda. The ride home was miserable. I was a shivering wreck.

I arrived in GBH[58] just before nightfall. The sky overhead was violently pink and dashed with clouds that looked like exploding horns of smoke. The cabby crunched down the dusty vein through town and up to my home. The minute I got out of the cab, Ali ripped open the waratan door and yelled "Boo." I laughed weakly and ruffled his hair. He slapped my hand away and glared up at me.

"What did you bring me?" he asked.

"Oh, just this," I said, reaching into my pocket.

He jiggled his bottom and held out his palm. I placed a wad of lint in the center of it.

"Very funny," he said, throwing the lint at me. "Now where's my *real* present?"

I chuckled and grabbed my bags. I paid the cabby and walked through the waratan door. Laika trotted up and barked. I gave him a pet and he scampered off. Merdan and my host mom Patma came out of the house. They were both smiling.

"How was Vietnam?" Patma said, in her screeching hen's voice.

"Good."

"Did you bring us some gifts?" Merdan asked.

"Of course."

I put my crap upstairs, then came down to the main house. I found Patma, Merdan, and Ali waiting for me in the front hall. Aziza and her sisters had locked themselves in the phone room. This was fine because I only had a box of candy for them to split. I sat down

---

[57] A soft, unleavened flatbread which is baked in a clay oven. It is often used with kebabs to make dürüm wraps.

[58] Gurbagahowda.

and reached into my bag. I pulled out three gifts, one for each person. I gave Ali a Vietnamese flag hat and Patma a pretty scarf. Then I handed Merdan his gift.

"Holy shit, what is it?" he asked.

He took the pear-shaped bottle from my hands and peered into its cloudy liquid. His eyes grew wide as saucers.

"Is that a dead cobra in there?"

"Sure is."

"Awesome."

Patma clucked and shook her head.

"Why in the world would those people put a dead cobra in a bottle?"

"Same reason you guys put goat colons in your soup."

"What?"

"Never mind. The cobra's for good luck. Enjoy."

I left and went back up to my room. I unpacked my bags and organized my books, clothes, trinkets, and piss bottles. I beat the rugs and made my bed. I swiped the walls and windows of their cobwebs and threw out the trash. I grabbed my paddy hat. I placed it on the outermost hook of my coatrack and stood back. Memories of my trip to Vietnam ran up my spine. As they filled my skull with tropical sex, I heard a knock at my door. I snapped out of it and turned around. I walked to the door and opened it. It was my host father Durdy. He was drunk and hiccupping into his shirt collar.

"Johann," he said. "You're back."

"I am, indeed. What's up?"

"Ohhh, '*up*, nothing. Just wanted to, '*up*, tell you that I heard about your girlfriend in Bitaraplyk."

"Yeah?"

"Yeah, it was her, '*up*, school director that raped her. The police just arrested him. They say, '*up*, he'll get twenty-three years in, '*up*, prison."

"Good. Well, I hope the fucker gets it '*up* the butt every single day."

"What do you, '*up*, mean?"

"Nothing."

I BOUGHT A fan and holed up in my room for the next week. If Durdy, with his erratic work schedule and frequent trips out of town, knew about Brooke then the whole of GBH did, too, and I didn't want them badgering the hell outta me about it. Plus, there was the heat. It was over 120°F in the sun most days, which meant that the sweat didn't collect on your skin, but evaporated, leaving your limbs thinner by the minute. Even in the confines of my room, I was sweating profusely and paralyzed. To avoid being reduced to a sack of bones I did like I'd done before—soaked my one bedsheet in well-water and draped it over my naked body as I lay on my bedroom floor, but this time with the fan breathing hot air all over me. As I did this, I stared up at my paddy hat. It was like some horrible talisman that transported me to the jungles and the mountains and the beaches of Vietnam only to send me back with a scream to the burning pockmark on Vulcan's groin when a fly landed on my forehead or a gust of wind blew across my balls.

One evening, when I could no longer stand it, I ventured out. The sun was slicing deep into the womb of the desert and shooting up leagues of reds and pinks and oranges that mingled with the tractor smoke and the dust to create a sky that just about pulled the eyes from my head. I stood and stared at it for a long moment. Vietnam was certainly more beautiful and fun, but above the waistline, it had nuttin' on this. I was almost glad to be back. I breathed in through my nose and smiled.

"Johann," someone yelled.

I looked over my shoulder. I saw Islam eating dinner on the tapçan with his family. He was smiling goofily and waving me over. I rolled my eyes.

"Yes, Islam?" I said.

"Come. Eat. Drink."

It had been weeks since I'd seen the guy. I couldn't refuse. "*Alright.*"

I wandered over to the tapçan and sat across from him. He elbowed his son out of the way and scooted up next to me.

"How Wet-Nam?" he said in English.

His breath reeked of vodka, animal fat, and cigarettes. I noticed a chunk of lamb stuck between two of his gold teeth.

"Wet-Nam was good," I said.

"Yes? What you see?"

"Oh, the beaches, the jungles, the mountains. Many pretty girls too. It was so much fun."

He scraped the drool from his lips with his forearm.

"Johann," he said. "Let's to . . . *burrrrrp* . . . have arak together."

"No, I think I'm good. My stomach is—"

He forced a shot into my palm. He clinked his glass with mine then whipped the arak down his throat. I put my glass to my lips and squinted.

"Aw, what the hell," I muttered.

I threw my shot back. It went blazing down my throat and into my stomach. I swallowed hard and shook my head. Then I looked back at Islam.

"*Gowy*," he said, slapping my knee. "Now tell me, how your fren?"

I noodled my eyebrows.

"Which friend?"

"You know, the fren who get rap-ed."

He said the "ed" so emphatically it was like a whip-tip cracking the teeth from my mouth. I had to pour myself another shot of arak and choke it down just to keep from punching him.

"She's in America now," I said. "She's fine."

"Oh," he spouted. "But you know story? It was school director. He give her arak then rap-ed. Now he have thirty-two years prison."

"I thought he got twenty-three years?"

"Thirty-two, twenty-three, *tapawdy ýok*. His life over."

He flattened his hand and sliced the air with it. His wife clucked. "*Wah-heÿ*," she said.

"*Wah-heÿ däl*," he spat. "This is bad man. He deserve."

His wife closed her mouth and concentrated on her food. I smiled at Islam and asked for another arak. He poured it and we took our shot. Ali called out from the waratan that dinner was ready. I glanced at the mound of oily potatoes Islam had to offer. One pile of shit was as good as the other.

"I'm eating here," I said.

Ali turned and walked away. I looked back at Islam. He grinned at me with every one of his gold teeth. I lifted a spoonful of potatoes and shoveled them into my mouth. They tasted like a *sadhu*'s[59] pickled ankle calluses. I swallowed them down with a shudder and slapped both knees.

"Welp, thanks for dinner," I said.

THAT WEEKEND, I left GBH. It was too hot and boring, and too many people were asking me about Brooke. I went to Lebap to visit Zack, a volunteer I'd traveled with in Vietnam. His host family were celebrating their baby's first birthday with a shindig of seismic proportions. On the morning of the third day, I said goodbye to Zack and got in a cab back to GBH. The whole way, I was hungover with my mouth open. I arrived at dusk. As I was dragging myself in through the waratan door, Ali ran up.

"Telephone," he said in English.

"Who is it?"

"*Brooooke.*"

My windpipe split. I dumped my shit off, ran inside, and grabbed the phone.

"Brooke?"

I heard sniffling. Then a raspy little voice said, "Johann?"

"Hey. How are you?"

---

[59] A *sadhu* is a holy person who has renounced all worldly ways and often wanders the land barefoot with little or no clothing.

She started crying. I held my own tears back.

"What's wrong?"

She blew her nose and cleared her throat.

"No one's told you, right?" she asked.

"Not outright, but I did guess it off Tex. I'm so sorry I wasn't there. I'm so fucking sorry."

The band of tension around my eyes cracked. Tears poured down my cheeks like hot tea.

"It's not your fault," she said, sobbing. "It's no one's fault but my fucking school director's. I could fucking kill him."

"No, I could fucking kill him," I screamed. "If I had half the chance, I'd cut his junk off and choke him to death with it."

She chuckled painfully.

"Well, there won't be any need for that. He's having his trial tomorrow morning in Tejen, and I'll be coming in to testify."

"Tomorrow? It's been going around that the guy's already been sentenced to twenty-three years."

I slapped my forehead. Brooke gasped.

"You mean, people in your village know?"

"Yeah, sorry, pretty much everyone knows. It's the *oba*. Nothing is secret."

"I guess I should have known. Anyways, whatever. I'm out of that fucking place after tomorrow. When the trial ends, PC is gonna come pick you up. We're partying in Aşgabat and forgetting all about this bullshit."

"Sounds good."

I woke up the next morning and packed. I went downstairs for breakfast and waited for PC. As I ate with Merdan, Patma entered the room. She asked me what was happening with Brooke. I told her she was testifying against her director.

She clucked.

"But he's a good man," she said.

"He's not a good man if he rapes women," I said through clenched teeth.

191

She clucked again and walked off. Merdan tapped me on the knee.

"How long do you think he'll be in prison?" he asked.

"Your dad told me twenty-three years. Then Islam told me thirty-two. I don't know what to believe."

"Well if it's any longer than three years, it doesn't matter."

"What do you mean?"

"Because in a Turkmen prison they feed you hard bread and gruel every day. Then at night, the guards come in your cell and beat you up and stick needles under your fingernails. No one survives more than three years in a Turkmen prison. Especially fat drunk school directors."

We chuckled. Someone banged on the waratan door.

"That's probably Peace Corps," I said.

I ran outside and opened the waratan. There was the snowy PC Jeep. It moved into the courtyard and parked. Brooke opened the side door and stepped out. She was wearing a faded maroon blouse and gray jeans. Her skin was pale and her once beautiful jungle of red hair was in a sad little braid down her back. Her eyes and nostrils were scarlet from crying. I ran up and gave her a hug.

"It's over now," I said, running my hand down her braid. "It's all over."

She sobbed into my collarbone. I let her continue for a minute, then I held her back and looked into her eyes.

"I know this motherfucking sucks," I said. "But I do have some good news."

"What's that?" she said, sniffling.

"We don't hafta drink arak tonight to get fucked up."

"Why is that?"

"Because I've got a liter of Jameson in my bag fresh from Bangkok."

She smiled.

WE MET UP with Tex and Dimuira in Aşgabat. We signed in at PCHQ then went to the Zip. I made up with Dimuira. I didn't want any tension between us after what had happened to Brooke.

We got a table in back and ordered beers and shashlik. While we drank and ate, I told the story of a street brawl Zack and I had gotten into in Vietnam. The story ended with me and Zack narrowly escaping on motorbikes from an angry mob of bleeding, chain-wielding Irishmen. Dimuira spit out her beer.

"That story just made me wanna be a dude," she said.

I chuckled and looked over at Brooke. She was staring into her glass. I nudged her with my elbow.

"Let's hit the Ak and crack open that Jameson," I said.

Her eyes brightened.

"I'm down," she said. "This beer is starting to taste like balls anyways."

We took a cab to the hotel and got a room. We went up and cracked the Jameson straight off. We took three shots in a row. We started chatting then slowly, Dimuira and Tex backed outta the room. Soon it was just me and Brooke. We were sitting on the bed facing one another. Brooke was going off about a trip she wanted to take to Thailand. She noticed the other two were gone and she grew silent. I let her gather her thoughts. She raised her eyebrows and looked at me.

"I guess I should tell you the whole story," she said.

I thinned my lips and shrugged. She poured a shot of Jameson and slugged it down.

"Well," she said, curling her mouth like a fist. "It all happened after school one day."

She told me how she'd had lunch with her director, how he'd pushed her to drink vodka and then driven her out to a remote lake under the pretense of having a "nice swim." On a muddy embankment, he'd pinned her down and raped her. She'd wanted to fight back, but she was just too terrified. She told Peace Corps what had happened later that night. The next day, she was on a plane to Washington, D.C.

"Everyone was extremely kind and understanding," she said. "The counselor I was talking with helped me a lot. She even gave me permission to go home and see my family for a week."

It took me a good minute to reassemble myself.

"Did you tell them what happened?" I asked.

"Yeah, they were really sad and upset, of course, but they also gave me their blessing to come back to Turkmenistan because they know I'm here doing what I love. Anyways, I know nothing like that is gonna happen again. Peace Corps has got my back big time, and I know that you do, too, Johann."

I bowed my head and stabbed my thumbs into my ducts. Brooke put her hand on my back and rubbed it in a circle. I looked up at her with teary eyes.

"Why can't we just be sweet?" I said.

She crinkled her eyebrows.

"Why can't who be sweet?"

"Men. Why do we have to be such pieces of shit?"

She dropped her shoulders and pulled my face up by the chin.

"Johann, do not feel guilty," she said, looking at me. "You're not even in the same universe as that motherfucker."

I yanked my chin away and started crying. She was silent for a moment.

"Is there something you want to tell me?" she asked.

The sadness filled my chest like a grave. I grabbed the whiskey and gulped it down.

"Nah," I said, wiping my lips with my forearm. "Let's just go down and find the others. We can't have them blowing up without us."

She laughed and we ran downstairs. We found Tex and Dimuira in the pink room drinking arak and singing karaoke. We ordered drinks and joined them. We did ridiculous duets and howled and got drunker and drunker and drunker. At 4:00 a.m. we went back up to the room. We grabbed what was left of the whiskey and each took a couple shots. Brooke's face turned into molten rock. She started shaking and sobbing. We rushed up to comfort her. She exploded and punched us back.

"Get the fuck away from me," she screamed.

She swung herself to the back of the room. She collapsed into the belly of the closet. We tried to approach her. She pulled her teeth out and her eyes went black.

"Who the fuck are you people?" she cried. "Who the fuck are you?"

Tex put his hand on her shoulder. She swatted it off. Dimuira got in there. She put her forehead against Brooke's and looked her in the eyes.

"We're all here," she said. "Me, Tex, and Johann. Just relax, Brooke. We've got'cha."

Brooke's eyes wound in a circle and snapped back to life. She shot up and pushed us away.

"Where's the fuckin' bottle?" she said. "I wanna chug it. I wanna go comatose. I wanna black this shit outta my head."

Tex grabbed the bottle and slipped it behind the nightstand. Brooke searched for it drunkenly but never found it. The clock hit 6:00 a.m. We all passed out in a haze.

WHEN WE WOKE up, Tex and Dimuira were gone. It was just me and Brooke. I told her what had happened the night before. She frowned.

"I'm so sorry," she said. "I didn't recognize anyone, and I felt like you were all my enemies and out to get me. I was pretty lucid when it all happened, but I still couldn't help myself. Can you forgive me?"

I reached my arm around her shoulder and pulled her in close.

"Of course. And I know it seems odd, but in some way, it's actually kinda healthy that you got it out."

"Yeah, that's what Sheri the new PCMO said. She even recommended I get drunk a bit to facilitate things. I just don't wanna end up like my crazy uncle who had a boating accident and almost drowned at sea. Now every time he gets drunk, he starts trying to do the breaststroke on the carpet."

I pinched my lips into a straight line.

"I'm sure that's not gonna happen to you, Brooke."

"I sure as fuck hope not."

We got ready and went to PCHQ. I wanted to talk to Harry about my vacation days, but he was in some meeting. I went up to the lounge and got on the phone with my folks. Brooke stayed downstairs and chatted with staff. An hour later she burst into the lounge. She was pink-faced and bouncing up and down, screaming "Eight. Eight. Eight." I had no idea what she was talking about. I finished planning my trip home for Christmas then hung up the phone.

"What's up?" I asked.

"Eight years," she cried. "My school director got eight years."

"Jesus, that's all?"

"Oh, it doesn't matter. Peace Corps said that's not the kind of jail you survive. It's over. He's done. And I didn't even have to watch him get beaten to shit by the KNB like the last rape victim here did."

We hugged and cheered. When we pulled apart, Brooke's face dropped.

"What about his family though?" she said. "Does this make me a bad person?"

I put my hand on her shoulder.

"His family isn't your responsibly. It's his. And when he did that horrible thing to you, he obviously wasn't considering them."

"Yeah, but his lawyer tried to convince the jury that it was my fault. He asked me how much I drank and how many men I'd slept with. I could tell he wanted to break me. And the whole time, the man who raped me was locked in a cage at the front of the room staring directly at me. His eyes were burning holes into my heart. And that fucking barred cage he was in. Jesus. It was so medieval and hideous."

She started crying again. Then she told me about how her host mother had lied on the stand and said that she, Brooke, was a drunk and that she went to Tejen all the time to party with strange men and have sex.

"She even signed a letter written by the KNB confirming it all," she said. "That fucking bitch."

"What about your director's assistant?" I asked. "Didn't she back you up?"

"Nope. In fact, she worked against me and claimed that she'd seen the whole thing from afar and that the bruises I had all over my body were from my school director trying to save me from drowning."

"Oh my god."

"Anyways, the fucker is in jail. And I hope he fucking dies there. But I can't stop thinking about his poor family and what they must be going through. I just hope this was all worth it."

Her face shrunk to a little black pool. I grabbed her by the chin and looked her in the eyes.

"This is just those assholes screwing with your head," I said. "And they're doing a good job. But there's one fact they can't fuck with."

"What's that?" she asked.

"That this man obviously had a system he employed on you. And the fact that he did it in broad daylight shows that he was operating without fear of repercussion. This means he'd probably done it before and not gotten caught. And if this is true, he's raped countless young girls who never got justice because they were too scared and too ashamed to come forward. You are their silent justice, Brooke. You stood up for all those nameless, faceless girls and gave them the closure they deserve. You took that bastard from the streets. And considering his position in the school, you can imagine how many more young girls he'd have gotten to had you not taken action. You should be proud of yourself. Because I sure as fuck am."

We hugged and cried again. This time our tears were joyous.

12

THE FIRST DAY of school came. I crawled out of bed, threw on some slacks and cut. School #17, although still a dump, was freshly painted. The students were lined up outside; the girls with their green köÿneks and braids, the boys with their oversized shoes and ties. They were waiting for the ceremony to begin. I recognized a few of my kids and waved to them. They smiled and waved back. One of the teachers clicked on an old ghetto blaster resting on a chair. The Turkmen national anthem blared from the speakers. The kids put their hands on their hearts and sang the words. The Turkmen flag went up and flapped in the dusty wind. I picked a zit on the underside of my chin and waited for the noise to end.

After an hour of garbled speeches and nonsense, I went and took a piss in the garbage pit. Then I walked to Azat's classroom. On the way, I ran into Jahan. She was wearing a red and white köÿnek that hugged her curves. I smiled and said, "Hello." She nodded and said "Hello" back.

"How was your trip?" she asked.

"Amazing. How was your summer?"

"Very hot and boring. I was here most days."

Her round face started to sink. I snapped my fingers.

"Hey," I said. "You still want me to teach you French, right?"

Her face lifted. I almost made out a smile.

"Of course," she said.

"Great. We can start next week."

We bid each other adieu. I went to Azat's class and opened the door. He was teaching his first formers the difference between 'a' and 'an.' He saw me and his eyes almost fell out of his skull.

"Oh, Johann," he said. "You are come back from Wet-Nam."

He ran over and shook my hand. I noticed a spot of drool glistening from the corner of his mouth.

"So, what you bring to me?"

I smiled and reached into my pocket. The man's nappy hair caught fire.

"Thought I forgot about'cha, huh?" I said, handing his gift to him.

He took it from my palm and studied it. A wall of wrinkles possessed his forehead.

"Hey, what is it?" he said.

"Twenty thousand Vietnamese dong."

"Twenty sousand? How much can I buy wiz zis?"

"At least a whole plate of manty. Maybe two."

He did his best to conceal his frown.

"Sank you," he said.

"No problem."

He went back to his grammar lesson. At break, we wrote my schedule. I penciled in five hours of teaching and clubs per day, with Fridays off. Azat wasn't too happy, but I'd met Peace Corps' minimum requirements of twenty hours a week, so he could say nothing.

I didn't have my first real lesson until a week later. I had to crack a few heads, but my students sewed their lips closed and fell in line. After that, it was easy. I could blow through my classes one after another without even busting a nut freckle. I even developed a routine. It went something like this: Wake up at nine-thirty. Piss in a Fanta bottle and read for half an hour. Take a bucket shower and get dressed. Walk to school and arrive at eleven sharp. Teach four lessons with breaks in between. At the first break, grab three potato fitçis from the old fart with the melting nose in back. At the second break, grab a *moroženoe* and an ice-cold Arçibil[60] from the little ladies who run the *kiçi çaýhana* nearby.[61] At the third break, bullshit with Azat as he smokes a cigarette out front. After school, do big or little kid clubs, depending on the day. Then cap everything off with an hour of French with Jahan.

It was amazing how comfortable this routine became. What had been impossible a few months prior was now as easy as picking my teeth with a clipped toenail. Not that I felt I was making a ginormous difference or anything. But Jahan's French was steadily improving, and a few students had twinkles in their eyes when they left my lessons.

I celebrated my little victory one weekend. I bought a big bottle of arak, some Ýetigen,[62] a bunch of bologna, cheese, çörek, and candy, and spent both Friday and Saturday night getting hammered in my room while watching videos of Vietnam and blasting Red Hot Chili Peppers. That Sunday, after my hangover faded, I went on a sunset walk. I observed camels lazily munching hay, kids kicking tin cans in the street, old dudes riding in the backs of trucks with their legs dangling in the dust, braying sheep, mooing cows, the sun dipping behind the pink horizon like a silent orb of fire. Afterwards, I did a slug of writing. It came out fast and wet and covered at least twenty journal pages. I went to bed feeling like things were finally clicking into place. I drifted to sleep with a wry little smile on my face.

I woke up and my head was clean. I jerked off to get the gears spinning, then I took a glorious dump and a hot bucket shower. I toweled off and went upstairs. I dressed in fresh clothes and shined my shoes. As I was getting my bag ready, a mite of doubt picked at my brain. I went through my papers without knowing why. Then I saw it: my expired registration.

I searched frantically for the renewal date. By some miracle, it

---

[60] A Turkish brand of bottled water.
[61] *Kiçi çaýhana* means little teahouse in Turkmen.
[62] A Turkmen brand of bottled soda.

happened to be that day. I threw my shit together and raced to school. I went straight to Azat's classroom and told him the news. He didn't look surprised.

"Go and talk wiz Islam," he said. "If he give permission, we go to *Bilim Bölümi*[63] then Tejen."

I nodded and ran over to Islam's building. I entered his creaking hall of birds' nests and portraits of Thug-B. I saw he was with a student. He was shaking a finger at his face and scolding him. He slammed his fist down and told the kid to scram. The kid scurried past me with a pathetic look in his eyes. I sat in the chair he'd been sitting in and folded my arms. Islam shuffled a few papers then looked up at me.

"Zis boy really annoy me," he said. "His faza send him next month to live in Aşgabat wiz his aunt. Bah. When he go, I sink I will take all teachers out for party."

I laughed perfunctorily. Then I told him the news.

"You will go after classmy?" he said in Turkmenglish.

"Yeah."

"*Bolýar*, zis fine with me."

I thanked him and shook his hand. As I was walking out the door he yelled, "Johann, I forget to tell you. Your boss Harry call. He come Wednesday for site inspection."

"Lovely," I mumbled.

AZAT AND I handled the nightmare of my registration. The next day, I prepared for Harry's visit. I dumped my piss bottles, dusted my floors, organized my books, and beat all my rugs to a shine. I scrubbed my walls bloody and meticulously folded my clothes. I knew I wasn't going to raise Harry's pecker with any grand secondary projects; at least I could raise his eyebrows with my cleanliness.

The following morning, I dressed in fresh work attire. I even wore a tie. I did a once-over of my room to be sure everything was

---

[63] Department of Education.

perfect. Then I packed my bag and split. On the walk to school, I was nervous. The feeling in me twisted my guts into knots like a psychotic clown making a balloon animal. I arrived at my first lesson and taught it robotically. It ended and Azat informed me that my other two lessons were canceled. I thanked him for the info and went to Islam's office. He was blathering on the phone in Turkmen. I grabbed a seat and read *Confederacy of Dunces*. A couple hours crawled by. I heard the crunching of gravel under wheels outside. An engine grumbled down, and two doors slammed shut. Islam hung up the phone and looked over at me.

"Zis probably your boss," he said.

I put my book away and fixed my tie. I brushed my slacks off and buttoned my sleeves. Aside from seeing Harry from afar during his introductory speech at the summer All-Vol, I'd never actually met the guy. I couldn't have him thinking I was an ill-kempt slacker on our first meeting. I stood in preparation to greet him. I heard English being spoken in the anteroom.

The door to Islam's office creaked open. Peace Corps' main secretary Maya entered first, followed by Harry. The man was considerably larger than I'd remembered. From tip to toe he was at least six two and easily half as wide. He wore a thick brown mustache that curled over his lips like a shoe brush. He had dense eyebrows but thinning hair and a cleft in his chin like a tiny upside-down triangle. His eyes were kind and sea green. They turned into little limes when he saw me.

"Hello there," he said, offering a hand.

I shook it and introduced myself. He did the same. Then he turned to Islam.

"You're lucky to have such a great volunteer in Johann," he said.

Islam nodded once and looked away.

"So," Harry said to me. "About those vacation days . . ."

Here we go, I thought. Not two minutes in and the man is fucking me square in the pooper. I cringed and prepared myself for entry. Harry glared at me then loosened his face into a grin.

"I've conferred with staff, and we've decided to let you keep them."

"Really?"

"Of course. The flight cancelation wasn't your fault. And you did spend all that time at Bangkok Airport after all."

"Yeah," I said with a withered smile.

"Anyways, enough of that. You know the T-16s are coming in next Tuesday, right?"

In all the commotion of the past couple months, I'd forgotten. I pretended I hadn't.

"Oh yes," I said. "Should be awesome."

"Yeah? Well, get this. We're putting a volunteer here in Gurbagahowda to serve with you. Whaddaya think of that?

My stomach turned to quicksand.

"To be honest, the thought makes me a bit uneasy," I said. "This person could be my salvation or my damnation."

The ends of Harry's mustache curled daintily.

"Well," he said. "You wanna come by and pick one out?"

"Uh, I'm not sure I'm allowed. But I wouldn't mind having a say."

He put his hand on my shoulder and chuckled.

"Why don't you just give me a tour of your school first," he said.

"Okay."

I took him to Azat's classroom. It was like any other in Turkmenistan; foggy windows with blue sills, five rows of eight chairs with chipping green paint, a rickety teacher's desk stacked with Russian, English, and Turkmen grammar books, a table in back set with Ruhnama propaganda, four walls lined with wood plaques bearing quotes by famous Turkmen, a jar filled with cloudy water for the kids to drink, a straw broom resting in the corner, and a big faded blackboard with a single photo of Thug-B smiling above it.

Harry soaked everything in and stroked his chin.

"Ya know," he said, "although this place is old and deteriorating, its owners have done a good job maintaining it and making it look presentable. This has been true for most of the schools and homes I've visited."

I asked Harry if things were the same in Afghanistan where he'd done his service thirty years prior. He chuckled and rolled his eyes.

"No way," he said. "The Afghans don't maintain their possessions nearly as diligently as the Turkmen do. Everything in Afghanistan is pretty much in a constant state of disrepair, which has been especially true since the wars with Russia and the US."

"Damn. I guess that's one point for the Turkmen."

"Indeed."

I showed Harry around the school a bit more, then we took the Jeep to my home. I introduced him to my host family, then I gave him the complete tour. I showed him the banýa, the kitchen, the outhouse, the chicken coup, the goats' den, the garden, the tamdyr, the well, and finally, my room. He nodded with satisfaction at the state of things. When he saw my books, he smirked.

"Don't you think it's a bit much that you have them stacked biggest to smallest?" he said.

I folded my arms and laughed.

"Nah, they're good."

"Those your journals?" he said, pointing to the last stack in the inner row.

"Yep."

"I've got a stack at home just like it. I wrote my butt off out in my village. Especially during the first year."

"Why is that?"

"Mostly because I was bored. Plus, my relations with my host family weren't the greatest yet so I was alone a lot."

"I know the feeling. How did you get over that?"

"I realized it was okay to feel upset by the way they did things. I also learned that to get them to listen, I had to explain my feelings in a nice way and just accept that maybe they'd never change."

"That's tough to do."

"Tell me about it. In two years of living with my host family, I never saw my host mother. Not once. She used to slip my meals under my door for God's sake."

"Jesus."

We left my room and went down to the Jeep. I thanked Harry for his visit and shook his hand.

"My pleasure," he said. "You gonna come in next Wednesday for the T-16 meet-n-greet?"

"Oh, hell yeah. I wouldn't miss it."

He shuffled his mustache and thinned his eyes.

"Only for one night though," he said.

"Haha, okay."

"And Johann?"

"Yes?" I said, smiling.

"Be good."

FOR THE NEXT six days, all I could think about were the T-16s. I was thrilled at the prospect of having fresh American blood in the country but terrified that they would all be douchebags or, worse, that one of them would be sent by PC to Gurbagahowda to corrupt my fun and keep an eye on me. I decided that I didn't want a new volunteer in my village proper. But I conceded that having one in Tejen, especially a cool dude or a hot chick, could have its perks.

That Tuesday, I woke up with eels in my belly. I taught a few classes, then went over to the kiçi çaýhana to grab a soda and a moroženoe. As I was enjoying my treats, someone whistled at me from the back. I looked over and saw Azat and two other male teachers. They were sitting at a table piled with empty plates and vodka bottles. They whistled at me again.

"Johann," Azat said. "Come to drink wiz us."

He flicked his neck[64] and waved me over. I shrugged and complied. An hour later, I was drunk. I bagged school for the day. I

---

[64] In Russia and other former Soviet countries, flicking one's neck is an invitation to come have a drink.

went home and called the PC lounge. I wanted to see if Brooke was in because I was having problems with my computer and needed her help. The phone rang a few times. Zack, the guy I'd traveled with in Vietnam, answered. I asked him why he was in. He said to greet the T-16s.

"Why would they want your dumb ass there?" I asked.

"Because, fucker, I'm on the peer support team. It's a good thing, too, 'cuz that means I'll get my pick of the girls."

"Haha, you know they're all gonna look like shit."

"Yeah, prolly. Anyways, you should come in today. Me, Stella, and some others will be meeting the newbies tonight at the airport, but your buddy Truman is here so you can play with his balls while we do our thing."

"Cluster Fuck's in?"

"Yeah, he cluster-fucked up and bought a train ticket for the wrong day."

"Haha. But won't Peace Corps be mad if I come in a day early?"

"Obviously don't tell them, dickhead. Just take your bags and go straight to the Zip. We'll meet you there."

"Alright. I'm already drunk anyways. It'd be a shame to waste it."

"That's the spirit."

I rushed upstairs and packed my bags. I told my host family I was out, then trotted to the awtostanzia. I was lucky enough to find a taxi to Aşgabat. I sat up front, plugged my headphones in, and we took off. I listened to acid techno and fantasized about the parties I was about to have. We arrived in Aşgabat and I had the driver take me straight to the Zip. He dropped me off out front with all my crap. I lugged it under the bamboo arches and around to the back. I found Truman at a table by himself. He was drained of weight and pale. His black hair was a mess and his glasses hung crookedly from his nose. His tits were down his bellybutton. I had half a mind to reach out and jiggle one.

"Hey man, you look great," I said, grabbing a chair.

He smiled cutely.

"Thanks," he said. "This is what I normally look like without all the fat."

"Wow. Where are the others?"

"They should be here soon."

We heard English being spoken from around the corner. Stella and Zack walked up. Stella had ditched the hippie garb for a beige three-piece. She'd recently taken a job with Peace Corps. Zack was in his same old board shorts and T-shirt. His blond head was shaved and the veins down his muscly arms were splitting with blood. He took the seat across from me. Stella took the one next to me. We ordered beers and chatted. The T-16s were the only thing on our lips.

"I hear you might get a new volunteer in your village," Stella said.

"Yeah, it's possible."

"Maybe it'll be a cute girl."

Zack pierced me with his mean blue eyes.

"Nah," he said, between beer swigs. "I'm gonna tell Harry to send you some zitty fat bitch or some dorky dickweed with glasses."

He opened his mouth and belched. I noticed one crooked canine.

"Fuck you," I said. "The minute any of the new girls gets a look at your nasty snaggle-tooth they're gonna run for the city dump."

He picked up a piece of shashlik and ripped it in half with his teeth.

"I don't give a shit who PC sends me," he said, chewing. "I'm already dating a hot local. And if it's some retarded dude, I'll just ignore him like I do the rest of the assholes in Lebap."

"Is that why I never see you?" Truman asked.

"Precisely."

We laughed and ordered more drinks. At nine-thirty, Stella looked at her glittery wristwatch.

"We'd better go," she said to Zack. "The fledglings will be in at eleven o'clock and Bartha gave us specific orders not to drink before we came."

I nearly choked on my beer. All the nice things Bartha had done for me flew out the window.

"That fucking bitch," I spat. "She's always shoving her fat ass into everything. What does she care if you have a few beers?"

"Oh, I told her I was gonna have a beer or two," Stella said, brushing off her three-piece. "She didn't like it much, but she had to accept it. I'm staff now. Plus, as long as I don't show up drunk, what difference does it make?"

Zack sucked off the last of his beer and slammed his mug on the table.

"You know what that bitch wanted us to do with the grunts?" he said.

"What?" I said.

"Turkmen fucking arts and crafts. Can you believe that shit? She wanted us all to dress up like Turkmen for the reception tomorrow and do lame-ass Turkmen arts and crafts with the newbies."

I downed a shot of arak I'd been nursing.

"God, what a dumb whore," I said hoarsely. "I mean, if she wants Turkmen arts and crafts, she should lube up a *hyýar* with *ýag*, stuff it in her fat ass and pose naked next to the Üç Aýak[65] with some *hoja* plucking away on the *dutar*. That'd really give the T-16s a flavor of this place."

The table erupted with laughter. Stella stood up.

"Okay Zack, we gotta go," she said. "Johann, we'll see you and Truman tomorrow at the reception."

"Cool," I said.

TRUMAN AND I woke up the next morning feeling like Death's oily taint. We'd been out that night on a double date I'd arranged, but Truman had fucked it up with his chick by asking her right when we got to the club if what she did for fun was drink. The girl got furious

---

[65] The Üç Aýak was the Monument of Neutrality in Ashgabat. Also known as the three-legged arch or simply the tripod. In 2010 it was dismantled by President Gurbanguly Berdimuhamedow.

and slapped him in the face. The rest of the night spiraled into the shitter.

We peeled ourselves out of our crummy hotel beds and went to PCHQ. We bypassed staff and went up to the lounge. Brooke was fiddling around on her computer. She was in a black dress and high heels with her red hair brushed to a shine. I gave her a big hug. She seemed in good spirits.

"You look ready to meet the newbies," I said.

"Yeah," she replied. "I mean, there might be *one* hot guy."

"True. But I'm still not getting my hopes up."

"Haha, shut up. Anyways, you look like crap. You should prolly shower and get some decent clothes on. There might be a hot girl too."

The woman had a point. I grabbed my bag, hit the banýa, and scrubbed my balls. I threw on some old cologne and a bit of deodorant. I went through my attire, but all I had were two T-shirts I'd bought in Vietnam. I settled on the one with fewer wrinkles. I slipped on that and my dirty jeans then placed my *kepka* on my scalp. I went back to the lounge and rounded up the volunteers. We made for the reception hall, which was right next to the Ors Bazar.[66] It was a ten-minute walk. The whole way my heart was jerking and gurgling in my chest. I was steeped in horrible thoughts about how the presence of new volunteers could ruin my life. We rounded a corner and hit a crosswalk.

"There they are," one of us yelled.

A stream of shaggy Americans were pouring out of the Grand Turkmen Hotel. They might as well have been a Yeti chain gang, they looked so out of place. I scanned their pathetic ranks looking for one cute chick. To my grand and terrible dismay, I saw none. We followed the grunts, maintaining a distance of fifty feet. We didn't want to meet them until absolutely necessary. We arrived at the marble-columned reception hall. We walked up the tall staircase to where the event was being held. The place was buzzing with nervous banter. It

---

[66] The Russian Bazaar in Ashgabat.

sounded like a colony of rabbits being threatened with ice picks. I machinated all the evil things I might like to say to those little rabbits. Then I ran into Zack. He was wearing a baby blue collared from JC Penny. He smiled weirdly.

"Dude Johann," he said, "I think it's finally hit them that they're here. You're prolly gonna hafta approach them, 'cuz they're fuckin' shitting themselves."

I nodded. Zack and I went into the room. It was filled with wandering bodies. They warped around us like we were two drops of blood in hot oil. I leaned into Zack's ear and covered my mouth.

"I'm gonna try and talk to a few of them," I whispered.

Zack chuckled.

"Be my guest," he said.

I left his side and approached two girls. Both were taller than me and had massive hands. One looked like Big Bird with Kenny G's curls. The other looked like Rush Limbaugh with a blond wig on. I extended my comparatively tiny hand and smiled.

"Hi, I'm Johann."

"Hi I'm XMLSIRT," said Kenny.

"And I'm QWCVKLU," said Rush.

My penis deflated with a sigh. Nobody said a word. The silence became unbearable. I held the smile on my face and inched away with it. As I neared the refreshments table, something brushed against me. I looked over my left shoulder and saw nothing.

"Down here," someone said.

I raised my eyebrows and looked down. I saw what looked like the female version of Marvin the Martian after she'd just spent five years locked in a pantry filled with Cheetos, chili, cheese, and one very depressed Bruce Willis. She was wearing a long purple skirt with an elastic waistband that made a bike tire's worth of pink fat pop out around the edges. Her neck, fingers, and wrists were drenched in Native American jewelry, and her dirty-blond hair was pulled back into an extremely tight ponytail. She had glassy green eyes and ugly red lips like a bullfrog. She curled her mouth open at me.

"Hello, my name is Leishankmarika," she said.

This wasn't her real name, of course. But my brain was so choked by patchouli fumes, it's a miracle it stored any auditory files whatsoever. I introduced myself then continued toward the refreshments table. I found the standard array of Turkmen pigswill: sliced honeydew and watermelon, somsas, fitçis, ham salad, parboiled palow, granulated tomatoes, and a big fat disaster bin of anonymous meat. I grabbed a plate and served myself. As I did, some poor cocksucker in a tahýa and tux sat plucking a dutar and crooning away in Turkmen. His singing sounded like the final moans of an eviscerated dumpster cat. I assumed that it, and the glorious refreshments, had been Bartha's idea.

I scouted for a place to eat. I spotted Zack chatting with two girls who looked decent. I walked over and joined them. Zack introduced the girls.

"This is Cammy," he said. "And this is Marissa."

Cammy was a cute little Asian with silky hair and a small mouth. Her legs were a tad big, but I knew a month of vomiting and diarrhea would take care of that. Marissa was a bit taller with blond hair and a round ass. She wore French tip nails and had a raspy voice. I introduced myself to the girls and we chatted. As expected, the topic of partying came up.

"Are you guys down to go big tonight?" Zack asked.

The girls looked at each other.

"I don't know," Cammy said. "A group of us went pretty big in D.C. Since then, Peace Corps has been really keeping an eye on us."

"Yeah," Marissa said. "Peace Corps has also been telling us all sorts of horror stories about oppressive cops and rape and all that. They made this place seem like a fucking danger zone and implied that if we screw up once, we're out."

Zack waved his hand lazily.

"Don't believe everything they tell you. Most times they're just trying to scare the crap outta you to save their own asses."

"Really?" Cammy said.

"Sure," I said. "I mean, some of that shit is definitely true. But if you party with us tonight, we'll have your back."

"Well, okay," Marissa said. "What did you guys have in mind?"

"I don't know," Zack said. "Maybe we could sneak up to your guys' room later on with some booze?"

"Yeah," I said. "What room are you guys in?"

"Four two nine."

"Okay then," Zack said. "This fuckhead and I will get some alcohol and come up to your room around eight. Sound good?"

"Sounds good," the girls said.

We were in. We were *in*. The only two decent-looking girls of the whole lot and Zack and I were fucking in. It was Vietnam all over again. It was Alpha male, stag party, motherfucking titty-slapping playboy, baller, blowing-the-doors-off-the-hinges shit all back up in that ass, *boyee*. I couldn't believe our luck. I couldn't believe how much the gods were just smiling down on our shoulders and spreading the hot legs of chance for us. I was ready to crack a champagne bottle. I was ready to turn to Zack and kiss him right on the stupid blond head. I felt a shadow on my back. It was long and wide and weighed over me like a metaphysical potato sack. I turned around. I thought I'd see Bartha, but it was something far more hideous. It had thighs like oak trees and tits like boulders. Its belly was a rumbling storm of lard and its arms were two writhing tentacles. Its face was many small faces screaming in agony. Its eyes were bulbs of scorching puss, and its hair, the fried snakes of the damned. It raised a suction-cupped finger and opened its cavernous maw. I put my hands up and cringed.

"*Nähili* Johann?" Mahym said.

"Gowy?" I squeaked.

She greeted Zack and the two girls. Then she plodded away. I breathed a sigh of relief. Zack stood and scratched his neck.

"I think I'm gonna go ask her what the policy on us hanging out with the newbies at this juncture is," he said.

He walked over and struck up a conversation with the Kraken.

Before a minute was up, I saw him frown. He walked back over to our group with his face two inches from the floor.

"What did she say?" Cammy asked.

"Absolutely not." He groaned.

I squeezed my fists into tiny white beads.

"Why the fuck did you even ask her?"

"I don't know. I'm on the peer support team. I didn't wanna get busted."

"Jesus Christ, man. But you don't go up there and ask. If we get caught, we play dumb. And anyways, what the fuck does Peace Corps care if we chill with the sixteens tonight? We're supposed to be living with them for the next fifteen months. Shouldn't we be getting to know them for fuck's sake?"

He glared at me and clenched his jaw muscles.

"Johann," he whispered, "Bartha is right behind you."

I turned around and saw the Wailing Wall. It had tits and earrings and a knock-off suit. It opened its red-painted mouth and wagged a stony finger.

"No, Johann," it bellowed. "You are not to party with the sixteens tonight."

I'd like to be a baller and say I defied the two ultra-beasts. I'd like to be a slick-daddy pimp and recount you a grand tale of wall-scaling and vodka bottles and naked dancing in the hotel lobby all under the nefarious sniffing nose of Peace Corps. The truth is, I ended up partying at the Ak with Zack, Brooke, Dimuira, and the like. Sure, we got hammered and destroyed the dance floor and sang Russian pop in the pink room till 4:00 a.m. But did we have the balls to flat out break the rules and be blood-guzzling bad-asses? Not this time around.

I WOKE UP the next afternoon feeling like a macaque's unwashed ass. I lay there staring at the ceiling for an hour, then I painfully rolled out of bed. I went to the bathroom and took a runny dump. I splashed water on my haggard face and checked the mirror. My eyes looked like little frogs' eggs. My cheeks were rubied and stretched apart by pillow marks. I coughed and blew a snot rocket into the sink.

"I gotta lay off the partying," I said.

I went back in the room and got dressed. I had every desire to return to Gurbagahowda and lock myself in my room for a century. I still had one bit of fluff to address; I had to go to the Aero Kasa[67] and buy my tickets to Istanbul so I could catch my connecting flight home for Christmas. I knew this would be no easy task. Many a volunteer had told me that it was a tremendous pain in the ass to even get served at the Aero Kasa and that oftentimes the ticket agents were so rude and so inept, the process of simply purchasing a single ticket could take hours. I found a vodka bottle on the floor and drained its last shot.

"Let's do this shit," I said.

I walked out into the hot sun and hailed a cab. I told the driver to take me to the Aero Kasa and he laughed. He drove me there and dropped me off out front. It was a small white building with opaque windows tinted blue. I paid the driver and went inside. The place was filled with fat Russophile Turkmen women wearing red lipstick, hoop earrings, knock-off heels, and spandex pants. They were clustered around each ticket window and clawing at one another with their press-on nails to get served first. I nearly elbowed six of them in their makeup-caked foreheads just to establish my place in the line.

After three hours of pushing and shoving and screaming and waiting, I made it up to the window. I pulled my passport from my pocket. The cunt ticket agent took one look at it and scowled.

"You need your Peace Corps ID as well," she snapped.

"But why? I have a long-term visa for Turkmenistan right here."

Cunt Face answered a call and waved me away. As I watched her gold teeth chatter off in chicken-speak, that old dyspeptic hatred for T-stan rumbled at the base of my guts. I could hear the screams of the idiots at my elbows pressing me to hurry up. I could feel the

---

[67] Where one goes to purchase plane tickets.

sweaty eyeballs of the security guards rolling up and down my spine. My skin shrieked and my head caught fire. I ran out of the building with my knees up and my hands in the air. I made it to the sidewalk, threw down my passport, and stamped it into the concrete.

"God fucking damn this fucking shit country straight to bloody fucking hell," I screamed.

An old man on the corner gawked at me. A passing family stopped and turned around. I flipped them all off and hailed a cab. I barked at the driver to take me to PCHQ. He nodded and did the job. I paid him and went in the building. I marched past staff and up to the lounge. I was panting and sweating and steaming. Zack was at one of the computers. He looked up from the screen and laughed.

"Now there's a man who's just been to the Aero Kasa," he said.

I ignored him and grabbed my PC ID from my backpack. Three hours and three hundred singed nerves later I had my ticket and was in a cab to Gurbagahowda. As we burned through the desert, I vowed not to leave my site for the next three weeks. T-16s or no, I needed a break.

13

I WOKE UP a week later in my own filth. I'd locked myself in my room on "sick leave" and refused to do anything but eat, sleep, shit, piss, and drink. My spirit felt like a starving tiger pacing in circles behind my ribs. I was in desperate need of release. I opened my journal and sucked in the room. I blew it all out in a hurricane of ink.

The next morning, I went to school. I taught a few classes and clubs, then cut. On the way home, I thought about my host family. I wanted to make a deeper connection with at least one of them, so I wasn't bored out of my skull. I knew my host mom was a no; besides serving me dinner on my stairwell or taking the rent money, the woman hardly cast me a glance. I knew my host sisters were also a no; Aziza hated the very tissue that constituted my intestines, Miwe and Ogulgerek were too young and timid, and Yazgül, well, we could sit on my steps and sing little Turkmen ditties together, but beyond that, there wasn't much bonding with the squirt. There was Ali, but the kid was a hellacious brat, and I'd just as soon take a toilet brush to my dickhole than attempt anything resembling quality time with him.

I got home and found Merdan in the courtyard. He had the family Lada on metal stilts and was picking away at its rusty underbelly. His knees were poking up from the side of the chassis. I walked up and kicked dirt on his shoe. He dropped his wrench and laughed.

"*Samsyk*," he said. "Stupid ass."

He crawled out from underneath the car. His face and hands were streaked with grease and his hair was a crumpled mess. He reached out with his palm and tried to dirty my shirt. I jumped back.

"*Ejeň sikeýn,*" I yelled. "You motherfucker."

We cracked up. Merdan grabbed a towel and cleaned his hands.

"So, what the hell do you want?" he said in Turkmen.

I put my finger on my lips and cast my eyes to one side.

"Oh, nothing. Was just thinking we could hang out."

"Oh yeah? You're not gonna lock yourself in your room and piss in your Fanta bottles?"

"*Nooooo*. I wanna kick it with you."

"Oh, so Yahtzee again?"

"No, not that either."

"What then?"

"Well, I know we're both tired of çorba. So why don't we go down to the bazaar and get ingredients for shashlik? My treat."

His eyes grew to the size of watermelons.

"You mean it?"

"Sure," I said. "But you build the fire and do all the grilling 'cuz I suck at that shit."

"Deal."

We walked down to the bazaar as the sun was setting. The vendors were just closing up shop, but we were able to convince a few to stay open. We bought a kilo of fresh beef from the butcher. We bought salt, pepper, and chili flakes from the spice lady, and garlic, onions, and tomatoes from the produce lady. The whole thing cost me around five bucks, 70,000 manat—a hefty sum in Turkmenistan—but it was worth it to get Merdan's old rocks off.

We got home and started the prep work. I sliced the produce and spiced the meat, and Merdan constructed our grill. I call it this because I don't know what the fuck else to call it. The thing was just a smoldering pile of embers with two old bricks on either side. I prayed to Allah and all the starving babies on earth that those bricks hadn't been appropriated from the outhouse. I thought of asking Merdan, but I didn't want to insult his taste in accoutrements. I grabbed some skewers from the kitchen and handed them off.

"You're on," I said.

He nodded and started in. Quick as the flick of a dick tip, he riddled up six big fat shish kebabs and balanced them across the bricks. As they sizzled and spat, we squatted on either side and watched. All around us, the life of the house unfolded. Patma was hunched over her black cauldron stirring God knows what. Ogulgerek and Miwe were scampering around the yard making Laika bark, while Yazgül sat on the steps to my room and squealed her little brains out. Aziza was in the living room jabbering away on the telephone with one of her girlfriends. And Ali, dear little snot from hell, was using the end of a stick to poke at the carcass of a mouse, for whose demise he'd almost certainly been responsible.

In the middle of all the chaos, Durdy came waltzing through the waratan door. He had on a white collared shirt and black slacks and his jacket slung over his shoulder. The bags under his eyes were visible even in the near dark. I was reminded of the times my own father came home exhausted and starving from work. It's funny to think of it because this was nothing more than a bricked-up barnyard in a forgotten desert on the other side of the planet, but with everything going on, all the laughing and the barking and the playing and the cooking, the fire and the good smells, the people wandering in and out, the closeness and the warmth and the miracle of it all happening in the same place at the same time under the same beautiful sky. Christ, dare I say it? Gurbagahowda was starting to feel like home.

Merdan finished cooking the meat. We grabbed some fresh çörek and took everything up to my room. We laid into our meal like twelve psychos on a single prosty[68] and didn't stop until the skewers were bare and the çörek had vanished. We sprawled across my carpet

---

[68] A prostitute. See Hans Joseph Fellmann, *Chuck Life's a Trip*, Russian Hill Press, 2019.

and gripped our bellies. Merdan faced me and smiled.

"We should do this again tomorrow night," he said.

"We'll see."

THE NEXT DAY after class, I schlepped home and crashed. I had a dream about burying my face in a pair of gorgeous black breasts. I was just about to suck the perfect black nipple. A machinegun spit bullets at my door. I cocked my eyes open and snarled. I dragged my ass to the door and whipped it open. Merdan was standing square in the middle of my threshold. He had a smile on his face the size of a merry-go-round. He kicked his knees in the air, one after the other.

"Are we gonna make shashlik again tonight?" he asked.

"Maybe. Now let me go back to sleep."

"*Please.* If we do, I'll give you a present."

"Fine. Just let me get some fucking sleep."

He leaped in the air and bolted back downstairs. I shut the door and collapsed on my bed. I woke up to the sound of knocking again. I walked to the door and opened it. Merdan was there smiling like before.

"Yes, yes," I said. "We'll make shashlik. But this present of yours better be good."

"*Hökman boljak,*" he said. "Of course, it will be."

We walked down to the bazaar and bought the stuff. We got back and did the same routine. Our meal was even better than before. As we lay there swirling our hands around our guts, Merdan laughed. I asked him what was so funny. He reached into his pocket.

"This," he said.

He pulled out a folded piece of paper and handed it to me.

"What's this?"

"Your gift."

"Really? What is it?"

He looked deep into my eyes. I thought he might cry.

"Dude, if this is some weird love letter or some crazy bit of bad news, I'm gonna be really upset," I said.

"Just open it."

"Fine."

I unpeeled the paper and flattened it out. It had a drawing of three stick figures. They were in an odd shape and seemed to be touching one another. I racked my brain then looked up at Merdan.

"What the hell is this?"

The seriousness melted from his face.

"It's you, Azat, and Islam lying naked on the ground in a triangle and sucking each other's cocks," he said smiling.

It took me a moment to process what he'd said. Then laughter ripped through me like a lightning bolt.

"Jesus Christ, Merdan," I said, heaving. "What in the fuck made you draw such a thing?"

'I don't know. I hear how you talk to your friends on the phone. And I hear the disgusting things you mumble. And I think that gross stuff is funny too. I always have, but I never told anyone because I thought they'd think I was weird or crazy."

I was flabbergasted. Not only by the fact that he was a deeply perverted son of a bitch like me, but that he'd actually understood some of the dirty English I'd used over the phone or under my breath. I put my arm around his shoulder and smiled.

"Well ya never hafta keep it from me," I said.

MERDAN AND I were now buds. We spent the rest of the week hanging out and cracking filthy jokes. I neglected school. That Monday, I got back on it. I dressed in my finest collared, kepka, and slacks. I strode to class, whistling and clicking my fingers at everyone who passed. I taught my kids; no sweat. I shot the shit with Azat during his smoke breaks and even bought the old fucker an ice cream.

School ended and I walked over to Jahan's. We hadn't had a French lesson in a while, so I was ready to drill the *S'il vous plaît* into her head. I rounded the last corner and went in. I found her sitting at her desk alone, as usual. She was in a blue paisley dress. Her hair was done up in a geisha bun and her lips were painted red. She had her elbow on her desk and her fist smashed into her cheek. With her other hand, she was bouncing a pencil by its eraser. I walked over and pulled up a chair. She glanced at me and smiled faintly.

"Hello, Han-Guly," she said.

"Hey, how are ya, Jahan?"

"I'm okay." She sighed.

"Just okay?"

"Yeah."

"Alright, well why don't we study some French? Maybe that'll cheer you up."

Her hazel eyes grew a little light. I opened the book to a new chapter. I had her read the first passage. It was about a French-speaking Senegalese author and feminist called Mariama Bâ who'd struggled to educate herself in a society that didn't believe females should attend school. As Jahan read the passage in her choppy French, I could tell it was getting to her. I sat and waited. She finished and I asked her if she had any thoughts. She dropped her head.

"I just realized something about myself that I don't like," she said.

"Really?"

"Yes. When I first started teaching, I was very motivated. I would work with my students day and night to help them learn English. I remember four years ago, I taught two of my best students, Göwher and Şemşat, two years of English in two months. I was so proud of myself. I did the same thing with many other students. But after three years, I started to see that my job wasn't taking me anywhere and that I wasn't succeeding. Then I just stopped trying. Now, I feel like I have no opportunities, and that I'm turning into the lazy teachers I used to hate. I need a change, Han-Guly. I really need one."

This wasn't the grand revelation I was hoping for. But at least it was something.

"Maybe you could become an LCF with Peace Corps next year?" I said.

The idea struck her head like a falling rock. Her face lit up with a mix of excitement and fear. She tapped her fingers across her desk. Then she crossed her legs and leaned back.

"How could this be possible?" she asked.

"Well, I could give your number to our language coordinator, Zoya, the next time I see her. How does that sound?"

"It sounds good, but will I even have a chance? I'm just an English teacher from this small village."

"Bah. Look at Baýram. He did it last year and he's from here just like you. Plus, don't tell anyone, but your English is better than his. And he even went to America for six weeks."

"But what about my mother? She is very sick."

"I know. But you'll only be in Aşgabat. During the week you'll teach Turkmen to the volunteers, and on weekends you'll go back and take care of your mother. Think about it. You can have both, Jahan."

"Okay," she said. "Give my number to Zoya and let's see what will happen."

"Yay. You're gonna be a great LCF. You'll see."

Her face bloomed with redness. She lowered her chin and widened her eyes.

"Can I tell you something?" she asked.

"Okay."

"I like you much more than Cyrus."

"Really?"

"Yes. He was always complaining about the Turkmen government and about how much he hated it here. Plus, he was a bad teacher and always yelled at the kids and hit them. But you are different. I see how much you love the children and want them to learn. And even if you are having troubles here, you still try to learn our language and culture very hard. You enjoy life, Han-Guly. And I am a chameleon for people's feelings, so when I am around you, I enjoy life too."

I was flattered beyond belief. I covered this by switching the focus.

"Yeah, well don't worry about Cyrus," I said. "He was an asshole."

She squiggled her eyebrows.

"An asshole," she said. "What's that?"

I cupped my mouth and leaned into her ear.

"*Haramzada*," I whispered.

She shrugged and puffed through her nose. She grabbed her notebook and opened it to a blank page. On the very top, in tiny letters, she wrote the word asshole. It was the first cuss word I'd taught her in English.

14

THAT FRIDAY I woke up at six. I'd gotten a call from Brooke the night before inviting me to her students' camps at her new site and I didn't want to miss a lick. I took a quick bucket shower and packed. I was down my steps and headed toward the waratan by six-thirty. Patma was emerging from her slumber. When she opened the door and saw me fit to wash the King's ass, she almost had a coronary. She rubbed the crust from her beady eyes and scowled at me. I smiled and saluted her.

"Be back in a few days," I said. "I'm going to Adalat to visit Brooke."

She muttered and shuffled down the steps. I strolled out the waratan door and to the taxi stand. I caught a Lada going to Aşgabat right away. I hopped in the front seat and we took off in a cloud of dust. As we sped toward the capital, I looked out the window. Every fleck of green, red, and purple that had survived the summer was now swallowed in an endless swamp of brown. The cabbie had me at PCHQ before ten. I paid him handsomely and walked inside. I went straight to Zoya's and knocked on the door. The old bag wasn't in. I wanted to give her Jahan's number in person. I decided to wait until later.

I took a cab to Adalat. It was an odd little town. Most of its buildings were apartment blocks that came in three shades—white, grey, and piss-yellow. Its two main avenues were bare except for a few scraggly trees and street lamps with popped-out bulbs. There were a half-dozen dükans and shashlik stands and a large, empty bazar.

It took me a tick, but I found Brooke's school. It was a communist bloc nightmare, but it was ten times the size of my school, and aside from the odd wall crack and ground puddle, it seemed to be in better shape too. The first person I met was Brooke's director. He was a thin Asian-looking man with leathery skin and black hair combed to one side. I shook his hand but eyeballed his throat. He said *Privyet* warmly and ushered me down the hall.

"Brooke is this way," he said in Russian.

I apologized in Turkmen and told him I spoke little Russian. He smiled and kept silent. We continued toward Brooke's classroom. As we got closer, I could hear the squeals of over-sugared children. We turned a corner and arrived. Inside were kids of every shape, size, hair, and skin color all bouncing and running around in a swirl of wigs, beads, big-eyed glasses, and Barbie dolls. Everyone was dressed like a different American celebrity. My favorite of the bunch was a 12-year-old Azeri girl who'd done herself up like Paris Hilton. The little thing was skinnier than a sick greyhound. She was wearing a ratty blond wig and ripped fishnets, plastic gold hoop earrings, and mock Gucci shades. Her lips were painted red and her nails, pink. She had adult-sized pumps strapped to her tiny feet and a tube top around her torso that was stuffed with two green balloons. I thought she'd collapse into a pile of bones. She managed a choppy, but not altogether graceless, strut around the classroom and even a flip of her wig. I laughed out loud. Then I gave Brooke a hug.

"This is awesome," I said. "Your kids look great. This would never fly at my school. I can barely get my kids to show up for a club."

"Haha, yeah," she said. "But this is hardly my doing. The kids did most of the work. I just made sure they didn't kill themselves in the process."

"At any rate, I'm impressed."

"Thanks. You wanna meet some of them?"

"Sure."

Brooke must have introduced me to forty of the little toads. They were all cute as buttons and seemed to have similar interests to their big American teacher, especially when it came to pop culture. At least half of them said they adored bands like The White Stripes and Panic at the Disco—two of Brooke's favorites. And most of them claimed they now watched shows like *American Idol, Jerry Springer*, and *Cribs*. Whether or not all of this was Brooke's doing— or even true—was up for debate. But it was clear her presence was at least encouraging their rapid Americanization. Part of me wanted to view it as a bad thing. It was sad to see hundreds of years of culture and tradition being crushed to bits by a tsunami of lip glitter, fake boobs, and cheesy guitar riffs. On the other hand, these kids did seem to be having a fuckload of fun, which was more than I could say for my "pure" Turkmen students back in GBH.

While the kids got ready for their performance, Brooke and I chilled outside. We chatted with a couple of older girls who looked Central Asian but swore they were full-blown Russian. They asked me where I lived, and I told them Gurbagahowda. By their facial expressions, you'd think my penis head was poking out through my fly.

"Where is that?" one of the girls asked.

I told her it was near Tejen. She still looked baffled.

"You know," I said, "the *one* city you hit on the highway before Mary?"

"Oh," the girl said. "That place is called Tejen?"

"Yeah."

"Wow. And what's your village like?"

"Well . . . It's very Turkmen."

"Yeah, I can see. I thought you were a Turkmen when I first saw you."

"Thank you," I said, smiling.

"Um, you're welcome."

I laughed and changed the subject. I complimented the girls on their near flawless English and said Brooke must've been the one responsible. They both nodded. Brooke shrugged.

"I'm not so sure about that," she said. "These kids had fantastic English before I got here. And this student of mine, Misha, he practically speaks like an American. Plus, he's a fucking wild man. You gotta meet him, Johann. He'll blow your mind."

Just then, a V-shaped dude came lumbering up. He was six foot three with a mop of brown hair crushed under a Virginia State hat. When Brooke saw him, her eyes widened.

"Misha," she cried.

Homeboy wrapped his massive arms around her. It was like a gorilla hugging a doormouse. They pulled apart and Brooke introduced us. I shook Misha's meat hook and studied his face. It was tan and angular and carried two sky-blue eyes and a toothy smile. It looked like he'd stolen it off a beach bum from Santa Cruz. I pointed to his hat.

"Looks like you were in the States," I said.

"Yeah, I was a FLEX student last year in Virginia," he said. "Fuckin' loved it."

The dude's English was perfect. He even had the twang down.

"I see you live in Turkmenistan," he said, pointing to my kepka.

I laughed. One of the girls chimed in.

"He lives in *Gurbagahowda*," she said.

Misha threw his arms in the air.

"*Really?*" he said. "How the hell do you like that place?"

"It has its ups and downs."

"Yeah, I bet. Anyways man, you gonna stay for the show today?"

"S'why I'm here."

"Cool. Because I'm performing too."

"Oh yeah? What's your act?"

"You'll see," he said, grinning wickedly.

We went inside. A little girl in a pink dress got on the mic and announced the acts. First up were the Gangstas. My favorite Azeri girl dressed as Paris and some other little turd dressed as Britney strutted onstage. They sat in chairs opposite one another. A child moderator suited up like Jerry Springer came out. He said hello to the girls. Then he screamed, "Attack." Paris reached out and ripped Britney's wig off. Britney pulled a knitting needle from her bra and stabbed both of Paris's boobs flat. The whole crowd went bonkers. The two girls turned and ran offstage squealing. The little girl in the pink dress got on the mic.

"Wasn't that awesome?" she said.

The crowd cheered again. The little girl introduced act two.

"Please welcome, Destiny's Child," she said.

A group of young girls walked onstage. They were all wearing ponytails, zip-up jackets, and skirts so short I could see their entire legs. They formed a straight line. The leader of the pack stepped forward. Judging by her curves and makeup, I took her for about fifteen. She stuck her toe out and cocked her ass to one side. Someone dropped the song "Baby Boy." The girls in back started doing a ridiculous version of "La Macarena." They looked like Gumby and Friends drunk and dancing on cross-dress night. Homegirl with the butt made up for it. She rolled her belly and ringed her hips gracefully. I watched with my chin touching my Adam's apple. I could feel my blood heating up. I reached down and popped my pecker under my boxer line. Brooke elbowed me in the shoulder. Before I made a fool of myself, the perverted show ended. I breathed a sigh of relief.

"Let's hear it for Destiny's Child," the little girl in the pink dress said.

As the girls trotted offstage, I clapped harder than I'd ever clapped in my life. I whistled and cheered and barked like a dog. Pink Dress announced the final act.

"Give it up for 'Misha the Detergent Guy,'" she said.

I snarled like I'd just sniffed a skunk's ass.

"What the fuck's so awesome about detergent?" I said to Brooke.

She giggled into her fingers. Someone clicked on "Ride of the Valkyries." A young girl walked onstage. She stood there blinking. Misha came out with a Jheri curl wig on and a box of detergent that read "Bingo." He strode up to the girl and bounced his eyebrows. He cleared his throat and the music cut off.

"Hello young lady," he said. "And how are you this glorious day?"

"I'm fine," she peeped.

"Wonderful. Now might I ask . . . what kind of detergent do you use?"

She crinkled her eyebrows like an ant had just kissed her anus.

"Tide?" she said.

Misha's enormous face twisted up in disgust.

"What?" he thundered. "You stupid fucking bitch. You should be using Bingo."

The girl zipped down to the size of a raisin. Misha cackled and pulled a giant machete from his waist. He raised it to the ceiling and swung it down hard. He narrowly missed the top of the girl's head. The girl jumped up and ran screaming offstage. Misha lifted his props and bowed dramatically.

The show ended and I was frazzled. I needed something to get my mind off all the boob-popping, machete-wielding, and pre-pubescent stripteases. Brooke and I hit a dükan for some Ýetigen and vodka. We did the twenty-minute walk back to her place, then called Tex and Truman. While we waited for them, I scoped the joint out. It was stark and commie, no doubt, but roomy and nice enough. Besides the master, it had a kitchen, toilet, banýa, and TV room. There was even a sizable storage room that I was certain Brooke would soon fill to the ceiling with empty diet soda and vodka bottles. After the tour, Brooke and I poured some drinks. We sat and sipped and chatted, then round about seven there was a knock at the door. We opened it and in walked Tex and Truman. They had vodka and soda with them too. We sat in the middle of the room with the music playing and proceeded to get hammered. The rest of the night slid away like slug guts down the drain.

THE NEXT MORNING was an exercise in toilet water. I ralphed my intestines into the shitter, took a long hot shower, then lay on Brooke's floor in agony for God knows how long. Later on, the three of us went to the lounge and diddled around. We met a few new T-16s and chatted with them over drinks. We got trashed again that evening back at Brooke's. I'd like to say I was a good boy and left the following day so as to make school that Monday morning, but I didn't. What I did was go to the lounge and goof around with two more 16s, Dave and Simon. The former was a skinny frat boy with a smile like a hyena and a penchant for whiskey guzzling. And the latter was a delicate Filipino boy who liked vodka martinis and shit-talking fat people. As I chatted with my two new buddies, Stella walked in. She was dressed in a gray V-neck blazer and black slacks with razor hems. Her feet were heeled in stiletto pumps and her hair was done up in a tight bun. She looked like the wicked principal from some corny 80s dramedy. I was saying something about how unfair it was that Peace Corps was trying to keep the T-15s away from the T-16s. She heard this and her face warped into a makeup-smeared knot.

"Why do you think that is, Johann?" she snapped.

I cocked my head and stared at her sideways.

"Are you implying that this is somehow my fault?" I asked.

"Well . . . If the shoe fits."

I was stunned. Here was this person who had taken me into her home, who had given me a place of refuge from my site when I was covered in spider bites and a knuckle-snap from going mad, not only implying that *I* was the reason Peace Corps was keeping T-15s and T-16s separate, but blatantly voicing her agreement with this behavior, and in front of everyone to boot. I was so furious I saw exploding stars. I was so good and goddamned pissed I could have gotten up, pulled down my pants, bent forward ass-out, and shot a rocket of putrid diarrhea all over Stella's new suit. I glared at her under pointed eyebrows. Her demeanor jellied and broke apart.

"You act like I'm some kind of evil being," I said coldly.

"Y-you're not an e-evil being, Johann," she stuttered. "You just do things that r-really get under Peace Corps' skin."

I steepled my fingers and clenched my teeth.

"I see."

I said goodbye to Stella. She scolded me playfully for not having called her as of late, and I told her that oh for sure, I would soon. I left with some other volunteers to have lunch at the Coffee House.[69] I was in a rancid mood the whole time. I tried to fix things by going back to Brooke's with Truman and drinking myself into a better place. This only made me more enraged with Stella's comments, and I bitched about them the night through. Truman tried to be a shoulder for me to cry on as best as his sour, cynical ass could. Eventually, though, he'd had his fill. He downed the last of his Ýetiballs[70] and looked me in eye.

"Ya know," he said, "you might be a happier person if you stopped hating people all the time."

His words rang out in my head like a klaxon. They were the last thing I heard before I hit the floor.

---

[69] In the 2000s, the Coffee House was one of the most expensive restaurants in Ashgabat.

[70] A cocktail invented by the T-15s, which contained vodka, pineapple juice, and Ýetigen lemon soda.

15

I TOOK A week off from school to recover. I spent most of that time at home, hanging out with Merdan, writing in my journal, and reading Beat writers: Kerouac, Ginsberg, Snyder, Burroughs. I did a lot of self-examination and a lot of masturbation; as it was November, I had to do the latter next to my *peç*. When I got tired of being a hermit, I ventured out. I hadn't seen Baýram in a while and was curious how his summer training in America had gone. I walked over to his house unannounced. He was surprised to see me but happy just the same. We went in his living room and sat down at the klionka. His hunchback mother with the one yellow tooth brought us çaý and cookies. We drank and chatted. I inquired about his trip. He told me he'd enjoyed it very much.

"Where all did you go?" I asked.

"Washington D.C., Lincoln, and Omaha."

"Those are an odd combination of places. How did you like D.C.?"

"It was okay, but we couldn't to leave the hotel. The people who gave us teaching seminar said it was in dangerous part of D.C. They said there were many black people and if they come to us, they would ask us for money and try to steal us."

"And you believed that bullshit?"

"No. I didn't understand why they would say this. A couple

times, I went out in taxi and I never see this. Maybe the city looked dangerous a little, but nobody harass or steal me."

"It figures they would tell you something stupid like that. They played it safe regardless of what dumbfuck stereotypes it might create about black people in the minds of foreigners."

"Yes. I also thought it was a stupid thing. That's why I didn't listen."

"Good. So after D.C., you went to Nebraska?"

"Yes. We were four days in D.C. Then we were six weeks in Lincoln and one week in Omaha. We were at University of Nebraska most of time. We stayed at Embassy Suites, a wonderful hotel. It had big rooms, Jacuzzi, sauna, pool, gym, even restaurant with pizza."

"Sounds awesome. And what about the people? Did you chat with any locals?"

His eyes softened.

"Yes, many. American people are so kind and different. I remember when I was at university with other teachers, many Americans would smile and say hello to us, and we wondering, 'Do we know these people?' because in Turkmenistan nobody smiles. When I came back and saw Turkmen people, I thought they were very rude to me."

"Yeah, I get that. Did people ask you stupid questions about Turkmenistan in America?"

"No, just ask me where is it and what is it like. Nothing bad. In fact, when I come back to Turkmenistan my own people ask me stupid questions: Did you take money from America? How much they pay you? What are cars like? I told them I go for education and learn to teach English better and they don't understand."

I laughed and gulped my tea.

"Yeah," I said. "People's values here are different and many Turkmen know nothing of the outside world."

"Yes," he said angrily. "People don't want learn here. They only have small mind of life. They get job to get money so they can buy house and Toyota car. Then they drive to town and honk at pretty girl, and then want sleep with prostitute and buy vodka and cigarettes. It is not a life. I look to Turkmen people and I think they are like animals."

"Well, what about the new president?" I asked, raising my eyebrows. "Do you think he is trying to help Turkmenistan?"

"At first I had many hope for him," he said, leaning forward. "I thought maybe he would be a good man and bring changes. But I don't see this. I work at school and president says he reforms education by adding one year to curriculum and raising pay to teachers. But this is not change. This just makes lazy teachers happier and give students one more year of bad school before they go to army or start stupid job. And so many things are still corrupt. Did you know that one year ago the government give two billion manat[71] to fix our main street in Gurbagahowda? It must be finished now, but after money goes through system and each man in power in Tejen and Gurbagahowda take some, it just disappear. No man fix anything. Just pour cheap sand and dirt on sidewalk."

"That's really depressing," I said.

"Yes. And this is everywhere in Turkmenistan. Nobody cares. In America things are clean. They have good roads and good stores, big hotels and good food. I love it there and I want very much to go back for one year or two years, not just small time. I think America is such good country."

I leaned forward and folded my hands.

"You are right," I said. "America has many lovely and fancy things, but do you know its history?"

"Not really."

"Well, lemme tell you ..."

I recounted the entire history of America, from the genocide of the Native Americans and the enslavement of Africans by settlers from Europe, to the Revolutionary War, the Civil War, WWI, WWII, the Korean and Vietnam wars, the War on Drugs, and finally, the War on Terror. I talked of America's crippling national debt and

---

[71] About 80,000 USD.

awful education and health care systems, of the media machine and its endless efforts to keep Americans fearful, angry, ignorant, and divided. When I finished, I looked Baýram in the eyes.

"Still think America is such a good country?" I asked.

He choked on his spit and cleared his throat. He thought for a minute and then spoke.

"Well at least Americans are individuals," he said. "I saw one black kid in D.C. wearing six very colorful T-shirts, and I ask him why he wear them, and he said, 'Because I want to be myself and not like other kids.' In Turkmenistan you do not have this. If I buy one shirt at bazaar and my friend likes it, he will buy it next day too. Then others will buy. In America, people try not to look the same, to be different and be themselves. I like this about Americans."

I chuckled and bit a cookie.

"I like individualism too. But buying a different color T-shirt doesn't make you an individual. In America, the media and societal pressures tend to create these materialistic people who think they are expressing their individuality by wearing different shoes and clothes. What they don't see is by prioritizing this crap, they're all acting the same."

Baýram grimaced.

"Well at least you can say what you are thinking in America," he said. "In Turkmenistan, if I start to make questions about the president or corrupt government, people ask me, 'Don't you love your country?' What kind of stupid question is that? Of course, I love my country. I love it so much that when I see these type bad things, I want to make it fix."

I laughed and pounded the floor. Baýram looked confused.

"Why you laugh?" he asked.

"Because. Do you know what my mom asked me when I said I was going to live in a Muslim country?"

"What?"

"She asked me if I hated America."

Baýram laughed.

"And that's not all," I said. "Every time I told someone I was going to live in a Muslim country for Peace Corps, they told me to watch out for terrorists and not to trust anyone. It was so silly. They think all Muslims are terrorists, and they don't understand that Islam is a religion of peace and unity and it's the fools that have given it a bad name. What's even worse was when I told people which Muslim country I was going to. One guy I worked with thought Turkmenistan was in Florida. He mistook it for the city of Tallahassee."

"They sound just as ignorant as we. Turkmen people only know about some Asian and European countries and then America. Some Turkmen also think America is European country or London and Paris are American cities."

"That sounds just as bad as the average American's geography. America is full of uneducated people who don't care to educate themselves."

"Yes, but your education is still much more good than our education," he said, raising a finger. "I don't mean to insult you, but look at school seventeen, your school. Islam is director but every day he drink and miss class or come to work with vodka on mouth. And many teachers don't teach, just sit and read while students write stupid sentences on board. But it's not only school seventeen. Many schools around Turkmenistan are like this. Even my school sometimes."

"Well, Turkmenistan does have one thing that America doesn't."

"What is this?"

"Fucking good watermelons."

Baýram grinned.

"You are right," he said. "I tried watermelon at Embassy Suites in D.C. They tasted like camel shit."

We both roared.

THAT MONDAY I started school again. I was in a bad place as Merdan had informed me that his cousin had hung himself the night before. I didn't know the kid. It was crummy news just the same. I arrived at Azat's class with my shoulders dropped. I disinterestedly helped the guy teach a few classes. I went out with him on his smoke break. He asked me what was up. I told him about Merdan's cousin. He gave his condolences and stubbed his cigarette out on the side of the school.

"I hate to tell you zis more bad news," he said, lighting a new cigarette.

"God, what now?"

"Inspector for Ahal Department of Education will come zis week. Please don't to miss school."

"Is that all?"

"Not all. She is wery *special* woman. You will see."

He said the word "special" like a spiteful waiter cordially offering his most hated clients a dish he knew the line cooks had jerked off in. I was gonna ask him what he meant, but I figured I'd find out soon enough.

I woke up that Wednesday to pounding on my door. I heard whispering then the clank, clank, clank of someone running down my metal staircase. I groaned and got up. It was two hours before class which meant whoever was fiddling with me had shaved an hour off my sleep. I contemplated grabbing my broom handle. I hobbled over to my door and opened it. No one was there. I heard giggling under my feet and looked down. In the middle of my balcony was a severed goat head. Its horns were dressed with yellow ribbons and its tongue was flopped out over its skinless jaw. I snarled at it in disgust. Merdan popped out from underneath my balcony and cackled.

"Is this what you fucking woke me up for?" I yelled.

He dropped to his knees and hugged his belly.

"Not j-just this," he said, panting. "Azat teacher is on the phone for you."

I curled my lip and grabbed my coat. I stepped over the goat head and went down into the main house. I answered the phone with a bark. Azat apologized for calling so early then said, "Hey." I knew good 'n goddamn well that "Hey" at the front of an Azat-sentence meant a train of bullshit was sure to follow. I waited for it with my fist against my cheek.

"Inspector is coming today," he said. "Please to dress nice and be on time."

"You know I always am," I said.

Azat chuckled and hung up. I ran upstairs and over the goat head to check my clothing sitch. I found some clean slacks and a collared. I was even able to scrounge up a barely wrinkled tie. I tacked everything together and laid it on my bed. I smoothed the ensemble with a discerning eye. It looked pretty darn nice; nicer than anything I'd worn in a while. I folded it all and put it to one side. I grabbed some dirty slacks, an even dirtier collared and a pair of week-old boxers that were so fetid I had to hold them at arm's length to keep my eyes from tearing. With much pain and deliberation, I got it all on my body. I skipped the tie and slipped on the previous day's socks. A pair of unpolished shoes completed the getup. I looked at myself in the mirror; face scruffy, clothes filthy, balls and cock unwashed. I grabbed my kepka and popped it on my head.

"Now I'm ready to meet this bitch," I said.

I walked to school with a whistle on my lips. I found Azat in front of the entrance, standing in the mud and smoking. He had a worried look on his face. I asked him what was up. He raised his hand.

"Zat her car," he said, pointing off to the left.

I followed the line of his finger. It stopped at a slow-moving black Mercedes. The car rolled by us and through the side gate. It came to a stop then the engine clicked off. There was a grand shuffling inside. I could see the silhouette of a large woman rocking in her seat. The passenger door popped open and homegirl stepped out. Large became ginormous when I got the full scope of her body. She looked like an irradiated warthog in a pink tent. She closed the door behind her and waddled up to us. The dimensions of her fat jiggled with unnerving earnestness. Azat lit another cigarette and scratched his neck. Hog Beast docked in front of us, widened her bloodshot eyes, and smiled.

"Hello," she said to me. "You must be Johann."

When she said the "aann" in my name, I got a good look inside her mouth. She had a tongue like a sofa cushion and two rows of corn-colored teeth fitted with meat and parsley flecks. Her breath reeked of garlic and turned lamb. It was clear she'd just engulfed lunch.

"Yeah, it's nice to meet you," I said. "And you are?"

"My name is Käkilik," she said. "But you can call me Käki."

"Okay Kaka," I said. "What's the plan for today?"

"Well, as I'm sure you know, I'm the inspector for the Education Department of Ahal. This means I inspect all the schools in the region to make sure they are up to code. My job is very difficult, so I must be very vigilant and make sure no matter is unchecked."

She paused after she finished. I almost shot off with, "You wanna a fuckin' medal?"

"I'm sure you work very hard," I said smiling.

"Now," she snorted, "since I am also a teacher at school four in Annau, I was wondering if you could write for me a letter of recommendation for the T-Program."

I raised my eyebrows to my hairline and looked over at Azat. He was sweating profusely and choking on his Adam's apple. I faced Kakalick again and looked her up and down.

"You want *me* to recommend *you* for the T-Program?"

My tone was teetering on the verge of sarcasm. The vein on Azat's forehead bulged. He walked in front of me and flashed his gap-teeth.

"*Davai,*" he said. "Let's go to sit in classroom and chat about zis."

"Wah-heý," I said.

"Why you say zis, Johann?" he asked, still grinning. "Zis is a bad sing you say about bad times. Today is wery good day. Za sun is out.

Is nice wehzer. I love zis day, don't you, Johann?"

"It's lovely, Azat."

Kakapants smiled in confirmation and we walked inside. We did a short tour of the school then went to Azat's classroom. Kakatits plopped down and pulled out the letter of rec. She handed it to me then gave me a pen from her purse.

"Please fill this out for me," she said. "I will come by on Saturday and pick it up. Thank you so much, Johann. You and I are going to be such good friends."

I stared at the woman like she'd just eaten my last curly fry.

"What exactly is the T-Program?" I asked her, knowing full well.

"Well," she said, "it's a program that lets teachers like me go to America to learn how to teach better. Your friend Baýram at school eleven also did this program."

I was stunned that she had the audacity to put herself in the same league as Baýram. I nearly laughed in her face.

"Ah ha," I said. "Well, I'll have a look at the letter and see if I can't get it back to you by Saturday."

"Oh, thank you, Johann," she cried. "And by the way, you and Azat have *such* a lovely classroom."

I looked at the cracked windows and the dusty floors. I noticed a pile of bird shit on the water heater. I smiled and put my hand on my heart.

"Why, thank you," I said.

We saw Kakalips to her Benz. She climbed into it with incredible effort, then squeezed the door shut. As the car rolled away in reverse, she jiggled an elephantine arm at us. We waved back and watched as the car squeaked around and putted off, leaning to one side. When Kakabreath was out of view, Azat turned to me and raised his eyebrows.

"Maybe you will want to make fun party wiz her?" he asked.

His question took me by surprise. I gave him an incredulous once-over. I saw the slyness in his eyes. I fell to the dust, laughing.

THE NEXT DAY I went to class later. While Azat taught my second graders, I perused the form Kakaballs had given me. It asked me not only how long I'd known the woman, but to evaluate her work. For the former, I put "One day" and for the latter, I put "N/A." I perfunctorily filled in a few more things. When Azat finished teaching, I handed him the form. He looked it over and gasped.

"Zis will be wery bad if you will write you only know him for one day," he said.

Azat had a tendency to mix up his pronouns. I usually corrected him, but this time I ran with it.

"I'm not going to lie for him, Azat," I said. "I've only known him for one day and that's what I'm writing."

He swallowed and adjusted his tie.

"*Onson*, zey will not like zis at T-Program and maybe no accept her."

"I don't care if they don't accept him. Furthermore, I don't know how he expects me to write an evaluation of his work when I've only known him for one fucking day."

Azat looked like he had a balloon of cocaine he'd previously been concealing in his butt, now concealed in his mouth as the police performed a cavity search on him. He didn't say a word for a whole ten seconds.

"Well," I said. "Spit it out."

"Hey, don't be angry wiz me," he retorted. "You say yesterday you will write zis one for her. Now if you will not, he may make problem wiz us."

"What kind of problem? What kind of man is he?"

"Hey, maybe one side good, one side bad. If you do what she like, maybe she make party and good. But if you will not cooperate, zen maybe no good and make problem for school and me and maybe you."

I mulled his statement over.

"Okay, so what you're telling me is that if I don't lie for this man, I . . ."

Azat's eyes widened.

"Hey, not man," he said. "Why you say man?"

I raised my eyebrows and shot him a look.

"Okay, maybe man," he said chuckling.

"Anyways," I said, "you're telling me that if I don't lie, Käkilik is gonna make problems for both of us?"

"Hey, I don't know. Maybe you will must speak to Döwlet mugallym at school eleven. He know Käkilik five years."

"Fine. Cover my classes. I'm going there now."

I walked to School #11 listening to "Changes" by Tupac. I felt like a used condom floating in a Las Vegas jacuzzi. It blew my stack that this fat whore wanted me to lie. So many better teachers like Jahan, Baýram, my two LCFs, Arzygül and Hurma, and even Azat, deserved to go to America instead of her. It was because of manipulative blob-monsters like Kakafart that real teachers like the aforementioned didn't get their shot. I had to do something.

I arrived at School #11 and walked up the steps to Döwlet's office. I found him outside the door checking his mailbox. He saw me and grimaced. I assumed this was because on the half-dozen occasions he'd approached me to teach at his school, I'd turned him down flat. Thinking back on it now, I guess I could have helped the guy out. But his general presence made me wanna gargle my own piss, plus he was always bragging about how wonderful his English used to be and how it just kept getting "lower and lower." To top it all off, he wiggled his fingers when he spoke and looked like the Turkmen equivalent of Rick Moranis with gold teeth. The whole thing was just a no-fucking-go. Even still, I tried to muster a smile for the prick.

"Hey Döwlet," I said. "How are you?"

"Hello Johann," he replied in his nasally voice. "I'm fine."

We shook hands and went into his office. The place was filled with well-watered plants and sparkling photos of Thug-B. Döwlet sat at his desk and I sat across from him. He poured me a cup of çaý then wiggled his fingers into a steeple.

"Johann, I am very surprised to you," he said. "You are not hard-working volunteer like Lenny Dunst."

As previously mentioned, Lenny was the first Peace Corps volunteer to ever serve in Gurbagahowda. Apparently, he'd done a bunch of amazing camps and clubs and even built a full-size replica of the Chrysler Building outside of town. I'd heard Islam blab about how wonderful the guy had been on a number of wasted occasions. I didn't pay it much mind because Islam was a drunk, and I had my own angle. For some reason, hearing that shit sail out of Döwlet's mouth rubbed me the wrong way. It cost me great effort not to peel the guy's scalp back.

"Well, Döwlet," I said. "I'm sorry you feel that way, but I have other obligations. First off, I work at school seventeen, not here. I teach a full schedule of classes, plus clubs and French. I devote the rest of my time to reading, traveling, studying Turkmen, and maintaining the other foreign languages I speak. I also write a considerable amount every day."

He looked stunned. Sure, half of what I said was bullshit, but he didn't know that.

"What do you write?" he asked.

"I'm writing a book about my experiences as a volunteer here."

His eyes glazed over.

"Ah yes, that's nice," he said. "But really, I am very angry with you because I invite you to teach again and again and you just say no, and this is terrible for me because my English, it was so good. But now it is terrible and when I hear my mistake, I want to beat my head and maybe kill myself and I just think . . ."

The man rambled on like this for a good five minutes. I contemplated slipping my shoes off and biting my toenails. When the rambling finally slowed, homeboy raised his eyebrows.

"Where are you from in America?" he asked.

"California."

"California? I visit Lenny in Chico. Oh, Johann, it was so wonderful. We smoke and drink and party and my English so, so good. I remember . . ."

The rambling continued. I thought about the shape and curvature of my nutsack. I wondered how many individual hairs grew on its surface. As I counted them out in my mind, I was interrupted by another question.

"You know I saw gay man parade in Chico?"

"And?"

"Well, it was crazy because these men wore dresses and women clotheses and many colors, and they kiss and hug and show penis, and Johann, I must ask you . . . Are these really gay men?"

I nearly fell out of my fucking chair.

"Yes, Döwlet," I slobbered. "They are really gay men."

He giggled like a little girl in church. He thought for a second then his eyes widened.

"B-but," he said, almost whispering, "does this mean they are really having sex?"

I looked to my right and saw that the window was open. I wondered what angle I would have to jump out to break my neck the instant I hit the ground. I clenched my teeth and looked Döwlet in the stupid face.

"No," I said. "This does not mean they have sex. It simply means they have special parties where they hold hands and hug and eat dograma and delicious watermelons together."

He crinkled his eyebrows and retracted his head. I waited for a minute.

"Yes," I yelled. "They have sex."

He giggled again. This time uncomfortably.

"Now," I said. "I came here to talk to you about Inspector Käkilik."

I explained the situation. When I told him the part about the form, he laughed.

"If you write you know her only one day and say you don't know her work, they will throw form in trash."

"Okay then. I'm not even going to fill it out."

"You can't lie?"

"No. The T-Program is for teachers who work hard and deserve to go to America. Not for teachers who teach six hours a week then try to muscle volunteers into vouching for them."

"You mean you never lie? Not even once?"

"I didn't say that. I'm just not going to lie for her."

"Okay, well Käkilik ask me also to write form but now I won't. I am like you, Johann. I will not lie. When you lie, God see you."

"I'm not doing this because God will see me. I'm doing this because *I* will see me. And then I won't like myself."

"Okay, I understand now, Johann. Anyways, what do you think . . .?"

The blabbing started up again. My meeting with Döwlet had accomplished nothing. I cut him off and thanked him for his time. He gave me his number and told me to call him. I told him I surely would and hit the door. On my way down the steps, I spotted a trashcan. I pulled out Kakafuck's form and tossed it in. My day was a mighty splendid one thenceforth.

16

THE FOLLOWING WEEK, I got a call from Ken. He told me his students were throwing him a COS[72] party that weekend and that I was invited. I told him about the Kakabuns incident and all the drama with Döwlet, Azat, and Baýram. He laughed.

"Sounds like you need to get the fuck outta Dodge," he said.

I agreed. That Friday, I packed my crap and headed out. It was nice to be back in Mary. The place was a real city with real food and entertainment minus all the PC bullshit of Aşgabat. The cabbie dropped me off at the American Corner. I ran inside and up the steps. I opened the door with a smile. I said hello to the receptionist then went to the computer room. I was expecting to see Ken fiddling around on the molasses-slow internet. Instead, I found Stella reading a book. She was dressed in her old volunteer garb: yoga pants, tennis shoes, a hand-knit sweater. Her hair was down, and her nails were unpainted. She looked like the Stella I'd known before Peace Corps had carved her into a robot. She looked like "Momma." I tipped my hat and said hello to her. She looked up at me from her book.

"Johann," she said, throwing up her arms.

She got up and gave me a hug. It was almost as if she had forgotten what had happened a few weeks prior. I hugged her back

---

[72] Completion of Service.

and pushed the memory away. When we pulled apart, she looked me in the eyes and smiled with embarrassment.

"Sooo, I want you to knooow," she said, "that I feel like I was kind of a bitch to you in the lounge the other day and for that, I'm sorry."

I was stunned. A few weeks ago, I was a criminal hell-bent on poisoning the virgin brains of the T-16s, and now I am a nice guy worthy of a hug and an apology? I figured her guilt had gotten to her. That, or she and Ken had gotten drunk the night before and he'd reprimanded her. Either way, I was ready to put it to one side. I accepted her apology and told her to forget about it. We chatted about the coming Thanksgiving party. As she rattled off the ingredients we still needed, I felt two giant hands slam down on my shoulders. I jumped up and turned around. Ken was standing there in slacks and a black collared. He had a big smile on his face.

"You made it buddy," he said.

We went in for the hug. I smelled his signature BO and cover-up cologne. I asked him when the party was gonna start. One of his little students walked into the room and tapped him on the leg.

"Ken teacher," she said. "The CD player is ready."

He smiled.

"Now," he said to me.

We piled into the main conference room and took our seats. Six young girls in hooded black robes walked in. They were carrying lit candles and bowing their heads. They shuffled to the front of the room and stood in a diamond formation. Someone clicked on the CD player. An ethereal techno song came wafting from the speakers as the girls danced in circles. I looked at Ken and raised my eyebrows. He lifted his hands and shrugged. The performance ended and people clapped. The MC came to the front and announced that we'd be playing a game. She divided us into two teams—volunteers and students. The former had to argue that Ken was bad and the latter, that he was good.

We got into groups and did our thing. Then we had the debate.

Our side went first. We argued that Ken was bad because he had a short temper, didn't know English grammar well, and would take a Turkmen wife if he *really* wanted to stay. We left out the part about him being a chain-smoking alcoholic womanizer who privately hated Turkmenistan, but hey . . . The other side argued that Ken was good because he was kind, generous, hard-working, handsome, and helpful. They won, of course.

Ken went up and gave a speech. He started with how much he loved his students and how much he was going to miss them after he left. He told a few stories about how students had cheered him up when he was down and inspired him. As he got more and more sentimental, I heard sniffles. I looked around the room and noticed that not a single student *wasn't* crying. Ken neared the end of his speech and even he started to cry.

After the first few tears fell, he said "These are not tears of sadness. These are tears of joy. Joy for the wonderful experience I've had here, and joy for the amazing things I know all of you will go on to do with your lives now that you've been given the gift of language."

He continued with examples of big things American Corner students had already done with their gift. Then he concluded his speech.

"I want you to know," he said, "that each of you is a very special person to me. You've enriched my life beyond anything I could have ever imagined, and you will forever be with me in my heart."

His students were crying harder than ever. I started thinking about my own students in Gurbagahowda. I asked myself if I felt the same way about them, and vice versa. The answer, I hated to say, was a resounding, face-slapping no. When I leave, I thought, I'll be lucky if my kids say a hearty goodbye to me. I might even get a hug from one or two of the girls. The boys, though, forget it. As for my host family, the only one who'll notice I'm gone is Merdan. Azat, Baýram, and Jahan might miss me, but they'll prolly be glad not to hafta deal with the burden of my presence anymore.

As these thoughts spiraled around in my head, Ken's students burst into song. They sang in almost comically broken English about how wonderful the guy was and about how much they were going to miss him. When the song finally ended, Ken and his little flock converged and cut the cake. As I'm not a big fan of sweets, I retired to the computer room and checked my emails. A few minutes later, Stella came in. She gave me a slice of cake and a plastic fork and pulled up a chair.

"What's up, stud?" she asked.

I sighed and slid my eyes away. She reached out and put her hand on my shoulder.

"Yeah, I know. Ken's a fuckin' rock star. Next to him, we all look like slackers."

"Whatever."

She thought for a moment. Her eyes brightened.

"Hey," she said. "I have some good news."

"What's that?"

"I heard through the staff grapevine that they're for sure putting a volunteer in your village."

"Really?"

"Yep. His name is Dave."

I remembered the frat guy with the hyena smile I'd met in the lounge. Thoughts of us partying and drinking and chasing girls filled my head. I was so excited I could barely keep my pants on.

"When is he coming?" I asked. "I can't wait to explode."

Stella looked at me cockeyed.

"Um, I think you're thinking of *Rave* Dave," she said. "I'm talking about *Asian* Dave."

"*Asian* Dave?"

"Yeah," she said, chuckling. "He's so excited about going out there. He seems like he'll be a good volunteer, but he's not much of a partier. You can use your ways and mold him though. Just don't tell Peace Crops I said that, haha."

I folded my arms and pouted.

"Well fuck. As long as he doesn't snitch on me or cramp my style, we'll be fine."

I WOKE UP the next morning covered in my own vomit and staring at a box that read "Barf." Memories of the night before came marching back into my head like mad soldiers waving their bloody bayonets. I remembered toasting with Ken at some shitty bar to the ass of one of his hot young students, thinking some Turkmen was Mexican because he wore a shirt that read "Esse" and Ken pissing all around but not into the urinal he was standing at. I remembered making Ken pose for glamour shots while drunk and yelling shit like "You're a lion," "You're a tiger," and Ken threatening a Turkmen cop that he was gonna cut him up, then us leaving and Ken telling me on the way home that I had huge balls for going after my dream to be a writer. I remembered puking bile all over one of his host mom's fresh diarrhea splatters in the toilet, chugging a shit ton of water, then passing out on the floor while Ken serenaded me with his snoring.

Much to my amazement, I had zero hangover. I figured it must have been due to all the puking and the water. I got up and took an enormous piss. Then I took a bucket shower and brushed my teeth. When I came back into Ken's room, he was still passed out on the floor. I kicked him square in the ass and he farted.

"What gives, dickhead?" he shouted.

"I'm hungry, fucker. Let's make something."

He rolled over and looked at me.

"How 'bout some cream of pumpkin soup?"

I rolled my eyes.

"I've eaten enough pumpkin soup to choke a hippo."

He jumped up and dusted his jeans off.

"Not like mine, you haven't."

We hit the bazaar and bought a bunch of ingredients: tomatoes, onions, garlic, pumpkin, *smetana*. We brought it all back to Ken's and got to it. Ken sliced, diced, chopped, and blended. I DJ'd and sipped a Yetiballs. We served the soup with hunks of warm çörek. We went into Ken's room, clicked on "Band of Brothers," drank, and ate. The soup was delicious; far better than anything my host mom had ever

251

made. We finished eating and went out on the balcony with our drinks. Ken chain-smoked and we chatted our brains to bits. We covered everything from ex-girlfriends to poetry, philosophy to family feuds, life, death, growing up. As the alcohol closed its liquid curtains on my consciousness, Ken looked at me with hardened eyes.

"Living in this place has made me a man," he said. "I know who I am now."

I felt stripped naked by this statement. It was as if Ken had lit my clothes on fire, and they were burning to ashes all around me without touching my body. It took me a moment to compose myself. I gulped the rest of my drink and stared at the blackened courtyard below.

"I think I've got the knowing-myself part down," I said. "But the man part? That I'm not so sure about."

Ken sucked his cigarette to the filter and blew out a cloud of smoke. He put his big arm around my shoulder and leaned in with a grin.

"Johann," he said. "You're closer than you think."

I FELL INTO a funk after Ken left. For a week, I didn't shower, shave, clean, or do laundry. It was like someone had cut off my arm, like I'd been kicked nude and bleeding into a ditch while the whole village stood around me and laughed. I taught when I had to, but I didn't do much. On my off time, I filled my piss bottles, read dark books, and curled up in my sweats next to my peç.

When Monday came, I felt a bit better. I had a fresh week to work with, plus I knew that in a few short days, a new volunteer would be joining me in GBH. I remembered what Stella had told me about the guy; that he wasn't much of a partier but that he was excited about coming, and that I could use my ways to mold him. This opened all sorts of avenues for me. My first thought was that if I wanted to, I could turn this fucker's world upside-down and scare the gum-smacking Christ outta him before he ever got a chance to sprout. I envisioned tormenting him with horror stories of rape, murder, and suicide, slamming him upside the head with sentences in Turkmen of immense grammatical complexity, then making him weep with disgust by showing him my collection of urine in various states of decay. I got a vein-slicked boner thinking about all this, but then I remembered how I'd been coaxed into this place by the ones who'd come before me, and how without their patience and care—hard-knock as it may have been sometimes—I'd have peed my jeans black and bolted for the windmills long ago.

On my walk to class, I had thoughts of a different nature. I decided, after much pondering, that I would teach the new guy everything I'd learned over the past thirteen months so he might one day pass it down to the next volunteer to come to Gurbagahowda. It now seemed almost a tradition to me. Lenny had done it for Todd and Nancy, the married couple who'd come after him, who in turn had done it for Cyrus, who'd then done it for me. Now I'd be doing it for Dave, and when the next volunteer after him came, he would do it for them. I was stoked to be part of this tradition. Unlike the others before me, I would have a year to teach my volunteer everything while we both grew alongside one another in this strangely beautiful place. I planned on showing Dave all my little spots; the uly çaýhana where Azat and I got drunk and ate manty, the park bench where I wrote poetry, and the Ruhnama room at school where I often escaped my students and read in silence, the bullfrog pit and the dirt oasis, the long stretch of desert behind my house that melted into infinity, and the various shashlik stands around town where I often had lunch, the old 50s-style phone house[73] which was the only place in town to make international calls, my favorite dükans and bazaar stands, and even the *dellekhana* (barbershop) with the awesome *dellek* who shaved my head perfectly for a buck. We would go to *toýs*, birthdays, and graduations together. I would teach Dave how to shoot vodka, flirt with girls, and dance like a Turkmen. If we got

---

[73] Where there was a switchboard and a phone booth. It was a relic from the Soviet era—most Turkmen villages had one.

really adventurous, we would go with Merdan to the bazaar to bang some hookers. But if not, I would still teach Dave the culture and the language, how to eat the food, squat, chew çigits and be polite. If he had questions about dealing with the woes of living in such a harsh, barren land I would ease them with wise words whose profound meaning was forged by months of suffering in hardship. I would introduce him to all my kids and all my friends and all the teachers at my school so that he might feel welcome and comfortable in his new environment. I would also make great efforts to learn who he was as a person; his accomplishments, his past, his dreams, goals, aspirations, fears, and troubles. It would be an immense growing experience for both of us, and I couldn't fucking wait to get my hands dirty with all of it.

I arrived at school, skipping with joy. I taught a couple classes then Azat let me use his cell to call Peace Corps. Our secretary Maya answered sweetly. I asked her who I should talk to about the coming volunteer.

"You will want to greet him?" she said.

"You got it."

"Let me switch you over to Mahym. She knows this information."

"Okay."

I was downright ecstatic. I didn't care if I had to talk to the fat slob monster cunt, I was getting a volunteer. The line clicked over. Mahym cleared her throat.

"Hello," she barked.

"Hey, Mahym. It's Johann," I said.

"Hello, Johann. What can I do for you?"

"Well, I was calling about the new volunteer coming to my site. I would like to know when and where to meet him tomorrow, so I can give him a warm welcome and show him around."

I heard a shuffling of papers.

"Johann, I'm in a meeting," she said. "You'll have to talk to Bartha."

Oh great, I thought. If dealing with Mahym's touchy fat ass wasn't enough, now I had to deal with Bartha's writhing beaver of a personality.

"Okay," I said. "Give her to me."

Bartha answered the phone a nanosecond later.

"Hello Johann," she said.

"Hi, Bartha. I'll make this quick 'cuz I know you guys are always so busy. *Spending the minuscule budget Washington reluctantly kicks us down on fancy apartments, lavish parties, tricked-out Jeeps, and literally tons of American food all for yourselves, while we volunteers rot away at our worthless sites on dollars a day.*"

I asked her about the new volunteer. She cut me off before I finished my sentence.

"Johann," she said. "No volunteer is coming to your site."

The blood raced out of my veins.

"What?" I said. "But I thought—"

"Well, you thought wrong. There's a volunteer, Dave, being sent to Tejen. But nobody is coming to your site."

My mind popped into red dots. Stella must have gotten the whole fucking thing mixed up. And to think, PC didn't even bother calling to tell me no one was coming. What a hose job. I coughed and gripped my neck. Bartha softened a little.

"I know this is disappointing," she said. "But we must take what rises to the top. Your site didn't. I'm sorry. Now, I hate to do this but I'm in a meeting. We'll talk later."

Then I heard a click and a long, drawn out beeeeeeeep.

There were no words for how I felt. I stood motionless with eyes like marbles of sky. Azat pranced up to me.

"What is news Peace Corps give about new volunteer Dave?" he asked, almost panting.

I looked at him blankly.

"He's not coming."

Azat's face dropped.

"Why he will not come?"

255

"Peace Corps is sending him to Tejen. My friend had it wrong. Nobody's coming here, Azat. Nobody."

He looked shattered.

"Hey," he said. "Now I feel wery sad. But one hour ago, I was so happy zat we will take new volunteer to uly çaýhana and have manty and beer."

"Well, we don't get to do that. And you know what? It doesn't fucking surprise me."

The clunky old bell rang, and a hoard of screaming children funneled inside the building. I stood at the brick entrance facing the road. I wondered if that disgusting hog of a woman Kakaturds had anything to do with this. So much for passing down the lame-ass tradition, I thought.

I SPENT ANOTHER week being a depressed little bitch. I'd describe my routine, but I've exhausted that number down to its very last cell. After school one day, I saw a big-headed club student of mine named Aman. I remembered grilling him a couple months back about why he wanted to go to America so badly. I'd asked him to write me a two-page essay on the subject. As the weeks passed and his club attendance became more sporadic, I figured he'd forgotten about the assignment. He ran up to me smiling and waving a piece of paper. I asked him what he had in his hand.

"This is essay you wanted," he said. "I finish it in computer room this morning."

I humphed and took the essay. It was two pages long and typed in double-spaced Helvetica. I skimmed it over. He rehashed his five original reasons for wanting to go to America: 1. Learn English better; 2. Travel; 3. Learn about a new culture; 4. Work with computers; 5. See a new country. At the end, he included one new reason: pizza. I read this and laughed. He looked puzzled.

"What so funny?" he asked.

I was going to explain to him how pizza wasn't even American, and how if he wanted to taste real pizza, he should go to Italy. It dawned on me that his chances of making it to Naples—arguably, the birthplace of pizza—were about as slim as his chances of making it to New York or Chicago or anywhere else in the US where pizza had roots. Then I got an idea. I smiled and handed him his essay.

"What are you doing tomorrow?" I asked.

"Just going to school and doing housework. We are very busy at home. This why my essay so late."

"If you're not too busy tomorrow, wanna have a pizza party?"

His cubic head turned so red and happy I thought Gallagher might materialize over it with a rubber mallet.

"Of course," he cried. "We can have it at my home. I will introduce you to my family. Then we will cook and eat and drink tea."

"Sounds like a plan."

"One more thing."

"What's that?"

"You will please bring your computer? I want to play games on it and see pictures of India."

"India?"

"Yes. You inspire me to visit other countries, and if I no go to America for pizza, I will go to India for interest."

"You got it," I said.

THE NEXT DAY, I met Aman at the bazaar. I already had tomato sauce, Italian seasoning, salt, pepper, and Tapatío[74] from a package my family had sent me, and Aman said his mom and sis had the dough on lock, so all we needed were tomatoes, onions, garlic, basal, kielbasa, and some of that horrendous plastic cheese that all the dükans sold. Once we had everything, we made our way to Aman's house. It was located on the outskirts of GBH, where the last bits of civilization crumbled into desert. Because of Aman's neat dress

---

[74] Tapatío is a hot sauce made from red peppers. It is produced in Vernon, California.

habits, intelligence, and slight British accent I'd been expecting his family to be somewhat wealthy. We arrived at his home and I realized that this couldn't have been further from the truth. His front yard was a square of cracked mud covered in piles of soggy hay. There was a dilapidated animal den straight ahead and an old outhouse to the left that was so crooked and smelly it reminded me of a dead bum I'd once seen in the streets of San Francisco. His actual house didn't look any better; it was a gathering of brick walls dressed at their crown with aluminum siding. By the graceful frown on Aman's face, I could tell he was ashamed. Still, that didn't stop him from ushering me inside and introducing me to his family. I met his mother first. She was tremendously fat with the eyes of a cow and arms that looked like legs. She greeted me sweetly then continued pounding the dough. I met Aman's sister who was a mini version of her mother. Aman took me to the back room.

"This is where I have my computer," he said.

I was stunned to hear him say this. I saw the computer and shock faded into pity. His computer was a prehistoric hunk of shit. Its plastic had yellowed from years of fingering and its screen was so tiny I could have covered it with a soda cracker. Aman walked over and clicked it on. The sound it made strummed up images of C3PO being sodomized against his will by Chewy. I smiled and waited. The thing finally seizure'd itself to life and Aman motioned me over with his big hands.

"Come," he said. "I will show you its features."

Its features were unremarkable. I'd have been more impressed had Aman's mother taken a crap in that outhouse without falling in than I was by anything on that computer. I feigned interest. Aman finished and grinned with all his poopy teeth.

"Now show me your computer," he said almost rudely.

"Okay," I said. "What do you wanna see first?"

"Games, please."

I showed him my games. All I had was Solitaire, Tetris, and Space Invaders. Aman dismissed them with a flick of his long fingers.

"I have seen all these before," he said Britishly. "Let's just see your pictures of India."

"*Okay,*" I said.

I busted out the photos. They were from the World Explosion 2006, the trip I'd taken around the world with my childhood buddies the summer before coming to Turkmenistan. Seeing them brought it all back. I thought about blasting away to exotic locales with limitless time and money, plus the girls, booze, drugs, and adventure. Aman ooh'd and aah'd. I clicked on the Chili Peppers and really got the shit rarin'. I felt like I was back out there with the boys, powdering Beelzebub's toenails with a razor blade and snorting it all up under crazy blue eyeballs. Soon the reverie started to bleed out along with the pictures. By forty minutes, I was left with nothing but a stale heart and the urge to piss. I asked Aman if I could use his shitter. He bent up on his skinny legs and slipped on his sandals.

"I shall take you," he said.

I got up and went out with him. He suddenly stopped.

"I want to introduce you to someone first," he said.

I stamped in place and gripped my crotch.

"Make it quick," I said.

He nodded and went in the den. I closed my eyes and gripped my crotch harder. I opened my eyes back up and saw Aman standing next to what looked like a Buick-sized lump of clay with a giant boner sticking out the top. He stroked its shaft and smiled.

"This is my camel," he said.

I was flummoxed that I hadn't noticed the two-thousand-pound creature in that tiny yard when I'd arrived. I didn't want to go anywhere near it.

"Come," Aman said. "It shall not bite."

I walked over and cautiously pet the camel's neck. It bobbled its head and moaned like a cyclops having an orgasm. I started to like my new buddy.

"So, what are you going to do with him?" I asked.

Aman blinked.

"I will kill him," he said. "Then I will sell the meat to the market for six million manat."

My mouth dropped open.

"You're gonna kill him?"

"Yes, of course. He has good meat."

"But I thought he was your friend?"

"A camel is not my friend. A camel is my food or my money. I pet him like this so I will show you he is safe."

"I guess that makes sense."

Now that I knew the camel was gonna be hacked into little bits and sold at the market, I gave him a proper neck scratch. I got in there with my nails and made his eyes roll around in his skull and his tongue come lobbing out like a big frothy eel. I leaned into his ear.

"This is your last hurrah, buddy," I whispered.

The camel let off a ginormous fart. It sounded like the engine of a tractor backfiring. Aman and I cracked up. I remembered I had to piss. I said goodbye to the camel and did my thing. I went back in the house and Aman's mother announced that the dough was ready. She gave it to us, and we took it in the back room. We sliced the toppings and prepared the sauce. An hour later, our pizza was ready. I won't say it was good, but I hadn't eaten all day, and this was Turkmenistan, so any friggin' pizza woulda done. Aman and I scarfed the thing while looking at more travel photos. When we finished, Aman rudely ordered his mother and sister to take our dishes and bring us tea and cookies. I ignored the offense and thanked the ladies. I put on *Caddie Shack*, during which Aman passed out snoring. I spent half the night squeezing my pillow around my head. I finally fell asleep at 2:00 a.m., only to be woken up at five by the call to prayer. As the *muezzin*[75] whined the entire Koran into my ears, I realized something awful. I had to take a dump.

---

[75] The person appointed to recite the call to prayer at a mosque.

17

THAT SUNDAY I got a call from my father. I hadn't spoken with him in two months. I knew from his emails that he was having heart troubles; something to do with atrial fibrillation and a series of failed surgeries. I asked him what the next step was. He told me his doctor had recommended he get a pacemaker. I asked him what the holdup was. He grunted nervously.

"Well," he said, "the delay is me. I'm the one who's holding back."

"Why?" I screamed.

"Because I wanna wait this thing out and see how it goes."

He grew quiet after this. I knew yelling and trying to prod him deeper would go nowhere. I changed the subject to Christmas and how much I was looking forward to seeing everyone. He mirrored my sentiments. We hung up the phone. I sat in silence hoping a heart attack wouldn't end his life and subsequently my service. I felt the urge to see Brooke. It had been a while since we'd hung out, and I knew if anyone could relate to my pain and worry, it was her. I needed an excuse to leave school in the middle of the week. I decided to call our PCMO Sheri and ask her for a mental health visit to Aşgabat. I went to the phone house in town and called her. She grilled me good, but in the end, she gave me a 72.[76]

---

[76] 24s 48s and 72s are one-, two- or three-day breaks away from site.

I woke up early the next morning and packed. I informed my host family and school that I was outro for the next three days then caught a cab to Aşgabat. I thought about what I was gonna tell Sheri. I knew I couldn't just come in and say, "Hey my dad is having minor heart problems," then ask her to rub my head. I had to make her feel needed. Furthermore, I had to make this visit sound warranted. I worked up a few good schemes. I signed in at PCHQ and walked to Sheri's office. She sat at her desk thumbing through a file. Her enormous ass was spilling over her tiny chair like a walrus in a martini glass. She grinned with her yellow teeth and waved me in. I gave her a hug, then sat down in the chair across from her.

"So, what's up?" she said.

"Well, I have a huge dilemma."

I told her about my father's condition. I mispronounced fibrillation so she could correct me. I mentioned the unsuccessful surgeries. I asked if A-Fib could lead to death. She told me it could in rare cases. I dropped the right amount of shock and awe. I brought up the pacemaker. I told her my father was reluctant to get one. She said this was understandable. I gave her a puzzled look.

"Why?" I asked.

"Because it means admitting that he's getting old," she said. "He may even think it means the end of his sex life. It doesn't, mind you, but he may think that."

"Oh my god."

"I know you don't want to hear that," she said, chuckling, "but it's true. You need to convince him that this is the best thing for him. You need to tell him that he needs to put his health first, otherwise, you're gonna consider coming home. Because that's what this is, right?"

I got the feeling that Peace Corps was shoving words into my mouth with its dirty fingers. I quickly spit them out.

"I don't even wanna say the word. I have every intention of finishing what I've started here and that's that."

"Then tell him you don't wanna have to plan his funeral with your mother. Tell him to put his health first, if not for himself, then for you."

"Okay."

"Now is there anything else?"

"No, that's all."

"Okay, I've put you down for three days. It seems you and your family have a lot to talk about."

"Boy, do we ever. Thank you, Sheri."

"No problem."

THE NEXT THREE days were a blur. I remember getting smashed off vodka at Brooke's and shoveling macaroni and cheese into my mouth, singing karaoke at the Ak till my lungs burst, then eating pistachios in a room full of sweaty Persian slimebags who'd just got done boning a pair of Russian hookers. I woke up on the floor in a ring of broken glass. My head was blistering with pain and I could barely open my eyes. I pried the suckers open and saw Brooke lying on the bed. Her fingers were cut and spots of dried blood were all down her pillow. I shook her gently and her eyes popped open. They were crazy with fear then softened into tiredness.

"What happened last night?" she asked.

It all came back to me.

"You freaked out again," I said. "You smashed a vodka bottle against the wall. I had to restrain you, so you wouldn't cut yourself with the shards. Then I guess you passed out on the bed, and I rolled down onto the floor."

"Oh jeez. I was hoping that was all a dream. Sorry about that, Johann."

"No worries."

She got up and walked to the bathroom. She turned on the sink and stuck her hands in. As she washed the dried blood off her fingers, I got anxious. I felt like a punctured spaceship in a vacuum that was collapsing in on itself. I tried to will the horrible thoughts back into my subconscious. When Brooke came out of the bathroom, one of my thoughts eked out.

"I don't know where the fuck my life is going," I said.

She sat down on the bed and crossed her legs.

"*Okay*. Tell me what's wrong."

"No, I don't wanna dump this all on you."

"You're not dumping anything on me," she said, laughing. "Remember last night? You were there for me. Now c'mon, tell me what's going on in your noggin."

I sunk my pulsating forehead into the cradle of my hands.

"I just don't know what the fuck to do with myself," I said. "I mean, I wanna be a writer but I'm scared shitless of it."

"Why?"

"Because I'll prolly just end up some poor, scruffy asshole sitting in some dark basement churning out crappy novels that nobody reads."

"Is that so bad?" she said, throwing her hands up. "Think about it. You'll be doing what you love. That makes you a helluva lot better off than some schmuck sitting in a cubicle who has to convince himself daily that he's not wasting his life."

"I guess you've got a point. But I don't wanna be broke and alone. What of that?"

"Well if that does happen, think about it this way. You'll have no wife, no kids, no responsibilities to anyone but yourself. You'll be free. And yeah, you might be broke and live in a rat-infested dung pit for the rest of your life, but hey, it can't be any worse than here."

I could have kissed the woman. Everything she said was spot on. I imagined myself as that poor scruffy writer. During the day I'd teach to make a buck, then at night I'd retire to my dank little room with a bottle of rotgut and write till the skin of my fingertips split and the keys below pooled with blood. But what would I write about? And what would be my signature style? I had something in mind, but I needed Brooke's take on it.

"I'm not sure people are gonna like my writing," I said. "I'm nervous that the style I'm developing might be too overblown and lame."

She flipped a curtain of hair over her shoulder and rolled her eyes.

"Well, tell me about it," she said. "Let me be the judge."

"Okay. Get ready for crap."

I cracked my knuckles and took a deep breath.

"I am absolutely tired of flat, stale writing," I said, exhaling. "I'm also tired of good writing, even great writing, that follows the same patterns. I say this mainly with respect to the thoughts and emotions an author tries to evoke with the scenes he creates. It seems to me that most authors are dead set on creating scenes that evoke emotions of a similar strain. For example, an author might create a scene whose primary emotion is hate, and along with it he might throw in fear or anger; sadness might even play a key role. If the scene is primarily about love, passion might go along with it, or friendship. It's always emotions complementing emotions, and the rest that could have been there or should have been there, are sublimated. Well, I wanna change that. I wanna write books that are so infused with contradicting thoughts and emotions that the reader doesn't know what the fuck to feel or think. I want to play the emotional spectrum like a piano, hitting all sorts of keys at the same time in weird and different and complex patterns till the reader doesn't know whether to laugh, cry, piss, or let his head explode. I want to create characters chock-full of striking contradictions . . . characters that'll murder one day and save lives the next. I want to fly up and down the greasy pole of philosophy with my ass in the air like a two-bit stripper on crank spraying ink from my cunt onto the page and making magic. I want to tweak people's minds in just such a way that they don't even know it's being tweaked until ten years later. I want to enlighten people with disgust and delight people with hell and whirl people around in waltzing spirals till they crash to the ground, sobbing. I want to finger my balls like a kook, then murder little girls in their sleep with cucumbers. I want to strain out complex thought and emotion, slice it up like sashimi, then serve it to the public so they can get their buzz on. I want to twang language like a ding dong, switch from slang to ping pong, back and forth, up and down, loop and around and there's the G."

I finished my rant with my hands in the air, panting. I felt like a complete fool. I retracted into myself like a poked sea anemone. Brooke was still sat on the bed listening silently with her legs crossed. She looked at me straight on.

"You're gonna be alright, Johann," she said. "Even if you are a fuckin' lunatic."

I blew back up into madness and gave her a hug.

"Thank you," I said.

MY TWENTY-SIXTH BIRTHDAY was that Friday. I had it in Aşgabat with Brooke and Stella and a group of 16s. I went back in a coffin to GBH. I gave Azat my permission slip to go to America and taught a few classes. I went home and wrote like hell. The next day was pretty much the same. Wednesday was my last day in town. I cleaned and packed for California. I went downstairs to say late to my host family. For some reason, they were all being nice to me. I got smiles from everyone, even Aziza. Patma wished me a safe trip. Ali begged me to stay an extra day for Gurban Baýram.[77] It was a sweet gesture. I wanted to believe his intentions were good. Then I remembered New Year's when he and his lovely little friends had thrown lit firecrackers at my crotch. I politely declined. I told Merdan to look after the family. He told me he would. He asked me jokingly if I'd bring him back a Playstation. I told him to kiss my butt. He laughed, and we hugged, and that was the end of that.

The next day, I got up early and walked with my crap in the

---

[77] Gurban Baýram, known as Eid al-Adha or the Festival of the Sacrifice, is a three-day Islamic holiday that celebrates Abraham's willingness to obey God's command to sacrifice his son. A lamb is sacrificed during this holiday because before Abraham could sacrifice his son, God gave him a lamb to sacrifice instead.

muddy streets all the way to the awtostanzia. I caught a cab to Aşgabat then a marşrutka to Adalat. I had to walk up five flights of stairs with bags hanging off me in all directions. I got to Brooke's place and she had me wait outside so she could clean. She finally let me in. Tex was there too. I hugged the man tight. Then I asked him what was what.

"Well, I'm staying in shitty Turkmenistan," he said.

I hugged him again.

"That's fucking great. What made you change your mind?"

"Eh, I figured I'd come this far. Might as well finish the fucking piece of shit."

"Good on ya."

"Anyways," he said, making a serious face. "You know Peace Corps is looking for you, right?"

"What?"

"Yeah," Brooke said. "Harry called here not too long ago and said you have to come in."

My heart started racing. It got about ten beats in then my brain clicked on.

"You guys are full of shit," I said.

They busted up. I threw a wad of snotty tissues I had in my pocket at them.

"Exceptionally hilarious," I said. "Now let's get slizzy."

I WOKE UP the next morning on Brooke's floor. I had a headache the size of a blue whale and a stomach full of bile. I yacked in the toilet and returned to the room. Tex was thumbing through some articles that had been submitted to the *Camel Turd*, our volunteer newspaper. I'd agreed to help him with the editing. We corrected a few articles together, then I handed in one of my own. It wasn't much; a how-to for managing the horrible outhouses in T-stan. I'd let Brooke read it beforehand and she'd said it was pretty good. It was another tiny step in my life as a writer.

We got a room at the Ak. We dropped our crap off, then went in the hall where a bunch of 15s and 16s were already partying. I sat with Rave Dave and Simon and started drinking. When we ran out of vodka, Dave and I went to his room to get more. As we did a shot, there was a knock at the door. We opened it and saw Iris—the tubby little redhead from the meet-n-greet that looked like Marvin the Martian—with her donkey-faced friend, Candice.

"Mind if we join you boys?" Iris asked.

Dave and I shrugged. The girls took this as a yes and attacked us. Candice threw Dave on the bed and started making out with him. Iris threw me to the ground and started sucking my neck. It felt like I was being molested by a defanged vampire. I looked up to see how Dave was faring. Candice was tonguing his balls. I pulled the leech of Iris's mouth off my neck.

"Let's take this to the bathroom," I said.

"Okay," she said.

We went in and made out. Then Iris slipped off her clothes. Her body was lumpy and spotted and white. It looked like a clear sack of milk with coffee beans floating around. I tried to smile. She took this as a green light and tore off my pants. She got on her knees and slurped at my cock. She went at it for a good fifteen then got tired. She told me to get on the ground then she stood up. She pulled down her pink panties and stuck her crotch in my face.

"Maybe this will help," she said.

Her pussy was fat and smelly and pierced in three places. I had to think fast. I remembered my father's heart condition and whipped up some tears. Iris pulled her hideous pussy from my face and frowned.

"You okay, Johann?" she asked.

"Yeah," I said sniffling. "It's just that I'm worried about my dad."

She lay down next to me and started slowly jerking me off.

"Whussa matter, baby?" she said. "C'mon, you can tell momma."

I told her about my dad and his heart problems. I trumped it up a little, but I really was somewhat worried. Iris crinkled her eyebrows lovingly.

"Want me to suck your dick again and make it all better?" she asked.

"Yes, please."

She went at it for another fifteen. I couldn't cum, so we put our clothes on and retired to my room. We heard a knock at the door. I got up and opened it. There was Candice with her donkey face.

"Dave is such a jerk," she said, crying.

"Why is that?"

"He fucked me and cummed on my tits and then he kicked me out of his bed."

"That asshole. Wanna join us?"

She nodded pathetically. She walked past me, and I noticed she had quite a nice ass. I ushered her into bed and dimmed the lights. When I came back, the two girls were already making out. I stood there and watched. They pulled each other's panties off and Candice straddled Iris. Candice kissed Iris's neck. Iris made a spearhead with her fingers and jammed it up Candice's cunt. She pulled in and out, in and out. The sucking noise it made reminded me of a plunger being worked under pukey water. I got an erection. I walked over to Iris and stuck my cock in her mouth. She sucked on it while spearing Candice. Then the girls separated and Candice went down on Iris. I pulled my cock out of Iris's mouth and went around to Candice's beautiful ass. She had it high in the air, and I could see the lips of her pussy between her thighs. I took the mounting position and gripped my penis. The head of it turned purple, and I could see little veins running up and down. As I was going to stick it in, it went soft. I felt a wave of alcoholic sickness rush through me. I staggered back. Iris looked over at me.

"You okay?" she asked, moaning.

"Yeah," I said. "Just woozy."

I went to the bathroom and drank a glass of water. I came back and the girls had stopped diddling each other. An idea popped in my head. I looked at Candice then at Iris.

"Since my buddy here isn't behaving," I said, flicking the head of my limp penis. "Would you girls mind sucking on him at the same time then letting me cum on your faces?"

Iris laughed out loud. Candice raised her eyebrows.

"I think I'm gonna leave you two alone," she said.

She got up and got dressed. She kissed me and said we'd revisit this later. I said okay and climbed in bed with Iris. We drifted to sleep as the sun rose.

MY EYES OPENED at noon. I looked down and saw that Iris and I were a tangle of sweat and juice and hair. I lay there for a minute blinking. I slowly peeled Iris's body from mine. She rolled over and farted softly. Then she looked at her little red watch.

"Oh shit," she said. "I hafta go. Swearing-in starts in an hour."

"So that's why all you 16s are here," I said.

"Yeah, we swear in today then get shipped off to our sites on Monday."

"Jesus. Good luck."

"You too."

She leaned in and kissed me. Then she stood and got dressed. She gave me one last look.

"Remember me," she said.

"How could I not?" I said, thumbing the painful hickey on my neck.

She chuckled and walked out. I scrubbed myself thoroughly in the shower then looked for my clothes. My jacket and kepka were gone. I had only a thin sweater to keep me warm. I left the Ak freezing and took a cab to Teke Bazaar. I bought a cheap jacket and kepka then took a cab to Adalat. Brooke was making lunch. She greeted me with a hug then floated an eyebrow.

"So, what happened last night?" she asked. "I saw Iris and Candice both go in your room."

"Yeah," I said. "We had a good time."

"Oooh, a little going away present? Maybe Turkmenistan ain't so bad after all?"

"Yeah maybe not, haha."

I hugged Brooke one last time and told her to be safe. She told me the same and I split. I took a cab to the airport and dealt with the security bullshit. It took a full three hours. I finally got on the plane to Istanbul. I was so exhausted my eyes were rolling over in their sockets. I took a seat and shut my lids. I was out before the plane lifted off.

I ARRIVED IN Istanbul at night. I went through security and hit the hotel desk. My father had booked me a night at the airport Holiday Inn. I asked the dude about my reservation and he frowned.

"We double book," he said. "I put you in Hotel Pimpajerk across the street."

"Whatever," I said.

He punched me in the system and gave me a keycard. I walked to the hotel and up to my room. It was the size of a security booth. It's saving grace was the comfy bed. I was drained from traveling all day with a hangover. I forwent both dinner and defecating for immediate sleep.

I woke up the next morning feeling decent. I took a scalding shower and shaved my balls then ordered a club sandwich from room service. I had a late checkout and my flight to Frankfurt wasn't until 3:00 p.m. I used the time to stuff my face and read *On Writing* by Stephen King. At noon, I packed my shit and wandered down to the airport. I wanted to avoid the check-in lines as they make me wanna gouge my eyeballs out with sporks. There was one dude ahead of me. I stood behind him and waited. An old couple came up next to me. They looked exhausted and were carrying a ton of bags. The lady called me to the check-in desk. Seeing as how I'd slept well and carried my crap all of two feet, I let the old couple go first. They thanked me profusely in German. I told them *Mit vergnügen* and felt

271

damn precious about it. The lady at the desk finished with the old farts and called me up. I handed her my tickets and passport. She clicked my info in.

"I'm sorry sir," she said, knitting her brow. "But your flight to Frankfurt has been delayed by five hours. This means you will miss your connecting flight to San Francisco."

"Oh my god," I cried. "What's the next flight I can get on?"

"There's one tomorrow, the twenty-fourth. But it will cost an extra thousand dollars, and you won't arrive at SFO until ten at night."

The blood drained from my face.

"Is there anything you can do? I've been abroad for fifteen months and haven't seen my family at all. They're planning a huge Christmas Eve party, which I'll miss. Plus, my dad is having major heart problems, so I don't know how much longer he'll be with us."

The woman's face turned the same color as mine. She bit her lip and clicked away. Her eyes popped. She looked over at me and smiled.

"Because you did that old couple such a sweet favor, I'm going to do you a sweet favor. There's a flight leaving for Munich today that'll put you on the ground with enough time to catch a connecting flight to San Francisco. You'll arrive at SFO at 7:00 p.m., two hours earlier than you would have. I'm going to put you on both flights. And it'll be business class because that's all we have available."

All the blood rushed back into my face.

"Thank you," I cried.

She laughed and handed me my boarding pass. It felt like gold in my fingers. I was so grateful, I'd have turned my mouth into her personal bidet.

"Is there anything I can do for you?" I asked.

She frowned thoughtfully.

"Well, your flight to Munich leaves in twenty minutes," she said. "So, I guess you could, um, run."

The word hit my ears like a bullet. I grabbed my shit and lifted my legs and sped off toward security. Homegirl had let the big dudes know I was coming through. It took me ten minutes with the whole computer-and-shoe bit then another nine just to get across the terminal. When I arrived at my gate, the lady at the desk was jumping up and down and waving her arms.

"Hurry up," she said. "They're holding the plane for you."

I handed her my boarding pass and ran through. My footsteps pounded down the corridor. The ladies at the door greeted me with a smile. They checked my stub and showed me my seat. I sat down in that bitch like a motherfucker. The door slammed shut and the plane took off.

I ARRIVED AT SFO at 7:00 p.m. on the nose. I went through the customs nightmare then out to the baggage claim. I grabbed my crap and walked into the arrivals area. I didn't see any of my family, but this was no cause for alarm; I was two hours early, after all. I decided I'd give them a ring. I strolled over to a payphone and slipped in a quarter. The phone rang twice. Then a voice answered.

"H-hello," it said.

It sounded like the voice of a sailor who had been lost at sea for a decade. I barely recognized it.

"Dad?" I said.

"Who is this?" the voice barked back.

"It's Johann," I said, scowling.

I heard wheezing on the other end. Then my father exploded.

"Johann?" he cried. "Oh, Jesus Christ. Oh, son, you don't know what we've been through."

"What the hell are you talking about, Dad?"

He started sobbing.

"Oh my god," he said. "It's a Christmas miracle. It's a goddamned Christmas miracle."

"Dad, please tell me what the fuck is going on. You're scaring me."

I heard shuffling, then the sound of a nose blowing.

"I'm embarrassed to tell you this, son," he said. "But I tried to monitor your whole trip home. I saw that you got on your flight to Istanbul, but when you failed to check into your hotel, and then failed to get on your flight to Frankfurt the next day, I panicked and thought you'd either been arrested or kidnapped. In an effort to locate you, I got on the phone with Peace Corps and the American Embassies in Turkmenistan, Turkey, and Germany. When they couldn't find you, I called the FBI. As we speak, all the aforementioned agencies are doing a search for you across three continents. I'm going to have to contact them after this and tell them to call it off."

"Jesus fucking Christ, Dad," I screamed.

"I know, I *know*," he said. "I panicked. And I want you home. I just sent your sister to come and get you. Please stay right where you are and don't move until she arrives."

"Alright."

My sister Hannah arrived an hour later. Her hair was a nest of frizz and her face and eyes were bright red. Tears were pouring down her cheeks. She hugged me so tight I thought a lung would split. We pulled apart and she looked me in the eyes.

"Where the fuck were you?" she cried.

The hickey on my neck burned.

"It's a long story."

On the ride home, I told her everything. I even told her the part about the near-threesome I'd had, and the hickey Iris had given me. As we turned onto our street, she handed me her cover-up.

"Put this on," she said. "I don't want Mom and Dad seeing that gross thing on your neck and figuring out you were off having a drunken three-way while they were on the phone with the FBI."

I laughed and took the cover-up. I spread it over my hickey as we pulled into our driveway. My mother and father were waiting on the front lawn. I could see the tears in their eyes twinkling in the headlights. I got out of the car and ran up to them. My father took me in his giant arms and lifted me in the air like a rag doll. I felt the warmth of his body suffuse my own. I was home.

BEING HOME WAS tough. Not only was I jetlagged, flabby, and pale, but my bowels were in an uproar, and every time I shat, it came out of me like frozen toothpaste from a tube. I had cramps and sweats and night terrors. My skin was ill-adjusted to the balmy climate, and I frequently broke out in rashes. I was bothered by the excess around me. Before I'd left, I'd figured we were a family of modest means, but now it seemed we were grotesquely rich. Our house was easily five times the size of my Turkmen host family's. We had two large fridges, a pantry, a fifty-two-inch plasma-screen TV, all the latest DVDs, leather seats and sofas, walk-in closets, multiple guest bedrooms, a perfectly manicured front and back yard, apple, orange, lemon, and pear trees, a garden fountain, a giant garage, a car for each family member, and a beautiful lake we could look out at while we sipped red wine and chatted on our front terrace.

I tried to get back into all this fancy shit. It was like trying to squeeze into a tuxedo I'd grown too fat for. I kept thinking back to my life in Turkmenistan. I missed my piss bottles and my tiny room, my host family doing chores and screaming at each other in the courtyard, my hilarious drunken lunches with Azat, my enlightening dinners with Baÿram, my somber but touching French lessons with Jahan, my bratty but coot kids, and my long walks around Gurbagahowda where I watched the desert melt into the endless blue sky. Above all, I missed the simplicity. In Turkmenistan, I had a routine, a schedule. During the week, I woke up, walked to school, taught a few classes and clubs, then came home and wrote. During the weekends, I went guesting or traveled to another city. Then the following Monday, I'd start the whole thing over again. In the US, I was a lizard. When I wasn't drinking to excess and smoking hookah in the garage, I was diddling myself to porn or fucking around with my buddies in some bar.

Then there was the food situation. In Turkmenistan, this was predictable; whatever was in season, that's what we ate. In the fall and winter, it was pumpkin and onion soup with sprinkles of goat and sheep meat. In the spring, tomatoes, and possibly a cucumber or two, entered the equation. In the summer, melons came out of the woodwork as did the odd piece of fish or chicken. In the US, however, any and all food items were possible at any time and in any combination. Lunch could be a rainbow of sushi, sashimi and sake, and dinner, a buffet of Indian curries with jasmine rice and flaky breads and all sorts of sweet and syrupy pastries. If you got wasted downtown and wanted to have the breakfast you missed at 3:00 a.m., no problem. Even a small town like Livermore had plenty of after-hours food options such as Jack in the Box, Taco Bell, In-N-Out, two burrito joints, Donut Wheel, 7-Eleven, and a little diner called Cindy's that served everything on their breakfast, lunch, and dinner menus 24/7/365.

If that wasn't enough, there was homemade food. My mother was convinced I was suffering from malnutrition, which I probably was. To cure me of it, she pulled every dish she could out of her Mexican arsenal: *huevos con chorizo y chile verde*,[78] *guisado con carne de res*,[79] *mole negro con pollo*,[80] enchiladas, quesadillas, chilaquiles, tamales, and her personal creation, speedy burros, which, if you recall my meal at Bartha's, are basically flautas stuffed with either chicken or beef and smothered with red sauce, cheese, sour cream, and homemade guacamole.

During the four weeks I was home, I gained ten pounds, which would have been twenty had I not been so stressed. Besides the aforementioned issues, there were my loved ones to deal with. My friends and family were intensely curious about my experience in Turkmenistan, and every opportunity they got they would ask me inane and often impossible to answer questions like, "What was the deepest thing you saw there?" or "How many camels have you petted

---

[78] Eggs with chorizo and green chile sauce.
[79] Beef stew.
[80] Black mole with chicken.

so far?" or "Where are the terrorists hiding out?" or "Do they even have cars in that damn country?" To make matters worse, only one in five of them had learned how to say Turkmenistan properly. The other four would still butcher it into hilarious mutations that came out of their mouths like half-chewed centipedes. One friend of my mother's even argued with me about the existence of Turkmenistan entirely. He was convinced that despite my having lived there for fifteen months, I was still confusing Afghanistan with Turkey. The ridiculousness of it all frustrated me to the point of insanity. Every time the doorbell or the phone rang, I would beg my mom to tell whoever it was that I was indisposed or out.

Our Christmas Eve party was the worst. I'd just flown in not twenty hours prior and already I was having to endure a house packed with eighty drunken, clueless, and festively-dressed Americans all looking to tear open their bag of moronic questions and dump it over my head. I must've gone upstairs a dozen times to soak my face in cold water and stare at my reflection in the mirror. All the while, I heard people downstairs yelling things like, "Where the hell's Johann?" "Does that kid even live here?" "Yo, Ganzo. Get down here and tell us all what you're doing in that terrorist-infested dump." Then I heard laughter. It crept into my room like a murderous clown. It told me everyone knew I was a failure, that I wasn't out there in the desert improving minds and saving lives but fucking, flouncing, and flailing, while drinking my youth from the neck of one bottle only to piss it into the neck of another.

One nightmare replaced another. The party ended and Christmas morning came. I tried to ensconce myself in the cozy little world that was our ritual. I poured eggnogs with brandy and handed out presents, but I felt like a robot disguised in human skin amongst a group of humans who despised robots. I sat by the fire and warmed my rashy toes. I hugged my family and smiled, but it was all a macabre charade. I announced to everyone that I might be staying for a month. In the delirium of the moment, my father gripped his chest and pitched forward. His face turned blue and his lips swelled. His eyes rolled back, and my mother panicked.

"He's having a heart attack," she screamed.

She and my sister Hannah rushed to his side. I rushed to the phone and called 911. The paramedics came and checked my father out. It wasn't a heart attack, but it was damn close. I got on the horn with Harry that evening. I asked him for permission to stay the month, and after scolding me thoroughly for the whole travel disaster, he agreed. I told my family the news. It brought the color back into everyone's cheeks.

Despite the tough stuff, there were some good points, the most basic of which was I could maintain my state of cleanliness. In Turkmenistan, this was very difficult. Just to keep my skin free of dirt and grime meant an hour-long process that involved chopping wood, lighting a fire, gathering and boiling well-water, then taking it into the banýa where I'd strip down and douse myself by the cupful until my body was clean. Afterwards, I'd have to worry about what to wear. I only had a few articles of clothing, and what I did have I had to wash by hand. This was a pain in my tan ass. I had to use a small plastic bucket with a bit of detergent and water, then sit for hours on end scrubbing out spots in extreme cold or blistering heat. Most of what I'd washed was dirty within half a week. This was due to mud slicks, cow pies, sandstorms, or raunchy body sweat.

Then there was the ordeal of going to the bathroom. When my piss bottles weren't an option, I had to slip on my sandals and hoodie and shuffle down to that god-forgotten outhouse at the end of the yard. To call it an outhouse is putting it lightly; it was more like a biohazardous coffin propped upright on a steaming pile of human excrement. Its walls were crawling with spiders. Its floor was a patchwork of diarrhea splotches. Its hole was a hell-mouth of stench, and the bricks on either side of it were caked with dried turds. Every time I stepped inside, the air choked my pores. A ten-minute shit behind closed doors was akin to having a brontosaurus point its anus at me and fart with everything it had.

In America, keeping clean was easy. I had a shower, tub, and toilet in my bedroom, a washer and dryer across the hall, a closet full of puffy and perfumed clothes, and just about every fucking toiletry imaginable. The discrepancy between all this was manifest the night I arrived. After the teary welcome hug, my folks took one look at me and gasped. My clothes were ratty and full of stains. My shoes were dented and coming apart. My face was scruffy and dotted with zits. And my hair looked like it had been blowtorched on one side and left to grow wild on the other. My mother grabbed me by the arm and dragged me upstairs.

"Give me your filthy crap and get in the shower," she said.

I obliged without protest. I unzipped my backpack and dumped a month's worth of unwashed clothing onto the carpet. It was a mound of matted and stinking fabric so foul I thought it'd melt the paint from the walls. I ran to my shower, and when I came out sparkling clean an hour later, I found my laundry spotless and folded on my bed.

Aside from the cleanliness, being home was good because I got to see my loved ones. Sure, they made stupid comments about Turkmenistan and bombarded me with questions, but they were my kin, my closest peeps, and just being in their vicinity, laughing, talking, drinking good booze and eating good food, healed the tragedy and illness of the previous fifteen months like glowing alien fingers on bullet holes. We did all sorts of stuff together. With my family, it was walks in the old sycamore grove behind our house, wine-tasting at the wineries around Livermore, and trips to the coast with our dog Buffster. With my friends, it was a lot of bar-hopping and getting smashed in the garage while smoking the hookah. And yeah, I felt like a slimy old Komodo doing all this. But sometimes, being a slimy old Komodo among other slimy old Komodos is just the thing a man needs to set his clock right and get his dick working again.

The night before my flight, my folks threw a going-away party for me. They invited all my buddies and extended family. We had a bunch of beer and wine and homemade dips. We ate four XL pizzas from Mountain Mike's then my mom busted out the cake. Across the top in blue frosting were the words *Bon Voyage Johann*. I'd be lying if I said a few of my tears didn't hit the frosting before I blew the candles out. Me and my homies watched some cheesy horror flicks by the fire and smoked one last bowl of double apple tobacco. Somewhere around three or four in the morning, I passed out drunk on the couch. I woke up five hours later to my father poking me with the remote. I wandered up to my room and packed my bags. I took a short nap and a shower. I came downstairs for lunch. My mother had made sandwiches and soup. We ate in silence. We packed the van and drove to the airport. On the way, we tried to be positive. We talked about my parents' possible visit in the summer. We reveled in my final return home the following winter. The truth was, I was going back to that gaping hole in the earth. And despite my tiny life and meticulously crafted routine, it was a whole universe away from what I knew and loved most.

IT WAS SNOWING when we touched down in Aşgabat. The sky was a canyon of mercury, and the cold was so intense it leaked through the seams of the plane. I grabbed my carryon and shuffled off. I entered the terminal and stood in line for security. It was long, grueling, and dull. The Turkmen officers maced me with every stupid question imaginable. I got through and grabbed my bags. I took a cab to PCHQ and arrived after staff had gone home for the weekend. I went up to the lounge to use the computers. I found Zack sitting on one of the couches reading a book on martial arts. I bumped his fist and asked him what was new. His blue eyes lost a shade.

"I'm ETing," he said.

My bags slid off my limbs and hit the floor in unison.

"Why?"

"Because. I'm tired of having to soldier my way through this place."

"But what about your kids? And your host family? And your Uzbek girlfriend?"

"Yeah, I'm gonna hafta leave all that behind."

"Well, what about finishing what you started? What about being a badass motherfucker like you were in Nam?"

"That's all well and good. And the way I see it, I *was* a badass motherfucker. I did my service, and it was a perfect sixteen months. Yeah, this is shorter than what I signed up for. But I know what I wanna do with my life now."

"And what the hell is that?"

"Go pro."

"At butt-licking?"

"Haha no, judo. I've always danced around it but never given it my all. I'm twenty-six now so I can't waste any more time."

"Jesus Zack, this is a huge blow."

"I know, man. But it's gotta be this way. I'm in town for four more nights. PC's got me up at the Ak while they get their shit together to ship me off. I've got an extra bed. Wanna play hooky?"

"I don't know, bro. Harry just gave me an extra two weeks in Cali to be with my pops because of his heart problems. Asking for another four days could be tricky."

Zack smiled.

"Who said anything about asking?"

ZACK AND I did our best to squeeze in a year's worth of time together over the next four nights. We drank to excess in his hotel room and watched videos of our trip to Vietnam. We ate at the best restaurants in Aşgabat and ordered the most expensive dishes. We partied at the nicest clubs and chased the nicest skirts. We splurged on room service and hit the wellness center a bunch. By the end, my bank account was teetering on zero. I went to Teke Bazaar to change my last twenty. I came back and found Zack on the phone. I asked him who it was. He held up a finger and said "Yep" a few times. Then he hung up.

"That was Peace Corps," he said. "They're looking for you again."

The blood in my brain froze.

"You're fucking kidding me, right?"

"Nope. That was Harry asking where you are. If you don't go in soon, there'll be trouble."

"Jesus man, did he sound pissed?"

"Yep."

I took a hot shower then a cab to PCHQ. I went straight to Harry's office and knocked on his door. He opened it and looked down at me over his belly. His fanny-mount wiggled.

"Hello, Johann," he said. "Come in and sit down."

I felt like a little chicken about to have a brick dropped on its beak. I walked over to the meeting table and pulled up a seat. Harry sat his big white ass across from me. He raised his chin, folded his hands and looked me in the eyes.

"What's the deal with you being four extra days away from site?" he asked.

I shrugged and lowered my gaze.

"Zack is leaving," I said.

"I'm aware of that. But why didn't you just ask me for the four days? I would have given them to you."

The word "bullshit" came to mind.

"I know you would have, Harry," I said. "But with my dad's heart surgery and the catastrophe with the FBI and coming back here to find that one of my best friends is ETing, I just didn't think to call you and ask. I'm sorry, but this is all so stressful for me. I feel like everything is falling apart, and I'm only halfway through my damn service."

I started to cry. Tears bled down my cheeks and snot dribbled from my nose. Harry ripped a Kleenex from the box and handed it to me. I took it and thanked him.

"I understand what you're going through," he said. "But you have to understand the position you've put me in. I was good to you and you made me look like a fool. Don't do it again."

I wiped my eyes and blew my nose.

"I won't."

I shook his hand and promised I'd leave for site that day. He told me that was fine and to have a safe trip. I thanked him again and went back to the Ak. I told Zack the news and he laughed.

"You're a smoothie," he said.

"Yeah, well now I'm on thin fucking ice. If I screw up again, they'll prolly admin sep me."

"Prolly."

"Anyways, at least I won't be ETing. Not like someone I know."

The reality that we wouldn't be seeing each other for a long time started to sink in. The room grew small and silent and it was just us, staring at one another. I felt that awful pain I'd felt when I lost Ken. It started at my extremities and worked its way toward my heart like spears of tar. I started to cry. Zack cried too. We hugged each other. Then I walked out.

18

I WOKE UP to a light clicking on over my head. I turned it off, plugged my ears with wadded tissue, and tried to fall back asleep. The light clicked on again.

"*Han-Guly, sen turmaly,*" Ali said. "Han-Guly, you need to get up."

The joy I had felt earlier at being allowed to sleep in the main house was now washed away by the realization that I was to be woken up every morning at the clit tip of dawn. I threw off the smelly flannel pajama bottoms I had wrapped around my head and elbowed Merdan in the gut.

"*Tursana,*" I said playfully. "Get up."

He rolled over and grunted. I elbowed him again.

"*Tursana haýwan,*" I barked. "Get up, you animal."

He shot his skinny leg out from under his *ýorgan* and dinged me in the thigh.

"Bah," he said.

It took me and Ali ten more tries to get Merdan outta bed. We ate breakfast together in the *kuhnýa*: fried eggs, çörek, ýag. The conversation turned to my exploded peç.

"We're sorry you have to sleep in the anteroom with Merdan," Patma said. "Five of our heaters are either rusted or exploded, and we have to wait till Durdy comes back from Aşgabat to replace them. You don't mind sleeping in the house, do you?"

Mind? Despite being annoyed that I'll hafta wake up and go to bed at a reasonable hour, I'm downright shocked and flattered. This is a clear sign that not only do you not hate me, you accept me as one of the family. So, to answer your question . . .

"No, I don't mind," I said casually.

"Good," Patma said, picking a soggy piece of çörek from her gold teeth. "'Cuz it may be about a month."

I nearly choked on my eggs.

"A month?"

She cackled. "I told you two days ago when you called me from Aşgabat to grab a heater from Peace Corps, but you didn't seem to hear me."

I vaguely remembered calling to tell her I was coming home. Plus, I had no idea that when I got home, I would find my peç exploded and my room so cold that the water in my filter was frozen solid. I rubbed my eyes and shrugged.

"Oh yeah, sorry about that," I said. "I guess I can get a couple of heaters next week from Peace Corps."

"No hurry," she said.

I RAN UPSTAIRS and got ready for a big day. I had to go to School #17 and tell Islam and Azat about my registration, which had to be done within the next forty eight hours lest I be charged 2.5 million manat, plus go to Tejen, get my *aýlyk*, eat shashlik, meet with the new guy Asian Dave, and try to make friends with him, possibly sit in on a few of his classes as a prelude to getting him wasted and cracking him open like a hot duck egg, all the while attempting to avoid Peace Corps, which might be in the area doing site visits.

I bundled up, said late to the fam, and split. I opened the waratan door and was slapped in the face by winter's tit. The trees were bones and the bushes, sticks. The telephone poles were hung with icicles, and the roads were frozen slicks. Patches of compacted snow were everywhere. They were whipped to a dull shine like blotches of phlegm. The air was so freezing it sparkled. My ears felt like rubber blobs stapled below my temples. I refused to pull out my scarf. Since Zack bitch-walked his ass home, I was the new thug of the tundra, and muthafucka, I had to act like it. I plugged my headphones in and clicked on Brotha Lynch.[81] The black coolness of his music suffused my blood, and I swaggered down the street with a grin.

I met Islam in the hallway of On Yet[82]. He was wrapped in a thick trench coat with a *telpek* on his head. I shook his hand and he thinned his eyes.

"He-hey," he said. "How are you?"

"I'm cool. How are you?"

"Good. Good. How is your faza?"

"He's okay, I guess. Better than he was but still not great."

The memory of my father on Christmas morning sprawled out on his Santa chair, mouth agape, heartbeat near zero as my mother tried to shake him back awake, filled my brain like wicked puss. I shuttered hard to keep it from swallowing me whole. Islam glared at me with his little Mongolian beads. He chewed the air for a second then threw his hand up.

"Bah," he said. "Your faza will be fine."

I chuckled and thanked him. I reminded him about my registration. He told me to go to the *garawul's*[83] office to wait for Azat.

Passing the buck, I thought.

I walked over to the garawul's little room. Çaý water was boiling in a rusty bucket on top of the peç. The garawul sat in his fluffy green don and telpek, gnawing on an old piece of *kolbasa*. He saw me and his ears and eyes grew three sizes.

"Han-Guly," he said. "Where have you been?"

"America."

"Ah right. Your father. I heard."

This blew me away. Even the garawul, whose name I couldn't

---

[81] Brotha Lynch Hung, real name Kevin Danell Mann, is a rapper and record producer from Sacramento, California.

[82] On Yet, short for On Yeti or Seventeen, was the nickname for School #17 in Gurbagahowda.

[83] Guard; deputy.

remember, and with whom I'd spoken all of two times in twelve months, knew about my father. I felt like a minor celebrity.

"We didn't think you would come back to us. Is he okay now?"

"He's better, I guess."

"That's good. Would you like some tea?"

"Sure."

He poured me a cup. I heard laughter coming from the hall. A gang of *mekdepdäki daýzas*[84] in flowery köýneks burst open the door. They fluttered in like giant electric butterflies, yipping and yapping and making all sorts of noise. They noticed me and stopped.

"Han-Guly," they said. "Is that you?"

It seemed my Turkmen name had really caught on. Now everyone was calling me Han-Guly, not just Jahan. I laughed and nodded. The daýzas plopped down next to me and yanked my guts out pull-by-pull with fatuous inquiries. I didn't care. In fact, I was quite content answering their questions about my father's health and the weather in California. I told them it was *maýyl* as fuck where I lived. I spun tales about board shorts, palm trees, and beaches. One of the heftier daýzas leaned in.

"Do you know Jean-Claude Van Damme?" she asked.

I jerked an eyebrow up.

"Nooo," I said. "But I might have seen him on the street one time in LA . . . maybe."

She clasped her meaty hands together and held them to her sparkling mouth.

"If you see him, Han-Guly," she said wistfully, "tell him Jennet Meredowa wants a piece of his delicious ass."

My jaw fumbled off my face. The daýzas exploded with laughter, bellies jiggling and teeth glinting in clouds of bad breath. She nudged me with her fat elbow and bounced her eyebrows lewdly.

"Tell that hunk'a meat I wanna make his acquaintance," she said.

I rubbed the sore spot on my ribs.

"Okay," I said.

---

[84] Old cleaning ladies that worked at the school.

I heard a familiar "Ooooooo." It was Azat coming in outta the cold. He was bundled up in a coat and telpek and blowing hot breath through his reddened fists. He saw me and brandished his toothy gums.

"Ooh, how are you, Han-Guly?" he said.

"I'm okay."

"We did not sink you will come back to us."

"Well, here I am," I said, stretching my arms out to a T.

"And how is your faza?"

"Better," I said. "Just after I left, the doctors put a machine on his heart to make it work right. It's called a pacemaker. You know it?"

"Yeah, I see it on TV. Zis is good news."

"Indeed."

I asked him about my registration. He said he'd take care of it. I told him I needed to go to Tejen to get my aýlyk and meet the new vol. He nodded and grinned.

"Did you get me present from America?"

I rolled my eyes.

"Yes, I got you a present, Azat."

He slapped his knee and hooted.

"But I'm not telling you what it is."

"Why?"

My reason was simple. I hadn't decided what I was going to give anyone. Except for Jahan, who was getting my old French books.

"You'll find out later," I said.

We made a plan to meet the next morning to fill in my registration forms. We shook hands and I said goodbye. I got a cab to Tejen. The driver spent an hour dropping people off all over town and running errands. When he finally took me to Asian Dave's, I was pissed. The map Peace Corps had drawn me was total shit. It took thirty minutes to find it. We arrived and saw the mayonnaise-colored Peace Corps Jeep pulling out of the driveway. The cabbie waited for it to leave. Then he pulled up to the house. I grabbed my shit and stepped out. I handed him a ten and he scowled.

"Give me another," he spat.

"No way."

"Do it. I just drove you around for half an hour."

I didn't want to argue. I handed him a five.

"That's all you're getting," I said.

"Give me another five or I'll crush your head."

He glared at me over the lip of the window. I glared back at him.

"We spent a whole hour doing your fucking errands, and I didn't complain. You're not getting another manat outta me."

"Give it to me," he shouted.

I ignored him and walked up Dave's driveway. I knocked on the waratan door, but nobody answered. I looked back and saw the cabbie still staring at me from his window. I was afraid he might get wise and smash me against the waratan with the teeth of his Lada. I turned and knocked again. The cabbie honked his horn and yelled out "Hey." I looked over my shoulder casually.

"What do you want?" I said.

He crumpled his hand into a rock and shook it at me.

"If I catch you in the street, I'm gonna kill you, motherfucker," he yelled.

I snubbed my nose at him and spit in the wind. He revved his engine and screeched off. I stood there breathing out clouds of steam. A man and his little boy walked up. I asked the man if he knew where the new American was. He told me he was Dave's host father and that Dave was at School #1. I thanked him and got a cab. I was hoping I'd miss Peace Corps and Dick and Dora, the married couple I disliked. We pulled up and I saw Dick standing with one of Peace Corps' goons. I asked the two of them where Dave was. They pointed to an adjacent classroom.

"He's in there observing Dick's counterpart," the goon said. "You are welcome to watch."

I nodded and walked over there. Dick's counterpart was starting her lesson, "The Greatness of America." Dave was seated at the front of the class. He was kind of a scary-looking dude. He had a gigantic head that bulged at the front like an upside-down gourd. His eyes were wide and almond-shaped and seemed to blink independently of one another. He sat motionless with his hands folded and his tiny mouth half-open. If I'd seen the fucker in a barn late one night, I'm sure I'd have mistaken him for an alien. I grabbed a chair next to him and tipped my hat.

"Nice to meet you," I said. "Name's Johann."

Dave's eyes took turns blinking.

"Hello," he said. "I'm Dave."

I reached out and shook his hand. It was clammy and limp like he'd just had it in the crack of his ass for the past hour. I tried to keep cheery.

"So, what's your plan for today?" I asked.

"I'm gonna observe these classes," he said, tilting his head to one side. "Then I'm going home."

Get this fuckin' card, I thought.

"Have you eaten?"

"Yeah."

I left it be. Dick and Dora had surely convinced the kid that I was a wormy hunk of dog shit. I focused my attention on the lesson. When it ended, Dave turned to me.

"You don't have to stay here, you know," he said.

I could have decked him. Here I was on a school day out in Tejen observing a shit class and trying to make friends and the son of a bitch couldn't even give me a chance. I stood and gathered my things.

"Nice meeting you," I said.

FOR THE NEXT week, I hunkered in. During the day, I taught my classes and dealt with the minutiae of my registration with Azat. In the evening, I chilled in the warm kuhnýa with my host family and planned my COS trip to Africa:[85] overland from Cairo to Cape Town in 100 days. I had dinner at Baýram's. We talked of the upcoming election and who would be the Democratic candidate—Hillary or Obama. I restarted my French lessons with Jahan. Our first lesson was after class on the day I'd brought my Christmas gifts to school. I'd already given Azat his gift: a wine calendar. He'd been nonplussed but I didn't give a hot fuck. I knew Jahan would like her French books. I carried them in my backpack to her classroom. A few little squirts were still lingering around. They said, "*Salam mugallym*" and "Good morning teacher," despite it being afternoon. I patted them on the head. They squeaked and scampered out the door. I laughed and turned around. There was Jahan. She was seated at her desk in a green velvet dress. Her legs were crossed neatly. She was looking at me with her big hazel eyes. I smiled at her.

"Wow," she said.

I got the feeling that I might have farted. I reached down and fanned the air near my ass. I brought my hand up for a sniff. There was no smell. I walked over to Jahan and sat down. I asked her how she was doing. Her face popped into a red smile.

"Han-Guly, I have such a good new," she said.

"Oh?"

"Yes. The government will give me money to rebuild my house."

"Really? How much?"

"I don't know yet. I will find out in February."

"Shit, that's great news."

"Yeah, and you know what other good new I have?"

"Huh?"

"I'm taking a test this summer to try and get into university at Aşgabat."

"Good for you."

"And if I work for Peace Corps like you said, I'll have a job and

---

[85] Many volunteers forgo a paid ticket home and use both their readjustment allowance and the dollar amount of their airfare on a big trip after completing their service.

school and soon a home."

"Hey, and if I get you into the T-Program, you'll be able to go to America like Baýram."

"I know. This year looks good for me, Han-Guly. Very, very good."

I got the sudden urge to call her a cunt. For some reason, I wanted to degrade her and put her down, to take her budding dreams and tear them from her stupid head and stomp all over them like spring flowers. I quickly shifted topics.

"So how was your New Year's?" I asked.

"Great. I have no friends, so I just sat at home and watch TV."

"Really?"

"Yes, but it's okay. My life is looking much, much better now."

"Yeah," I said, wincing. "Once you have a good job and an education and a ticket to America, things will fall into place. Plus, I'm sure you'll make a bunch of international friends, so it won't matter that you don't have friends here. The people that shunned you will be stuck in this turd pot forever, and you can just show them your middle finger and be on your way."

Jahan smiled. I smiled with her. When it started to hurt, I reached into my backpack. I pulled out the French books and handed them to her. She took them and held them to her chest.

"Are these for me?" she asked.

"*Oui*, Merry Christmas."

"Oh, I was right. My life is getting much better."

I didn't say anything.

I WALKED HOME feeling terrible. I knew the reality of Jahan's life would make it almost impossible for her to break free. Had she just been a dim-witted switch-chewer, GHB would have been enough. But no, she had to go and get herself a bunch'a freakin' dreams and plans and goals and stack them all on top of one another till they formed a grand rainbow staircase leading all the way up God's cloudy asshole. Fuck. I needed something to distract me. When I got home, I changed into my sweats and went into the kuhnýa with my travel books. I set to planning my Africa trip in earnest. After COSing, I was gonna get about eight grand for my readjustment allowance,[86] and I figured what better way to readjust than by leaping into the black heart of Africa with two crummy shoes and my head on fire. I read about Ethiopia and Kenya and Tanzania. As I was getting to the part about the crystal-clear waters of Zanzibar, I heard a knock at the door. I thought it might be Merdan fucking with me.

"*Kim?*" I spat. "Who is it?"

The door opened and Azat poked his head in. All four of his little gravestones were showing.

"I already gave you your wine calendar," I said.

"Haha. Zis not about Christmas present," he said. "Please, come outside for one minute."

I threw my pencil down and stood up.

"What's this about then?' I said, slipping on my coat.

"You will see."

I smirked and followed him outside. I was praying this wasn't about my damn registration. I walked through the waratan door. A black Benz with tinted windows was parked in the street. The air around me was freezing. I crossed my arms over my chest and rubbed my shoulders.

"Will you please tell me what the hell this is about?"

Azat grinned.

"We find zis man," he said.

"Which man?"

"Za man who you say yell at you and say he will kill you. Za man from taxi in Tejen."

The ugly incident popped in my head. I vaguely remembered having mentioned something to Azat. I never dreamed the fucker

---

[86] Volunteers are given a readjustment allowance after they finish their service so that they may financially readjust themselves to life, either back home or somewhere abroad.

would go out and find the guy. I was skeptical but curious.

"You really found that cabbie who threatened me?"

Azat made a goofy face and nodded. He pranced over to the Benz and yelled, "Ho." The driver's side door clicked open. A log cabin of a man stepped out. He was so heavy that the car grew a foot taller. When he stood all seven feet erect, I got a look at him. He had a crew cut and a wide steel jaw. His hands were the size of stingrays and riddled with silver rings. He was wearing a black leather jacket that sucked around his stony muscles. His eyes were two angry slashes that burned into mine. I scratched my neck.

"Who is this guy?" I asked.

"My friend," Azat said.

He nodded to Humungo. Humungo opened the passenger side door and reached in with his giant hand like he was reaching in the fridge for a can of Pepsi. He pulled out another, smaller man. The man was messing with his hair and shivering. I squinted at him. It took me a second, but then I recognized him as the Tejen cabbie who'd threatened me. Azat went over and put his hand on the man's shoulder. He flinched.

"Han-Guly," Azat said. "Zis man has somesing to tell you."

The cabbie darted his eyes from me to Azat to Humungo. He tried to speak but his chin was quivering so violently he couldn't get the words out.

"*Oňa diýsene*," Azat shouted. "Tell him."

The cabbie looked down at the ground. He made a circle in the dirt with the tip of his shoe.

"*Diýsene*," Azat spat. "Do it."

The cabbie looked up at me. I could see the fear swimming in his eyes like little sharks. He opened his mouth, but nothing came out. I think he thought he'd said everything required of him but didn't realize he hadn't said a word. Humungo clipped him on the back of his head with his airplane wing of a hand. The cabbie spit his words out.

"I . . . I'm sorry," he said in Turkmen. "I didn't mean to be mean.

It's just that I drove you around a lot and I thought, well, maybe you would give me some more money. I am very, very sorry."

I looked the cabbie in the eyes. I looked all the way down through his skull and neck and into his ribcage where his miserable yellow heart fluttered and flopped. I wanted him to understand that if he ever did anything like this again, I'd sic Humungo on him. I mean, you just don't go around threatening somebody's life over a measly twenty-five cents. Once I felt he'd gotten the message, I eased my glare.

"I forgive you," I said.

The cabbie let out a sigh of relief.

"Oh, thank you," he said, bowing his head and shuffling backwards.

He bumped into the wall of meat behind him. He shrieked, slipped back in the car and shut the door. I looked over at Azat.

"What's going to happen to him?" I asked.

He put his hand on my shoulder and made a little O with his mouth.

"You won't worry about zis man again," he said.

He got in the car. Humungo started the engine and pulled up to the intersection. I thought he'd turn left into town. He made a right and peeled off into the desert.

THE WEEK ROLLED by. Azat and I never mentioned the cabbie again. We finished my registration and taught our classes together. I was glad when the weekend hit so I could drink and write and forget about all that shit. That Sunday I got a call from Peace Corps. It was Maya, our secretary, reminding me to come into Aşgabat for MST[87] the following Thursday. I thanked her and hung the phone up.

Thank God, I thought. Five full nights of blowing up away from this place.

I taught happily for the next two days. That Tuesday night, I

---

[87] Mid-service training.

cleaned my room and packed. I cut early the next morning. I said goodbye to my host fam and our dog Laika, who'd been extra nice to me lately for some reason. The little guy was lying by the waratan door licking his balls. I walked up to him and scratched his belly.

"Good *booooooy*," I said.

He stopped licking his balls and licked my hand. I patted him on the head, then left for the awtostanzia. I got a cab directly to Adalat. I went up to Brooke's place with all my crap and knocked on the door. She opened it in her pajamas. She rubbed her eyes and blinked.

"Gelr," she said.

This was a nickname she'd given me after the threesome incident. It came from the Turkmen word *gelmek*, which means to come. I'd given her the nickname, Learnr. I'm not sure why.

"Learnr," I yelled back.

We hugged and closed the door. Brooke raised a finger and bounced off into her room. She came back holding a bottle of Jack Daniels.

"I got this for Christmas," she said, smiling.

I dropped my bags and slapped my forehead.

"Jesus Christ, Brooke. It's only noon."

"And?"

MST WAS A joke. When we weren't being water-boarded with safety and security rants, we were playing silly cultural games, watching inspirational videos, or listening to star volunteers brag about their accomplishments. The only thing good was that Harry promised to do away with 24s and 48s.

"You are all adults," he said. "This means that during the week, you will work at your sites. But the weekends are yours to spend as you see fit. All you have to do is call and tell us where you'll be."

We took this with a pinch of salt. At the very least, we'd have a bit more mobility. The other aspects of our MST aren't even worth mentioning. We washed everything away with booze in the evenings.

As we drank, two topics were on our lips. The lesser of the two was my threesome. People wanted to know what had actually transpired between me, Iris, and Candice in that little room before Christmas. My answer every time was, "I don't kiss and tell." The greater of the two topics involved Truman. Rumors were going around that he was to be admin sep'd. He hadn't been present at any of the meetings. When we asked Harry about it, he said, "I told Truman to go to his site and get me something. That's all you need to know."

On our last day, I got word that Truman was at the Ak. I asked the reception what room he was in, and it took the idiots twenty minutes to find him. I went up there and pushed the door open. Truman sat on the bed with a group of volunteers in a circle around him. Everyone was crying. Truman saw me, wiped his eyes quickly, and slipped his glasses back on. I sat down next to him and put my arm around his shoulder.

"Please tell me this isn't what I think it is," I said.

A volunteer broke down and left the room. The others followed her and left me and Truman alone. Truman took a moment to gather his thoughts. Then he glanced at me tenderly through his glasses.

"They're admin sep'ing me," he said.

"Fucking assholes," I screamed.

I pitched a fit in the middle of the room. I threw pillows and cushions and bottles all over the place. One bottle had some alcohol of unknown provenance still left in it. I swigged it down and sat back next to Truman.

"You finished?" he asked.

"Yes, now tell me what the fuck happened."

"Well . . ."

He told me about how three weeks prior he'd stayed four nights in Mary with his T-16 girlfriend Tammy without informing Peace Corps. He'd thought it was all good until PC called him in under the pretense of giving him a dental exam and then had given him the boot. I was in shock. Not two weeks prior, I'd pulled a similar move with Zack. I told this to Truman. He shrugged.

"There might be other reasons that they're admin sep'ing me," he said.

"Oh?" I said, raising my eyebrows.

"Yeah. Harry said he'd received a letter from my site decrying all my shortcomings as a volunteer. He said the letter mentioned my only teaching nine hours a week with no clubs, and that I once puked in the bushes at a toý."

"Good Lord, that's nothing. I hardly teach more than you, and I've puked in a dozen bushes at a dozen toýs."

Truman pulled out a cigarette and lit it. He filled his cheeks with smoke then made a tiny O with his lips and blew the smoke out slowly. He ashed his cigarette and fixed his glasses. Then he looked me in the eyes.

"There might have been one other thing," he said.

"Yeah, I thought so. Spill it, you little turd."

"Well, over the summer, I had an incident with the host sister of one of the volunteers in my welaýat."

"Oh?"

"Yeah, I was drunk one night, and she came over in a miniskirt."

"Uh-huh."

"And basically, one thing led to another and she went down on me."

"Jesus Cluster Fuck. How old was she?"

"Sixteen."

"Shit. And lemme guess, word got around and eventually, someone told Peace Corps."

"Exactly. Peace Corps sent a guy to get the girl's statement, but she wouldn't snitch. This infuriated them, so they waited for some other excuse to throw me out."

"You gonna fight it?"

"Yep."

"How?"

"I'm going to concentrate on the letter. I'm of the opinion that Harry solicited it from my *oblastnost* so he could obtain grounds to admin sep me. If this is true, I'm going to find out."

"How the fuck are you gonna do that?"

"I'm going to use the Freedom of Information Act. Everything Peace Corps has ever written, recorded, said on the phone about me, I'm going to demand access to. If after receiving all this information, I find sufficient evidence to suggest a conspiracy against me, I'm going to hire a lawyer and take staff to court."

"Damn, that's intense."

Truman stubbed his cigarette out and crossed his legs at the knee.

"You've never seen me really pissed off, have you, Johann?" he said.

"I guess not. So, what's the first step?"

"I'm going to write a missive explaining myself to Peace Corps. It will be a testament to my innocence. If they don't accept it, I'll hand them a copy of the FOIA."

"Wow. So, this is pretty much Cluster Fuck's Last Stand?"

Truman grabbed his laptop and unfolded it.

"Yes," he said. "Now please get out and don't bother me for the next three hours. I have to write this shit."

TRUMAN FINISHED HIS missive in time for all of us to have an early dinner at the Zip. We ordered piles of steaming shashlik and washed it all down with tons of icy piss-water beer. We got a bottle of arak. We poured a bunch of shots then each of us gave a teary-eyed toast to Truman.

The rest of the night was a blur of discos and dancing and hard drinking. My only real memory was of me and Truman at the Ak Mezzanine bar, pounding flaming sambucas. After our fourth, I nearly choked. My vision went hazy and I wiped my eyes. I pulled my fingers away and the tears were dislodged. They ran down my cheeks in droves. I put my arm around Truman and hugged him close.

"I'm going to fucking miss you," I cried. "You were the first person I got in trouble with all those months ago when we played hooky at the Daýhan and now your little ass is leaving."

I buried my face in his shoulder and sobbed. He lit a cigarette and sat there looking annoyed. I could feel his heart beating rapidly through his jacket. I never told him.

19

Truman was admin sep'd. I spent the next three days lamenting. I slept till noon and filled my piss bottles. I ate all the granola bars and beef jerky and Velveeta Cheese shells my folks had sent me. I sat by the crummy peç I'd gotten from PC and planned my Africa trip. On occasion, I snuck out into the freshly fallen snow and petted Laika as he lay in a little ball on the pile of hay behind the torture chamber/outhouse.

When February 14 rolled around, I decided it was time to teach. I walked through the frozen mud to On Yet and did five lessons back to back. Afterwards, I did a Big Kids Club. Aman was there, and he'd brought some old English test written by some Turkish dimwit who'd used the most convoluted and complicated grammar he could. I tried my damnedest to unravel it all for my students. There was to be an Olympiad[88] the following week, and according to Aman, they had to know "all grammars."

I walked home feeling marginally decent about myself. I figured a nice long nap followed by a bit of good writing was in order. I went to the torture chamber and took a dump. As I walked out, I heard a clamor behind the wall. It sounded like wet wood being split. I went around back to the trash field to see what was up. I found Merdan

---

[88] A competition in various subjects among students from different schools.

standing next to the wall. He had a blood-soaked butcher's knife in his hand and was wearing a white T-shirt streaked with red. All around him in bowls were pink and purple cubes of organ meat. The sheep he'd just slaughtered was dangling by its hind legs with a hollowed-out torso and no skin or head. Merdan kicked his chin at me and went back to it. He hacked off the legs and ribs and spine and put them in the bowl with the head and hooves. It dawned on me that this would have been an awesome thing to have videoed. Hoping Merdan would kill another sheep, I ran upstairs and grabbed my camera.

When I came back, Merdan had finished dismembering the sheep. He was hunched over a yellow brick and sharpening his knife across it. He heard me walking toward him and looked up. A streak of dark blood was across his cheek. His eyes caught my camera and turned the color of the blood.

"What the hell is that for?" he asked.

"Nothing. Are you gonna kill another sheep?"

"No. I'm going to kill a goat this time. But you can't film it."

"Why not? It'll be really interesting for my family in America. They never get to see stuff like this."

"Oh, bullshit. You told me people in America eat meat."

I scrunched my eyebrows. Then I eased them.

"Yes, we eat meat," I said. "But that doesn't mean we kill the animal. The butcher at the big bazaar does that for us. Then he packages it and we buy it."

"Well, I don't care. I don't want you filming this."

"Merdan, please."

"No," he said, swiping the knife downwards.

"Why?"

"Because . . . I don't want your family to think I'm a bad person."

His face tightened. I smiled.

"Merdan," I said, "they're not gonna think you're a bad person. They know you're killing this goat to feed your family and not just for fun."

His face loosened. I put my hand on his shoulder.

"It'll be cool. Don't worry."

One of Merdan's neighbors came staggering up. He was cradling a goat with its hooves tied together. He plopped it on the ground in front of us and dusted his hands.

"Welp," he said. "Here it is."

It was a smaller goat with carrot-sized horns. It had a burgundy coat that tapered off into white around the legs. Its eyes were milky and dumb. They stared off into nothingness as their owner lay there silently. I clicked my camera on. Merdan flashed an irritated look and grabbed the goat by the tie. He dragged it through a bed of rocks and over to a bloody hole in the ground. He placed its neck over the hole and grabbed his knife. I pointed the camera at him and pressed Record. He looked up at me.

"Turn it off," he said.

I lowered the camera. I was starting to feel like a dick. Just the same, I couldn't let this moment pass. I strained to think of a way. I remembered Merdan's weakness; the one thing that made him buckle at the knees with goo-goo eyes and a mouthful of drool. I leaned into his ear and cupped my mouth.

"I'll buy you some shashlik," I whispered.

"Promise?" he said, standing up.

"Yes."

"Two times?"

"Only if you let me film the whole thing."

"Deal," he said, slapping his hands together.

He crouched back down over the goat. He dug his fingers into the fur around its neck and felt for its arteries. The goat remained silent. It looked almost content. This must have seemed like another part of regular farm life: being moved from one den to the next, being tied up while the younger goats fed first, being sold and riding in the back of a truck to another farm. The goat had no reason to think anything bad was about to happen.

Merdan took a deep breath and picked up the knife. He grabbed the goat by the left horn and sawed at its throat. The goat screamed like a little girl. Its body jiggled and jerked as its neck opened up into a steaming right angle. Every time Merdan hit a new artery, it sprayed blood everywhere. I jumped back so it wouldn't hit my shoes. My hands were now shaking. I could barely keep the camera steady. Merdan sawed and hacked and sliced. The goat stopped moving and the blood-flow trickled. Merdan pressed down and cut through the last piece of skin. Then he gripped a tuft of fur between the goat's horns and raised its head for me to see. Its eyes were two white marbles. Its tongue was the tail of a dead fish. Its neck was a dripping flower pot. Its ears were two sad twigs. I filmed it with pain in my heart. Merdan smirked and dropped the head into a bucket. He went over to the body and started cutting. He removed the hooves and genitals then sliced away the coat. When the goat was naked, Merdan hung it by the hind legs against the wall. Then he turned and faced me.

"Are you sure your family is gonna wanna see this part?" he asked.

"Oh, yes."

He shrugged and turned back. He lifted his knife and stuck the point to the belly of the carcass. He made a wide incision all the way down to the ribcage. A basket of grey alien fruits came bulging out. I opened my mouth and pointed.

"Are those its guts?"

He glared at me over his shoulder with one eye. I closed my mouth and concentrated on filming. He moved on to the organs. He sliced them out one by one and placed them in a series of bowls. The stench was horrific. It smelled like a dumpster full of soiled bum skivvies. I wiped my eyes and cupped my nose. Merdan put the knife down and grabbed a bucket of water. He set it next to the bowl with the intestines. Then he reached in and grabbed a string of gut. He pulled it through his clenched fist. As he did this, he whistled "Twisted Nerve" from *Kill Bill*. A pile of slimy brown pellets formed on the other end of the string. It terrified me to think that in a few short hours the intestines that carried those pellets would be floating around in my soup.

We took the organs and quartered carcass to Patma. She called the girls out and they sliced it all up and put it in the cauldron. That night we had dograma with boiled liver on the side. I ate as much as necessary to assuage my guilt, then I slipped the rest in a baggy. Once everyone had gone to bed, I snuck outside. I went over to Laika's hay bed and put the baggy in front of him. He buried his snout in it and sauced away. I pet him down the spine.

"Happy Valentine's Day, buddy," I said.

LAIKA WALKED ME to school the next day. It wasn't the first time he'd done this, but this time an extra little something was in his step. Every car that drove by, he barked at. Every person that walked too close to me, he snarled and growled and bumped away. When another dog crossed my path, he chased it off into the dirt. When a bird or even a bug flew into my space, he jumped up and tried to snap it from the air. For twenty solid minutes, he was my personal bodyguard. And even though he was stout and dirty and weak in the bones, he had heart and packed a helluva bite, and for that, I felt safe.

When we arrived at On Yet I went to the kiçi çaýhana and bought him a fitçi. He took it from my hand and wolfed it down in chokes. As he ate, I petted him down the back. A year prior, he'd have bitten my fingers off for attempting such a stunt, but now he was all about it. He finished eating and rolled over onto his belly. I scratched him up and down. He kicked his hind legs and whimpered. His tongue flopped out of his mouth like a wet sock. His eyes went goofy and melted with gladness. The passing Turkmen gawked.

"What the hell is the American doing to that dog?" one of them mumbled.

Laika's pink worm poked out. I almost ran with the comment. It tickled me that I could shock the rubberneckers on my own terms. Still, I decided against giving Laika the time of his life in public. I finished scratching his belly and patted him on the butt. He jumped up and licked my mouth and left a trail of hot slime across my lips. I laughed and pushed him away.

"I've gotta teach now, boy," I said. "Time to go home."

He cocked his head and stared at me. His eyes grew sad as I backed up and walked off. I contemplated playing with him for a few more minutes. When I turned around, he was gone.

For the rest of the month, I made it a point to spend more time with Laika. Not that I hadn't spent any time with him before, but I just felt like going out of my way seeing as how he'd been an extra good boy as of late. I took him with me to the dükan to buy my snacks and booze. I let him sit next to me on my special frozen bench while I wrote my poems. I hung out with him on his haystack while he snorted and licked his balls. I even took him on my walks way out into the desert where the ground was like freezer-burnt cookie dough and the sky hung over us like an infinite block of ice. I watched the sun set with him from my balcony. I gave him all my food scraps and even some of the good stuff. I whistled tunes to his barking while I crapped in the outhouse. And every night before bed, I sat with him on the tapçan in the blistering cold and we pointed our noses in the air and looked up at the billions of twinkling stars.

One evening I got a phone call. Patma answered it but didn't recognize the voice. I picked it up expecting to hear Brooke on the other end. A man spoke instead.

"How's it hangin', partner?" he said.

I was baffled at first. Then the twang hit me.

"Jimmy," I cried. "How the fuck you been?"

"Purdy good. Just out here in Türkmenhalk freezin' ma' nuts off."

"Yeah, I hear ya. How long has it been since we've kicked it?"

"Since the camping trip last spring when yer ass got bit by that spider."

"That's right. Fuck, we're long overdue."

"That's what I was thinkin'. You wanna roll out here this

weekend, get fucked up, maybe make some burritos?"

"Sounds like a plan."

I woke up the next morning feeling grand. My head wasn't clouded from drinking or lack of sleep and the knowledge that I was going to Jimmy's that weekend had me feeling happy as a motherfucker. I was determined to make it to school on time. I hopped out of bed at nine-thirty, took a refreshing bucket shower, and threw on my suit. I plugged in my earbuds and switched my iPod to "Disco Hits." As I strolled out the waratan door, the Bee Gees were bumping under my feet. As always, Laika was lying on the adjacent dirt mound with his back to me. He looked like a slab of filthy marshmallow. I funneled my hands around my mouth and inhaled.

"*Gooooood booooy.*"

He lay on his side. I squinted my eyes and scratched my head.

"You coot boy," I said. "You're so lazy this morning."

I hiked up my pack and walked up to him. I reached down to pet his hind legs. He didn't seem to be aware of my presence. In fact, he didn't seem to be aware of anything at all. I pulled my hand back and stood above him. I hoped he would suddenly jerk to life with one leg like he usually did. He just lay there like a pressed shirt. My face sagged.

"Laika?" I said.

There was no response; just a rustling of fur as the wind blew over his body. I noticed that one of his legs was so stiff it didn't even touch the ground. My eyes welled with tears.

"Get up, boy," I said.

He didn't move. My face cracked apart.

"Laika," I cried.

I stood for a moment and stared at his lifeless body. His eyes were closed tightly as if he'd forced himself into a deep, troubled sleep. I wanted to wake him from it, but I knew I couldn't. I did the only thing I could do.

"Goodbye buddy," I said.

I imagined a little smile descending across his lips. It was as if his miserable cage was unlocked and he was finally set free.

SCHOOL WAS A blur. I taught as much as my mind could bear. As I walked home, I wondered about Laika's body. Patma had told me after hearing of his death that the street sweepers would come and take it away. This had shocked and infuriated me. I'd wanted to give him a proper burial, but I knew it would only incur laughter and ridicule from the Turkmen. Dogs were regarded as nothing more than appliances to be made vicious for protection from thieves. Burying one with any kind of ceremony would be like doing so for an alarm clock or a radio.

In an act of avoidance, I stopped by the dellekhana. My hair was long anyways, and I needed a shave. I went inside and sat down. Six people were in front of me. Their eyes were on me as I waited. I wanted to slug them all black. I looked up with a grimace tattooed to my face. The first person I saw was Aman. He looked exactly the same: the same hiked-up slacks, the same pointy shoes, the same puffy brown jacket, the same cubic head, the same sloppily parted hair, the same patches of bright red acne. He gawked at me with his fish-tank eyes.

"Hello Han-Guly," he said.

"Hello, Aman."

His eyes darted around the room.

"What's wrong?" he asked.

"Nothing."

I tucked my chin under my collar and faced the floor. Everyone in the place was now staring harder than ever. I could feel my bones unhinge. I wanted the conversation to stop, but Aman, being the social genius that he is, missed all my signals. He shifted his long legs and leaned in.

"Are you well?" he asked.

"No, Aman. I'm not well. In fact, I'm very shitty."

"What happened?"

"My dog died," I said, looking him in the eyes.

His face jumped with astonishment.

"I am sorry," he said.

His voice was replete with sympathy. It was almost as if he knew the depth of my pain. I started to feel guilty for having been so curt with him. Just as I was about to apologize, his eyes widened.

"Wait a minute," he said, with a little smirk. "Did you say, 'dog died?'"

There was a moment of silence between us. His smirk grew into a full-on smile. When I didn't return it, he cupped his mouth. I could tell he was on the verge of laughter.

"Yes," I said. "My fucking dog died."

I was teeming with rage. If I'd had a knife, Aman's future as a father would have been shaky at best. I could tell he was scared. Before I did anything stupid, I left. I walked through the park and to my house. Laika's body was gone and I was glad. I went up to my room and threw off my stuff. I collapsed on my bed and tried to nap. Before I passed out, Patma rapped on my stairs. She called me for dinner in the family room. I wasn't that hungry but figured I'd eat. I went down and grabbed a bowl.

Dinner was as expected. Everyone was slurping their shitty çorba and laughing at vapid Turkish sitcoms without the slightest bit of sadness over Laika's death. Seeing this blatant display of heartlessness sent me into a stupor. I just sat there, sipping çorba from my çemçe and staring at the wall. Merdan tried to snap me out of it by being silly and cracking jokes. I ignored him.

I finished my food and went upstairs. I entered my room and sat on my bed. My eyes crumbled into hot water. I raised my hands to my face and spasmodically sobbed into them. My head was flooded with memories of Laika. Each one jabbed at my heart and sent me further and further down the spiral of grief. No longer would he greet me in the morning with his sharp bark and wagging tail. No longer would he accompany me to school and chase other dogs and cars and people away to protect me. No longer would I get to sneak him treats after dinner and pet him on the snout while he wolfed them down. No longer would I get to go to the outhouse in the middle of the night and see him sacked out on his favorite stack of hay. No longer would I get to wrestle with him and bounce around the yard. No longer would I get to have him rest his chin on my thigh while we sat on the tapçan together and looked up at the night sky.

Losing Laika wasn't just losing a dog, it was losing a friend. And in this place, friends were hard to come by. It was a tragic and unnecessary loss. The only thing I had to console me was that no matter what, up to his very last horrible moment, Laika knew he was loved.

In the days after his death, I found out that Laika was most likely poisoned. Patma informed me that in Gurbagahowda, as in other Turkmen villages, the police control the stray dog population by driving around in their squad cars and tossing old meat laced with strychnine out the windows. Since dogs in Turkmenistan have no collars, licenses, or ID tags, the police have no way of knowing if the dogs they are poisoning have owners. Laika was probably just hungry and looking for food and some shithead cop saw this and decided to end his life for it.

I WOKE UP the next morning feeling groggy and sick. Laika's death was weighing on me like a sack of dead fish. Thankfully, it was Friday and I had Jimmy's to look forward to. I took a bucket shower, packed a small bag of crap, and split. My time with Jimmy helped. We cooked good food and guzzled cheap booze and wandered all around his hood. I did a bit of filming. Jimmy was paranoid about this because of the KNB. In the end, nobody bothered us. I left with some great footage of Türkmenhalk and all the shrubland, muddy lakes, and creepy, busted-ass Russian cemeteries on the outskirts.

I was still somewhat depressed when I got back to GBH. I did almost nothing. I may have taught a class here and there, the odd club, but other than that it was pretty much me clipping my nut hairs and popping zits on my taint. I got a letter from Iris, the hickey threesome girl. It started off with her asking how I was, then it devolved into a three-page explanation of how what happened between us was entirely her choice and how she wasn't a loose woman, but one simply trying to quell her loneliness and sexual hunger with my nicely shaped cock. I farted on the letter and returned it to its envelope. Later on, I was informed by Merdan that Laika had not been poisoned but stabbed through the stomach with a long needle by someone who intended to rob our place and didn't want to have to deal with a dog. The whole thing made me ill. A healing dinner at Baýram's was in order.

That Friday I cruised over to his place. He wasn't expecting me, but he welcomed me just the same. His wife served us two beautiful plates of palow. I told him I'd recently visited Jimmy, one of his language students during training. He was pleased to hear this and asked how he was. I told him he was fine and mentioned our walk. I told him how Jimmy had been paranoid about me filming because of the KNB. This brought us to the topic of freedom. Baýram gave me his full mind on this one.

"The difference between Turkmen peoples and the rest of the world," he said, sipping his çaý, "is that Turkmen peoples don't want fight for their freedom. They are scared to getting hurt or killed. So long time we have had no war, and nobody wants to start again. Just keep a quiet life. But this is problem because with just quiet life, we cannot have change, but only same presidents who do same things and not take care of our country like they should."

This made me think of the rival faction I'd heard about during training. They had attempted a coup against Türkmenbaşy's regime but failed. Peace Corps hadn't explained much more than that. The truth of the whole matter had been burning a small hole in the back of my head.

"Didn't somebody try to overthrow Türkmenbaşy a few years ago?" I asked.

Baýram looked up from his palow.

"Yes, but he was failed."

"What happened? Who was this man?"

"His name was Boris Shikhmuradov. He was half-Armenian, half-Turkmen man from Aşgabat who worked as ambassador to China. Later he quit because he did not like Türkmenbaşy's government. He believed it was 'oppressive state.' He was right."

"What did he do about this?"

"He gathered all information about corruption and went to Europe to make plan for coup and for new government. He was there for many years and he talk to the Turkmen people with radio and told them their government is bad and that Türkmenbaşy do evil things and that we should join him to fight against this."

"Jesus. What did you think about that?"

Baýram curled his fingers and shook them in the air.

"I thought it was great thing," he said. "I wanted this man to be president because he was smart, and he had good plan. He wanted new education system, new roads, open borders, many things. He wanted to make Turkmenistan open, modern country. Not like Türkmenbaşy."

"So why did he fail?"

"Because he did not know the people. He worked with government and traveled a lot, so he was not with locals much. So, when he comes to radio telling them to start revolution, they think, Who is this man? And they are scared to fight."

"Did anyone support him at all?"

"Some, maybe one thousand people. But this is not enough. When he sneak back to Aşgabat to start revolution, he saw that only small number of people will want to help him. He was brave man, so he continued anyway because he thought if people will see him and others, they will join to fight for their freedom. But they didn't. When Boris went to protest in streets with others, nobody came except police and they arrest everyone. We think now that they kill them all in desert, including Boris."

"Holy shit," I said, pinching the bridge of my nose. "And no one's done a fucking thing since, huh?"

He looked down at the klionka.

"I am afraid no one will ever."

IN THE DAYS after that dinner with Baýram, I wondered about Boris Shikhmuradov. I was inclined to ask my host family and a few neighbors, but I thought better of it, lest the KNB catch wind. As there was no internet in GBH, I consulted my Encarta encyclopedia. My extensive search for the man turned up zilch. I decided to ask Azat. I knew he'd been in the military and was thus privy to the comings and goings of the Turkmen government, and that no matter what, the guy wasn't a snitch. I invited him out to the uly çayhana one afternoon. After we'd finished a few plates of manty and *stakans* of vodka, I brought up Shikhmuradov. Azat clicked his tongue.

"Hey zis man is terrorist," he said. "He sell weapons for money to fight against our government."

"Really? I thought he did radio broadcasts from Europe to unite the Turkmen against Türkmenbaşy's oppressive regime? Then when he came to start a revolution, no one joined because they were too afraid."

He put a cigarette to the corner of his mouth and lit it.

"Bah," he said, blowing smoke out the other corner. "He was terrorist. He even write book confessing all crimes."

"Seriously?"

"Yes, I have zis book. I will give later."

"Okay."

Now I was boiling with curiosity. The following night, I went to Baýram's again for dinner. I mentioned the book to him. He laughed.

"That is false book," he said. "The government give it to us to read when they catch Shikhmuradov. It is propaganda that government says he wrote, but they really wrote. It says, 'I am Boris. I am terrorist. I try to kill Turkmen peoples and ruin government. I apologize.' It is so big lie. Even Osama bin Laden will never say he is terrorist. I hated that book so much. When they give it to me, I ripped it and threw it to trash."

That was the end of the discussion. A few days later Azat gave the book to me, but from what I could understand, it was pretty much as Baýram had said. I stopped halfway through and put it aside. Doing the same with thoughts of Boris Shikhmuradov was not as easy.

20

THE FOLLOWING MONTH was uneventful. The biggest thing that happened was a tiff I had with Brooke during which she laughed at my lack of computer skills and I laughed at her lack of Turkmen skills and she called me a dick and I walked out on her, and a week or so later we both said sorry and drank down a full two bottles of vodka to heal the wound.

Besides that, Merdan brought home a new dog. It was a puppy of about three weeks that he'd found in the streets, and the little thing was dead within days because Merdan had poured a poisonous solution all over him to kill his fleas but ended up just killing him. I also bought a cell phone. I had my folks call me on it while I was in Aşgabat as that's where it worked best. I told them about my trip to Africa. They were none too pleased but accepted it without protest, especially since I was already working hard on the itinerary for the trip they were planning to see me in July. I visited a few volunteers and they visited me. On one such occasion, everyone but yours truly took their shirts off and Tex made out with a guy and Dimuira made out with a girl and I sat back with my drink and videoed the whole thing. It was an okay month for the most part, but I did spend a lot of it thinking about old Boris and the conversation I'd had with Baýram about freedom. This invariably got me thinking about Jahan. I knew she badly wanted to escape the clutches of this place but just didn't know how or when. Since January, I'd seen her a number of times. Besides writing a letter of recommendation for her to go to Kazakhstan on a two-day teacher training program, which would be her first time out of Turkmenistan, not much happened between us.

On a Tuesday toward the middle of April, I went to her classroom for our French lesson. She was sitting at her desk in a faded flowery dress. I walked up next to her and sat down. A Turkmen newspaper was opened across her lap. She smiled at me and said, "Hello." Then she pointed to an ad in the classifieds.

"This is opening for English/Turkmen translator at Ministry of Foreign Affairs in Aşgabat," she said. "I read it and I have all criteria except one."

"What's that?"

"I don't know how to use a computer."

I squared my lips and thought for a moment.

"Well, I'm no expert with computers, but I can bring my laptop over to your house next week and at least teach you how to use it. That is, of course, if you can convince your mother to let me."

Jahan's mother had been married to my host father Durdy's brother, Nedir. One night, Nedir had a heart attack. My host family claims that because of money issues, Jahan's mother had refused to take him to the hospital, a move that had resulted in his death. After that, the families split apart and cursed one another. Since I lived under Durdy's roof, I was unwelcome at Jahan's.

Jahan looked up at me solemnly.

"I will let you know next week," she said.

"Great. We can work on your résumé then too."

For the rest of the week, I familiarized myself with the programs on my computer. I was determined to see Jahan leave Gurbagahowa, even if it was for a crappy job with the government in Aşgabat. I'd already spent an inordinate amount of time getting hammered, fucking women, and feeling sorry for myself. In my mind, doing this one decent thing for another person might in some small way put the disaster that was my service on an even keel.

THAT MONDAY, I went to see Jahan. I was in good spirits as she'd called me the previous day and told me that her mother had okayed the visit. I wanted to ask her if I should bring any gifts for her mom. I found her sitting at her desk drooping like a dog ear in the sun. I sat down next to her and put my hand gently on her shoulder. She flinched, and a tear jerked loose from her eye. She grabbed a napkin and wiped it away immediately. Then she forced a smile.

"What the hell is it?" I said. "Did your mom change her mind?"

"No," she said. "It's my brother."

"What about him? I thought he was in the army."

"He was. But he came home this weekend. My mother told him that you will come over to teach me computers and write résumé for job in Aşgabat. He got very angry and said I don't need to know computers and that I must stay home and be a stupid *öý hojalykçy*."[89]

She buried her face in her hands and sobbed.

"That asshole," I screamed. "What the fuck does he care what you do with your life?"

My blood was sizzling. Had I been even half-drunk, I might have gone over to Jahan's house and beaten the sour sack of bile out of her brother. I took a few deep breaths and calmed myself.

"He is always this way," she said. "Since I was a child, he tells me what to do and where to go. And even I am older than him three years, but he doesn't care because my father is dead, so he is man of the house and now makes all rules."

"Jahan," I said, axing my hand at her. "He's a twenty-three-year-old illiterate ditch-digger. How the hell does he know what's best for you? You're a gifted English teacher who speaks five languages and received a degree from one of the most prestigious universities in the country. That asshole doesn't know his dick from a stick."

Jahan giggled. The tears around her eyes jiggled like jelly. I ripped a tissue from the box and handed it to her. She took it and blew her nose.

"You know the meaning of the word asshole, right?"

---

[89] Housewife.

"Yes," she said, wiping her eyes and giggling again. "You taught it to me."

"Well, that's what your brother is. He's an asshole."

I yelled the word out with all my lung power. Jahan cracked up.

"Oh, fuck it," I said, slamming my open palm on the desk. "I'll bring my laptop to school tomorrow, and after class, I'll teach you everything I know about computers, which isn't a lot. Plus, we'll write your damn résumé. Howzat sound?"

Jahan grinned. I grabbed my crap and stood up.

"Be sure to give your asshole brother a hug for me," I said. "See you tomorrow."

I SPENT THE following afternoon teaching Jahan how to use the computer. By evening, she had a working knowledge of Word, Excel, Explorer, Photoshop, and Encarta. I taught her how to set up an email account, and how to write and send emails. I even managed to type her a decent résumé, which I loaded on to my memory stick and gave to her to take to Aşgabat. The next day, Wednesday, was the last day she could apply for the job. I was pissed at her for having waited so long but glad she'd decided to tell her brother to go fuck himself. I wished her the best of luck and cut home. I crashed early that night and spent the next day fiddling with my dingleberries and worrying. I prayed Jahan hadn't bungled the whole thing or frozen at the gates. I slept fitfully then woke up the next morning and went to school. I taught a few lessons and clubs. At 4:00 p.m., I went over to Jahan's. Her classroom was empty except for one student. I asked the little guy where she was, and he told me the computer room. I raced over there with my heart glugging syrup. I was terrified I'd find her slouched over and sobbing, her arms hanging lifelessly, her hands curled into little balls of defeat.

I arrived at the computer room door. I pushed it open and looked in. I saw Jahan sitting at the back monitor. She was wearing a dress that was so blue it made the blue walls around her look white.

She turned away from the monitor and looked at me. For the first time since I'd known her, she was wearing lipstick and blush and eyeliner. She had a long gold chain draped around her neck. It sparkled in the sunlight coming through the open window. I threw my hands in the air.

"Jahan," I cried.

She flinched a little. Then she smiled. The whole room bent around her smile. I smiled too. I sat down next to her and asked her the news. She squared her shoulders and raised her chin.

"I had such a good day yesterday," she said.

"Yeah? What did you do?"

"I set up two email accounts. I emailed Rob, my old American friend. I went to the ministry and gave them my résumé, and they gave me the application for the translator job. Then I went to the store to buy groceries. I even ate at a fancy restaurant and bought a cell phone."

"That's awesome."

"I did so many good things, Han-Guly," she said. "I felt like I was sleeping for five years. Now, it's like I wake up again. My life is a new life. I have hope."

"I'm so proud of you, Jahan. I told you that if you just kept pushing, you'd finally get what you wanted."

"I know, and you were right. I just have one more small favor to ask you."

"What's that?"

"Will you please help me to write my application and turn it in to the ministry for me tomorrow? The headquarters is right near the Peace Corps office."

"Absolutely."

For the next two hours, I helped her with her application. I made sure all the appropriate boxes were ticked, and that every sentence was grammatically correct and fluid. Jahan went to have her photo taken. An hour later, she called me on my cell phone with her new cell phone and told me she was in front of my waratan. I went out there in my shorts and slippers. The blue of her dress and the red of her lips and the gold of her chain were all lit up in the sun. She handed me her application with her photo attached.

"Thank you for this," she said. "You saved me."

FOR THE NEXT two weekends, I cut loose. The first weekend, I got wasted with Brooke in Aşgabat, and the second weekend, I got wasted with Jimmy in Türkmenhalk. I also did a bunch of work on the trip with my folks. The plan was for them to come to Aşgabat for the Peace Corps' Fourth of July party at the embassy, then spend a night at my site. Afterwards, we'd travel through Uzbekistan, seeing cities along the way. Then we'd take a plane from the Uzbek capital, Tashkent, to the Kazakh city of Almaty, where T-16s Simon and Rave Dave would meet us. After four days in Almaty, my folks would fly back to the States. Simon, Dave, and I would then spend a week with Truman in Kyrgyzstan, where he was teaching English. The logistics of the trip were a bit of a nightmare. Besides needing a visa for each country, my folks needed a letter of invitation from each government, and they were required to have a guide present at all times while traveling through Turkmenistan and Uzbekistan. To handle this crap, my father had gone through an agency called Silk Road Junky. They appeared to be doing their job.

On a Friday in early May, I went out to buy booze and write some poetry on my little bench. I came back and Ali informed me that my father had just called. He told me he'd call back in an hour. I chilled in my room for forty-five minutes. I went down to the living room to wait. Patma glided up in her purple köýnek.

"You don't have to wait here," she said. "Aziza will answer the phone, and if it's your father, we'll let you know."

I knew this was true. However, a part of me wanted to hurt both Patma and Aziza for having hung up on my father so many times in the past. I told Patma I was fine waiting. She huffed and walked off. Ten minutes went by. The phone in the living room never rang. I worried that it might be out again. We had a new phone in the TV room, so I went in there. Aziza was sat with her back to me and her face glued to the screen. Patma was at the wardrobe gathering her sewing items. I asked her if she'd heard the new phone ring. She pushed her eyebrows into a deep V.

"Why are you asking me this?" she said. "Did *you* hear the new phone ring? You're in the next room. If it rings, Aziza will pick it up, and if it's your father, you can come in here and speak to him."

I nodded and flipped the old bat off behind my back. I returned to the living room. Patma came in with the new phone. She unplugged the old one and connected the wire to the new one.

"You don't have a very good personality," she mumbled.

"Really?"

She walked out and slammed the door. I was one fried nerve away from telling her what a wretched old cunt she was. I took a deep breath.

Seven more months, I said to myself.

The phone rang. I grabbed it up.

"Dad?" I said.

"Johann?"

"Yeah, it's me. How's the trip lookin'?"

"Well . . ."

He explained the troubles he was having. The biggest of which was that Brad, the head honcho at Silk Road Junky, hadn't gotten the ball rolling on the letter of invitation from the Turkmen government. His excuse was that since I lived in Turkmenistan, he figured I was the one who'd do it—a fair assumption. However, he hadn't made this explicit until recently. This was a problem because a letter of invitation could take weeks or even months to be processed, and the date of my folks' departure, July 1st, was fast approaching. To make matters more complicated, their visas and LOIs[90] for Uzbekistan and Kazakhstan hadn't arrived either. A miracle wasn't in order yet, but some fast action sure as fuck was. My father said that if we didn't get

---

[90] Letters of invitation.

everything settled in time, we might have to explore a Plan B. This about made me throw the phone across the room.

"There'll be no fucking Plan B," I shouted.

"Why not?" he said exhaustedly.

"Because I want to show you this damn country and Central Asia as a whole. Plus, I've already made plans to meet up with two other volunteers in Almaty and to visit another volunteer with them in Kyrgyzstan."

I waited for his response. He remained silent.

"We're gonna make this work," I said. "Tell Brad today to get everything ready: LOIs, visas, tickets, guides, so that by the time July rolls around, you'll have it all in the bag. Push him, Dad. Make it happen. If he's got any sense in his head, he'll do it. Because if he doesn't, there's a lot of volunteers here who are gonna get the word from me that Silk Road Junky blows ass."

My father coughed and cleared his throat.

"Alright," he said.

We hung up. I walked into the anteroom. Patma was squatted and sewing something. She saw me and swallowed her anger like a large pill. She looked up at me with a thin smile.

"How's your father?" she asked.

"He's good," I said, swallowing my own anger. "We're trying to get everything ready for their trip out here."

She grumbled softly. "When are they coming?"

"They arrive in Aşgabat on July second. I'll be coming here with them on the fifth."

She didn't respond. I could tell she was hurt. I started to feel guilty.

"Look," I said. "Please don't be offended by what I did earlier. I hadn't spoken to my father in a long time, and I needed to get all the trip planning done. I don't want you to think I don't trust you. And I especially don't want there to be a problem between us."

A palpable softness was in the air. Patma's face loosened and a beam of controlled warmth emanated from it. She stared at me with her hard but kind eyes.

"*Men bilýän*," she said. "I know."

I grinned. She looked down and continued sewing.

"So, what are you going to do now?" she asked.

"Haha, what I usually do at around this time."

"Write?"

"Yup."

"Just be sure you write good things about Turkmenistan. I want America to know we're a good country."

"Oh, I will," I said, almost choking. "But first, people have to read my book, and that's not at all guaranteed."

She looked back up at me.

"They'll read it," she said.

FOR THE NEXT 72 hours, I hit the writing and the booze hard. When Monday evening rolled around, I was a sloppy old zombie with a missing nose. I schlepped down to the courtyard to get some air. As I sat on the tapçan scratching myself and smashing mosquitos, Durdy drove up. He parked the Lada in front of me and stepped out. He was visibly drunk and could barely stand upright. He staggered toward the front door, hiccupping the whole way. He noticed me on the tapçan and his eyes lit up.

"Han-Guly." He burped. "I hear your folks are visiting."

"That's right," I said. "They'll be here on July fifth."

The front door opened and Patma stepped out. She looked irritated.

"Well hey," Durdy said. "When they get here, I'm gonna . . . hup . . . slaughter a goat in their honor and invite all the neighbors."

He cackled wildly. Patma shook her head in disgust and helped him inside. A few minutes later she came back out. She told me my father was on the phone. I raced inside and took the call.

"Dad?"

"We got the tickets," he said.

"Really? That was fast."

"Yeah, your mother and I said the hell with it and pushed the whole thing through. We've got Brad working on the visas, guides, and LOIs. He assured us we'd have everything in time, so we went ahead and paid for everything."

"How much did it all cost?"

"Ten grand."

"Jesus. It'll be worth it though. My host dad says he's gonna slaughter a goat for you guys when you get here."

"What the hell does that mean?"

"It means you might hafta eat a little guts and liver and stuff."

"I ain't eating dick."

"Don't look now," I said, laughing. "'Cuz they might serve that too."

My father hissed with laughter. I could hear the phone scraping against his beard.

"Jesus, son, this trip's gonna blow my mind," he said.

"That it will."

THAT FRIDAY, I went to Aşgabat early to handle my visa crap. I hit PCHQ to check my email, then I met up with Rave Dave downtown. Homeboy wanted to hit the embassies for Kazakhstan and Kyrgyzstan first, as those were the countries he'd be visiting. I insisted that we do the Uzbek one first because I knew it'd be the biggest pain in the ass. He reluctantly agreed. We walked over there and found that the doors hadn't opened yet. It started to rain. We waited on the curb and got soaked. Four hours later they opened the doors. A guard led us to a tiny hot room where we spent another two hours dealing with all sorts of bureaucratic nonsense. I finally got up there. The guy at the service window was a massive prick. He demanded that everything be filled out perfectly and in block letters. I must've rewritten my visa and LOI applications a half-dozen times. I handed him the final versions and he sneered.

"That'll be two hundred dollars," he said.

I nearly gagged. I gave him the money, and he informed me that if my applications were accepted, my visa would be good for six days, and *only* for the *exact* dates that were specified. He told me to come back in three weeks. I wanted to flick a butt hair in his stupid mouth, but I thanked him kindly instead.

Dave and I headed to the Kazakh embassy. The lines and wait were less of a nightmare, but the lady at the front desk only spoke Russian, which about filled my keister clean up. A pretty young Turkmen girl who spoke both Russian and English was behind me. She told me by way of translation that since I'd be entering Kazakhstan twice—once by airplane via Tashkent and once by bus via Bishkek to catch a flight back to Aşgabat—and would be staying on both occasions for no longer than five days, I would need a double entry transit visa instead of a standard tourist visa. To obtain this, I needed proof in the form of a tourist visa that I'd be visiting Kyrgyzstan; a major problem considering I hadn't even applied for my fucking Kyrgyz visa yet. I was furious to the point of incontinence. I still managed to thank the ladies. Dave and I went over to the Kyrgyz embassy. As per usual, it had already closed and wouldn't be open again until Monday. There was only one thing left to do.

"Shall we get fucked up?" I asked Dave.

"Most definitely."

The next 48 hours were a haze of booze, women, and Russian pop. I'm not sure about everything that transpired, but I'm fairly certain that while drunk at the Ak, I made out with a butch lesbian volunteer who told me her three goals during Peace Corps were to give head, get penetrated, and taste cum—none of which I helped her with. I believe I also told another volunteer the story of how at fourteen, after having finished *Way of the Peaceful Warrior* one night, I climbed on my roof, got buck naked, and jacked off under the full moon as a proclamation of my desire to dedicate my life to conquering all fears. I think Harry and his wife Lonnie took me out to a nice lunch one hungover afternoon. I assume I barfed afterwards, but I can't be sure.

I APPLIED FOR my Kyrgyz visa and returned to site. My host family were in a stupor as Patma's mother had passed over the weekend. We had her seventh-day sadaka that Saturday. The next morning, I started feeling sick. By nightfall, I was aching all over and squirting fire out my ass. I skipped school for the next few days to heal. I lay in bed in my boxers and watched episode after episode of *Dexter* from Chinese bootlegged discs. I sweated, puked, pissed, and shit ten pounds of liquid. By Friday, I was feeling good enough to go to class. I slung my work clothes over my skinny frame and hobbled to On Yet in the blazing heat. I taught a few classes and clubs. The kids were in a frenzy, as their last day of school was the following Monday.

I finished teaching and went over to see Jahan. She had a bright red köýnek on and her hair in a tight bun. Her face was done up nice. When she saw me, she rapped her pencil on the top of her desk.

"Han-Guly," she said, "Monday is the biggest day of my life."

"Why's that?"

"Because. All my students I have taught since very small will be graduating. I work so hard with them for many years, and now I will see them become adults and enter world."

"Wow, that is a big deal."

"Yes. And you have to promise me one thing."

"What's that?"

"That you will come and be with me on this day."

"No problem."

And it really wasn't. I had no plans to go anywhere that weekend and no obligations. I taught Jahan a bit of French. On my way out, she reminded me to be at On Yet at 8:00 a.m. on the dot that Monday. I smiled and promised I would. I grabbed a few bottles of vodka and Ýetigen and some snacks from the nearby dükan. I spent the next two days binge-watching *Dexter*, drinking heavily, and pondering my own adulthood. I realized that in my life there were three things I couldn't live without—traveling, languages and, most importantly, writing. I thought about my plan after Peace Corps. I knew my father wanted me to pursue graduate school as he'd done. I considered applying for a master's program at either Berkeley for linguistic anthropology or Bloomington for Central Asian studies. I knew these things would pave the way for good teaching gigs and afford me the time and opportunity to focus on languages and travel. As for the writing, I could squeeze it in during the summers or make it part of my studies. It seemed like a reasonable compromise. I knew there was a GRE[91] testing center in Aşgabat. I decided to apply when I went for my visas.

On Sunday night, I had trouble sleeping. I popped a couple Benadryl to knock me out. I woke up the next morning feeling groggy. I checked my watch and my grogginess warped into terror.

"Eight thirty-six?" I screamed.

The end-of-the-year *çykyş* was no doubt in full swing. I leapt outta bed and ran to the banýa. I took a lightning-fast bucket shower and shaved my face. I ran back to my room and threw on my clothes. I was out the waratan by nine-fifteen. When I arrived at On Yet, I saw a group of students and teachers in the quad. The DJ was dismantling his gear and teachers were pulling down decorations. It was almost as if they were breaking up the party just to spite me. I felt like an enormous tool. I dreaded seeing Jahan and having to explain to her that I'd missed the "biggest day of her life" because I'd gotten drunk all weekend and popped too many antihistamines. I walked to her classroom. I found her slumped over in her chair, staring dejectedly at a sheaf of papers. The color from her green dress was bleeding onto the floor. Her face was waxy and her bun was a mess. I swallowed my tongue and scratched my scalp.

"Hi, Jahan," I said.

She looked up at me with a thin smile.

"Hey, um, I'm sorry I'm late. I know how much this meant to you. I just fucked up and overslept."

"It's okay."

---

[91] Graduate Record Examination.

"So . . . have you heard anything about the teacher training in Kazakhstan or the translator position at the ministry?"

"Nope."

"Okay well, I'm going to Aşgabat this weekend to get my visas. If I see Zoya at Peace Corps, I'll give her your info and tell her you're interested in the LCF position."

"Thanks."

My efforts were going nowhere. I apologized once more then went to Azat's. He was throwing a little *uçurym* party for his sixth-formers. The boys were all in their loud ties, pinstriped pants, and rhino-horned shoes, and the girls were in their sparkly green köýneks, long braids, and *Wizard of Oz* slippers. When they saw me, they all screamed, "Teacher. Teacher." They wrapped their little fingers around mine and dragged me to the center of the room. They bounced around me like little frogs and demanded that I dance with them. I must've danced for an entire hour. The kids all called me Michael Jackson and swore up and down that I was the best dancer in the world. I'd only popped my kepka and done a few twirls, but hey, it was a nice thing to hear anyway. We busted out the cardboard cake and took some group photos. When my eyes were burnt out by the flash and my belly was full of frosty gunk, I bid Azat and the kids adieu. I saw Aman in the hall. He ran up to me panting and put his Frankenstein hands on my shoulders.

"Han-Guly," he said. "I've been waiting—"

"For a girl like me?"

"What? Yes, I've been waiting for you today."

"Why's that?"

"Because . . . Do you remember the test you have help me with in February? The one for Olympiad?"

"Vaguely."

"Well, I did well at Olympiad because of you. Then they let me take English test at Turkmen–Turkish school in Tejen."

"That's awesome."

"Yes, it is. And now they will say this week if I will go to study

English in Istanbul."

"Really? Jesus, that's great. How do you think you did?"

He hung his cubic head.

"Ay, I don't know. Maybe I did not passed. I think I have missed many questions. It was difficult test for me."

"Don't talk like that," I said, slapping him on the back. "You're a smart guy. I'm sure you passed. When do you find out the results?"

"I don't know. I will wait for their call."

"Well shit man, when you find out, call me and I'll take you out to celebrate your trip to Turkey."

He smiled.

"You really think I did pass this test?"

"Hell, yeah."

He thrust his hand into mine and shook it. His face was tight with excitement and I could see tears in his eyes.

"Thank you, my friend. I will call you and tell you good news."

I gave him a hug and wished him luck. I turned away and my ten-buck grin depreciated to a two-cent frown. I looked out the door and into the dust.

How dare you give him false hope, my inner voice said.

THAT THURSDAY, I went to Aşgabat. My first order of business was to see Zoya. I went up to her office and knocked on her door. I heard the shuffling of paper and the clinking of glass.

"*Gel*," she said. "Come."

I opened the door and walked in. She sat at her desk in a green velvet dress. Her hair was in a spiraled bun. Her angular face was caked in makeup, and her long earlobes were dangling pearl earrings. She moved a stack of papers from one side of the desk to the other. Then she lifted her teacup.

"What can I do for you, Johann?" she said.

I watched as she opened her big ugly lips and sipped tea through them. When she pulled the cup away, a mark of menstrual red lipstick was on it.

"I came to ask you about an LCF position," I said, grimacing.

"You want to teach Turkmen to the T-17s?"

"No," I said. "I want my counterpart from Gurbagahowda to teach Turkmen to the T-17s."

"Oh, this makes sense. Your Turkmen is very good. But it is not good enough to teach."

"Thank you for clarifying that. Now, my counterpart's name is Jahan. Here is a copy of her CV."

I handed her the paper. She took it and held it in front of her face. The expression in her eyes went dead. It was almost as if she were checking for ink smudges instead of actually reading. She looked at me over the rim of her glasses.

"This looks okay," she said.

"Really?"

"Yes. But is hard for me to believe this is just your counterpart. Are you dating this woman?"

"What? No."

"Okay. I am only check. I will call her next week and we will see."

"Thank you."

I left her office wanting to strangle her with one hand and finger her with the other. I prayed she would call Jahan and not make me look like any more of an idiot than I already did. I flushed these thoughts from my mind with a hot shower. I met up with Rave Dave in the lounge and we hit the Kyrgyz, Kazakh, and Uzbek embassies. I got my visas from the first and third and applied at the second. I was told by the huge Russian-speaking Kazakh woman, whom I'd dealt with before, that my visa would be ready on Tuesday. This gave me an entire five days to play with my testicles. I thanked the lady and immediately called Brooke. She was thrilled at the news and invited us over. We went to her place in Adalat and dropped our crap off. We hit a nearby dükan, bought provisions, and proceeded to cook, drink, and laugh our way into the weekend. Much of what transpired, I've forgotten. I do remember that at one point during the first evening, Dave and I went down to the dükan to buy more beer. We were almost arrested for breaking the Adalat curfew of 10:00 p.m. Luckily, it was only a hair past the hour. We gave the cop who stopped us a few beers and he let it slide. We went back up to Brooke's and told her the story. Our near arrest was the running theme of the weekend.

THAT TUESDAY, I got my Kazakh visa and applied for the GRE in October. I tried to squeeze in another day of debauchery, but Harry caught me scheming in the lounge and sent me packing. I went back to Gurbagahowda and fiddled around. I took Merdan out to shashlik for his birthday and watched a whole butt-load of *Dexter*. I got a call from my father on Monday. He informed me that he'd just paid twelve hundred bucks to have his visas expedited and to put extra pages in his passport. He sounded pissed and worried. I assured him that everything would go smoothly. We said our goodbyes and the phone rang again. This time it was Aman. He greeted me in a lowly tone. I asked him what was wrong.

"I failed," he said.

My heart collapsed like a bag of water stabbed by a hot knife.

"You mean your test to go to Turkey?"

"Yes."

"Oh my god, Aman. I'm so sorry. Can't you retake it?"

"No. This was last chance. Next year, I am too old."

"What about another program? Something in Russia or the Ukraine?"

"I don't know," he said. "I think I will just must accept that I am stupid in English and I will stay in Gurbagahowda forever."

"Don't say that."

"Is true, Han-Guly. I am nothing."

He thanked me for my help and hung up. I slammed the receiver down and kicked the cradle away. I thought of Jahan and my eyes brightened. I vowed to see her the next day.

I WOKE UP the next morning with a plan; I would get Jahan a job at Peace Corps, and I would make her known to staff and every volunteer by working on an important project with her. I tossed around a few ideas. I decided I would use her superior knowledge of Turkmen to help me with the grammar book I'd pitched to Mahym as my secondary project so many months back. The premise of it was simple. I would take 501 of the most common verbs in Turkmen, list all their meanings in English, then provide example sentences in both languages using all possible prepositions and noun cases. It would be called *501 Turkmen Verbs*. I was sure it would be a success, as Peace Corps' material on the Turkmen language was both meager in quantity and execrable in quality.

I walked to On Yet with a whistle on my teeth. I went to Jahan's classroom and found her at her desk. Her cheeks were red and her eyes were glimmering. I asked her what was what.

"I just got a call from Zoya," she said.

"Really? What'd she say?"

"She said that she will call me back in August and that there is good possibility I will become LCF at Peace Corps."

"You're kidding."

"No. Thank you so much, Han-Guly. I feel even more like I have a chance now."

I congratulated her. I also privately thanked Zoya; the old ostrich had come through. I finally didn't feel like so much of a honking fucking moron. Once the laughter and the cheers died down, I told Jahan about my idea for the book. She thought it a swell one and told me we could start on it right away. We agreed to meet in her classroom at 9:00 a.m. the following day. I went back home and used my Turkmen–English dictionary to compile a list of what I felt were the 501 most useful Turkmen verbs. I worked through dinner and into the night. As the clock hands spun, mine typed and scribbled and flipped with blurring speed. By 3:00 a.m. I had the list. I saved it on my USB and hit the sheets.

The next morning, I arrived at school at eight forty-five. I printed out two copies of the list and went over to Jahan's. She was standing at the door with her arms folded. Her floor was being cleaned by some dáyza with a long mop. I asked her when she'd be finished. She said at least an hour, but that we could use the cleaning room for our meeting. We rolled our eyes and went over there. The place was filled with scraggly mops and hardened rags and buckets of dirty water. We sat down on a couple of broken chairs. I handed Jahan the list of verbs and began explaining the details of the book. She seemed very distant. I finished my spiel and asked her what was wrong. She fluttered an eyelash and smiled plastically.

"Nothing," she said.

I raised my eyebrows to a bed of wrinkles.

"I'm not gonna let you get away with that," I said. "If you don't tell me what's wrong, I can't help you."

"It's nothing," she said.

"Tell me," I said, glaring at her.

Her faced went flush. I could see tears collecting around her eyes.

"It's about the job you are trying to get for me at Peace Corps," she said.

"Okay?"

"You won't be upset with me?"

"No."

"Promise?"

"Yes."

"Okay . . . Two years ago, Cyrus tried to get me the same job. I was very excited, and I went to the meetings and gave big presentation. I tried very hard, but Zoya told me I would not get the job because I was not assertive woman. Now I am afraid to go because it will probably be the same."

I was smoking with anger at Zoya for rejecting Jahan based on some asinine Peace Corps-constructed definition of how a female LCF should behave, and at Jahan for actually taking this bullshit to heart. I wanted to tear my ears from my head.

"I wish you had told me this before," I said through my teeth. "I wouldn't have wasted my time if I had known you had already tried and weren't willing to try again."

"I will try again," she said. "I just think I will fail again, like I always fail, like last time, like Kazakhstan, like the translator job at the ministry, like my life. I only fail."

She broke into shakes. The tears she was holding back were now dangerously close to ripping free. She gripped her elbows and rocked back and forth. I took a deep breath.

"Look," I said, exhaling. "I know you feel like a failure, but you're not. It's just that what you want in life is not what most Turkmen women want. Most Turkmen women are content with getting married, having children, and being öý hojalykçys for the rest of their lives. But that's not for you, is it? You want to see the world, learn different languages, meet new people, and have adventures. And that's difficult because so few people here understand that, especially when it comes from a woman. I know realizing your dreams will be much harder than it was or is for me, but I can tell you my story if it'll help."

She was fidgeting with her gold rings. I snapped my fingers to get her attention.

"You in there?"

"Yes, Han-Guly," she said. "Tell me your story. I am listening."

I proceeded to tell her about how my mother and father were both highly educated chemists, how they always encouraged me to study the sciences as it would afford me a decent job and a family. I explained that my father pushed me the hardest, that when he found out I wasn't like him, he was very unsupportive.

"I told him I loved languages, travel, and above all, writing," I said. "His response was, 'These are good hobbies, but they won't make you any money.'"

"What did you do?" she asked.

"Well, at first, I listened to him. I went to university, even though I didn't want to, and I studied political science instead of linguistic anthropology—the only subject I could see myself enjoying—because, by that point, my father had given up on his dream of me becoming a world-class chemist and felt that political science was at least a science in name and could lead to a lucrative career with the American government, in which I could employ my talent for languages."

I could see Jahan's eyeballs reeling. I brought it down.

"The point is, my father didn't and still hasn't accepted that I want to be a writer. In fact, he's done everything in his power to go against it, which is part of the reason I'm here. I've needed this space and time to collect my thoughts and figure out how the fuck I'm gonna break it to the man. To be honest, I'm still struggling with it. But at least I have a strong idea, and I think if you're able to get away from your family and try something for yourself, you'll have a strong idea too."

Jahan looked down at her lap.

"I would like to go away from my family and try something for myself," she said. "But they don't make enough money. My youngest brother fixes brakes on cars. My second brother has no job because he finishes army. And my sister sweeps at hospital. I have best job, and I must work so I can pay for my mother's medicine. She is in much pain if she can't have it and no one else makes enough money."

I rolled my eyes and sniffed.

"So, what? You're going to spend the rest of your life taking care of your family?"

"I don't know," she said. "Once my mother told me I could go to Aşgabat for university. She was very sick, but she told me to go so I could get my diploma and become a good teacher and make good money. I was so happy. I went and made my dream. It was wonderful time, but when I go back to Gurbagahowda things were the same. I tried very hard to stay with my family and be a good girl, but I got very bored and sad. Finally, I told my mother about this and she said, 'You may go to the city to find job and travel and do as you like.' But I was too afraid, so I stayed."

"Wait," I said, slapping my forehead. "Your mother told you to live your dreams, and you were the one who said no?"

"Yes," she said, pulling her neck in like a spooked turtle. "But I am afraid because I think maybe she is testing me to say the right answer, which is I will stay. But if I will say I want to go maybe she will hate me, and my brothers and sister will, too, and I will lose my family."

"Well, what kind of a fuckin' family is that?" I said. "Families should be proud of their children for succeeding, not try to shoot them down. That's bullshit."

I was now screaming. I could hear the cleaning ladies outside clucking and gasping with fright. I didn't give a squiggly duck dick. I was furious and, furthermore, convinced that Jahan needed this.

"Tell me something," I said. "How long have you been taking care of your family and paying for most everything?"

She held up seven pudgy fingers.

"Seven years?"

She nodded.

"Gee, that's interesting," I said. "And you have three other perfectly capable adult siblings, two of whom are male, and all of whom have enough brains to at least get decent jobs, yet they don't. Why is that, Jahan?"

"I don't know," she said, almost giggling.

"Well, I do. Because you fucking pay for everything. You do all the work, earn all the money, and they sit back and collect. Don't you think it's time they got off their asses and started helping out a bit? You did your piece. You supported your entire family for seven years. It's time for them to start taking a little initiative. Why doesn't your loser army grunt brother get himself an education and a real job? And don't tell me 'I don't know.'"

"I don't know," she squeaked.

"Ahhhhhhhh, Jahan. You have to get over your fear of confronting people and start demanding the things you want, otherwise, you'll never get them. And tell people how you feel once in a while, for Christ's sake. You look like you're about to explode."

She thinned her lips. I could tell she was thinking hard about what to say next.

"I'm afraid to open myself to people," she said. "Especially you, Han-Guly."

"Why?"

"Because in six months you will leave, and then I'll be alone again. I feel like now I am dead inside, but at least there is no pain. But if you make me alive again and then you leave, I will feel so much pain and fear. So maybe I think it's better to just stay dead."

My heart melted in two.

"Look, Jahan," I said. "I didn't just come to Peace Corps to run away from my dad and all my problems. I also came here to help people. And when I arrived in Gurbagahowda, I realized that no one here needed my help. You were the only one who asked for it, and you were the only one who continued asking. But if you don't open up and tell me what's going on in your life, the most I can do is teach you shitty French and bitch at the walls."

She remained silent.

"And about me leaving," I went on. "It's true. I am going to leave. But if you can open up a little and let me pour some of this energy into you, then you'll have that piece of me forever, so whenever you're feeling sad or depressed or lazy, you can use that energy to get on your feet and start moving again. And I want you to know something because maybe this'll make you realize how important it is that you follow your dreams."

Jahan looked at me and waited. I centered my expression between concerned father and loving friend.

"I want you to know," I said, "that saving you has been the only thing that's kept me here through all this bullshit, and I'm asking you to make it worth it. I'm asking you not just to make your dreams come true, but to make mine come true as well. Because it is my dream to see you get outta this hellhole and do something with your life."

She folded her hands and bowed her head.

"Thank you," she said. "I needed to hear this."

FOR THE NEXT two weeks, Jahan and I worked on *501*. We made considerable progress on it, but not on anything else. I went to Aşgabat both weekends; the first, to party, and the second, to read and write emails. My buddies from back home informed me that they'd all be coming on the Africa trip. Brooke and Tex were thinking of coming as well, so that would make eight of us, at least for the first month. I found out from my father that he'd received both the Turkmen and Kazakh visas. He was still waiting on the Uzbek visas but was hopeful he'd have them soon. That Thursday in Gurbagahowda, I got a call from him. He sounded exhausted.

"What's going on?" I said. "Did you get the visas?"

"Nope. I just talked to the guy at Visa HQ and he said that supposedly the computers at the Uzbek embassy are down."

"Oh, that's bullshit. They're just jerking you around."

"Yeah, well, that may be so, but there's nothing I can do about it."

"Did you try calling Brad? Isn't it his goddamned job to iron out these sorts of things?

"I did call him, and I told him I was pissed with the way things had been handled thus far, and you're not gonna believe this, but he blamed me."

"What?"

"Yeah, he blamed me. He said it was me who wanted to go through Visa HQ and not through him, so this was all my fault. Can you believe that fucking guy?"

"I'm astounded. And I'll tell ya what, if our trip gets screwed, I'm gonna see to it that every PCV, government hack, and embassy goon in Central Asia knows what a pile of donkey shit Silk Road Junky Tours is."

"Well, don't do anything yet," he said, chuckling. "Lemme call you tomorrow at nine and tell you if we get the visas."

"Okay."

The next morning, I woke up at 9:00 a.m. on the nose. I ran downstairs to the main house and my father called shortly thereafter. He did not sound good.

"The computers at the Uzbek embassy are still down," he said, sighing.

I slammed my fist on the ground.

"What the fuck do we do?" I shouted.

"I don't know. But if those visas aren't issued by tomorrow, we're screwed. As it is, I'm already gonna hafta drop four hundred bucks to have them couriered to our house."

"Did you talk to Brad?"

"Yeah I did, and he said he was gonna start working on the LOIs, but that still doesn't handle our problem. If we don't get these visas by tomorrow, we're gonna be spending most of our time in Aşgabat chasing them down, even with the Uzbek LOIs."

I was on the verge of tears.

"But if that happens, we're really fucked 'cuz my Uzbek visa is only good from the sixth to the twelfth, so if we try to enter or exit even one day later, they won't let us. Plus, if we miss our day here in Gurbagahowda that'll be a huge disappointment because I've already told everyone at my site that you guys are coming, and they all want to meet you. Christ, my host family is about to slaughter a goat in your honor."

My dad sighed. He said he'd call at 10:00 a.m. the next morning. I spent the entire day worrying. It drove me mad to think that months of planning and thousands of dollars would all spiral down the puke tubes over a single pair of visas. I was furious at the Uzbek government for being so pigheaded. At the same time, I understood their position; for the average Uzbek citizen, it was next to impossible to get even a non-immigrant visa to the US. An immigrant visa was unheard of. There were likely thousands of Uzbeks applying and being rejected for both each year. On the flip, there probably weren't more than a handful of Americans applying for Uzbek visas during any given year. Our case may have been seen by the Uzbeks as a chance to get even. If so, I prayed that someone at that embassy had a heart.

I COULDN'T SLEEP that night. I tossed and turned and panted till what little hair was on my head stood on end. At 4:00 a.m. I went outside to take a piss. I looked up at the soot-black sky and saw a crescent moon smiling down on me. I don't know if it was my delirium or my desire to sleep, but I took the moon as a good omen. I choked down three Tylenol PMs and sunk into a fitful sleep.

I woke up groggy. I checked my watch and it read nine fifty-five. I threw on my shorts and raced down to the living room. The phone rang five minutes later. I picked it up.

"Hello? Dad?" I said.

There was a crackling on the other end. A voice came through.

"Johann?"

I could tell it was my father, but just barely. He sounded like a sad cat drowning in whiskey. I asked him the news and cringed. He sighed so hot and deep I thought the receiver might melt.

"So, do you wanna hear the bad news first?" he said. "Or the *really* bad news?"

I dropped the phone. I picked it back up and wiped my eyes.

"Christ, Dad. I guess just gimme the *really* bad news first."

"Well, we got the fuckin' visas."

Imagine Janet Leigh in *Psycho* after the first tit-stab.

"Ahhhhhh."

My father laughed. I pounded the floor.

"You've got to be fucking kidding me," I shouted.

"Nope. I just talked to Visa HQ and the guy said we got the visas and that they're being couriered to our house as we speak."

I heard the doorbell ring in the background.

"In fact, that's gotta be him at the door now."

I heard the door squeak open and my mother say, "Hello."

"Son," my father said. "It's the guy, and he just handed your mother our passports. We're coming to Central Asia."

"Hot shit."

21

I FINISHED THE itinerary for my folks' visit to Gurbagahowda. It was tricky due to various people's schedules, but I devised a solid plan. That Monday morning, I was packed and ready to go. I said goodbye to my host family, then Merdan drove me to the awtostanzia. We pulled up and he patted me on the back.

"Have a good trip asshole," he said, smiling.

I assured him I would. I found a cab straight to Aşgabat and sat shotgun. The ride was surreal. I was a blooming mess of emotions. Part of me was stoked to see my folks. Another part was worried they'd see the work I was doing and be disappointed. Another part was spiteful they hadn't come earlier. And the deepest part, the one shading his eye in the bastard labyrinth of my sniveling heart, was terrified that he and I both wouldn't have the guts to admit to my father once and for all that we wanted to write.

I arrived at PCHQ at noon. I checked my emails then took a marşrutka to Adalat. I consulted the dükan for booze and food. I went to Brooke's and found that she, Tex, and Rave Dave were already there drinking. The night hit me like a tumbling rhino. I woke up the next morning hungover and sallow. I availed myself of Brooke's facilities. I went back to HQ for some lame TEFL meeting then hit the Ak. I was expecting my folks at midnight. It was twenty past five o'clock. I went to Dave's room for a drink. People were playing Edward Baklaşka Hands, which is a game where you tape a 2-liter *baklaşka* of cheap beer to each hand and can't remove either until you consume the contents of both. I got in on the game. I downed the first beer and my phone rang. I ripped the empty baklaşka off my hand and took the call. It was Katarina, the woman who'd been hired by Silk Road Junky Tours to pick my folks up from the Aşgabat airport. She told me their flight from Baku, Azerbaijan, had been delayed; they wouldn't be arriving till 5:00 a.m. I asked her if there was anything I could do. A female volunteer behind me screamed out, "Suck my cock."

"You seem to be wery busy," Katarina said. "I vil khendl it."

I thanked her and hung up. I swigged my second baklaşka and flipped on the music. The last thing I remember is Iris dragging me to her room and asking me if I wanted to be her "bitch." I'm pretty sure I said, "Yes."

I WOKE UP in Iris's bed. She was wrapped around my legs like a wet towel. I kissed her on the forehead then pried her off me. I went to my room, shit, showered and shaved, then hobbled down to the banquet hall. All the vols and staff were there. I took my seat and suffered through four hours of mind-blackening nonsense. At lunch, I called the Grand Turkmen where my folks were to be staying. I wasn't even sure if they'd made it to Aşgabat. The receptionist plugged me through to the room they'd booked. A bullfrog with laryngitis answered the phone.

"Hello?" it said.

"Dad. You guys made it."

"Yeah, we sure did, but it was a pain in the fucking ass with all the lines and delays and everything. At least we're here though."

"Did you guys get some sleep?"

"Some."

"Are you ready for the embassy party tonight?"

"We'll be ready."

"My meetings end at five and I'll be over at six. Sound good?"

"Yeah, but there's one problem. We don't have our luggage."

"What?"

"Yup, Lufthansa lost it. Won't be in till tomorrow night."

"Fuck."

I told my folks to go to Yimpaş, the Turkish mall in town, to buy some clothes. They said they would, and we ended the call. I went back and suffered through my meetings. Every chance the volunteers got, they asked me if my folks had arrived and what they were doing and where they were staying and what color their latest joint bowel movement was. I dealt with the questions as best I could. When I was on my last nerve, Divine—Truman's corpulent site mate who'd given a tearful speech at his wake—approached me and smiled seductively.

"I hear your dad's a big guy," she said, unclothing her blubbery shoulder.

"Yeah."

"Well, you know what? I might just hafta dance with him at the party tonight."

"Oh?"

"And if he dances good, I might just S his D."

She licked her chops. I spat out my sparkling water. The volunteers at our table cracked up. Harry gave us all the eyeball. The clock ticked five and the world cheered. I met Brooke outside. I invited her and her dumpy new T-16 squeeze Harlow to the hotel to greet my folks. We changed into our party clothes and went over there. My folks were on the second floor. We took the elevator and knocked on their door. My father answered it in nothing but his underwear.

"Jesus Christ, Johann," he screamed. "You didn't tell me you'd be bringing guests."

He slammed the door on our laughter. When he opened back up, he was decent. He invited us in and introduced himself. My tiny mother introduced herself as well. She was in a pickle about what to

347

wear. She'd bought an oversized purple köýnek, some black capris, a black shirt studded with rhinestones, and a black pair of open-toed sandals. I looked the whole mess over and laughed.

"You should go with the Barney costume and the hooker sandals," I said.

She frowned and tried everything on. She settled on the capris and the rhinestone frock. She looked like a menopausal Russian housewife who refused to abandon the idea of her own sexiness. She slouched and looked up at me.

"How do I look, Goosy?" she asked.

"Perfect."

We chilled for a bit then went to the Ak. All the volunteers were outside waiting for the PC vans. I went around and introduced my folks. Everyone wanted to be first in line to meet them. It was nerve-racking. I felt like I was rationing bits of cheddar to a gang of starving mice. My irritation was compounded when my father insisted we take a group photo. I didn't want to have to smile alongside my enemies in the crowd. I gritted my teeth and bore it. My father snapped the photo and the vans rolled up. They drove us through the heart of Aşgabat. My folks looked like two lost dogs staring out the window at the gold statues and the marble buildings and the massive fountains that gushed neon water.

We arrived at the embassy at seven-thirty. Harry greeted us in a periwinkle suit and polka dot bow tie. He walked with my father up the long grassy lane. I stayed back with my mom to chat. I told her how much it meant to me that she and my father had come. She slipped her arm around my elbow and held it tight.

"You're our baby boy," she said. "We'd go to the ends of the earth for you."

I nearly lost it. I changed the subject and ushered her up the hill.

THE PARTY SCENE was decent. There was Tex-Mex food and cowboy hats and a dancefloor with a band playing country. The only snag was that the embassy goons got their food first. When Harry casually announced this, my folks boiled in their seats. I cooled them down with a slanted smiled.

"Get used to it," I said. "We do the most difficult job and get the least credit."

They bit their tongues. After a few plates of marginal enchiladas and more than a few glasses of even more marginal cabernet, they forgot they were angry in the first place. For some ungodly reason, both Iris and Dimuira came to our table after dinner. I had no intention of subjecting myself to that shitshow, so I pounded two Jacks and Cokes, thus exceeding the volunteer two-drink limit by four and stumbled out to the dancefloor. I shook my legs to a few jams. My folks followed the act. The second my father stepped foot on the tiles, Divine lurched at him from the crowd. She grabbed his huge hands and held them up like a baby chimp's. I cupped my mouth and leaned into my father's ear.

"Be careful," I whispered. "She told me earlier she might S your D."

His face fell red. He exploded with laughter and the night followed suit. The last thing I remember is drooling on a sofa at the Ak disco while Dave and Dimuira made out in front of me. It was a pathetic end to a grand evening.

THE NEXT TWO days were a barrage of lame meetings. The only things worth mentioning are that Dave fucked Dimuira's mouth and my folks got their clothes. There was also the lunch with Harry and his wife Lonnie. We had it on Harry's invitation to a Turkish joint in town. My father was furiously ill with diarrhea. He kept getting up to go to the bathroom and couldn't finish his slice of bread. Other than that, the lunch was fine. My mother and Lonnie exchanged shopping tips and Harry regaled us all with wild tales of his service in Afghanistan. The meal ended and Harry paid. I was almost in a spot to think him nice. On our way out the door, he put his hand on my shoulder. He shuffled his mustache and looked me in the eye.

"I know you're going to visit Truman in Kyrgyzstan," he said.

"Okay?"

"Don't get me wrong, I think that's wonderful, but I feel I must warn you like I warned Simon and Dave. Truman is nothing but trouble."

I felt a loud fart coming on.

"Not because he's a bad person," he continued, "on the contrary, he's a good person. It's just that his irresponsible lifestyle creates problems all around him and those who associate with him eventually fall victim to whatever mess he's created for himself."

He waited for me to respond. I nodded once.

"Thank you," I said. "I'll keep that in mind."

"Good," he said, patting me on the shoulder.

Harry and Lonnie left. My folks and I took a cab to the bank, as my father needed to exchange money. The cabbie kept complementing me on my Turkmen. I couldn't understand half of what he was saying, but my responses were enough to keep the conversation going. My folks were in awe. My father kept repeating things like, "That's amazing, son," and my mother held my hand and beamed. I felt proud, like the fact that I'd learned enough Turkmen to chat with a drunken cab driver really meant something. I reveled in my own glory for a moment. Then our car stalled.

"Fuck your mother," the cabbie yelled.

We rolled to a stop by the side of the road. The cabbie got out and checked the tank. He told me through the window that it was empty. I nodded my head like "no shit." My folks looked at me with doe-eyes.

"What do we do now?" my mother said.

I kicked open the door.

"We walk down the road and hail a new cab."

"Great," my father said.

We got out and paid the cabbie a buck. The sun was bearing down on us like a flaming truck. My parents looked like such tourists;

both were wearing black sunglasses, white sneakers, and those stupid cowboy hats from the embassy party. My mother had her camera slung around her neck. Every time she saw a flower or a beetle or a dead butterfly, she clicked a photo of it. A cop was on the corner staring at her. I barked at her to stop but she didn't hear me. I went back to hailing a cab. I got one before we were all arrested for gross idiocy or fried to boogers on the pavement. We went straight to the bank. A tall gold statue of Türkmenbaşy was out front. His sparkling hand was in the air greeting those who came. As we walked under it, I muttered the word "prick." Inside, the air conditioning reconfigured my bowels such that whatever log was in there got pushed to the lips of my anus. I clenched my cheeks and widened my eyes.

"I gotta take a fuckin' dump," I said to my dad.

He chuckled and waved me on. I went in the john and picked a stall. There was a real porcelain toilet. I dropped my pants and covered the ring. The turds flew out of me like drunken sailors from a freshly docked ship in Bangkok. My toes shook uncontrollably. The plopping stopped and I reached for toilet paper. I touched nothing but cardboard.

"You gotta be fucking kidding me," I said

I looked on the lid and around the base. There were no more rolls. I contemplated shuffling to another stall. Someone walked in and washed their hands. I waited for them to finish. Another guy walked in and popped a squat in the stall next to me. He grunted out his first turd. When it slapped the water, I saw red.

"Fuck it," I said.

I reached into my pocket. I grabbed whatever was in there and held it up. It was a crumpled 10,000 manat note. I uncrumpled it and saw Türkmenbaşy's face. I thought of Boris Sheikmuradov and his failed coup. I thought of his thousand followers who'd been murdered in the desert and the families they were survived by. I thought of the KNB and their wicked minions. I thought of Jahan and Baýram and all the other Turkmen who suffered under their boots. I felt a swelling sense of pride in my bosom. I looked The Great Leader in his pixelated eye and winked.

"Here's to you, baby," I said.

I reached between my thighs and scraped his face across my hole. I did it once more for good measure then I dropped the note. I stood and pulled my pants up. I turned around and looked down. Türkmenbaşy's face was decorated in shit. A tiny wrinkle where his mouth was made it look like he was smiling goofily. I smiled back and hit the lever. Homefry spiraled down the tubes and joined his family. I washed my hands and walked out. My father was waiting for me by the door.

"How'd it go?" he asked.

I told him what had just happened. He cackled like a jackal on ice. We got the dough and hit the curb.

"Let's get the fuck outta here," I said.

I WOKE UP on the floor at seven-twenty with a crick in my neck. My folks were ready to go so I was the one holding up the show. I showered, dressed, and shuffled down to the lobby. Our guide was already waiting for us. He had neat black hair, a strong jaw, and brown eyes. His demeanor was soft and playful, and he seemed to greet life with a court jester's nonchalance. He introduced himself as Myrat. He saw we were struggling with our bags and immediately helped us. We took everything out to the van where our driver was waiting. We stacked it up, shut the doors, and hit the road.

On the way through Aşgabat, Myrat chatted with us. He welcomed my folks to Turkmenistan. Then he started in about himself.

"I'm a student of English for ten years," he said. "I study at the International Institute of Foreign Language at Aşgabat, and I must say, I just receive some very good news."

"What's that?" I asked.

"In one month, I will go to study international relations for four years at institute in Geneva, Switzerland."

I thought of Jahan sinking deeper and deeper into the pit of quicksand that was Gurbagahowda while her dreams dissolved in the wind.

"Good for you," I said.

"Thank you," he said. "It is big deal for me. I have many plans for afterwards too."

"Such as?"

"I want to fight world hunger because if people aren't hunger, they won't commit crimes, and if there is no crime, that means there is peace."

"Brilliant."

"Thank you, thank you."

He rambled on. We left Aşgabat and peeled out into the desert. The Ladas whipped by us like crazed banshees. My mother crossed her legs and gripped her elbows. I put my hand on her shoulder and told her it was okay. She nodded softly and stared out the window. The mountains of the Kopet-Dag swelled then faded. The sky got bluer and bluer and the sun burned above us like the eye of a cosmic snail. Before we hit Tejen, we stopped on the side of the road to buy melons. The ladies who ran the stands were wrapped in purple rags and squatting on box lids. They stared at us through slits as we walked up. When they realized we were there to buy their produce, they broke into a frenzy. They fussed and squawked over which melons to sell us. They settled on two watermelons and two *kyrk günlük* (cantaloupes). We thanked them and handed over the cash. We got back in the van and took off.

We arrived in Gurbagahowda at 11:00 a.m. As per my itinerary, we stopped at On Yet first. Jahan, Azat, and Islam were waiting outside. They greeted us with handshakes and warm hellos. Islam was the most excited of the three. He assumed the role of guide and ushered us in the door. He led us through the halls of his rickety little school. He showcased the fabulous paint job and the portraits of T-Bag, Thug-B, and various exemplary students. He took us to his office and sat us down for tea. A few other teachers were there, and they gawked at my folks like they had green genitalia growing from their cheeks. I could tell my father was the most uncomfortable with this. He must have repeated the words, "What a wonderful school," three dozen times. Islam bowed and lapped it up. I tried not to cringe.

After our cockeyed cup of tea, I took my folks to see the classrooms. They ooh'd and aah'd the whole time. My mother remarked that everything was "all so lavish." I couldn't tell if she was being polite or sarcastic. Either way, it made me feel like I'd been serving at a McDonald's Play Place. Nothing eviscerates a Peace Corps volunteer more than telling them how lovely their site is. I choked down the comment and continued the tour. Next on the list was the computer room. My mother walked in and gasped.

"Oh, Goosy," she said. "The Turkmen government must really care about its people. This is absolutely wonderful."

I looked at the three junk-box computers. Two were dead and the other had a flickering screen. I nodded and clicked off the lights.

"Indeed," I said.

We said our goodbyes and got in the van. As we did, I saw Jahan lean in and whisper something to my father. When we were in our seats, I asked him what she'd said. He turned around with a strange little smile on his face.

"She said she wished her mother had had a son like you."

I blushed. He asked me why she'd say such a thing.

"Her brother is a dick and won't let her do anything," I said. "He's part of the reason she's stuck here and not off traveling and living her dreams."

My father snorted.

"Why don't you kick his ass?"

"Believe me, I've thought about it."

He chuckled. I told Myrat to tell the driver in Russian where to go. We hit all the spots: the uly and kiçi çaýhanas, the bazaar, the dükan, the dellekhana, the phone house, the park, the bench where I wrote my poems, the trail into nothingness that I often walked. I wouldn't say my folks were impressed with Gurbagahowda, but they seemed at least satisfied that their son was living in a place of some civilization, even if it was stuck decades—and in some cases, centuries—in the past and surrounded on all sides by flat, brown fuck-all.

Our next stop was Bayram's. We parked in front of his gate and got out. He greeted us with a smile and a handshake. We were an hour early, but he didn't seem to mind. He took us inside to meet his family. His wife and four kids stared at us with glistening eyeballs as we walked in the door. You'd think the A-Team had just arrived. Nope, it was just three Americans with heatstroke, sweating themselves to puddles. We said our hellos and went into the dining area. When my father saw the spread on the floor he choked. The man is six feet six, 330; inviting him to sit Indian-style would be like inviting the Dalai Lama to twerk nude. Out of sheer politeness, my father gave it a crack. I mean this quite literally for as he lowered his massive torso over his paperclipping legs, his cavernous ass crack came smiling above his pant line. I tried desperately not to laugh. I could tell Bayram and my mother were doing the same. My father tipped forward and crashed down on his heels. The teacups in front of him jumped. He rocked from side to side and straightened his back. He looked up and grinned like an eel.

"Comfy," he said.

We laughed and sat around him. No sooner did we pour our tea than Gözel came in with the food. She brought sliced veggies and salads and meatball soup. Bayram held out a hand and said, "Please enjoy." Both of my folks were now battling knee-buckling diarrhea. They each ate a slice of tomato and a spoonful of soup. A few minutes later, Gözel came in with the main course. It was chicken palow with raisins and carrots. Bayram took the bowl and made each of us a plate. I assume he was going by size because he gave my mother one helping, me two, and himself three. When he got to my father's sixth helping, I looked at my father's eyes. I'd only seen the man cry once before, but if Bayram had put a single grain of rice more on his dish, I knew I was in for an encore.

Once everyone was served, we started in. We sipped our tea and chewed our food. The silence in the room was deafening. I contemplated lighting my dad's twelve hairs on fire just to dash a little spice in the afternoon. I did the next best thing. I mentioned that Baryam was an English teacher and that he'd recently gone to the States for training. I was hoping this would at least get my mother talking; she'd been a substitute teacher of both chemistry and Spanish for many years. I finished listing all the places Baýram had visited in the US. My mother stared at the fruit bowl.

"Wouldn't it be great if Turkmenistan could ship its delicious melons all over the world?" she said.

Baýram looked at her like she'd just unknowingly queefed in his face. My father and I nodded and chewed. My mother realized she'd done a non sequitur. Her face went cranberry and she tried to cover it up by eating spoonful after tiny spoonful of food and repeating the phrase, "This is so delicious." By the twentieth repetition, I cut her off. I suggested we watch some TV and Baýram agreed. He clicked the thing on and gave us pillows. Gözel cleared our plates and we leaned back. Within minutes, we were out. The last thing I heard was the air conditioner buzzing.

WE WOKE UP two hours later. We gave Baýram the melons we'd bought and thanked him and his family. We arrived at my house at 5:00 p.m. My host family came outside. They walked up to my folks and said, "Salam." They shook their hands and fell silent. I could tell my folks wanted desperately to connect. My father fanned his face and looked at me.

"Tell them I said it's very hot."

He almost screamed the last two words. I guess he figured if he increased the volume of what he was saying, he'd also increase its comprehensibility. He only succeeded in terrifying my host sisters. They ran back in the house and locked the door. Patma started watering the garden. I translated what my father had said, and she chuckled.

"Why don't you show them around the yard," she said. "We'll take their bags up to your room."

I nodded and thanked her. I led my folks around the complex. I showed them the fried garden and the ratty chicken coup, the tamdyr and kettle-stand where Patma did her cooking, and the rusty pipe that glugged our only water. I showed them the crumbling brick wall atop which I sat and watched the sunset, the kuhnýa where I warmed myself in winter, and the banýa where I often contemplated suicide. The penultimate treat was the goat den. I introduced them to my favorite goat *Aky* (Whitey), who'd narrowly escaped our dull butcher's knife. He took a liking to my father right away. I chalked it up to kindred intellects. The final scar on the list was the torture chamber. I walked up to the door and held the knob.

"Feast your eyes," I said.

I threw open the creaky door. A swarm of flies came billowing out. They pulled the shit particles with them. My folks cupped their faces. My mother closed her eyes. My father kept his open. He squealed when he saw the oozing hole and the jiggling mound of feces underneath. I laughed and clapped my hands.

"Who's ready to eat again?" I said.

My folks turned and walked up to my room. I giggled and skipped behind them. Myrat and the driver joined us. My father busted out his little DVD player and put on the movie *300*. A minute later, he fell asleep. The driver and my mother followed his act. Myrat and I stayed up and watched. I wasn't so keen on the film, but Myrat dug it. Every time there was a fight scene, he raised his fists and shouted things like "Oh my god." and "Fantastic." He sounded like a motivational speaker getting a blowjob.

The film ended at dinnertime. Patma and my host sisters served us a feast. They brought sliced honeydew and watermelons, meatballs, and stuffed pepper çorba, lamb and chicken palow. They even brought Agy Serdar, my favorite brand of spicy ketchup. Once everything was on the klionka, they closed the door behind them. Myrat, the driver, and I dug in. My folks barely ate. If they got half a dozen bites between the two of them, I'd be surprised. After the plates were cleared, my mother grabbed her suitcase. She unzipped it and started pulling things out of its belly.

"We got all your favorites," she said.

She handed me bags and bags of Skittles, roasted peanuts, beef jerky, Rice Krispy Treats, and granola bars. I gave her a giant hug and thanked her.

"We also got you some practical items," my dad said, tossing me a duffle bag.

I unzipped it and looked inside. It was filled with T-shirts, boxers, socks, toothpaste, deodorant, dental floss, and razors. It felt like Christmas in Reno. I gave my dad a hug and thanked him as well. My mother took out another bag.

"I also bought each of your little host family members something nice," she said.

She pulled everything out and displayed it for me. She'd brought hand lotions and soaps for Aziza, Ogulgerek, and Miwe, Beanie Babies and a Mickey Mouse purse for baby Yazgül, a San Francisco Giants cap and a deck of cards for both Ali and Merdan, a beautiful set of teacups for Patma and Durdy, and a hardcover picture book of California for the whole family. Seeing what efforts my mother had gone through choked me up. I rubbed her on the shoulder and thanked her again.

"Think nothing of it," she said.

We brought the gifts down together. We went into the anteroom and I called my host family. They gathered around us. My mother handed out their gifts, and they smiled and thanked her. Patma whispered something to Ogulgerek. She ran into the other room and came back with a shopping bag. She reached in and pulled out a beautiful brown shawl. She handed it to my mother and smiled.

"I knitted this for you," she said in Turkmen.

I translated. My mother blushed. Tears were now filling her eyes.

She straightened her back and put her palms on her knees.

"Johann, translate what I say for your host mother," she said.

I nodded once.

"Thank you so much for inviting us," she said. "You have a wonderful home and a wonderful family, and my husband and I are honored to be here. Thank you for the lovely dinner and the beautiful shawl, and thank you . . ."

She started crying. The tears spilled down her cheeks like clear pollywogs. She made a tiny circle with her mouth and breathed in deep.

"Thank you," she repeated, "for taking care of my precious boy."

She sunk her face into her palms. I looked at over at Patma. She too had tears in her eyes, but her hard old pride refused to release them. To avoid embarrassment, I got up and said goodnight. I lifted my mother—who was still crying—and led her out the door. My father followed. I suggested we all go to bed. Myrat and our driver had beaten us to it. They were catatonic on the tapçan with their mouths open to the stars. It was cool and breezy out. My room was hot and stuffy. My folks looked at one another.

"Mind if we join them, son?" my father asked.

"Not at all."

I ran in the house and grabbed pillows and blankets. When I came back out, my folks were already asleep. My father was splayed out and ripping logs. My mother was curled up and purring like a little bird. I wrapped her in a blanket and kissed her forehead.

"G'night," I said.

WE WOKE UP at four thirty the next morning. We packed our crap, said goodbye to my host family, and cut. We were out of GBH by five-twenty. We had fifteen hours of travel ahead of us, if everything went right. The second we hit the desert, our driver hit the gas. We floored it to Tejen then cut left toward Mary. The Ladas and the camels and the sheep and the tractors all whizzed by us in streaks of dusty colors. My folks gripped their seats and tried not to barf the bananas they'd eaten out the window. We arrived in Mary at seven. We make a quick pit stop, then cut to the ancient city of Merv. It may once have been a great Silk Road city. But after Genghis Khan's son, Tolui finished with the place in 1221, it wasn't much more than a few bars of sand collecting shrubs. We toured around and checked out the nearby mosque. A prayer was in session, which a bearded imam wearing a red tahýa and a long green robe was conducting. He raised his hands and closed his eyes. The sea of worshipers in front of him dropped to their knees and prayed. It was a moving and beautiful sight. Then a group of pudgy, pink-faced Americans in fishing hats and "I Love Aşgabat" T-shirts came waddling in. I clenched my jaw and curled my lip. I told Myrat we were ready, and we got in the van and split. We sped through the sandscape for another bit. At 1:00 p.m., we stopped for lunch. The restaurant was on the side of the road. Its roof was sunken, and its doorway was dangling with dried bones. My father took one look at it and grunted.

"I'm not eating at this fucking shithole," he said.

My mother slapped his shoulder and forced him outta the van. We went up there, and the server seated us outside next to a slick of smelly green water. We ordered shashlik and beers. Some old drunk staggered over to the water slick. He farted loudly and whipped out his dick. He started pissing and a rabid dog bolted across the street and tried to bite his crotch. The guy ran off squirting and cussing in every direction. My father laughed so hard he almost fell out of his seat.

We ate and left. We blew through Türkmenabat and greater Lebap. We made it to the Uzbek border by five. The crossing closed at six. Loads of trucks and cars were in front of us. Myrat suggested we walk. We said goodbye to him and the driver. We grabbed our crap and hit the street. We made it to the crossing in ten minutes. Everyone behind a desk or holding an AK asked to see our passports. We must have had them checked twenty times. We wiped our brows and walked out. We were expecting to see our new van. All we saw was another row of trucks. It disappeared into the desert.

"What the hell is this?" my dad said.

We walked a ways. There were a few families dragging their bags. I asked a guy what they were doing. He turned to me and smiled.

"We are walking to the Uzbek border," he said in Russian. "It's two kilometers ahead."

I dropped my chin and slapped my cheek.

"What did he say?" my dad said.

"He said, 'Tie your shoes and swig some water, 'cuz you've got a helluva walk yet.'"

"Great."

We hit the Arçibil and got to it. The air was so hot and dry we felt like three earthworms crawling across the floor of a giant blazing oven. By kilometer one, our faces were blood-red. Our clothes were blossoming with sweat and our eyes could barely see. I was terrified my folks might die. I gave them the rest of my water and they chugged it down. We pushed and pushed and pushed. When we made it to the crossing, we looked like death. A man with a stethoscope walked up to us. He checked our heartbeats and felt our heads and gave us cups of water. The water was warm and tasted of wax. None of us gave a black rat's ass. We sucked it down and asked for more. The man poured us three more cups then handed us our forms. The fucking things were all in Russian. We struggled with them for two solid hours. I'm certain we filled them out improperly. The lady behind the desk took them anyway. She stamped our passports and shooed us out. The guards locked the doors behind us. We walked down the road in search of our van. The only vehicle we found was a tiny white Lada. We asked the driver if it was for us. He smiled and said it was. My father stamped his feet.

"That asshole Brad said we'd get a luxury van, not this pile of shit," he shouted.

He dropped his bags and pulled out his cell phone. As he gave our tour operator a piece of his mind, my mother elbowed me.

She pointed to a billboard above my father's head. It read, LET HAPPINESS BLOW ACROSS YOUR FACE.

We both roared with laughter.

UZBEKISTAN WAS BEAUTIFUL. We toured some of the world's best-preserved ancient cities: Bukhara, Shahrisabz, Samarqand. We saw mosques and mausoleums and bazaars. We ate tons of juicy shashlik and washed it down with ice-cold beer. Our tour guides were informative and sweet. Our hotel rooms were better than expected and even boasted ground floor bookshops and restaurants. Despite the cramped Lada, it was a smooth ride. It'd have almost been a perfect time, were it not for the ugly thought in my mind. It crept up my brainstem like the tentacle of a malignant tumor. It spread through the guts of my head, tearing down good feelings and saturating them with fear. It was the thought that my father would hate me, the idea that if I admitted to him clear and final that I wanted to write, he wouldn't accept me. I didn't see this as a far-fetched thing. My father had graduated from MIT[92] with a Ph.D. in organometallic chemistry, and it was arguably his thesis that had served as the springboard for the research that won his supervisor the Nobel Prize in chemistry in 2005. The man ate, drank, and breathed chemistry. He read magazines and books on chemical compounds, tinkered with theories on ultra-clean energy, and had even created a 90-proof liquor that was so pure and so sweet it went down without a burn and left without a hangover. As I child, I revered my father. I tried to be like him and do the chemistry thing, but I didn't have the brain for it. My gears were more attuned to the word. And it took me grade school, middle school, high school, and college, five summers traveling the world, and two years roasting in the belly of hell to come to terms with this.

When we arrived in Almaty, I knew I had to tell him. It was the last stop on our trip, and I didn't want him to go back home and start

---

[92] Massachusetts Institute of Technology.

extrapolating a spider web of plans to trap me in after my service. I waited for a time when it was just us. It came on a bright hot day. We were walking down the street looking for a soda stand. I'm not sure how, but the topic of the future came up. At first, it was casual chitchat. We went back and forth about all the great wine and steaks and stories we were gonna share when I got home. Then things got quiet. My father stopped walking and looked me in the eyes. I could feel the question coming. I could see it resting in his throat like a poisonous rose. I hunched my shoulders and lowered my chin. My father spread his lips.

"What's your plan?" he said.

Those three little words hit me like bricks. I went spiraling backwards into the chasm of myself, screaming and clawing and flapping the whole way. I saw the madness of my youth and the struggle of my service. I saw all the horrible monsters—fangs, eyes, scales, claws—that had brought me to this day. I'd be a chickenshit if I ducked out; a yellow-blooded, fish-gutted, cock-mongrel who sucked pea soup through a straw and raped babies on Wednesdays. I hit the bottom of my spirit and groaned. My body was a knot of limbs and my fingers were out, curling. I untied my joints and stood up. I dusted myself off and swallowed. The answer came from one mouth and out the other. I heard it through the walls of my flesh.

"I want to write," I said.

My four words were bigger than his three. They hung in the air like bagged cadavers swaying gently in the breeze. I could see my father processing them. I could hear the gears of his giant mechanical mind churning and spinning and straining. His cheeks twitched. His beard grew darker and his specs glinted. He took a deep breath and let it fly.

"It's your life," he said.

I'm not gonna say this didn't hurt. Truth be told, being stripped naked and dipped in hot tar would have been preferable to the old man's response. Anyways, it was what it was. I took it in the gullet and moved on.

The rest of our trip was so-so. I said goodbye to my folks and hello to Rave Dave and Simon. We went to Kyrgyzstan and visited Truman. We drank like pirates and fucked women and Simon blew a dude. We traveled to Issyk-Kol[93] and all through the mountains. We ate good food and smoked good smoke and even saw a fight or two. It was a reckless, crazy, wild ride. Our CD Harry would surely have disapproved. When we got back to Aşgabat, we were all bumps and bruises. Dave even had white polka dots on his tongue from smooching some Korean hooker's twat. We hocked a real laugh over that. We had one last night together and drank it dead. In the wicked blue morning, we said our goodbyes. I went to the old airport[94] and caught a cab. We hit the desert at sunrise. It burnt my eyes to scabs.

---

[93] Issyk-Kol is a lake in the Tian Shan mountains in eastern Kyrgyzstan. It is the seventh-deepest lake in the world.

[94] An old airport in Ashgabat, the parking lot of which now serves as a large taxi stand.

22

FOR THE NEXT week and a half, I did very little. Highlights included dealing with the heat, eating tons of shitty çorba, registering with Azat in Tejen, and drinking heavily with Brooke in Aşgabat. I also worked on *501* with Jahan. We made progress on it, but as far as Jahan's personal life was concerned—the teacher training in Kazakhstan, the translator job with the ministry, the LCF job with Peace Corps, her house, her French, her goals, her dreams—there was no progress.

On a roasting Tuesday afternoon in early August, I went to Jahan's classroom to work on *501*. She was looking her usual depleted self—dress pale, face paler, eyes like two little hazel swamps—but at least she was ready to work. She had her example sentences written and her dictionary out. She'd sharpened every pencil on her desk and had placed them all in a neat row above her notepad. I sat down next to her and we got to it. We translated sentence after sentence in a surprisingly short amount of time. I thought we might have a shot at putting a full day in. Then the gangly garawul with the round eyes and the Dumbo ears banged on the door.

"Jahan," he yelled. "Get your ass out here."

She clenched her teeth and stood up.

"What is it, sir?" she asked.

"You have a meeting to go to. Now move."

"But sir, I went to the meeting last Friday like you told me to, and Islam said it was okay if I skipped today's meeting."

The garawul's saggy face turned the color of beet juice. He stormed into the classroom and speared his hand out.

"It's absolutely not okay," he screamed. "You will go to today's meeting and that's final."

Jahan straightened her back and raised her chin.

"Sir," she said. "I'm working on a book right now with Han-Guly, and he and I have a lot left to do, so if you don't mind—"

"I do mind. You can work on your worthless book tomorrow."

The veins on the garawul's neck were wriggling like frog's legs. I wanted to take my pencil and pierce one. I folded my arms and scowled. The garawul turned on his heel and stormed out. Jahan slumped down in her chair and bit her lip. She looked like she was about to burst.

"You okay?" I asked.

She slammed her fist down and shot out of her chair.

"It is always the same," she shouted. "They lie to me and they don't listen, which means they don't respect me."

She fiddled with her gold rings and paced around her desk. I didn't know how to comfort her and part of me didn't want to. It was nice to see her get angry. I was hoping she'd get angrier and tell the floppy-eared garawul to fuck himself. She never did. She just came and sat down and packed her things. I could see she was on the verge of tears. I had to say something.

"How 'bout I call Zoya today and ask her about the LCF position? I know she said she'd call this month, but we can show initiative and call her first."

Jahan shrugged.

"I guess you can. We can meet tomorrow morning at nine and you can tell me any news."

"Deal."

We said our goodbyes and split. On the way home, I started feeling ill. I hit the outhouse and took a runny dump. I drank a bottle of Arçibil and had a nap. I got up and ate some slimy çorba. I went into the living room and called Zoya. She answered in her waddling ostrich voice. I asked her about the LCF position, and she snorted.

"The deadline for the application is in three days," she said. "If you don't turn it in by then you will have no chance."

"Are you serious?"

"Of course."

"Why didn't you tell me this before?"

"I mentioned it during July All-Vol. You must not been listen to me."

"Well, what can I do to fix this?"

"You can give me Jahan's phone number now and I will call her and try to make her come to Aşgabat to fill out application."

"What happens if she can't come?"

"Then you will come and fill it out or she won't get job."

"Fine."

I gave her Jahan's number and thanked her. I ran to the outhouse and took another dump. I spent the rest of the night shitting. I didn't sleep till 3:00 a.m. I woke up the next morning at ten-forty. I figured Jahan had already gone home. I took a horribly painful crap and ate lunch. I went to the phone and called Jahan. I apologized for being late. She sighed.

"I waited till noon for you," she said.

"I'm sorry," I said again. "I am very sick and woke up very late. Did Zoya call you?"

"Yes."

"What did she say?"

"She said I must go to Aşgabat to fill out application, but I cannot because of finances."

"What? Jahan, you have to."

"I cannot. I don't have my salary yet. Maybe we can ask Zoya for special extension?"

"That'll never work. Zoya is very strict. It must be by Friday or we can't do it."

There was a long pause. I could hear Jahan clinking her rings on the other end. I closed my eyes and waited for it.

"Can you go in and get the application?" she asked.

This was truly a test of my zeal. For me to make this happen, I would have to leave for Aşgabat that day, diarrhea guts and all, come back the next day with the application, meet with Jahan at school, have her fill out the application, then return to Aşgabat the following morning to hand the damn thing in and make the deadline. Knowing me, I'd stay the weekend and party. This would mean the whole ordeal would end up costing me a million manat or more. I rolled it over and over again in my head. I knew what I had to do.

"Okay," I said.

"Thank you, Han-Guly," she said, sounding almost disappointed.

"No worries. I'll see you at school tomorrow at 3:00 p.m. with the application."

I spent the next two hours trying to get a hold of Zoya. I must've called a dozen times. Our poor secretary, Maya, had to deal with my ass. After my twelfth call, she finally asked me what I needed from Zoya. I told her about the application. She clicked her tongue.

"I have the LCF application right here," she said. "I can just read you everything and you can write it down. Then you can have your counterpart write the answers and you can bring them to Aşgabat and fill the application out yourself."

It was a brilliant idea. Though had there been internet or even one miserable fax machine in GBH, the whole thing could have been avoided. I praised Maya anyway and told her to fire away. She obliged then mentioned that on top of answering the questions, Jahan had to provide three letters of reference. I groaned and hung up. I called Jahan and gave her the news. I told her to be over by 4:00 p.m. She said she would.

At four on the dot, there was a knock at the waratan. I opened it and saw Jahan. Her head was wrapped in a green ýaglyk. Her eyes were little slits. I invited her inside, but she refused. I had to sit on a dirty rock outside and explain everything to her while she leaned over me and breathed. I got to the part about the three references. I told her she could use me, Baýram and Islam. She nodded her head and hmmm'd. I heard her rings clink.

"What's wrong now?" I asked.

"My mother doesn't want me to do this job," she said.

"Jesus, why not? It'll only be for three months."

"Because Zoya told me that it was two hundred and fifty dollars a month. And my salary here is three hundred dollars, so that's one hundred and fifty dollars I will not have for my family. And my mother is still sick . . . and my brother has no job."

A hundred and fifty bucks for Jahan could mean the difference between life and death. For me, it simply meant downgrading from a steak and a bottle of wine to a burger and a bottle of beer. I still needed the money for my trip to Africa, and because of my drinking problem, my funds were running rather short. I mulled the whole thing over in my head. Then I sighed.

"Don't worry," I said. "I'll give you the money."

Jahan's ýaglyk slid down and her round face turned red.

"No," she said. "It's too much money."

"Not for me," I said, handing her the information. "Go home now and tell your mother your salary at Peace Corps will be the same as your salary now. Then come back here tomorrow at 9:00 a.m. and give me your answers and references to take to Aşgabat."

"Okay," she said.

JAHAN CAME AT nine twenty-six the next morning. She was wearing a lavender ýaglyk and köýnek and carrying a stack of papers. She handed them to me with a frown.

"What in God's name is wrong now?" I asked.

"I spoke with Baýram teacher," she said. "He told me that when he came back from working as LCF for Peace Corps he had to work very hard to find a job and it took him many months. This will be very hard for my family and my mother says she doesn't want me to take this job because I will lose more money."

I was one spark away from exploding. I clenched my jaw and folded my hands.

"Jahan," I said, "what is it that you want to do?"

She looked down and drew a line in the dirt with her toe.

"I want to go. But—"

"Look. You hate being a teacher, right?"

She nodded.

"Okay, well this is the only opportunity you're gonna get for a long time that could help you become something other than a teacher. If you don't at least try, you'll be stuck here forever. I understand your concern about finding a job when you get back, but we'll worry about that later. Right now, I'm going to Peace Corps, turning in this damn application, and getting things organized with Zoya. Then you can go to the orientation and decide afterward what you're going to do. Okay?"

"Thank you, Han-Guly," she said.

"No worries."

I went upstairs and packed. I grabbed a cab to Aşgabat and made it to PCHQ by noon. I spent half the day in the lounge filling out the application. I had to doctor a couple of Jahan's responses, so they fit the essay questions. One of the entries she wrote really touched me. It read:

"Johann is not only my co-worker, he's my best friend too. I know he wants to help me all the time, and I'm happy to have someone around who understands me."

I typed this and tried not to cry. Harry wandered in and saw me. He shifted his pussy-tickler and bounced on his heels.

"What are *you* doing here?" he asked.

I explained that I was trying to get my counterpart a job as an LCF with Peace Corps.

"Good," he said. "We need LCFs badly. There are eight slots and we've had twelve applicants, so she's got a good chance. How's her English?"

"Good. Great, in fact. Right now, I'm using what she wrote to fill out her application. There's also these essay questions and I'm—"

"Writing them for her?" he said, raising his eyebrows.

"No," I said. "I'm typing them for her. That's why I came in. She wrote them. I'm typing them. We're keeping it honest. Have a look for yourself."

I handed him the essays. He looked them over with a sour face. He handed them back and said, "Hmm." Then he sauntered off.

"Fucker," I mumbled.

At 5:00 p.m. I finished Jahan's application. I went to Zoya's office and handed it to her. She smiled like a wicked cuckoo over a quail egg. She told me she'd contact Jahan soon. I thanked her and breathed a sigh of relief. I spent the next three nights drinking myself into a coma.

THAT MONDAY I met up with Jahan to work on *501*. She seemed in decent spirits. I told her I'd turned in the application. She didn't respond.

"Are you going to the orientation?" I asked.

She folded her hands on her lap and frowned.

"I will think about it," she said.

"You'll think about it? Jahan, I didn't go all the way to Aşgabat, write out your entire application, and lick Zoya's nasty butt crack for you to think about going. Besides, just because you go, doesn't mean you hafta take the job. But I can assure you, if you don't go, you won't have a snowman's chance in Tejen of getting the damn job."

"Please let me think about it," she said.

I shrugged and pulled out my materials. We worked on *501* for the rest of the afternoon. I went home and got naked. I dumped a bucket of water on myself then lay in front of the fan and binge-watched *Dexter*. The next morning, I met with Jahan again to work on the book. No sooner did we start than Islam marched in like a tiny mongoloid goblin.

"Jahan," he barked. "Get to my office now and attend this meeting."

I spiked him the devil eyes. He ignored me and walked off. I turned to Jahan wearing a concerned face. She was smiling and bouncing her fists on her lap.

"What are you so happy about?" I asked.

"Because," she said, grabbing a piece of paper.

She scribbled something down and handed it to me. There were two words, "People's Council." I looked back up at her. She was glowing like a vile of radium.

"So?"

"So, Islam told me that maybe I will be elected to serve on this."

"What's that mean?"

"It means I will be on the Council and just make decisions for Gurbagahowda and the school. I will just sit and not work and have an easy life."

"That's what you want?" I said. "To sit around at meetings all day and do nothing? I thought you wanted to get out of Gurbagahowda and see the world. You know, travel, explore, get a cool job."

"I do want those things," she said, still smiling. "But this job will mean more money, and I will have influence and respect in Gurbagahowda."

"What about the orientation? Has Zoya called yet?"

"Yes, she has. She called me yesterday after you left and said she wants to see me there."

"Great. And what did you tell her?"

"I told her I would see."

"You told her you would see? Zoya is not a person you say, 'I'll see' to. If she offers you something, you take it and be glad."

"Han-Guly, I want to go," she said, firmly, "but I must think about it still."

"You don't have much longer to think, orientation is in six days."

She nodded and went to her meeting. I packed my crap and left. On the walk home, I thought about the whole mess. The way I figured it, she was just stalling. Every time I asked her about going to the orientation, she was gonna tell me she was still "thinking." Then when it came time to go, she'd flake. The excuses she'd give me would be finances and this new job on the People's Council. But underneath I knew it was just plain ol' fear. I shrugged it off and kept walking. I got home and went straight to my room. I spent the rest of the day sweating and masturbating. The next morning, I went back to On Yet to work on the book with Jahan. I made no mention of the orientation. I didn't want to have a volatile work environment like the previous day. I pulled out my materials and got to it. I translated page after page of her Turkmen sentences into English. My hand started to sweat. My pen slipped from my fingers and rolled across the desk. I reached for it carelessly. My elbow bumped Jahan's breast. She lost her breath. The sound she made—like a little fish sucking air—tinged the base of my spine and sent blood rushing to my face. Electricity crackled between us. I thought of kissing her. I knew the consequences would be devastating. I composed myself and continued working. Jahan did the same. We never mentioned the incident.

The next day we worked on *501* again. I wanted to ask Jahan about the orientation, but I refrained. The day after that I could no longer contain myself. I asked her if she was gonna go and she bit her lip.

"I will think about it," she said.

I closed my book and looked at her.

"I know what you're doing," I said.

"What?"

"You're going to keep postponing until the orientation is over. Then you're gonna blame it on finances and the new job here."

"No, I'm not. I just need to think."

"Bullshit. You've had forever to think. Now there are only three days left. Are you going or not?"

"Ay, Han-Guly, please."

Her eyes teared. She wiped them dry with her thumbs. Her face was now cracking. She spoke to keep from falling apart.

"I want to go," she said. "It's just that I'm having financial troubles, and—"

"I told you I'd cover the difference in your salary," I said. "Hell, I'll even pay for your whole trip to Aşgabat. Just go to the damn orientation."

She looked up at me and smiled weakly.

"But if you give me this money it means I am—beggar."

"No, it doesn't. It just means I'm helping you. Think of it this way. You've worked with me on this book for a long time now and this is your payment. If your mom has any questions, just tell her I'm paying you for your work and that's it."

"Okay. But I still don't know if I will go. I must attend teachers' meeting tomorrow and ask permission. If they give me, I will go to Aşgabat for orientation."

"Fine."

I SPENT THE rest of the day and night flipping around in my sheets, naked and worrying. There was nothing I could do. At midnight, I went out to look at the stars. They were all a bunch of dim bollocks hanging up in the sky. I urinated on the chickens and went to bed. I woke up the next day at noon. I ate a crappy bowl of pumpkin soup. I went into the house and called Jahan. Her mother answered the phone rudely. Then Jahan got on the line.

"I have good news," she said.

"What is it?"

"The council approved. I can go to Aşgabat."

I nearly barfed up my lunch.

"Holy shit, that's fantastic. Do you need anything from me?"

"Yes, I will need money."

"How much?"

"One-fifty."

"Dollars?"

"No, Han-Guly. One hundred fifty thousand manat."

"Phew. Okay, come by tonight and pick it up."

"Thank you," she said softly.

I was a butterfly on the piano the rest of the day. I wrote twenty pages in my journal, jerked off three times, and did somersaults around my room. I watched the endless orange sunset from my balcony. I sang little Turkmen songs with Yazgül and bullshitted with Patma while she cooked her swill. At eight-thirty there was a knock at the waratan. Patma yelled out *"Kim?"* No one answered. I knew it was Jahan. I ran up to my room. I grabbed the money, stuck it in an English book and ran back down. As I passed Patma she looked up at me.

"Who in God's name is at the waratan?" she asked.

"Sorry," I said. "It's Jahan teacher."

"Can't she speak up and say it's her? That's only polite."

"Sorry. She just needs a book."

Patma clucked and went back to her cooking. I brushed her off and opened the waratan. Jahan was standing there in a bright pink dress. I handed her the book and smiled.

"The money's inside," I said. "Now go to Aşgabat and kick some ass."

She giggled. I raised my hand in the air.

"Gimme a high five," I said.

She raised her hand. I slapped mine against hers. She forgot to push outward. I ended up shoving her shoulder back. She looked terribly confused.

"We'll hafta work on that," I said, chuckling.

She smiled and nodded. I told her good luck and to call me after the orientation. She said okay and split. I went back to the courtyard and Patma bitched some more. I ignored her and went up to my room. During dinner, Merdan bitched about Jahan, too, and called her and her mother whores. I switched my ears off and concentrated on my çorba. Jahan was going to orientation and that was all that mattered

THE NEXT DAY was the most pleasant day of my service. I woke up and had a long and satisfying wank, then I went to the outhouse and flushed my guts of their flowers. I emptied my piss bottles and took a nice cold bucket shower. I went for a walk through town with my arms behind my back and my chin up. Everything I saw bore my fingerprints. The mosque, the poçta, the phone house, the theater, the çaýhanas, the barbershop, the Ladas, the goats, the crooked phone poles, the camels, the dirt roads and the rows of spidery trees—all were speckled with the grease of my touch. I walked to the end of town. The sun was there, floating in the sky like a sphere of burning hay. I smiled grandly at it and flashed my teeth. They sizzled and glinted and popped like diamonds in the microwave. I walked back home and masturbated again. A woman with green skin and the blackest hair and eyes carried me through the valley until my prick shed tears. I wiped them up and had some dinner. I ate downstairs with the boys and enjoyed my meal, even though it did taste of boiled rat hair. Before bed, I slid in a DVD. It was a romantic comedy about a guy who watched films and masturbated a lot but then found a girl who did the same and they got married in some desert on the other side of the planet and lived happily ever after. I fell asleep cooing and sucking my thumb. It was the perfect end to a day well played.

The next afternoon, I awoke to birds chirping. Really it was my host mom screaming that I had a phone call, but it was still birds chirping to me. I clothed myself and came downstairs. I took a pillow for my elbow and lay across the floor. I picked up the phone and cleared my throat. Then I blinked twice slowly.

"Hello?" I said.

A tiny mouse helloed back.

"Hey Jahan," I said. "How's the orientation going?"

There was a long pause. I figured she was just trying to recall all the synonyms for "fantastic" that she knew. I waited with a smile. I heard a little sigh.

"Han-Guly," she said. "I know for sure I will not take this job with Peace Corps."

My heart coughed open like a dried pumpkin.

"Why?" I screamed.

"Because it is too much risk."

"You called just to tell me that?"

"Yes. And to ask your permission."

"For what?"

"Zoya will have us do a presentation in two days, and since I know I will not take this job, I want to know if I can just come back tomorrow."

I don't like to use my gender as a force to gain leverage. But I knew that in Turkmenistan if a man said "no" to a woman with enough conviction, she'd have to listen. I gathered what few scraps of testosterone I had left in me.

"No," I shouted.

Jahan cringed audibly.

"Okay," she said. "I will stay."

I apologized for yelling at her and said I just wanted her to finish the orientation. I told her that once she did, I'd never bother her again. She made a little popping sound with her mouth.

"You're not bothering me," she said. "You're helping me."

I thanked her, and we said our goodbyes. The next morning, I got a call from Maya at Peace Corps. She told me she and Harry were coming out in two days to check my site. She said they might put a new T-17 in with my family, and she wanted to know if I found them suitable. Patma and three of my sisters were in the room with me. I told Maya this and she proceeded to ask me a series of Yes or No questions. From what I remember they were: Do you feel like part of the family? Does your host mother treat you like a son? Do you get along with your host siblings? My answer to all these questions was, "Sort of." Maya laughed and told me my host family was one option.

She said PC was considering a few other families, but that no matter what, a T-17 was coming to GBH. I said that was swell and hung up.

FOR THE NEXT forty-eight hours I fretted about Jahan and her flailing resolve and about having to deal with the coming fledgling. My COS date was December 23rd. This meant that I'd be forced to spend at least three weeks with the little cum-gobbler. If they lived with a host family on the other side of town it might not be too terrible. Sure, they'd corrupt the beauty of a few of my fingerprints, but that was to be expected anyways with time and rain and all the horrible çorba dumps. What would really get my goat was if staff put the newbie in with my family. I guess I could tolerate it if it were an *extremely* hot chick, but such creatures were as common in Peace Corps as unicorn clit bracelets in Scranton, thus I was pretty sure I was gonna hate the fucker with a hot-split-pea-soup passion, plus they'd probably be staying in my room with me, stinking the place up with their dirty feet and pathetic little tears, so yeah, fuck all that noise.

Peace Corps came that Thursday. I took them around town and showed them all my haunts. We went to the uly çayhana for lunch. As we chewed our manty, we chatted about the coming T-17. I answered a few more questions about the suitability of my host family. Then I asked about Jahan. Harry took a tiny bite of his manty and dabbed the corner of his mouth with his napkin.

"I think she made it to the final round," he said.

My face grew pink with happiness. Harry thinned his eyes and smiled cutely.

"But a lot of good teachers are there," he said. "So, to be honest, I don't think she'll make it."

I felt like pitching my beer in his face. I thanked him for his candid response and grabbed my wallet. He stopped me at the pass and paid the bill. I thanked him again and grabbed my hat. I went outside to see him off. He put his hand on my shoulder and leaned into me. I could smell the lamb on his breath. I could see the tiny red veins in his eyes. He looked down into my pupils for a long second. Then he smiled.

"Now don't go anywhere this weekend," he said. "Wouldn't want you getting into any trouble just before your COS."

I simpered and nodded once. Harry released my shoulder and slid into the Jeep. I waved him off and walked home. The minute I arrived, I called Jimmy. I told him my woes and that I needed an out. He laughed out loud like a good ol' country farm boy jus' seen a bull get his balls clipped.

"You just get'cher ass out ta' Türkmenhalk and we'll drink that whole shit away," he said.

I happily obliged. The next day I went out there and we sure did drink that whole shit away. I was a hot mess when I got back on Monday. I fell asleep at 8:00 p.m. and was out for a clean twelve hours. I got up the next morning and took a freezing bucket shower. I threw on my wrinkly clothes and walked to school in the heat. I went to Jahan's classroom to see if she was in. Sure as a cow in Texas ends up between a bun, she was at her desk. She was scribbling something on a sheet of paper. I sidled up next to her and folded my hands.

"So, how'd it go?" I asked.

She looked over at me and smiled.

"Zoya called yesterday," she said. "We had a long conversation about my performance, and at the end, she told me I will not get the job."

I wanted to scream. I wanted to wring my hands at the sky and curse the lightning from the clouds. The blood in me was dry and gray. All I could muster was a miserable, "Why?"

"Because," she said, "I made a mistake on my presentation."

"What mistake?"

"I froze on stage," she said, still smiling. "All the other candidates did their presentations and Bartha watched them. Then when I did my presentation, this woman called Mahym came, and I got very nervous. Zoya told me yesterday that this was very

379

unprofessional. She said I couldn't adapt to change."

The anger rushed back into me like a tidal wave.

"That's fucking bullshit," I screamed. "I knew this was going to happen. And what the fuck was Mahym doing there? Was she judging you? That bitch."

"No, not judging. She was watching. Zoya was judging."

I was shaking with rage. Jahan looked me in the eyes.

"Han-Guly, please," she said. "Many good teachers were there. I don't feel bad that I lost. I made a mistake."

"I understand that. But I feel like this was my last chance to help you, and now you'll be stuck in this goddamned village forever."

"This is a problem," she said, fiddling with her rings.

"What do you mean?"

"I mean, I have more bad news."

"What now?"

"The school will take all of my good students and give them to another teacher. It happens every year. I teach my students well and then the senior teachers take my best and give me stupid ones. They want to make my life harder and harder, and I don't know how to stop them."

Her lips began to quiver. A few tears broke from her eyes and dribbled down her cheeks. She wiped them and stared straight ahead.

"I know what I must do," she said. "I will stop loving my students. Then I won't hurt when they are taken."

"Jahan," I said, "if you refuse to love your students, your life will be even colder and more boring than before. At least if you love them, you'll have some joy."

"But Han-Guly, it is very hard to find even one student to love because all of them are so stupid. Most don't want to learn. And the ones who want to learn are mostly too stupid to learn what I teach them. It is very rare to find students who love to learn and are smart to learn. And when I do find them, the senior teachers take them from me."

Her face was soaked with tears. I evened myself as best I could.

"Jahan," I said, "I really think you should—"

"Can we please work tomorrow?" she said. "I am very upset right now."

I grabbed my bag and stood up. "That's fine."

23

I DIDN'T SEE Jahan for the rest of the week. She seemed to be avoiding me, but I couldn't be sure. I sucked it up and worked on *501*. I took walks around town and went guesting when I could. One day I was invited to a toý. It was a riotous affair that had my ears bleeding halfway through. I took a break to grab some *gazly suw*. As I sat on a bench drinking and nursing my ears, Aman walked up. He greeted me pleasantly with his big square face. Then he started in about how he wanted to attend some international university in the Ukraine and how the entrance test was really hard but if he just had two thousand bucks, he could pay off the testers and go automatically. I felt like the top Beanie Baby in a claw machine; everyone was desperate to hook my goods. I knew I had the dough to make it happen. Christ, for what I'd be spending in Africa, I could send Aman to that university four times over. I decided not to give him the money. I told myself it was because I didn't want to set a bad precedent for the new volunteer. This was half the truth. The other half was that I wanted those two Gs so I could blow up extra huge on my trip. As a consolation prize, I offered Aman my story. I told him about how during my senior year in high school, I worked a shitty pizza delivery job for a full nine months to pay for my graduation trip to Europe. I told him what a harrowing journey it was, but that after all, I succeeded. He ate it up like French fries with dreams in his eyes. The next day we made manty at his house and listened to American tunes. As Mike Jones[95] rapped on my computer, Aman told me of his mystery friend in Kiev who might be able to get him into the uni. I told him that was great, and we clinked our Sprite glasses. I felt like the greatest fraudster in the universe.

That Sunday I got a call from Peace Corps. It was Maya reminding me that our COS conference was the coming Tuesday in Türkmenbaşy City. I thanked her for the info and hung up. The smile on my face was wider than a Detroit junkyard. According to the T-14s, the COS conference was the best damn shindig in Peace Corps Turkmenistan. Not only was it held in a seaside city with beaches and bars and leaking oil rigs, but there were more fieldtrips than meetings, and the rooms, food, and booze were all comped. The guilt of failing Aman and Jahan and everyone else at my site receded. The giddy happiness of escape washed in. I picked up the phone and called Brooke. We squealed about the conference, then I asked her if I could crash at her place tomorrow. She laughed and said no problem. She told me Tex would be there, too, and we both screamed. I got off the phone and did my laundry. Ali pointed a boogery finger at me and cackled, but I didn't give a fuck. I just hung up my skivvies and went for a stroll. As I passed the dry ditch that was Bullfrog Pond not two months prior, a little student of mine walked up. She was wearing a bright green dress and black shoes. Her hair was in two perfect braids tied off with white lace. She danced around me and grabbed at my finger. I patted her on the head and asked her, "What's up?" She smiled and told me the first day of school was tomorrow. I smiled back like "Oh that's nice," and continued walking. She frowned and stamped her feet.

"Aren't you coming to the performance?" she asked.

"Um, I'd love to," I said, "but I have a meeting tomorrow in Aşgabat."

Her eyes grew heavy with tears. She poked her lip out like a

---

[95] Mike Jones is a platinum-selling American rapper from Houston, Texas. In 2004-2005, his breakout singles "Still Tippin'" and "Back Then" garnered him national fame.

teaspoon and dropped her chin.

"But teacher, I love you," she said.

If you've ever seen a grown man almost break down and bawl, you'll know what I looked like. I knew that if I didn't say I'd come to the silly çykyş, I'd be the most towering bonfire of an asshole the world had ever seen. I squatted and pinched her cheek.

"Okay, I'll come."

She squeaked and cheered and hugged me around the neck. Then she bounced off into the dust like a tiny frog. I groaned and went to the dükan. I bought the biggest bottle of vodka I could find then walked back home. I gathered my crap and packed it up. I'd be gone for almost a week, so my luggage was double. I finished and hit the sheets. Within minutes, I was dead asleep.

THE NEXT MORNING, I said late to the fam and went to On Yet. Everyone was outside in their Monday finest, waiting for the çykyş to begin. I looked among the students for the little girl who'd invited me. She was nowhere to be seen. I pulled out my camera and did some filming. After the fortieth fiery speech and ninetieth whirling dance, I got bored. I said goodbye to Jahan and others. Then I grabbed a cab to Aşgabat. I went straight to PCHQ. I made a phone call to my sister, as my father had mentioned on our trip that she was getting married soon. Neither he nor my mother liked the guy. I congratulated my sister anyways and apologized for missing the wedding. I hung up and went to the lounge. Tex and Brooke were already there chatting about COS. I hugged them both and flicked my dime in. Then I got on the computer and checked my emails. A bunch was from my friends back home. Everyone was pumped about the trip to Africa and writing shit like, "See your ass in Cairo, bitch." I told this to Tex and Brooke. They both decided to come. We got on the net and looked at tickets. We found a sick-ass deal for fifteen hundred bucks: Aşgabat to London to Cairo, overland to Cape Town, then from there to the States via Dakar. Since we'd be leaving on the twenty-third of December, we decided to spend Christmas in

London. Afterwards, we'd meet up with my buddies and spend New Years in the shadow of the pyramids. The whole damn thing made us freak. We danced outta the lounge, pointing our fingers in the air and singing Toto's "Africa." As we passed the reception desk, Tex reminded us that we had to sign in.

"It's Peace Corps new thing," he said, holding up a clipboard. "Supposedly, we can come to HQ all we want, but we need to sign in."

As I'd already signed in at the gate, I figured it was no big thing. I mean, why the fuck would I sign two clipboards, when one did the trick just fine? While the others gave their John Hancock, I took a piss.

We all grabbed a marşrutka and blew off to Adalat. We arrived and bought provisions: vodka, beer, Ýetigen, and all the fixings for ghetto Tam Yum soup and chicken pineapple rice. We took it up to Brooke's flat and got to it. We clicked on the Manu Chao and before Jesus knew it, we were spilling oil over Satan's dick in a flaming hot pan. The whole place filled with the smells of curry and garlic and fried onions. We danced to the music in our bare feet and slid alcohol down our gullets.

I was so fucking happy I could have unzipped my skin. Just before the food was ready, I went out on the balcony to soak the night in. I gazed into the bellies of the black mountains in front of me. I felt the stars on my body like a billion twinkling eyes. I thought of Africa and the adventure that lay ahead. I thought of Peace Corps and the great struggle I'd endured to get to this point. I was a self-made man pulled up by a shoestring; a golden king amidst the ashes of his foes. I smiled at the perfection I had crafted. I reveled in the beauty of my fingertips and all the hearts they'd touched. I felt my buzz spike and then wane. I walked inside in search of more booze. When I couldn't find any, I asked Brooke. She crinkled her nose and cocked her head.

"Think we're out," she said.

This simply wouldn't do. I grabbed my wallet and hit the door.

Tex said he'd come with me. Brooke looked down at her watch and tapped the face.

"You guys be careful," she said. "It's past curfew."

We blew her off and slipped our thongs on. We bumbled downstairs and out into the swamp of shadows with talk of Africa on our lips. We spoke of wine binges in Zanzibar and gorilla treks in Uganda. We laughed about the other volunteers and what suckers they were for going home after COS. As we neared the bright lights of the dükan, two figures came into view. They were tall and gaunt and blacked-out except for two silver badges glinting in the moonlight. They swished toward us like bayou crocodiles. I heard the distinct crackling of walkie-talkies. My mouth ran dry and my heart tightened. I elbowed Tex to let's go, but the figures caught up with us.

"Where the hell do you think you're going?" one of them said to me in Turkmen.

I stopped in my tracks and shrugged.

"Nowhere special," I said. "We were just on our way to that dükan to get some . . . um . . . water."

"Vodka's more like it," he said.

The figure who'd spoken stepped out into the light. The darkness on his face peeled away. He had a razor-thin nose and beady eyes. A hare-lip exposed his two front teeth which were the color and shape of corn kernels. He got within kissing distance of us and pointed a gnarled finger.

"Sit down," he said. "I've got questions."

We dropped our heads and obliged. For the next hour, he and his ghoulish little sidekick grilled us scalp to toe about everything from our birthdays to our underwear size. We told them we were English teachers from Peace Corps and that treating us this way would just hurt their country. They broke out laughing like two sick hyenas and slapped their thighs.

"We don't give a shit who you are," Harelip said.

"Yeah," Ghouly agreed. "You guys are gonna pay."

I gulped and looked over at Tex. He was scratching his long arms and gritting his teeth. I put a hand on his shoulder. The instant I touched skin, he shot up and got in the cops' faces.

"Why don't you give us your fucking information," he barked. "C'mon, both of you. Your names, your badge numbers, chop-chop."

Tex had crazy bats in his eyes. His fists were tight and ready to strike. I knew if he decked one of the cops it was all over. I stood and pulled out my phone.

"I'm calling my boss," I said.

Everyone jerked out of their craze and looked at me. I fake-dialed a number and pretended to have a conversation with Harry. As I spoke, it dawned on me that this was a bad move. Sure, it kept Tex from punching our way to prison, but it brought superiors into the whole mess, which meant the chance of us talking or even bribing our way out was almost zilch. When I saw my little ruse wasn't working, I hung up the phone.

"Look," I said to Harelip. "Why don't I give you three-hundred-thousand manat and we'll call it square, okay?"

He twisted his mouth, so all his yellow teeth were exposed.

"We're way past that," he said. "Now I'm calling *my* boss."

He got on his walkie-talkie and called in. As he spoke to his boss, the fear of Zeus hit me. I got on my phone and called Peace Corps for real. I spoke to our new security officer, Oraz, and told him the deal. He said to be patient while he readied the Jeep. I told him to hurry and clicked off. Just then a little cop van came blaring up. It stopped in front of us and the driver squeezed out. He was fat and pink and pug-nosed. His resemblance to a sow was so striking I almost laughed out loud. He walked up to me and Tex and pointed a sausage-finger at us. He told us he was the police chief and demanded to know what was what. My phone went off in my pocket. I picked it up and handed it to him.

"This is probably for you," I said.

He took the phone and barked hello. He said "Bolýar" a few

times then handed it back to me. I got on and asked what was up.

"Johann, you must go with them now or you will have big problem," Oraz said. "Don't worry though, I will come in Jeep soon."

I said okay and hung up. I told Tex the news and he grunted. Miss Piggy walked to the van back and opened it. He raised a hand and smiled.

"Have a seat," he said.

The space could barely fit a duffle bag. Tex and I groaned and squeezed ourselves in. Our limbs were bowtied sideways. Miss Piggy slammed the door. He got in the van with Harelip and Ghouly and cranked the engine. We bumbled off down the road. My phone rang again. I eked my fingers into my pocket and grabbed it out. I clicked Answer with my pinky. I pressed the phone to my chin and said, "Hello."

"Where the hell are you guys?" Brooke said. "I'm starving."

I glanced over with my left eye. I could see the light of her window fading out of view. I remembered the food and the booze and the damn good time. When it all vanished behind a rock line, I frowned.

"We're in the back of a police van," I said. "We got arrested."

Brooke cackled.

"Sure," she said. "And I'm up here braiding my ass hairs with a zucchini."

I didn't respond for a whole ten seconds.

"You're serious," she said.

"Yes."

"Oh my fucking God, what can I do?"

"Nothing. I've already called Peace Corps. They're gonna bail us out."

"Okay."

I could hear her voice shaking.

"Relax," I said. "Everything's gonna be fine."

"Okay."

We arrived at the police station. I hung up with Brooke and slipped my phone back in my pocket. Miss Piggy came around and opened the doors. Tex and I got out and dusted ourselves off. We followed Miss Piggy and his minions into the station. They forced us to sit on the floor next to the cage that housed the drunks. The fluorescent lights burned down on us. Mosquitos flew in through the open windows and bit our legs. We scratched and slapped and cursed. We looked like two street dogs waiting for the needle. An hour later, some hoary old cunt with a trunk for a nose and bushy eyebrows walked up. He said he was the police captain then he shook his finger at us.

"This is not okay," he said. "Turkmenistan has laws which you must follow, laws which were written to protect people. You think that just because you're from another country you can come here and break our laws? Well, you can't. You're drunk, you broke curfew, and now you will suffer the consequences."

My phone rang. I tried to answer it but Captain Cocknose ripped it outta my hand.

"I'll take that," he said.

I told him it was my boss and that I had to answer it.

"I already spoke with your security officer," he said. "He'll be here shortly. In the meantime, you can help me with my fax machine."

My mouth swung open.

"What?"

"You heard me," he said. "Get around here and help me with this thing. It's been broken for weeks."

I had a mind to protest. I decided not to lest I put myself, Tex, and Brooke in worse standing with the Adalat police. I went behind the counter and over to the fax machine. It was a tremendous hunk of shit with a long plastic tongue. I screwed with its buttons and cranked its levers. I'm not really the MacGyver type, but I diddle a mean nutsack, which I guess helped me out. I somehow got the thing working. Captain Cocknose slapped me on the shoulder.

"You're a genius," he cried.

He ushered me back to where Tex was sitting. Then he folded his arms.

"Now before I let you two gentlemen go," he said, "let's see what's in those pockets."

I suddenly remembered I had a Swiss Army knife my dad had given me in my pocket. The blood evaporated from my face. I doubled over and groaned. Captain Cocknose raised his eyebrows.

"What is it?" he asked.

"It's my *stomach*," I said. "I'm going to be sick. I need a bathroom, now."

He smirked and waved Ghouly over.

"Take him to the bathroom," he said, "and make sure he doesn't go anywhere else."

Ghouly nodded and took me to the outhouse. The whole way there I croaked and crooned. I went inside and closed the door. I pulled out my knife and popped a squat. I took one last look at the thing and frowned.

"Sorry, Dad," I said.

I held the knife under my asshole and grunted. I waited a full five seconds then let it fly. It smacked the feces below like a turd would. I pushed out a few real turds for good measure. I grabbed some newspaper and wiped my asshole. I stood and pulled my pants up. I walked outta the outhouse smiling. Ghouly looked perplexed.

"You okay?" he asked.

"Fabulous," I said.

I went into the station and emptied my pockets. Tex did the same and we got the okay. A few minutes later Oraz arrived. Captain Cocknose made an enormous show of it, patting me and Tex on the back and raving about how wonderful we'd been.

"This one here even fixed my fax machine," he said, shaking my torso.

Oraz smiled and nodded. He signed us out then took us to the Jeep. The captain followed. Before I got in, he handed me my phone.

I saw the battery was dead. I looked at him and scowled.

"You be good now," he said.

I pinched my lips and sat down. I closed the door and we drove off. On the way to Brooke's, I turned to Oraz. I asked him if we were in trouble and he laughed.

"Not at all," he said. "This is normal occurrence in Turkmenistan. I know you're not drunk and that you do nothing wrong. Please don't worry about this."

I thanked him for his efforts. He dropped us off at Brooke's and we ran up there. She threw open the door and showered us with hugs. We told her what had happened and how close it was. She phewed and wiped her brow.

"Well I'm glad that shit's over," she said. "You guys hungry? I waited for you."

The Tam Yum soup and the chicken pineapple rice were sitting on the klionka untouched. They were an unbelievable welcome after our near butt-fucking by nightstick. We heated everything up and dug in. We turned on the music and drank some flat beer we'd found and laughed and laughed. The old ghosts of the night slowly returned. It was almost as if nothing had happened.

I WOKE UP the next morning with a mild hangover. It didn't bug me because I knew that in a few short hours I'd be on the beaches of Türkmenbaşy with my dawgs, splashing, and barking and blowing up. I took a shower and organized my things. Tex went to the office early to check some emails. I was a bit apprehensive that he might get hounded by staff. I reassured myself that it was all okay. I waited an hour after Tex left. Just to be a hundred percent, I called him with Brooke's phone at the lounge. He told me everything was fine.

"I haven't even *seen* Harry," he said.

I leaped for joy and hung up. I picked and poked at Brooke, raving about COS and our Africa trip. I ran down the list of countries we'd be visiting. For each, I asked her what she was gonna do the second she stepped across the border. She responded with things like, "Quaff goat piss," and "Tie my tits to a bridge and jump off." We rolled around on the floor and roared. Later, we made a little breakfast. We ate and chatted about when to head over. The talk of PCHQ still made me nervous. I dropped my fork and knitted my brow.

"You really think everything's gonna be alright?" I said.

"Oh yeah," she said. "I mean, if they haven't called by now, nothing's wrong."

As if by some strange cosmic divination, her phone rang. I figured it might be Tex so I wasn't too scared. Brooke picked it up and held it to her ear. Then her face sank.

"Oh, hello Oraz," she said.

The fear bloomed in my chest like a tropical disease. I shot up from the floor and paced back and forth. Every three seconds I asked Brooke what Oraz was saying. Each time, she held up a finger and shook it at me to shut up. After five agonizing minutes, she got off the phone. I knelt in front of her and clasped my hands together.

"What the fuck did he say?" I asked.

She frowned like a melting rainbow.

"He said you're not to go to Türkmenbaşy. You're to go home now and wait for Harry to call you."

A mass of hornets ballooned in my head. I ran around Brooke's flat, punching at the air and wiping sweat from my brow. I could hear and see nothing; just a screaming white facsimile of reality. This lasted for a good ten minutes. I came to and caught myself shouting the words "I'm fucked." over and over again. The self-pity washed in like a noxious wave. I switched my repeating phrase to, "I didn't do anything wrong." I belted this out about three dozen times, all the while hoping and praying that a member of some godly tribunal in the clouds would hear my cries and realize that a clerical error had been made in the bad karma rationing department and rush over and correct it, thus rendering this whole fucking catastrophe nothing more than a mean ol' dream.

Brooke watched me, her face sagging with pain. When she could no longer take it, she stood and clapped her hands.

"Johann," she shouted. "You have to calm down."

I ignored her and carried on with my madness. She walked up and wrapped her arms around me. I unhooked them from my waist and pushed her away.

"This is bullshit," I said. "Absolute fucking bullshit. I did nothing wrong. We did nothing wrong. How can Harry do this? How can he kick us out?"

"*Johann*," she said, "Harry never said he was kicking you out. He only said for you to go back to site. You can't just give up like this. You still have a shot."

"No. This is just like what they did to Truman. They told him to go home and wait to hear from Peace Corps. Then before he knew it, he was packing his shit and on a plane home."

I was crying now. The tears were bleeding down my cheeks. My body trembled, and my knees buckled. I collapsed like a matchstick under a brick. Brooke rushed to my side and wrapped herself around my arm. She was shaking and crying too.

"It's all over," I said. "All this work and I'm getting booted out for a trip to the fucking dükan. That's two years of my life. Two years and I have nothing to show for it. I'm finished, Brooke."

"You're not finished," she said, sniffing. "Your kids love you, your co-workers, your host family. And that's way more than Truman had. His site didn't even want him. But yours does. That's your strength. That's how you can beat this."

The strength left my body. My eyes were cracked marbles and my heart was an old loogie. I shrunk deeper within myself.

"I haven't got it in me, Brooke," I said. "I've fought and fought to make it through this fucking bullshit, and now, the day before my COS conference, I'm forced to fight the biggest battle of my service. Fuck that. Last night, I was a god, Brooke. A god. And now look at me. Everything is unraveling before my eyes and I can't do shit about it. I've got nothing. I am nothing."

I trembled and sobbed. My nose and eyes gushed warm liquids. My limbs contorted themselves into strange bows. I sunk to the lowest part of myself. As I jittered in the darkness, a memory came. I voiced it to Brooke through a stuffed nose.

"One night about a week ago," I said, "I was sitting in my room with the light off, wondering what the fuck I was doing here. I struck up a conversation in my head with God and I asked him, 'Why did you make me this way? Why did you give me a talent with words and then never tell me how to use it? I mean, at least give me some sort of sign that I'm going the right way and doing the right thing.' I went on like this for hours. And do you know what he said? Nothing. Fucking nothing. And on top of that, He decided to make me feel like I was the king of the world last night, to build me up above the clouds and then knock me down in one fell swoop. What kind of sick fuck does that?"

My lungs cracked. I could no longer speak in high tones. I just lay there and groaned. Brooke pulled at my arm.

"Johann, you have to snap outta this," she cried. "I need you here with me. You can't give up. You've got a shot. Please, Johann."

I was a slug in the dark. I crawled around with my little eyes out, fishing for something. I moved over a spot that was raw and vibrating. It felt like a tiny vein of energy. I wrapped around it and used it as a rope. I slithered up and up and up till I made it out of my hole. I was badly beaten but something was left of me. I wiped the tears from Brooke's cheeks and looked her in the eyes.

"I'll be okay," I said. "I'm gonna fight this bullshit."

I got up and took a cold shower. It shocked me into reality and cleared my mind. I came back into the room and grabbed Brooke's phone. I dialed Harry's number and waited.

"Hello," he said sharply.

"Harry, this is Johann," I said. "Oraz told me to call you."

"Johann, I'm sure he didn't tell you to call me," he said. "Anyways, you are not to go to Türkmenbaşy. Go back to site and I'll call you on Friday."

He hung up. I put Brooke's phone on the desk and looked at her.

"What'd he say?" she asked.

I told her. She crumpled her hands into fists.

"That fucker," she screamed. "This whole conference is gonna be one big piece of shit. I can guarantee you everyone's gonna be pissed, and boy if we get drunk enough, you can bet the lot of us are gonna be screaming 'Mass ET. Mass ET.' at the top of our lungs and I'll be right there leading the chant. We'll teach those assholes to fuck with us. From now on, it's us against them. Let the cold war begin."

I was flattered at the gesture. But I couldn't let Brooke ruin her service over this too. I put my hand on her shoulder and smiled.

"Please don't do any of that," I said. "Just go and have a good time. This is your COS conference. It's supposed to be fun."

"I know," she said. "But without you and Tex it won't be dick."

I laughed and got my crap together. Brooke did the same and we took a marşrutka to Aşgabat. We ran into Jimmy and Divine at the awtostanzia. They were ecstatic about the upcoming conference. I told them what had happened, and they gasped. Jimmy kicked the dirt and Divine started crying. I hugged them both and told them it'd be okay. I said goodbye to everyone and got in a cab to Tejen. I told the cabbie my woes. He eased them by telling me that he too was arrested once for being out past curfew. When I got to GBH, I told my family what had happened as well. Ali made me laugh by telling me he was gonna dress Harry up in a pink köýnek and have a camel fuck him up the ass. I went to bed with this image in my head. I tried to sleep, but I had a helluva time. I was terrified of being kicked out of Peace Corps. It felt like I was being force-fed a spoonful of my own feces. At around 3:00 a.m., I finally swallowed. I resolved that if they forced me to ET, I'd go to Europe, teach for three months, then meet up with the group in Africa for the big trip. It was an acceptable solution. I drifted into a fitful sleep with visions of Harry in a pink dress being raped by barnyard animals.

24

FOR THE NEXT two days, I built my case. I gathered letters of good faith from Jahan, Azat, and Islam, wrote my defense, and created a timeline of events for the night in question. I covered every angle and every argument. I even cast a spell of good luck that Jahan had told me, via her mother, in which I waved a five-thousand-manat bill around my head three times and then used the money to buy cookies for my students. By Friday, I felt confident. I was gravy on both the physical and the spiritual planes. I waited in my bedroom for Harry's call. I knew if it didn't come by 5:00 p.m., I was in the clear, as this was the time staff left.

Five o'clock came and went. I oozed with relief and had some dinner. At 7:00 p.m. I got a text from Brooke. She wanted me to call her at the lounge. I went down to the phone house and made the call. The first words out of her mouth were, "Harry is a royal dick."

I laughed and asked her what had happened.

"Oh, at COS he saw me weeping after one of those stupid meetings," she said, "and he came up to me with that fatherly concerned look on his face and asked me if I was okay. I told him I wasn't, and his response was, 'Don't let those two idiots ruin your COS.' Then I told him I didn't agree with what he did, and he stormed off mumbling something about how I didn't know what the hell I was talking about."

"What an asshole. Did anyone else say anything?"

"Yeah. Oraz said he'd talk to Harry and tell him you guys didn't do anything wrong. And Sheri said she thought it wasn't fair, and that had it been anyone else, they would have been at the conference. She was really sweet."

"That's cool. So, what do you think is gonna happen?"

"I think you're chill. Oraz and Sheri have your back, plus pretty much all the volunteers. Harry isn't stupid. He knows it would create a shit storm if he kicked you guys out. He might punish you bad and it might suck for the rest of your service, but I think you've got an eighty percent chance of staying."

Hearing the confidence in her voice made me feel even better. Plus, the fact that Harry hadn't called that day like he'd threatened to, told me things were okay. I thanked Brooke for her support and hung up. I went home and decompressed. Not much happened over the weekend. I got a few texts from both Iris and Candice and they told me that all the volunteers in Daşoguz were rooting for me. Come Monday, I felt like a gem. I took a nice cold bucket shower and donned my finest threads. I walked to school with flames in my steps. I was so sure the bullshit had passed, I texted Brooke that we should have a little COS party of our own the coming weekend. She jumped at the idea. We made a tentative plan to meet in the lounge that Friday.

When I arrived at school, I went to Azat's classroom. He greeted me with his checkered smile and shook my hand. He helped me write out my schedule for the fall semester. He asked me the latest on the Harry situation and I told him. I asked him what he thought.

"I have no bad dream about you," he said. "So, I sink your boss, he is calm now and he will want not to make you problem."

I thanked him for his vote of confidence. I went to Jahan's and she mirrored Azat's sentiment.

"My mother said many prayers for you to make everything good again. I think they will work."

I turned up a thumb.

"She gave me that spell, too," I said. "Looks like it worked after all."

We both laughed. I told her I'd be back around four to work on the book. I split and walked to the dükan. I bought a Pepsi and a Snickers and went to my favorite bench. I wrote a few poems and enjoyed my snack. I went home and took a crap. When I got to my room, I threw on *Buffy the Vampire Slayer*. I watched episode after episode, scratching my ballsack through my boxers and drooling. I drifted to sleep; I was just at the point of kissing death's feet. Ali screamed my name. I got up and opened my door. I asked him what the fuck he wanted. He put his little fist to his hip and cocked it.

"Peace Corps is on the phone," he said.

I rolled my eyes.

"Are you lying?"

"Yeah Han-Guly, I'm lying. I got up from my afternoon nap just to mess with you about Peace Corps calling."

The brat had a point. I slipped my thongs on and walked downstairs. I wasn't worried at all. In my mind, the worst that could happen was Harry would chew me out and then give me site restriction. I went into the house and grabbed the phone. It was Maya on the other end.

"Johann," she said in her sweet voice. "Harry would like to speak to you."

I pinched the bridge of my nose.

"Okay. Put him on."

I heard the line click over. Harry got on the phone immediately.

"Johann," he said. "I want you to pack your things and come to the office tomorrow. You're going home."

My heart vanished in a blip.

"You're kidding," I said dryly.

"No, Johann, I am not."

That hot panic swelled inside me again. It blanketed every facet of my rational mind. Thoughts became bullets and dreams became knives. I lifted my hand and slapped at my eyes.

"Why?" I screamed.

"Because, Johann, I can't do this anymore."

I could hear his voice cracking. I tried to wedge my way in.

"But Harry," I said, "you haven't even heard my side of the story."

"I don't need to. I already know that you were out of site without permission and that you got arrested. That's enough."

"But at least let me explain myself."

"You can explain yourself when you come in," he said miserably. "Now please pack your things."

I could tell he was about to hang up. I panicked.

"Wait. Is there anything I can do to set this right?"

There was a long pause. Harry responded in a low and sorrowful tone.

"It would take something absolutely momentous."

I tried to ask what, but he hung up. I dropped the phone and stared at the carpet. My blood turned to starch in my veins. My head became a block of Styrofoam with ants gnawing at the corners. I picked up the phone and called Brooke.

"Hey Gelr," she said. "What's up?"

I asked her if she was sitting down. She told me she was at the chalkboard writing out sentences. I told her she might wanna leave class and find a bench. She asked why, and I flew into a rage.

"Just do it," I screamed.

I heard chalk drop and kids mumble. I heard a door open, feet shuffle, then another door open. I heard gravel being scraped then meat being plopped.

"Okay," she said. "I'm outside sitting. Now tell me what the hell is going on."

I took a deep breath.

"Harry is kicking me out."

I heard sniffling.

"Why?"

"He says it's because I was out of site without permission and got arrested."

"But it wasn't your fucking fault. And it's not like you were trying to trick the goddamned asshole. I mean, you came into the office and signed in at the front, for Christ's sake."

"I know. But Harry won't listen to me. He's hysterical right now."

Brooke was sobbing.

"None of this makes any sense," she cried. "You guys didn't even fucking do anything."

"I know. Christ, I know. I'm just fucking numb."

"What are you gonna do?"

"The only thing I can do. I'm gonna go around to more of the people I know in town and see if they'll write me some letters. Fuck, maybe I'll even ask the chief of police. I don't know."

Brooke was weeping hysterically. I almost felt like she was taking this harder than I was.

"I'm sorry to leave you like this, Learnr, but I gotta go. It's getting late and I wanna get this shit done."

"Is there anything I can do?" she asked.

"Just call people and let them know what's going on. Especially the people you know will be sympathetic to my plight."

"You got it. And Johann?"

"Yeah?"

"Try your best to stay afloat."

"Will do."

I said goodbye and hung up. I forced myself to my feet and walked out the door. Patma was outside washing dishes. She looked up at me.

"What's going on?" she asked. "I heard you screaming."

I stared at her blankly.

"Peace Corps is kicking me out," I said.

"Over what happened in Adalat?"

"Yes. My boss is angry at that, and also at what happened when I got back from America."

She clicked her tongue.

"But he shouldn't kick you out for these things."

"Well, he is. But if you guys write me a good letter, that might help."

"We will. I'll have Merdan do it for you tonight. I'd do it myself, but I can barely write."

Patma smiled. It was the first time I'd ever found her smile beautiful.

"Where are you going?" she asked.

"I'm gonna go get some more letters. It's the only chance I've got."

"Good luck," she said.

I thanked her and walked out the waratan. The first person I had in mind was Baýram. On the way to his school, I ran into my old Russian teacher, Sonya. I'd only had three lessons with her, but I remembered her spunk and her crazy black hair. The moment she saw me, she furrowed her brow.

"Han-Guly," she said. "You're not smiling like usual. What's wrong?"

I told her what had happened. She agreed to write me a letter on the spot. We went up to her office and she wrote the thing in the most beautiful Russian cursive. She handed it to me with a smile.

"Give this to your boss," she said. "And don't worry. Whatever happens, I know you'll be okay."

I thanked her and gave her a hug. I stuffed the letter in my pocket and walked out the door. I got a text from Candice. She asked what had happened and I told her. She responded back within a minute. Her text read:

"None of this makes any sense, Johann. I've called everyone in The Gouz[96] and they're all shocked and angered. Not only do we feel bad for you, we're afraid for ourselves. What kind of message is Harry sending? Get arrested unjustly, get kicked out of Peace Corps?"

I thanked her for her support and told her to lay low. She responded back asking me if there was any way Harry would change his mind.

---

[96] What we called the region of Daşoguz.

It would take a miracle, I wrote.

She responded with a sad face and good luck. I thanked her again and continued my walk to Baýram's school. His co-worker told me he was in a meeting. I decided I'd visit him after he got home from work. I had two hours to kill. I went over to On Yet to see Jahan. I must've been wearing a sour face. The first words out of her mouth were, "What's wrong?" I sat down next to her. I chose my words carefully so as not to alarm her.

"Jahan," I said, "I want to tell you something and I don't want you to get upset."

"What is it?"

"My boss called today. He's sending me home."

Her cheeks tightened into a fake smile.

"What?" She sounded dazed.

"I'm leaving tomorrow, Jahan. I'm so sorry."

We sat in silence for a moment. I couldn't believe this was the end of things. All that work I'd put into helping Jahan turned out to be nothing more than a frustrating and abortive mission. I was a paragon of PCV failure.

"What did your boss say?" Jahan finally said.

"Not much. Just to pack my things and come in tomorrow because I was going home. He sounded very upset and when I tried to explain myself, he said that nothing else mattered except that I was out of site without permission and that I got arrested. Then he hung up."

Jahan was quiet for another minute. I could tell by the swirls of redness on her cheeks that she was processing what I'd told her. When she finished, she pinched her eyebrows to a V.

"Asshole."

I laughed out loud. "You said it."

"I'm serious," she said. "This is not fair. I had something I wanted to give you, but it is not finished."

"What's that?"

"It's a tahýa I'm knitted. I just started, and my mother told me to start early so I could finish soon but I didn't listen. I just thought you will leave in many months and I will have much time to finish and now you are leaving tomorrow, and I can't give it to you."

I felt like a wad of gum on a cabbie's shoe heel.

"That's so sweet," I said. "I guess all I can do is give you my American address and you can send me your tahýa once it's finished."

"Okay," she said, looking down. "I will do this."

It got quiet again. That hornet's nest of rage swelled inside me. I was furious at Harry for his pigheadedness and refusal to hear my side. In my mind, I had done nothing wrong except walk down to a fucking dükan an hour past curfew and I was paying for it by losing the one decent thing that came out of two miserable years of service: my friendship with Jahan. I could have bashed the man's head in. I started scribbling on the newspaper in front of me to distract myself. I heard Jahan sniffling beside me.

"That son of a bitch," I screamed.

I flung my pen across the room. It ricocheted off the window and stabbed the adjacent flowerpot. Jahan jumped.

"Sorry," I said.

I looked down at the newspaper. I saw that I'd circled the words *täze, halkara,* and *ykbal.* In English they translate to "New international fate." The irony sucked my lungs flat.

"Look at the words I circled," I said.

She looked where I was pointing. A tear wiggled its way from her eye and slid down her cheek. She wiped it away and tried to smile.

"Maybe," she said.

I said goodbye. I told her I'd be back tomorrow to say goodbye again. I still had an hour to kill before Baýram finished work. I went home for a spell and called Brooke. She told me she'd contacted my sympathizers and that they were all shocked and upset.

"Most of them will call you tomorrow at the lounge," she said.

I thanked her and told her I'd call her later. I took a sad little dump and went over to Baýram's. I told him the news and he flipped.

"What a stupid boss," he said. "And what a stupid country. Why do we have such stupid curfews? And why do we have such stupid police?"

I'd never heard the word "stupid" used so many times. I almost laughed.

"Did your stupid boss even allow you to explain to him what happen?" he asked.

"No. He just said I was out of site without permission, and I got arrested and that was enough for him."

"Well, that is very stupid. Have you packed?"

"Not yet."

"Okay then, I will help you."

We went into his computer room. We grabbed a duffle bag, some boxes, and Scotch tape. We said goodbye to his family. They gave me hugs and wished me good luck. As we walked out the door, they all stood in a row on the porch. Everyone had a somber face, except little Kakajan. He was grinning wildly with a finger in his left nostril. I walked up to him and patted his head.

"Bye, you coot boy," I said.

I could feel the tears coming on. It was time to leave. Baýram's ancient mother gave me one last hug.

"Sag aman bar," she said sweetly. "Go safely and in good health."

"Thank you."

I turned around and followed Baýram. We walked to my house slowly. It was a cool evening. The sky was a tapestry of orange and pink glass. We both looked up at it.

"What will you do when you leave?" Baýram asked.

"Either go to Europe and teach English or go home and enjoy the holidays with my family. After that, I will go on my trip to Africa."

Saying this out loud sounded surprisingly nice. Sure, I wouldn't get to finish my service, but teaching in Europe or being home for the holidays, followed by a kickass trip to Africa with all my best buds wasn't a boot to the groin by any means. Baýram said he pitied and envied me at the same time. In a way, the same was true for me of him. When we got to my room, we started packing. We dismantled everything I owned and filled eight boxes, four bags, and five pieces of luggage. We stuck it all in the middle of my room and stared at it.

"How will you get this all to Aşgabat?" Baýram asked.

"I don't know. Hopefully my boss will send me a car."

I went down to the waratan with Baýram. He smiled painfully.

"I will miss our fun nights together," he said.

"Me too."

"Here," he said, reaching into his pocket. "This is for you."

He pulled out a photo and handed it to me. It was of his children lined up in the living room. Like before, all of them wore somber expressions except baby Kakajan. He was smiling brightly in his little Spiderman jammies. On the back of the photo, Baýram had written his info.

"Please write me," he said.

I promised I would. I gave him a hug and we parted ways. I went back up to my room to do some final packing. I opened the door and saw Merdan sitting on my bed. He was crying. I started crying too. I sat down next to him. We put our arms around each other and cried together. Neither one of us said a thing for an entire hour. We just cried and blew our noses and cried some more.

When we finally stopped, I explained to Merdan what had happened. He was furious at Harry and had some choice things to say about him. I told him we shouldn't spend our last night together talking about my asshole of a boss. I reached into my bag of goodies and pulled out a DVD.

"How bout we watch some porn instead?"

He nodded and clapped his hands. I slipped the disc in and for the next two hours, we watched all sorts of raunchy shit. Merdan made us some tea. We sipped it and cracked jokes until 3:00 a.m. Before he went to bed, he gave me a letter he'd written. It was tough to read, but from what I gathered it explained how I meant the world to his family and how Harry just had to let me stay. I hugged him and told him I'd see him in the morning.

"I'll drive you to the taxi stand," he said. "We can say our last goodbye there."

I felt a lump in my throat. I told him to go before we both started crying again. We hugged once more, and he left. I texted Brooke and Candice just before bed. Brooke said she'd see me tomorrow at PCHQ. Candice wished me good luck. I responded with, "Why bother?" Just before I drifted to sleep, she responded with, *"Because I'm counting on a miracle."*

I WOKE UP the next morning at seven thirty. I took a long, hot bucket shower to calm my nerves. Then I went back up to my room and selected my outfit. I was going to wear my regular old jeans, T-shirt, and kepka ensemble. I decided against it. If I was going to go out, it had to be with a bang that would blast the teeth out a motherfucker's mouth. I rifled through my bags. I found my nicest pair of jeans and a black Armani Exchange shirt I'd folded and saved aside for a special occasion. I uncrumpled everything and put it on. I left two buttons open on my shirt, so my chains were visible. I slipped on a pair of black leather shoes I'd bought in Almaty. I donned my rings and my watch and my aviator shades. I felt like I was dressed for my own funeral. I knew my man Johnny[97] would be proud. I stepped outta my room like a smooth black cat. I floated down the steps and out the waratan door. The air around me was unearthly. The sky was powder blue, and the clouds were wispy as tea steam. I walked along the dirt road and soaked it in. This was the last time I'd see this place and I wanted it to take. I hit the mosque, the theater, the library, the park, the dellekhana, and the dükans I frequented, as well as my favorite manty joint, the uly çayhana. I said goodbye to all my friends. Each one was more heartbroken than the last. The little dude at the uly çayhana that always gave me my food hot and fresh almost cried.

---

[97] Johnny Cash. People used to tell him he was dressed like he was going to a funeral, to which he'd respond, "Maybe I am."

"But you haven't even finished your service yet, Han-Guly," he said.

I told him this was true but that I still had to go. I gave him a firm handshake and went over to On Yet. Azat's class was already in session. I stood up front and relayed the news. Some of the children gasped. Others started crying and had to be consoled. I felt like I didn't deserve such a response. Sure, I'd taught them English for the past twenty-one months, but I'd never visited any of their homes despite their constantly having invited me, and on top of that, I'd never come through with the summer camps or any other secondary project.

I swallowed my shame and said goodbye. On my way to Jahan's, I ran into two more of my students. They were walking hand-in-hand in their little green köýneks. Their braids were down the front and tied off with white lace. They smiled when they saw me. I smiled back sadly and told them the news. Their mouths crinkled and their eyes watered.

"But teacher," they cried. "You haven't even been here a year."

I didn't have the heart to tell them I'd been there almost two. I told them I knew, and that they'd been very good students. I gave them each a hug and patted them on the head. I said goodbye before I lost my last bit of resolve. I walked the rest of the way to Jahan's. I found her at her desk staring dead at her students. Her hair was a mess and her eyes were red. She had on a threadbare dress and a shoddy pair of sandals. She looked like she'd been dragged through a dump by a hook in the belly. I decided to give her a minute. I turned to her students and looked them over. They were her seventh-formers—my favorite group. They were sitting in metallic silence with their hands folded. I took a deep breath and gave them the news. I saw a few chins quiver and a few eyes water. I could tell they were trying to be tough. I thanked them for always being good students. I told them I would miss our trips to the kiçi çaýhana for ice cream and our after-school clubs, our laughing and joking and playing poker in the rain. They told me the same and I turned to Jahan. I sat next to her and tried to smile. She looked down at her hands and wiggled her rings.

"I can't believe you will go today," she said. "I thought you will stay and that your boss will change his mind."

"I thought so, too, Jahan. But he didn't."

"You will write me?"

"Of course. And you can send me that tahýa."

"Okay."

We exchanged information. Then Jahan looked up at me.

"Han-Guly, can I ask you one more favor?"

"Sure."

She reached into her bag and pulled out a stack of photos. She handed them to me, and I thumbed through them. They were of her and her family and her students. I got choked up looking at them.

"These photos are for you," she said. "Now if you could please give me some photos of you as well, plus a copy of the book we were working on, I would be very happy."

Luckily, I'd had the foresight to bring my USB. I told her no problem and went with her to the computer room. I printed a few choice photos and burned *501* to a CD. I gave her everything and walked her back to class. I wanted badly to give her a hug. I knew if I did, especially in front of her students, word would go around GBH like a grass fire and it could spell hell for her reputation. I opted instead for a handshake. It was cold and clammy, but it was something. As I was turning to leave, she let out a little breath. I looked at her face and could tell she was about to cry. I handed her a tissue and smiled.

"I'll call you and give you the final word once I've talked to my boss," I said. "Who knows, maybe I'll get lucky."

We both chuckled. I said one last goodbye to the kids and hit the door. On my way out, everyone, including Jahan, stood in unison. I knew from having seen them do this for Islam, the garawul, and other senior figures, that this was a tremendous sign of respect. I felt wobbly in the knees. I left before the shame of my pitiful service consumed me entirely. I ran into Azat in the courtyard. He'd just finished class and offered to help carry my crap down. I accepted and walked to my house with him. We got to the waratan and Aman sauntered up. He told me he'd come to see me the day before but that I'd been out. I said I was sorry and that something had happened. His square face dropped.

"What is it?" he asked.

"I'm being sent home," I said.

"What? Why?"

I told him the story of what had happened. When I finished, his eyes were flaming, and his mouth was an apoplectic hole. He looked up at me and sneered.

"What's your boss's name?" he asked.

"Harry Donaldson. Why?"

"Because I will remember this name. And when I become president, I will fuck him."

His mouth ejected the word "fuck" like a pistol shot. It scared me a little but mostly it made me laugh. We chatted a bit more. Then my phone rang. It was Maya from Peace Corps.

"Johann," she said. "Harry will not be sending you a Jeep. It is unfortunate, but you must find your own way here."

I could tell by her voice she felt bad. I thanked her for the info and hung up. I told Azat and Aman the news. They offered to find me a cab. I thanked them, and they left for the taxi stand. In the interim, I texted Brooke. I told her about the Jeep situation.

"What?" she wrote back. "This is insane. Truman was a terrible volunteer, worlds worse than you and PC at least had the decency to give him a fucking vehicle. What assholes. Again, Johann, this is terribly sad and terribly scary."

I told her I couldn't agree more. I said I was running a bit late and that I'd meet her at the lounge at three. She said she'd be there. A minute later, she sent me this text.

"On second thought, fuck PC. Tell them you're out of cash and that they have no choice but to send a car. What does it matter?

They're kicking you out anyways. Why not go out dragging your feet like the criminal they're treating you as?"

It sounded like a tasty bit of revenge. I knew it would be to my detriment though. I decided to honor my pimpin' black getup; I'd play it cool.

Azat and Aman returned with an empty cab just for me. I thanked them for their efforts, and we went up to my room and grabbed my crap. Merdan and Ali came up and helped us. We brought everything down and filled the entire cab. I gave all the guys hugs. I shook hands with my host sisters and patted little Yazgül on the head. She wiggled and squirmed and bounced away. I had to laugh, otherwise I'd cry my fucking eyes out. I wrote down all my info and everyone wrote down theirs. We all promised we'd write each other and tried to smile. As I was getting in the cab, Patma walked up. She grinned at me and put out her hand. I took it with one and put the other on my heart.

"Thank you for taking care of me," I said. "I will miss you."

"We will miss you, too, Han-Guly. As far as we're concerned, you're family."

25

THE RIDE TO Aşgabat was strange. I thought I'd be a train crash of emotions, but I just sat there peacefully and stared at my hands. I guess it's because I knew what was going to happen; I'd arrive at PCHQ, lock my things in storage, go to Harry's office, listen to him bitch at me for an hour, and then drink myself to sleep before waking up to get on a plane. The more I thought about it, the less I understood what I'd been dreading. Was it Harry's temper flaring up? What the fuck did that matter? I'd dealt with the cops in Adalat, endured the disappointment of missing COS, completed the rigorous task of preparing my case, however indefensible it may have been, and broken the painful news of my early departure to my host family and all my friends. The hard stuff was over. What lay in front of me was either a badass time in Europe or Christmas with my loved ones, followed by Cairo to Cape Town by backpack with all my best buds. Fuck a chew out. This was a blessing. The drawback being that I didn't get to finish what I'd started.

I looked out at the desert. Its emptiness was somehow liberating, and I could almost feel myself being lifted out of my seat. I stuck my head out the window to look at the sky. It was a morass of blue crystal streaked with white clouds. I mused at it with a smile. Memories of my service, both good and bad, shuffled through my brain, kicking up a tangle of sublime emotions. I felt the beautiful death of something inside me.

"This is the end," I whispered.

In Aşgabat, I directed the cabbie to Peace Corps, and we pulled up at the gate. I got out of the car and asked the guards if we could park next to the storage unit so I wouldn't have to carry all my crap across the lot. They folded their arms.

"It's against Peace Corps policy," they said.

I knew they were just being hard-asses because staff were around. I thanked them anyways and got my crap. The cabbie helped me with it. Once we'd unloaded everything, I dropped him an extra twenty Gs and sent him on his way. As he was driving off, Brooke walked up. She was wearing a tattered pair of jeans, an Iron Maiden T-shirt, and a pair of black bug-eye shades. Her red hair was in a ratty ponytail. She looked like she hadn't eaten or slept for days. She came over to me slowly, never looking up. She buried her head in my shoulder and cried. I put my arms around her and stroked her hair.

"I can't believe this is fucking happening," she said, sniffling.

An older volunteer walked by. She looked at us and frowned.

"Is Harry kicking you out?" she mouthed.

I responded with a slow nod. Her face dropped.

"That asshole."

She stormed into headquarters. Brooke looked up at me and smiled.

"See?" she said. "Everyone loves you."

"Yeah, I'll miss them too. Any word from Tex?"

"Nah, he's probably back at his site doing the same thing you just did. I'll let you know when I hear from him though."

I looked at my watch. It was almost three o'clock. Harry was no doubt back from lunch. I figured this was a good thing as he was less likely to be a prick with a full gut. I unlaced my arms from Brooke and wiped my eyes.

"I'd better get in there," I said.

"Okay. I'm gonna see Sheri. I'll meet you in the lounge. Good luck."

"Ha ha, thanks."

I walked to Harry's office. I could see through his glass door that he was entertaining two embassy goons. I looked at him and raised my eyebrows. He glanced at me sourly then returned to his conversation. I shrugged it off and went upstairs. I got on a computer and checked my email. It was mostly my friends raving about the trip. I hadn't told them or my family that I was being kicked out. I figured I'd let the guillotine blade drop across my neck before I informed anyone of my failure. Part of it was shame and part of it was just me not wanting to spike their good time with my shitty news.

I played along like everything was alright. As I typed my last "Woohoo," Harry walked in. I jumped like a spider had just bitten my flank. I composed myself with a deep breath then looked at the man. His eyes were dark and downcast. His face was redolent with fatherly condescension. His sleeves were pulled back like he was about to get in a street brawl. He was rubbing the skin of his left temple with his thumb. Once he'd cracked his headache, he wiggled his index finger at me. Then he turned around and walked off.

"Here we go," I mumbled.

I gathered my bearings and followed him. I went down to his office and through the glass door. He closed it behind me and offered me a seat. I sat down and waited for him to say something. He perched himself across from me and folded his hands. I was expecting him to be scowling, but he was smirking. His cheeks were filled with an almost good-humored ruddiness. I searched his eyes for malice but found an aloof playfulness. It was like he was musing at some wry little tidbit he'd read in the newspaper. He sat there staring at me like this for a long minute. Without warning, he broke the silence.

"Do you even know why you're here?" he asked.

I was stunned. For a second, I thought that this might all be some elaborate joke. I scratched my neck and cringed.

"Um, yeah? At least I think I do. But don't you wanna know what happened?"

"No," he said daintily.

"I'm confused."

"I know you are, Johann. And that's what pisses me off so much."

His face shed its playfulness and hung a curtain of steel.

"I mean, really," he said. "How *stupid* do you think I am?"

"Um, I don't understand," I said, shrugging.

"And that's exactly what I'm talking about," he screamed. "It's your *arrogance* that boils my blood."

"I'm sorry, Harry, I still don't understand."

He leaned forward and scrunched his mustache into an M.

"Well, lemme help you," he said. "First off, you are never at your site. You leave it constantly and without any regard for your responsibilities as a volunteer. And you always do it in the sneakiest way; never quite breaking the rules but *bending* them just enough so you get what you want. And you think I don't notice, don't you? The way you always call after working hours and leave a message so we don't get a chance to tell you 'no.' Then you come into headquarters at lunchtime and leave before everyone gets back, only to return again with Brooke and Hal and God knows who else after working hours so you can goof around on the internet instead of being at your site and working."

I opened my mouth to yawn. Harry screamed it shut.

"And I don't even wanna hear about what happened last weekend because I don't care. I already know what I need to know. You came in without calling first. You didn't sign in, you didn't let anyone in PC know your whereabouts, and why? Because you knew if you called us, we'd tell you 'no.' And you knew if you signed in, we'd be on your ass about being here without permission, so you figured you'd just skip that step too. I mean really, Johann. What were you thinking? That I wouldn't notice? That I wouldn't bother to look? Well, I'm sorry to disappoint you, but I'm not that dense. Not only did I look, I called your director and he informed me that you didn't even show up that day for the first day of class."

"He's lying to you," I said.

"Oh, is he?"

"Yes. He is. And I can prove it. When I went to school that morning, I brought my video camera and filmed most of the opening ceremony. I've got it with me. Would you like to see the tape?"

"No, I wouldn't. And how long afterwards did you stay?"

"An hour or so."

"Well, that's not going to school for the day, now is it?"

I didn't bother mentioning that there were no classes or solid schedules and that all the students and faculty members left no more than half an hour after I did.

"And anyways," he said, "it doesn't matter. You still came in without calling and you still were arrested for Christ's sake. I mean, why in the world couldn't you just come in the next day like the rest of the volunteers? What was so damn important that you felt you needed to be here a day early?"

"My sister's getting married. I wanted to have time to talk to her on the phone without all the other volunteers being here. Plus, I'm arranging our whole trip to Africa and I needed to get online to buy tickets and—"

"Oh Jesus, Johann," he cried. "You're so self-absorbed. First off, none of the stuff you mentioned has anything to do with why you're in this country. And second, just who do you think you are? You're organizing the entire trip? Everything revolves around you, right? Everyone is at your beck and call, is that it? You live in a goddamn dream world."

I felt a fart coming on. I clenched my butt cheeks to keep it from escaping.

"I don't," I said.

"Well, you sure act like it. And my phone may be off the hook with all your little friends calling in to try and save your ass, but I'll have you know that not everybody appreciates the 'Johann Show' all the time."

The fart almost squeaked out. I widened my eyes.

"That's right, Johann," he said, with a smug little smile under his mustache. "As much as I know you hate to hear it, there's people who don't like you and who don't appreciate your constant crap."

I shifted cheeks and crossed my legs.

"I'm aware that there are people who don't like me," I said.

"Yeah? Well, that makes you doubly selfish. And did you know that you completely ruined everybody's COS? The mood at the conference was so somber and so low, and it's all because you didn't have the consideration to think about anyone else but yourself before you went and did what you did."

My fart was raring to fly. I waited for it with a rumbling asshole and dull eyes. Harry scanned me up and down and fidgeted with his fingers. He ran a palm over his mustache and scratched his chin. Strange waves were emanating from him. I was afraid he might pitch back in agony and a baby alien would burst from his stomach. The anxiousness went on for a full minute. Then Harry steadied himself and looked at me sadly.

"I don't know what to do here, Johann," he said. "I told you you were out, and by God, you're this close to it, but I want to see you finish your service. I want to see you succeed. I see a lot of myself in you when I was your age, and I want very much for you to complete what you've started as I did in Afghanistan. But right now, all I see is you going down the same horrible path Truman is, and I really don't like that. Honestly, if I let you stay, what the hell am I supposed to tell the next guy who screws up because he thought it would be okay since Johann got off so easy? What am I supposed to tell Dave and Simon when they sneak out and get arrested for God knows what? Really, please tell me."

I knew I had the man. He was a wriggling little worm on my plate. I gripped my asshole with one hand and my fork with another.

"Harry," I said, "I can tell you with complete certainty that if you let me stay, no one in Peace Corps is going to think that I got off easy. I mean, I missed COS—a PCV's biggest conference—got banished to my site, sweated it out for a week, was told I was being sent home, after which point I had to pack all my things, say heart-breaking goodbyes to my host family, co-workers and friends, come to headquarters all on my own with all my stuff and face the firing squad. Now does that sound like being let off easy?"

Harry leaned back in his seat and raised his eyebrows.

"There's still one problem," he said. "Even if you do stay, your disrespect for our out-of-site policy can't go unpunished. What do I tell people when they ask why you were able to leave site all the time without permission and never got kicked out?"

"Harry, before I answer that," I said, sweating, "I want to inform you that since the episode with Zack at Christmas, I've never left site without telling Peace Corps."

"Oh no? How many times have you snuck away to Mary without telling anyone?"

"Okay, it's true. I used to do that a lot. But since our agreement, I have not gone anywhere, even Mary, without telling Peace Corps first. And as far as last week is concerned, I wasn't trying to hoodwink you or put one over on Peace Corps. I simply forgot to call, and I figured signing in at the front would be enough. Think about it, if I was trying to trick you, I wouldn't have come to headquarters in the first place. I would have avoided it entirely. And as far as what you'll tell people, you can just say, Johann leaving his site without permission is not a problem anymore because he's been restricted to it. And if you're worried about me sneaking out, you can call me randomly to check. I'll be there."

Harry's eyes were murky with exhaustion. His head was nodding back and forth. He stuck his fist under his chin and put his elbow on the desk. Then he leaned forward for support.

"I'm not going to make my decision now," he said drearily. "I've had a very long day and I need some rest and time to think. What I want you to do is go to your hotel room—I've made you a reservation at the Aşgabat—and just think. Don't go out, and especially don't hang out with Brooke; she's only made things worse by fueling your anger and rebelliousness. Just go to your room, think long and hard about all this, and tomorrow, you'd better have something good for me."

The fart in my rectum was now gasping like a violated lamb. I squeezed my cheeks together as tight as I could and offered Harry a hand. He shook it and told me the rest of the day was mine to relax and think. I thanked him and bolted for the door.

"Just remember, Johann," he said. "You may think of Brooke as your friend, but friends don't just come to your aid when you're in trouble, they keep you from getting into trouble in the first place."

I nodded obsequiously and leapt past the threshold. I bounded to the shitter and slammed the door. I poked out my butt and arched my back. I uncoiled my asshole and let the fucker fly. It blew out of me like a storm cloud. The lightbulbs flickered and the mirror cracked. A few tiles came loose and clanked to the floor. I slid down there with them and slapped my forehead.

"Good Christ." I said.

A half hour later, I walked out. I was two sizes thinner and had a grin cheek-to-cheek. I walked up to the lounge and found Brooke. I told her I still had a chance and she leaped in the air.

"That's fucking awesome, Gelr," she said.

Before we could celebrate, Harry came marching into the room. He pointed an angry finger at Brooke and swished his twat-rack.

"Time for you to leave, missy," he snapped.

He turned around and marched back out. Brooke slammed her fist down on the table.

"I fucking hate that man."

I put my hands on her shoulders and looked her in the eyes.

"Just go," I said. "If you get pissed, it's only gonna make him wanna separate us more."

"I guess you're right."

I gave her a hug and told her I'd call her with the verdict. She said okay and left. I spent the next few hours sending off emails. I made no mention of my possible ejection from Peace Corps. On my way out, Harry called me into his office. He asked me if I'd be able to go the next three months without seeing Brooke. I told him I would because she'd be going to Africa with me for hella days.[98] He seemed satisfied with my answer and sent me on my way. I took a cab to my hotel and had a crappy pizza for dinner. I watched an episode or two of *Buffy* to decompress. Afterwards, I thought about what I was going to tell Harry. I knew if I fed him a line of bullshit or acted like I wasn't still at his mercy, I'd be out on my ass so fast my jeans would split. In the end, I could only come up with one thing; seeing people's reactions when I told them I was leaving showed me what they really thought of me. Some people, like Islam, the garawul, and other members of staff, didn't give a shit. But the people closest to me, namely, Jahan, Merdan, Baýram, Azat, Aman, and even my host mom, reacted strongly, and it showed me that they cared. That alone made it worth staying. And this is what I'd tell Harry.

THE NEXT MORNING, I went into headquarters early. I met Harry in his office and told him what I'd come up with. I thought I had it in the bag. He yawned and rolled his eyes.

"Oh, Johann," he said. "That's all well and good, but you're still failing to realize how your actions are affecting Peace Corps."

A spike of fear shot up my heart. I figured this was where he told me I was toast.

"Anyways," he said, "I've decided against my better judgment to let you stay, Mr. Felmanstien. But I want you to know that I'm putting my career, my standing at Peace Corps, and the future of this program and every volunteer in it, on the line for you. So, what I want you to do is go back to your hotel—you're staying another night—and write me a good solid proposal about what you are and aren't gonna do with your next three months and bring it to me tomorrow."

A wave of relief washed over me. I sat up straight and smiled.

"I'll do everything you've asked. And I promise to make my

---

[98] NorCal slang for a long time.

punishment reasonable and to clearly express my understanding of just how much my bad decisions have affected Peace Corps."

He yawned and waved me on. I left and went to the lounge. I called Brooke and told her the news. She screamed my ear dead on the receiver. I told her I'd call her later and we hung up. I called my host family and told them I'd be coming home. Both Patma and Merdan were ecstatic. They said they'd make a dinner in my honor. I thanked them and we hung up. I grabbed my cell phone and texted Candice.

"Believe in miracles?"

She texted back immediately with "Holy shit." She said she'd spread the word and that felt good. I went back to my hotel room and thought about my statement. I wrote everything I knew Harry wanted to hear; that I'd stay at my site unless given explicit permission, that Peace Corps had the right to randomly call and make sure I was there, that if I wasn't I would be kicked out no questions asked, that I was sorry for all the bad things I'd done and all the stress I'd caused Peace Corps, that I was a punk and a buffoon and a no-good dirty rotten cocksucker with turds for ears and a cunt for a face.

I saved my statement on my USB and brought it to headquarters the next day. I printed it and gave it to Harry. He read it with a smirk. When he finished, he took off his glasses.

"This is a very good statement, Johann. But before we both sign it, I want to run you through the ET Handbook."

I raised an eyebrow. "The ET Handbook?"

"That's right. Because you fuck up again, and this is the last thing you'll be given before I boot you out the door."

I nodded, and we went through it. It basically said how all the perks I would have gotten by completing my service, i.e., extra access to all the latest gumballs, full dry-cleaning service for a month, free doggy bags at Chinese restaurants in Schenectady, so on and so forth, would be taken away from me, were I forced to ET. I said okay to the whole lot. Harry closed the book, and we both signed my statement. I headed to the door. Harry looked at me and curled his mouth into a princely smile.

"Johann," he said, "can I ask you something?"

"Sure," I said, opening the door a crack.

"Why exactly do you leave your site so much? Are you running from something?"

I almost laughed.

"No," I said.

"Oh, Johann, I don't buy that," he said, walking toward me. "No one would leave their site as much as you do unless they were running from something. And I'm willing to bet it's something personal. Am I right?"

I wanted to give him the real answer. I wanted to say, "Yes Harry, I do it because my site is fucking boring and I hate teaching English and I'd rather get drunk and party with my friends than waste my time helping people who either don't care or are too stupid to be helped. So please keep paying my bills and looking the other way while I accomplish absolutely nothing."

But Harry didn't want the truth. He wanted a lie to back the lie he had already formed in his mind about me and the rest of the volunteers. Because it was that lie that juiced his bones in the morning so he could get up and do his job. It was that lie that he had scribbled on his application so he could get this job in the first place, and I suspect it was that lie that got his sniveling ass through Peace Corps so many years ago. I decided not to disabuse him of that lie. I told him I did know what I was running from and asked if I could talk about it with him later. He smiled brightly and shook my hand.

"Of course you can," he said.

I thanked him and walked out the door. I spent the rest of the day going through my boxes and throwing out crap. When I was all re-packed, I went to the old airport. I found a cab straight to GBH and passed out for the ride. I got home and found Ali and Patma in the courtyard. Ali ran up and hugged me, almost tripping over his own feet. Patma walked behind him and smiled like a flaming skull.

"We're glad you're back, Han-Guly," she said in her crackly warm voice.

"Me too," I said.

Merdan must've heard my voice. He came bursting through the front door and tackled me. Miwe and Yazgül followed behind. They grabbed my legs and hugged them as I walked. Ogulgerek and Aziza came last. They gave me the standard cold handshakes but at least they smiled. I smiled back and Merdan slapped my shoulder.

"*Gudrat boldy*," he said. "A miracle happened after all."

He threw a jab at my stomach and romped away snorting and laughing.

It felt good to be back.

26

I SPENT THE next five days readjusting. It was rough on the nerves, but the fact that I had a new life to work with made it bearable. I went around town and told everyone the news. I chilled with my host family and wrote and fucked with the goats. I did my walks in the desert like always. I looked up at the sky and smiled and the big blue bastard smiled back. I was happy on these crutches of mine. The horizon was an ethereal egg yolk of gold, punctured and bleeding sideways. I swam in its wake and danced on the camels. I stood at the precipice of the trash yard with a stick in my hand, staring down the sun. I was gleefully evil, and boy was it fun. The man with the stache may have locked me up, but motherfucker, my smile could still run.

I remember the first time I saw Jahan. It was the day I got back, after school. She was sitting at her desk in a red dress. She saw me and grinned.

"I knew you'd come back," she said.

"Really?" I said, sitting next to her. "How?"

"Because of the cookie spell."

I threw my head back and laughed.

"But I had so much trouble."

"Yes, because you used half-cookies, not whole. If you used whole, you would have no trouble."

The woman was right. I had used half-cookies. Who the fuck

was I to say that this wasn't the reason for my troubles?

"Well, hot balls," I said. "Anyways, how you been?"

"Okay. Three teachers came by today to say me *gözüň aýy*."

"Congratulations? Why?"

"Because you are back. It is their way of insulting me. They are make me sound like bad girl."

"What? Those fuckers. Who was it?"

"I won't tell you."

I wanted to protest but I refrained. No sense making hay on a scorching, raging hot day. I unzipped my pack and pulled out my *501* materials. Jahan pulled hers out, too, and we got to work. We blew through the alphabet like gangbusters. We knocked off letter after letter after letter and didn't even stop for water. We repeated the process over the next few days. We were really getting into our old rhythm. One afternoon things got weird. Jahan seemed tired and I couldn't place why. I asked her the matter and she told me no bother. I shrugged my shoulders and pulled out my junk. We got a few minutes into our groove. Then Jahan's cell rang. She picked it up and scratched the back of her neck.

"Hello? Oh really?" she said.

She got up and walked away. As she did, I heard the voice on the other line. It was an older woman's. In the hall I could hear Jahan telling the woman thank you and that she "appreciated the offer." She walked back into the room.

"I'll have to call you back tomorrow, ma'am," she said.

I instantly knew who she'd been talking to. She hung up the phone and sat next to me. I folded my arms and dangled an eyebrow.

"That was Zoya, wasn't it?" I asked.

She nodded shyly. I leaned forward.

"And she offered you the job with Peace Corps, didn't she?"

Jahan stared straight ahead. I knew the answer was yes. My blood turned into a lake of happiness. Angels stood at the edge skipping rocks across it. My heart tap danced at the center with a hat in the air. I was the silliest damn fool there ever was.

"That's fucking great," I cried. "You're gonna take it, right?"

Jahan grabbed a ring and wiggled it mechanically.

"I don't know."

"You don't know? Well, why the hell not?"

"Because, Han-Guly, I am scared."

I looked down at her hands. They were burning white and shaking as she gripped her cell phone. I ignored this and continued.

"Shit, Jahan, I told you I'd pay for your loss in salary. I'll even pay for your damn trip to Aşgabat. Just take this fuckin' job. It's your only opportunity to get outta this miserable place. And it might even land you a permanent position with Peace Corps, which will for sure mean travel. I mean, look at Zoya, she's been to thirty-six countries, makes good money, lives in Aşgabat, and has a daughter who's studying in America. She's got it made and so could you. All you gotta do is . . ."

I droned on and on. She sat still and processed my speech. When I finished, her countenance cracked.

"Han-Guly," she said, "if I take this job, I may lose my job here. It's a very big risk for me and my mother needs her medication and . . ."

"Oh shit, Jahan," I said. "I'll pay for your mother's fucking medication. And I'll have Peace Corps convince Islam to let you have your job back if need be. Now, that should fix everything, damn it."

A deafening silence started to swell. I cracked the tip of my tongue at it.

"You're always talking about how much you wanna leave this place. And you're always telling me your dreams to see the world and about how you're dying inside because you're stuck in this sand trap. Well, this is your chance to get out and make those dreams happen. Yes, it's a risk, and yes, it'll be hard, but I have money and connections and I'll help you. Really, Jahan, I don't see what the fucking problem is."

Everything had burst out. I prayed no one else had been in the building. I looked down to make sure Jahan was still there. She was crouched into a ball like a frightened roly-poly. When she was sure my tantrum was over, she raised an eye. Then she sat up straight and looked at me.

"Han-Guly," she said. "I have not been honest with you."

"Whaddaya mean?" I said frowning.

"I mean, I have not told you all of my reason."

"Well, what is it? Your money? Your house? Your mother? Your job? Whatever it is, I can help."

A deadly certainty filled her eyes.

"You cannot help me with this," she said.

"Oh horseshit. I can help you with anything. Just tell me what it is already."

She took a deep breath and exhaled a column of air.

"I was in trouble with the law many years ago."

My shoulders dropped. The first thought that came was that Jahan had been a prostitute in Aşgabat. I scolded myself and brushed the notion from my brain.

"The law?" I asked. "What happened?"

"I was arrested."

"Why?"

She looked down at her desktop.

"I'm very embarrassed to tell you the reason."

"Jahan, you don't have to be embarrassed to tell me. You may not know this, but I've been arrested before too."

"Yes, but that was certainly for getting with girls and drinking. This was much more serious."

Her words stabbed me in the belly. It was almost as if she'd been waiting for the chance to scold me for what she perceived were my profligate ways. I tried not to take offense. I swallowed hard and blinked.

"No," I said. "Those were not the reasons. I, too, was arrested for something pretty serious."

"What?" she spat.

"Well, I was sixteen and my buddy was gonna fight someone

after class. I came to back him up and I had a knife on me. I didn't even know it because it was this lame little fishing knife that fit right in my wallet, and I had forgotten it was there. Anyways, when the cops came, they searched me and found that stupid knife. I was arrested and charged with a felony. Luckily, I was underaged and had really good grades, so the felony was wiped from my record. Just the same, the incident screwed me over pretty bad, as I was suspended from school for a week and almost expelled. Now, was what happened to you worse than that?"

I leaned back in my chair and smiled confidently. Jahan stared straight ahead.

"Yes," she said. "It was worse . . . much, much worse."

I was blown to sticks. I searched for the words, but they scattered away from me. It took me a minute to find them.

"Much worse?" I said.

"Yes."

"What the hell could be much worse?" She remained silent. "Jahan, you have to tell me."

Again, she said nothing.

"Well at least tell me what the hell it was about."

I looked down and noticed she was writing on a scrap of paper. When she finished, she stared hard at what she had written. She handed the paper to me. I lifted it to my eyes and read its content. It was a single word in tiny red letters.

"Political?" I said, reading it out loud.

Never in my wildest fever dreams could I have imagined Jahan being a political activist, and in one of the most oppressive totalitarian dictatorships in the world, no less. Before I had a chance to reread the word and prove to myself that it hadn't all been a mirage, she snatched the paper from my hand and ripped it into pieces. She rolled each piece into a tiny ball then piled one ball on top of the other to form a little pyramid. She sat back in her chair and squeezed her hands together so they wouldn't shake. I wanted to say something, but I just sat there with my mouth agape. I couldn't wrap my mind around it. This shivering little schoolteacher in front of me was once, I supposed, an active political opponent of the great Türkmenbaşy. And here was I thinking that unknowingly bringing a pocket knife to a fight at school was a big deal. What a fucking buffoon. I knew something terrible must have happened to her to make her so afraid. I was intensely curious as to what it was but hesitant to ask. She was still visibly shaken. I decided to go the indirect route.

"I don't know what happened to you, Jahan," I said. "But I will say that I'm shocked and amazed. You've got guts I'll probably never have. I understand now why you're afraid to take this job. You're afraid that working for the American government might in some way make your own government mad at you again, right?"

She nodded.

"Well then, all I ask is that you think hard about your decision and make the one that's best for you."

"Okay," she said. "I promise."

We worked on the book for an hour. Then we went our separate ways. The next day she told me what I already knew—she'd declined the job at Peace Corps. I tried to be supportive, but my face betrayed my disappointment. Jahan covered me with her big hazel eyes.

"I know you don't understand, Han-Guly," she said. "So, before you leave, I promise I'll tell you my story."

"Okay."

THE NEXT SIX weeks were hardly eventful. Sure, the first black president was elected, and yeah, my sister was planning her wedding, but other than that, it was drab, drab, drab. I guess I could mention that I took the GRE and bombed it with flying colors; a reality that I was okay with because one drunken night, I'd decided that I was gonna skip grad school and write until my fingers crumbled to dust no matter what measures my father took to prevent me. I guess I could also mention that a few volunteers called, and two even came to visit; a relief to be sure, as I was flailing naked in a stream of my own yellow boredom, but still, not much to tell. Then there was my little spurt with Aman. I went over to his house a few times and tried to get him into an English program in Kyrgyzstan, only to find out that the tuition was eight grand and that it was a hundred and fifty bucks just to take the entrance exam. The kid begged me to "help him with his dream." I told him that was all good and gravy, but that he'd have to come up with the dough himself.

As for Jahan and me, we just worked on the book. I tried not to bug her about the political thing, and I know she noticed because she rewarded me by giving me other insights into her life. One lesson, she told me about how her uncle used to write children's stories with political messages. She said he'd read them to her as a child, and that they'd inspired her to write stories and journals of her own. This made me very excited and I asked if I could read them. Then, of course, she told me that this wasn't possible as she'd burned them all. Another conversation we had revolved around a man who was courting her. He was a GBH cop and apparently he'd been calling her a dozen times a week.

"One day, I decided to meet with this man," she said. "I went to police station and he came out to see me. He looked very angry. I asked him what's wrong and he said, 'You should be ashamed. I heard from whole village that you are bad girl and that you will cheat me if we see each other or get married. I didn't want to believe that, so I made a test for you. I thought for a long time you would pass, but since you come to me today, you failed.' I asked him why I failed, and he said, 'Because if I want to see you now, how do I know you will not run to some other man if he calls you like I did?' Then he said, 'So I wanted to tell you today that I think you are a bad girl too.'"

This was a needle in my heel. I wanted to go over to the police station and string that pig up by his testicles over a vat of boiling lead. I opted instead to go home and fill out my third and final trimester report. It was a glorious hunk of shit but at least it gave me a legit excuse to go into Aşgabat. I called Harry and asked for permission. He tried to convince me to come the following weekend. I asked him why and he grunted.

"Don't you remember that today I'm sending the newbie out there?" he said.

"No," I answered honestly.

"Well, that figures. I wanted you to show him the ropes this weekend, but if you promise to be back by Sunday, that'll still give you till Wednesday morning with him, which should be plenty, knowing you."

I gritted my teeth.

"Thank you so much, Harry," I said. "See you in a few."

I packed and took a cab to Aşgabat. I texted Brooke and let her know I was coming. She said she'd meet me in the lounge. I told her that was cool and that we could finish up the trip. The cabbie dropped me off in front of headquarters. I slipped him a bill and went in. I pulled out my trimester report and knocked on Harry's door. He waved me in with a fluttering of fingers. I twisted the knob and stepped inside. Harry greeted me with a handshake and a phony grin.

"How are ya?" he asked.

"Pretty decent," I said. "Here's my trimester report."

I handed it to him. He took it, looked it over and smirked.

"Thanks," he said, placing it to one side.

The room got quiet. I put my hands in my pockets and raised my shoulders and eyebrows.

"So, who's this new guy you're sending me?" I asked.

He ruffled through the papers on his desk and produced a photo of all the T-17s.

"This guy," he said, pointing. "Raymond Tung."

The guy was a nerd if he was a day old. He had black hair parted down the middle, a tiny chin, and glasses that covered his entire face. I looked him over and spiked an eyebrow.

"Looks like a really cool dude."

Harry put the photo away and offered me a seat. He sat down in front of me and folded his hands.

"Now," he said, "Raymond is a very *good* kid, so I don't want you to go putting any silly ideas in his head."

"Oh, I won't."

He eyeballed me like my grandmother used to when I told her it was the Cookie Monster who'd hit my sister. He lifted his finger and shook it in front of my face.

"And just so you know," he said, "Raymond is allergic to alcohol, so no drinking."

"Got'cha."

"Plus, his LCF says his Turkmen is the best of all the volunteers so you might have a little competition."

"Swell."

"As long as you give him advice, and I mean *good* advice, everything should be okay between you two. Wouldn't you agree?"

I nodded and smiled. Underneath I was a smoldering barrel of spite. Raymond was a nerdy, hard-working, language whiz with an allergy to alcohol. Peace Corps had found their golden child to send to my site. I wanted to protest but I knew it'd be useless. I shifted tracks instead.

"So, tell me," I said. "What are some of the new sites you're sending volunteers to?"

Harry grinned like a parched coyote. His eyes filled with quixotic power. I thought his tongue might come rolling out.

"Oh, tons," he said, jumping up.

He went over to his desk and grabbed a map of T-stan. He brought it back giddily and set it in front of my face. It was riddled with green thumbtacks. But since the interior of the country is nothing but sucking desert, the riddling only ran around the edges of the map. Harry sat back down and named off all the new volunteer sites. I pretended to be interested. When he finished, he made his mouth into a proud little determined smudge.

"It really gets me that we can't be in more places," he said. "I mean, what's to say we can't expand into . . ."

He started naming off more places that he could barely pronounce. When he said each name, he used big hand gestures to

433

emphasize his desire to expand there. I wondered if other country directors developed the same sense of mild megalomania that Harry was experiencing. In my mind, it wasn't that far of a stretch. Most of them are in third-world countries where American, and even foreign, presence is minimal, thus making them the head cheese when it comes to PC and all the volunteers. Of course, Washington surpasses the CD in rank. But their headquarters is thousands of miles away and their influence is barely noticeable. And while policies and such are set by Washington, the CDs, because of their remoteness, are seemingly given free rein to enforce policy how they see fit.

Harry finished rambling. I thanked him for his time and went up to see Brooke. We booked hotels in London and Cairo. Then we left for the Zip. On our way out, Maya stopped me. She looked nervous as all hell.

"I have a big problem with volunteer to Gurbagahowda," she said. "We had one host family but last minute we change from girl to boy volunteer so when we bring Raymond today and they see he is boy and not girl they say it was problem because only mother and three daughters with no man in the house, so they say they cannot take him."

"Okay? What does this have to do with me?"

She scrunched her shoulders and cringed.

"Well . . . Please don't be angry, Johann, but I had to tell driver to take him to your house to stay for all of site visit. Is this okay?"

Maya looked terrified. She was biting her lower lip and scratching her upper arm. I hate to say it but it turned me on. I let her squirm for a bit then I defused the bomb.

"That's fine," I said.

"Thank you," she cried. "You are a very kind man."

I shrugged like "Sure, you're right." I told her I was gonna call my host family to make sure everything was cool. As I walked back up to the lounge, I had a disturbing thought. What if they put that little gimp in my fucking room? Normally, I wouldn't have had this thought, but today was different. For the first time in . . . I couldn't remember how long . . . I had given Patma my key before I'd left. My peç was broken and the repairman was coming on Saturday to fix it; my key was the only one they had to let him in the room. The thought of Raymond going through my journals, books, lotions, piss bottles, and pornos soured my stomach. I raced upstairs and called home. Patma answered in her crackly voice.

"Alew?" she said. "Hello?"

"Hey, it's Han-Guly. Is the new volunteer there?"

"Yes. He's in your room."

I gasped.

"Could you please get him?"

The line went silent. I waited for a long minute. Someone picked up the phone.

"Hello?" a dude said.

His voice was bottled up and nasal. I immediately recognized it as Taiwanese–American.

"Is this Raymond?" I asked.

"Yeah, you're Johann, right?"

"Yes. Look, I don't mean to be a dick or make any assumptions about you, but I'm going to ask you not to touch anything in my room, okay?"

"Oh, okay," he said, giggling.

"Like I said, I'm not trying to be a jerk or pass judgment, but as I'm sure you've noticed I'm extremely particular about my things and I keep my room very tidy. I also have my private journals and books in plain view. Had I known you were coming, I'd have put things away. But due to Peace Corps' royal fuck-up, I didn't."

"Oh, I understand. I won't touch anything. I saw your journals and I know that stuff is personal. You can trust me."

"Good. It was not my intention for you to see this side of me first. Usually, people meet the wild, globetrotting party guy first and it isn't until months or even years later that they meet the neurotic, book-polishing, neat-freak, but for some reason, you're seeing this side of me first, so I have to deal with it."

The line went silent. I rapped my fingers on the desk.

"Johann?" Raymond finally said.

"Yes?"

"Please don't be angry, but I did look at one of your books already."

"Which one?"

"The one on Islam. It looked so interesting and I'm so bored. I promise I'll put it back. I know right where it goes."

I was irritated but not terribly.

"Look," I said, "if you promise to put them back the way they are now, you can look at the books by my bed. But only those ones. Don't go searching through my stuff. Got it?"

"Yes . . . and Johann?"

"What is it?"

"Well, I suppose you don't want me sleeping in your bed."

I could almost hear the guy cringing on the other line.

"You've supposed correctly," I said.

Raymond said okay and that he'd use a düşek. I told him that was fine and that he could use my electric heater as well. He thanked me, and we hung up. I went with Brooke to Zip and we started drinking. The next two days were full of red debauchery; that and me trying not to think about Raymond jerking off in my bed to Muslim religious texts.

THE CAB RIDE on Sunday was long and dreary. I slept for most of it. I arrived and found the house full of workers. They were removing our old busted heating system and installing a new one. The courtyard was cluttered with the half-painted remains of a dozen peçes. I stepped over them carefully and went inside the house. I said a cordial hello to my host family. Then I asked about Raymond.

"I don't like him," Merdan said. "He's boring and quiet."

I laughed.

"Did you even try to talk to him?"

"Yeah, but he barely speaks Turkmen. It is like when you first came here."

"Oh c'mon, he'll get better. Do you guys want him to live here?"

"No. Mom says we will only take a girl and Dad says no, period. The girls don't like him and neither do I. And Ali *says* he likes him, but he just wants him around so he can fuck with him."

"That's probably true," I said, chuckling. "Where is he right now anyways?"

"He's in your room being boring."

"Alright. Well, I'd better go chill with him."

I walked upstairs and opened the door. Raymond was there in his long-johns and sweater sitting Indian-style on his sleeping bag and reading the PC newspaper, *Camel Turd*. His tough black hair was shooting up in all directions. He had patches of stubble growing all down his jowls. His cheeks were puffy and his eyes were wide. He wore the expression of a prepubescent boy selling lemonade he'd made himself. When he noticed my presence, he lifted his tiny chin. His thick glasses glinted below my one lightbulb.

"Hey, I'm Raymond," he said.

"You mean, I'm not?" I replied.

The joke splattered against his face like a wet fig. He just sat there blinking.

"Anyways, sorry I was such a dick to you on the phone," I said. "It just weirded me out to have someone in my room I didn't know."

"Oh, I totally understand. I would have been weirded out by it too. And just so you know, I didn't look at your journals, and I only looked at a few books, all of which I put back in their proper places."

"I appreciate that. I see you've met my host family."

"Oh yes, we had dinner together the first night. They were nice, though I can't understand your host mom. Ali was the only one who said more than a few sentences to me. At one point, he told me I should speak up, which made me really uncomfortable."

I chuckled under my breath.

"If that made you uncomfortable, be glad you're only staying here a few more nights."

"Why is that?"

"Well, the term 'spawn of Satan' comes to mind."

Fear flashed in Raymond's eyes.

"Really?" he said.

"Oh, yes. That kid is the most horrible little shit I've ever had to deal with in my life. I mean, there's a small part of me that feels bad for him 'cuz his father is a neglectful drunk. But most times I just wanna strangle his fuckin' face blue."

"Gosh."

I knew I was dropping too much reality on him. I switched tracks and asked him the basics. He told me he was from Fremont, California, which is forty minutes from Livermore. He said he'd had a good Christian upbringing, and that'd he'd traveled very little before Peace Corps.

"I came out here to get a new perspective on things," he said.

I could tell there was more to his story. I didn't want to push him. I asked if he'd had any trouble adjusting to Turkmen life.

"Well, I was arrested," he said.

"Oh? Do tell."

"Actually, it was all very funny."

Actually, it all wasn't very funny. Basically, his training host brother took him out under the pretense of seeing the Üç Aýak, but really he just wanted to meet up with his squeeze so he could make out with her. Raymond waited behind while they did their thing. Then before the poor bastard knew it, the sun was down, and his host brother had disappeared with his chick. Raymond didn't know what to do so he started walking home. That's when the cops stopped and arrested him.

"It was so funny," he said. "When Safety and Security Oraz came to the station, the police were so nice to him. They let me go right away."

I nodded blandly. It was obvious the motherfucker had a lot to learn about Turkmenistan and life in general. I was inclined to give him a good schooling, but I was too chuck.[99] I wished him goodnight and crawled into my comfy bed.

WE GOT UP early the next morning and walked to On Yet. We went straight to Azat's classroom. The children stared at Raymond like he had a busted antler for a head. I could tell it made him uncomfortable. Azat finished his lesson and we made the rounds. We introduced Raymond to all the teachers and students, plus Islam and the cock-gobbling garawul. Then we took a cab to Tejen. We went to the bank to activate Raymond's account, only to find that Peace Corps had opened an account for him at a small bank in Gurbagahowda. Raymond called Maya to confirm this. I told him to let her know that I'd arrived safely in GBH the previous night. He did so and hung up. We walked over and did the fool's registration, and that was the end of that.

To celebrate, we went to the restaurant and ordered the pork shashlik. As we waited for our food, Raymond tried to say something to Azat in Turkmen. It was clumsily formed but not altogether incorrect. Azat smiled with his cracked dominos and responded in English. I could tell Raymond was insulted. He bit his lip and stared at the tablecloth. I could almost hear the gears of his mind spinning. It was a mite unnerving. The food came, and we scarfed it down. Then we took a cab back to GBH. At 3:00 p.m. I got a call from Harry.

"I'm gonna beat you bloody," he said playfully.

"Why?"

"Because you didn't call in when you got back."

I rolled my eyes.

"But I just told Raymond to tell Maya I'd made it home safely. He called in to ask about the bank account, so I figured I'd just kill two birds with one stone. I'm sorry. Next time, I'll do it myself."

"Okay, okay, don't panic. Everything's fine," Harry said. "It's

---

[99] The adjectival form 'chuck' means highly relaxed, comfortable, tired or exhausted. See Hans Joseph Fellmann, *Chuck Life's a Trip*, Russian Hill Press, 2019.

probably just a matter of staff not letting me know what's going on around here as usual. Anyways, how are things with Raymond?"

"So far we've gotten along swimmingly."

"Good. Now remember what I said. Give him *good* advice."

"Oh, I shall."

We said our goodbyes and hung up. I walked straight to the outhouse and took a putrid dump. I went up to my room to chill with Raymond. We got a little nap in, then Patma served us dinner. It was boring-ass pumpkin soup. Ali was there to eat it with us. The whole time, he gloated about how much he was gonna fuck with me before I left. I almost belted him in his stupid little mouth. He finished his dinner and I shooed him out. Raymond got very quiet. He looked down and pinched his lips together. Then he looked up at me and blinked.

"So, tell me, Johann," he said, "what are your thoughts about your Peace Corps experience?"

I could tell he was looking for a sugary answer; one that was glimmering with hope and dripping with goals. I decided not to give it to him.

"I'm going to level with you," I said. "And I want you to hear me out."

He sat up straight and put his hands on his knees.

"Okay," he said. "Go ahead."

"I'll start with staff because they're the biggest pain in my ass. But remember to take what I say about each person with a grain of salt, okay?"

He nodded like an obedient puppy.

"Good, so here's goes . . ."

I blew through the gauntlet. I did Mahym, Zoya, Oraz, Maya, Bartha, Sheri, the lot. Most I disparaged, but a few I praised. Raymond just sat there soaking everything in with wide eyes and a thumb in his mouth. When I got to the end, I slowed my flow.

"That pretty much covers all the bases," I said. "Except, Harry."

Raymond shifted closer and leaned in. I opened my arms like I was about to drop the bomb murder tale at a campfire.

"The man is truly annoying," I said. "You can never totally hate him, and you can never totally love him. On one hand, he's an honest, hard-working guy who genuinely cares about the volunteers and will really go to bat for us. He'll stand up to bitchy policemen, KNB agents, school directors, education ministers—he doesn't give a shit. And for the most part, he's a decent guy . . . until he throws one of his fucking tantrums. Then he can be one of the most hurtful, mean-spirited pricks on the face of the earth. And I speak from experience. His rage is almost never commensurate with the severity of the situation. On top of that, he can be extremely condescending and overbearing. He tends to treat the volunteers like his little children rather than his co-workers, which is especially irritating for people like me who have cut up and now have to endure him viewing us as his 'wayward sons and daughters.'"

"Yeah, I kinda got that impression from him during hub days. I remember when I first saw him, he was just wandering around with a father-face, overseeing everything, and I remember thinking, Who is this guy?"

"Yeah, well I'm sure he'll be cool with you. Just don't get on his bad side."

"Oh, I won't. So, would you say your experience has been bad because of staff?"

"Absolutely not. This has been one of the most incredible, life-changing experiences I've ever had. I know I haven't had the best relationship with staff, nor have I been the star volunteer they hoped I'd be, but I've helped change a few lives, including my own, and to me, regardless of what PC expected of me, that made it all worth it."

"Wow. And how exactly would you say this place has changed your life?"

"Being out here all alone with no distractions, no chaos, and only the desert and the sun and the memories to comfort me, I was forced to look inward, to examine who I was and what I stood for. It was a long, hard fuckin' road and half the time what I saw was anything but flattering, but in the end, I came to like myself, even love myself, and I'm better off for it. I'm sure you'll experience something similar out here too. You better be ready though, 'cuz when those demons come'a knockin', they ain't fuckin' around. They mean to end your sweet ass."

Raymond gulped. Little creases threaded across his brow.

"That's actually why I came out here. I know it's a bad reason, but it's the truth. I feel like I know you, Johann, so I can tell you my story." He sat there for a moment and stared at the ground. Then he looked me right in the eyes. "About two years ago, I had a break in my faith. I was watching TV downstairs at my parents' house and I saw two people having sex. It only lasted for a minute before the channel went dead, but it was enough to excite me. I spent the next two hours searching through the channels to find sex. When I couldn't, I got so furious I ran upstairs and went in the shower and—"

Raymond paused and lowered his head. A guilty expression spread across his face. He blinked away a few tears. Then he parted his lips.

"I masturbated," he said.

I wanted to burst out laughing. Little did the poor bastard know he was sitting inches from a stack of raunchy pornos that would probably send him to the loony bin if he were to watch even one. I clenched my teeth and straightened my shoulders. Raymond continued.

"I masturbated," he repeated, "to the images I saw on TV. When I finally finished, I had a horrible epiphany. I saw my two sisters. Both were happily married and had higher educations and good jobs. I saw my mother and father. Both were successful businesspeople with plenty of money and a good house. I saw my friends, all with wives and good jobs and graduate school degrees. Everyone was happy and successful. And then there was me: wet, naked and cold, masturbating in the shower alone. I felt so empty inside. Usually, Jesus filled that emptiness, but he wasn't there this time. I was all alone. I felt like I had been abandoned. I didn't even know who I was anymore. I thought about it the whole day. I decided I was going to rededicate my life to Jesus. I was going to do everything I could to fill my hole with his love. I worked hard and was very committed. That summer I involved myself in everything. I even reaffirmed my status in the Christian community as a youth leader by doing Vacation Bible Camp."

"What's that?"

"Well, that's where I learned to teach English," he said proudly. "It's a Christian-run organization that goes to third-world countries to teach English to kids in impoverished neighborhoods."

I spiked an eyebrow. "And?"

"Well, and the government of whatever country lets us teach English. I was sent to Taiwan since I'm Taiwanese and know a bit of the language. But I didn't work with the Taiwanese. I worked with the native Polynesians on the island. Many of them are extremely poor and their illiteracy rate is really high and most of their communities are plagued by alcohol and drugs and domestic violence."

"How does teaching English solve all that?"

"We do other things, too," he said, standing up. "Like we just start teaching them little songs about Jesus and Heavenly Father. They're so simple. Like I remember one that goes, 'He is strong. He is mighty. Step into the light and feel His . . .'"

Raymond was now lumbering across the room and grimacing like a caveman. He seemed completely entranced by what he was doing. In the middle of it all, he looked up at me. When he realized I wasn't a classroom full of poverty-stricken natives who were desperate for any kind of help, his goofy expression melted away. He sat back down Indian-style and continued.

"Anyways, many of them convert," he said. "They are looking for hope and we provide that for them. We also provide schools, books, education, community centers, and churches. It really does improve their standard of living."

I was tempted to ask him why VBC couldn't just provide social infrastructure and education without all the dogma. I didn't want to offend him.

"All in all, I liked my experience in Taiwan," he continued, "but when it was over, I still felt that emptiness inside. Then I saw an ad for Peace Corps online. It looked pretty good; free travel, a chance to get away and figure things out, plus help people. I started the application process. And while I was working on it, I asked people in the community what they thought of the idea. A lot of them were negative. They felt like I was jeopardizing my faith. It was so funny. I went to the library one day and ran into this girl I hadn't seen in years. I told her about my idea to join Peace Corps and she reacted almost angrily. She said, 'Is that really what you wanna do? Throw away two-and-a-half years of your life in some third-world country when you could be making money and starting a family? Not to mention, you'd be separated from the community. And what about your faith? You're putting that on the line too.' Not everyone was as harsh as her though. She was a recent convert and before that she was really into drugs and suicidal. Then she found Jesus.

"Anyways, towards my leave date, I got extremely panicky. All these voices in my head were telling me to do different things, and I kept trying to figure out what God was telling me, what He wanted me to do. I asked Him for many nights to send me a sign, but nothing ever happened.

"I talked to my parents about it and they were a little shocked, but my father told me there was a time in his life when he, too, had these questions and was searching for answers. He said this phase would soon pass, but that he supported my decision to join Peace Corps. My mother said the same. Eventually, our pastor and the rest of the community came around too. I took this as my sign to join. Shortly thereafter, I got my blue package that said I was going to T-stan. But when I dialed Peace Corps to accept, the call didn't go through. I thought it was weird, so I tried to call again. And again, the call didn't go through. Then I thought, 'Is this God telling me not to go? Is this the sign I was asking for?' I hung up and decided not to call that day. That night I asked God if I should go, and a voice in my head said, 'No.' I couldn't believe it. I was so confused. Was that voice God? I had no idea what to do. I tossed and turned for hours. Then finally at dawn, I realized something: The only person I should have been asking was myself. I decided right then that I would go. I got on the phone that afternoon and accepted."

"Are you glad you did?" I asked.

"Yeah, so far. And I'm glad I'm in a Muslim country, even though Turkmenistan isn't very Muslim. Part of the reason I'm doing this is to understand other religions better. That's why I was so interested in your Islam book."

"I see."

Our conversation tapered off. We made our beds and got in. Before we clicked off the lights, I remarked that it was 2:00 a.m. Raymond told me that this was the latest he'd gone to bed in years.

THE MONTH AFTER Raymond's visit was for tying up loose ends. I saw a bunch of volunteers for the last time, made huge progress on *501*, and even helped Peace Corps find a host family for Raymond. During the first week of December, I started looking at my Description of Service (DOS). I knew I had to have it in soon, but I didn't have any way of getting it to HQ once I'd completed it. I called Harry and asked him if I could come in that weekend to turn it in. He sounded irritated.

"So, you'd come in on Friday and leave Sunday?" he asked.

"Yeah."

"Well, okay, but you'd better get the rough draft to Bartha before you go back to site because both of us are leaving for vacation shortly thereafter."

"Okay."

"And just so you know. You and Brooke are the last ones to turn in your DOSs. And are we surprised? Nooooo."

I wanted to counter with, "Yeah, ya fuckhead, 'cuz we're the last ones to COS." I left it at a polite chuckle and a goodbye.

THE NEXT DAY, I packed and went to class. I spent a couple hours teaching so I could tell Harry if he asked, plus I cracked off a gang of sentences for *501* with Jahan. After that, I took a cab to Aşgabat. I was pumped; not because of the DOS, but because this was the swearing-in weekend for the 17s, which I knew would mean some major blowing up. I arrived at headquarters and went to Harry's office. He sat me down and started grilling me.

"Have you even looked at the list of things you have to do before you go?" he barked.

"Yes, some of them. But I'm still unsure about a few."

He grunted and pulled out the list. He told me I still had to set up appointments for my language test, medical exam, and exit interview. The first two he told me to arrange for my last weekend in the country. The last, he told me he would conduct himself that day. He told me to be back in his office at 5:00 p.m. sharp. Then he raised a finger and wagged it at me.

"And you'd better be making your appointments and working on your damn DOS in the meantime. I mean it, Johann. That thing better be in Bartha's hands by Sunday or you're dead meat."

I wound my cheeks into curlicues. I said goodbye and walked out. I arranged my medical exam with Sheri and my language test with Zoya. I made them both for the weekend before I COS'd. I went up to the lounge to work on my DOS. The place was packed with 17s coming, 15s going and 16s looking to blow up. I saw Raymond in the mix. He was positively glowing.

"Johann, you missed my performance at swearing-in," he said.

"Oh yeah?"

"Yeah. I played the guitar in front of everyone and sang a song in Turkmen. The whole crowd loved it. I was a real hit."

I turned my mouth into an upside-down U and patted him on the shoulder.

"I'm sure you were," I said.

I sidestepped him and got on the computer. I tried to bang out as much as I could of my DOS, but it was tough with all the commotion and laughter. I got about a quarter of the way done and gave up. I went to the Turkmenistan Hotel where the 17s were and booked a room for myself, Simon, Rave Dave, and Brooke. I thought of calling Tex. Brooke informed me that although he'd also been spared the knife, he'd decided not to leave site until COS.

I came back to PCHQ. I was at Harry's office at five on the tip. This time he waved me in graciously and smiled.

"I want you to know before we start," he said, "that Peace Corps really appreciates all the hard work you've done."

His comment stunned me, but I knew where it was coming from. Harry wanted to make nice with me before I left so I wouldn't have a foul taste in my mouth about Peace Corps. The Central Asian program was in jeopardy, and what with the recent canceling of the Uzbekistan program, the region couldn't afford any more bad PR. The butt-licking went on for a few more minutes. Then Harry started in on the questions. He asked me what the best thing about my service was. I told him my relationships with my counterparts and host family. He asked me what the worst thing was. I told him the culture shock and ensuing anger. He asked me if I would ever do Peace Corps again. I smiled and told him, "Yes." This concluded the questioning. As I stood up to go, Harry looked me in the eye.

"Something tells me you thought that Peace Corps would be just like your travels," he said.

I knew the answer he wanted. I gave it right to his shit-eating grin.

"Oh, for sure," I said. "And boy was I wrong."

He nodded like, "Boy, don't I know." He shook my hand and I hit the door. After that, it was party, party, party. I'm pretty sure I dirty danced with a bisexual T-17 and pounded Sambucas with Rave Dave and maybe even sang some drunken karaoke. The next morning, we all crawled our way to Harry's Annual Christmas Party. We'd been expecting a huge delicious spread seeing as how the man lived in a marble palace and it was Christmastime, after all. Instead, we got finger-food, coffee, and OJ; a fact made hilarious when

Brooke looked at it all and said, "Gee, it's nice to be appreciated." We had a good gut laugh over that one. We availed ourselves of a few treats and chatted with a few 17s then said *adios* to Harry and his dumb ol' Santa hat. After that, we worked on our DOSs. We got about halfway done before the blow-up train came chuggin' on down to the lounge. We hit the Zip first and then the Turkmenistan. We tried to get the 17s to do our little tradition where we put on the song "Ghost Ride It" by Mistah Fab and danced around the room with sheets and sunglasses on our heads, singing and pretending to be cool ghosts. Only two of them participated. The rest just silently watched, which made Simon stop dancing and scream, "The 17s suck." This put a nasty squirt in everyone's drink. And it got even nastier when I tried to dance salsa with some little 17 chick, but she just clapped her hands at me and yelled, "Dance, Monkey. Dance." Brooke heard this and told her to cool it. The girl stood up and sneered.

"Who the fuck are you?" she shouted.

Brooke's eyes turned to flames and her red hair to snakes.

"I'm the bitch that's gonna kick your ass," she screamed.

The 17 shrank to a dot and shivered.

"I'm sorry," she said. "I'm new. I'm fucking nothing."

Brooke squeezed her fist in front of the 17 until it cracked.

"You're goddamn right, you're sorry," she said.

I stepped in and broke it up. The night was a blur after that. The next morning Brooke and I were outrageously hungover. We hugged Dave and Simon goodbye and said we'd see them on the flip. We grabbed a bite to eat. Then we went into headquarters and worked on our DOSs. We put a solid five hours in. Harry came to say goodbye. I got up from the computer and shook his hand. His eyes were teary, and his mustache was drooping. I could tell he wanted a hug. I opened my arms and leaned in.

"Oh, my Johann," he said like a senile grandmother.

We hugged. Harry held me longer than I cared for. We pulled away and he looked me in the eyes.

"This is the last time we'll ever see each other," he said.

I raised my eyebrows and nodded. His hands were still on my shoulders.

"But we'll still talk on the phone a few more times before I go on vacation, right?" he asked.

"Oh, of course," I said.

He let go and smiled. He gave Brooke a hug then walked down the hall. As he turned the corner, I noticed a piece of toilet paper clinging to his left heel. It was the last I saw of him.

FOR THE NEXT ten days, I was on a deserted spaceship. The reality that I'd be leaving soon was setting in and everything was suspended in an awful white hue. I tried to distract myself by helping Raymond integrate. I gave him some pointers and taught him some phrases and showed him around town. I even introduced him to Baýram and Aman. They both seemed to like him, and I hoped he could provide them with the opportunities that I couldn't.

When I wasn't with Raymond, I was with Jahan. We worked diligently on *501* and finished it with time to spare. One night, she invited me to her house to celebrate. I thought I might get ambushed by her family, but they welcomed me warmly and served me a good dinner. I can't for the life of me remember what we spoke about; maybe my trip to Africa, maybe my life back in California. I know I gave Jahan a burnt copy of *501*. In return, she gave me the tahýa she'd knitted for me. It was red and black and ringed with white lace. It looked like something an imam would wear. I put it on my scalp and smiled.

"You looked just like a Turkmen," she said.

I thanked her kindly. I told her I wanted to give her some more French books in return, but really I wanted to ask once and for all what political dealings she'd been involved in and what had happened to her after she'd been arrested that had made her so terrified. I met her at On Yet the next morning. It was the day before I left for good. She was sitting at her desk as usual. I could tell by the look on her face and the way she was resting her chin on her thumb with her index finger pointing straight up her cheek that she already knew what was coming. I sat down next to her and handed her the books. I took a deep breath and exhaled.

"I know what you want," she said. "And I've made a decision."

"Okay?"

She folded her arms and looked at me plainly.

"I will not tell you what happened to me, Johann."

I was stunned. Every nerve in me was screaming for revenge. I almost cut it all loose in a rash of hellfire. Then I saw the look in Jahan's eyes. It was a look that said it didn't matter. A look that told me I knew what I needed to know and that was that. I swallowed it like a plug of concrete. I told her I'd come to school the next day to say goodbye, and then I left.

I packed that night and hung out with my family. I think we had palow but I can't be sure. The next morning, I took my last horrible dump and bucket shower. I had my last stale çörek and bal, my last glass of tongue-curling çal. I grabbed my crap and took it downstairs. I said goodbye to my host family and Laika's ghost. It was incredibly unceremonious, partly because it had already happened once before and partly because, at that point, I was so deflated with the sense of my own worthlessness as a volunteer that all I wanted to do was get as far away from any reminders of it as I could. I walked to the awtostanzia and arranged a cab. I told the cabbie to give me ten minutes while I did something at On Yet. I walked over there and said goodbye to Azat first. He was sad to see me go, but truth be told, I think he was sadder that I hadn't given him some big parting gift. I went to see Islam next, but he wasn't in. His secretary said he was in a meeting at another school, but if I had to guess, he was passed out drunk at the kiçi çaýhana with his face planted square in the center of a giant lamb pie.

I went to see Jahan last. She was stood at the windowsill watering her dying plants. I walked over to her to say goodbye. She never turned around.

GLOSSARY

Glossary of Turkmen terms

Entry type

In this glossary, there are eleven classifications: *adj.* (adjective); *adv.* (adverb); *conj.* (conjunction); *excl.* (exclamation); *interj.* (interjection); *interr.* (interrogative); *n.* (noun); *num.* (number); *phr.* (phrase); *pr. n.* (proper noun); and *v.* (verb). Please note that (R) indicates a Russian word or word of Russian origin.

Pronunciation guide

Turkmen Letter	Approximate sound in English
a	like the "a" in c*a*r
b	like the "b" in *b*ox
ç	like the "ch" in *ch*urch
d	like the "d" in *d*og
e	like the "e" in p*e*t
ä	like the "a" in *a*pple
f	like the "f" in *f*at
g	like the "g" in *g*oal
h	like the "h" in *h*at
i	like the "ea" in s*ea*t
j	like the "j" in *j*azz
ž	like the "z" in a*z*ure or the "s" plea*s*ure
k	like the "k" in *k*ick
l	like the "l" in *l*et
m	like the "m" in *m*at
n	like the "n" in *n*et
ň	like the "ng" in si*ng*
o	like the "o" in c*o*t
ö	like the "e" in h*e*r (but with pointed and narrowly rounded lips)
p	like the "p" in *p*et
r	like the "r" in *r*at (but 'rolled' as in Scottish English)

s	like the "s" in *s*it
ş	like the "sh" in *sh*ut
t	like the "t" in *t*en
u	like the "oo" in sh*oo*t
ü	like the "u" in h*u*ge (but much shorter)
w	like the "v" in *v*an or the "w" in *w*orld
y	like the "e" in h*e*r mixed with the "ea" in f*ea*r
ý	like the "y" in *y*et
z	like the "z" in *z*ebra

Source: Turkmen: Turkmen-English, English-Turkmen Dictionary & Phrasebook By Nicholas Awde, William Dirks, A. Amandurdyev.

Glossary

A

adalat *n.* justice; fairness.

Aero Kasa *n.* plane ticket agency.

ak *adj.* white; pale.

akmak *adj.* foolish; stupid.

akylly *adj.* smart; clever; intelligent.

alabai *n.* a Turkmen mastiff.

Alew? *interj.* Hello? (Used by Turkmen when answering the phone.)

altyn *n.* gold; golden (*adj.*).

aman *adj.* safe; unharmed.

arak *n.* vodka.

Arçibil *pr. n.* a Turkish brand of bottled water.

asylly *adj.* noble; well brought up.

asyr *n.* century; age; era

awtostanzia (R) *n.* taxi stand.

aýak *n.* foot; leg.

aýal *n.* wife; woman.

aýlyk *n.* salary; wage.

B

Baaaay *excl.* an expression of disbelief, frustration or dismay.

baklaşka (R) *n.* plastic bottle.

bal *n.* honey; jam.

balak *n.* pants.

banýa (R) *n.* bathroom.

barmak *v.* to go; to arrive.

baýram *n.* holiday.

bazar *n.* bazaar; market.

bilim *n.* education; knowledge; science.

bilmek *v.* to know; to be able.

bitaraplyk *n.* neutrality.

bok *n.* feces; shit.

Bolýar *interj.* okay; fine; alright.

boş *adj.* empty.

bölüm *n.* department; section; branch.

Bu näme? *interr.* What's this?

burç dolamasy *n.* stuffed peppers.

bürgüt *n.* eagle.

Ç

çal *n.* a beverage made from camel's milk.

çaý *n.* tea.

çaýhana *n.* teahouse.

çemçe *n.* spoon.

çigit *n.* (sunflower) seed.

çopan *n.* shepherd; cowherd; cowboy.

çorba *n.* soup.

çörek *n.* bread; food (Ahal dialect).

çüýşe *n.* bottle.

çykyş *n.* speech; presentation; performance.

D

Davai (R) *excl.* *Let's do it; Come on Okay; Sure; Buy.*

daýhan *n.* peasant; collective farmer.

daýza *n.* aunt; old lady (among PCVs).

dellek *n.* barber; beautician.

dellekhana *n.* barbershop; beauty salon.

däl *adv.* not; is not.

däli *adj.* insane; crazy; mad.

dil *n.* tongue; language.

diýmek *v.* to say; to pronounce.

doctor (R) *n.* doctor.

dograma *n.* Turkmen national dish made of stuffing, onions, and sheep's head. Sometimes broth is poured over ingredients to make it into soup.

dutar *n.* two-stringed traditional Turkmen musical instrument.

dükan *n.* store; shop.

düşek *n.* bedding; mattress.

düýe *n.* camel.

E

Ejeň sikeýn *excl.* Motherfucker; Son of a bitch.

Eneniň agyzyny siksene *excl.* Go fuck your grandmother's mouth.

erbet *adj.* bad; wicked; vulgar; evil.

et *n.* meat.

F

fitçi *n.* meat pie.

G

garaşsyzlyk *n.* independence.

garawul *n.* guard; deputy.

garpyz *n.* watermelon.

gatyk *n.* yogurt.

gawun *n.* melon.

gazly suw *n.* carbonated water.

geçi *n.* goat.

Gel *excl.* Come

Geldiňmi? *interr.* Did you come? (This is the Turkmen way of asking if one came to a certain place, safely and in good health.)

gelmek *v.* to come.

gitmek *v.* to go; to leave; to run.

gowy *adj.* good; well (*adv.*).

goýun *n.* sheep.

göt *n.* butt; ass.

Gözüň aýy *excl.* Congratulations.

greçka (R) *n.* buckwheat, usually boiled and served with chucks of meat and eggs.

gudrat *n.* miracle; providence.

Gudrat boldy *excl.* A miracle happened after all.

gum *n.* sand; desert.

gurbaga *n.* frog; bullfrog.

gurluşykçy *n.* construction worker.

gutap *n.* meat-stuffed, halfmoon flatbread, which is fried in oil or baked in a clay oven.

Gutly bolsun *excl.* Congratulations; May it be blessed.

gyzykly *adj.* interesting.

H

halkara *adj.* international.

haramzada *n.* rascal; imp; asshole.

hawa *interj.* yes; yeah.

haýwan *n.* animal.

hiç zat *n.* nothing.

hoja *n.* holy man.

holodilnik (R) *n.* refrigerator.

hoş *adj.* good; fine; okay (*interj.*).

howda *n.* pond.

Hökman *excl.* Definitely; Of course; For sure; undoubtedly (*adj.*).

Hudaý *n.* God; Allah.

hyýar *n.* cucumber.

I

içmek *v.* to drink.

Iňglis dili *n.* English language.

işlekli *n.* big meat pie.

it *n.* dog.

iýmek *v.* to eat.

J

jaň etmek *v.* to phone.

jaý *n.* house; building; lodging; room.

jelep *n.* whore; prostitute.

jüýje *n.* chick.

K

Kak dyela? (R) *interr.* How are you doing?

kelle-baş aýak *n.* boiled sheep's head and hooves.

kepka (R) *n.* cap.

kädi *n.* pumpkin; squash.

kän *n.* a lot.

kiçi *adj.* junior; minor; small; little.

kiçi çaýhana *n.* the little teahouse (in Gurbagahowda).

Kim? *interr.* Who?; Who is it?

kitap *n.* book.

klionka (R) *n.* tablecloth (usually placed on the floor).

kolbasa (R) *n.* sausage.

köp *n.* a lot.

köwüş *n.* shoe; shoes.

köýnek *n.* shirt (male); dress (female)

kuhnýa (R) *n.* kitchen.

kunti *n.* whore.

kyrk günlük *n.* Turkmen cantaloupe.

L

lavash *n.* A soft, unleavened flatbread which is baked in a clay oven. It is often used with kebabs to make dürüm wraps.

lüle kebap *n.* ground meat kebab.

M

manat *n.* the unit of currency in Turkmenistan (and Azerbaijan).

manty *n.* dumplings of Central Asia.

marşrutka (R) *n.* transport van.

maşgala *n.* family.

maşyn (R) *n.* car.

maýyl *adj.* warm; mild.

mekdep *n.* school.

mekdepdäki daýza *n.* an old cleaning lady who works at a school.

molla *n.* mullah.

moroženoe (R) *n.* ice cream.

mugallym *n.* teacher; master.

müdir *n. director.*

müdür *n.* principal (of a school).

myhman *n.* guest; visitor.

N

nahar *n.* food; meal.

Nähili? *interr.* How are you?

O

oba *n.* village.

oblastnost (R) *n.* region.

okamak *v.* to read; study.

okatmak *v.* to teach.

okuwçy *n.* pupil; student (at school).

onsoň *conj.* so then; then.

Ors *adj.* Russian.

otag *n.* room.

Ö

öwrenişmek *v.* to adjust to (a situation); become accustomed.

öwrenmek *v.* to learn; to study.

öý *n.* home; house; lodging.

öý hojalykçy *n.* housewife; homemaker.

P

pagta *n.* cotton.

palow *n.* rice cooked with carrots, cherries, onions, and meat.

Parahatçylyk Korpusy *n.* Peace Corps.

peç *n.* heater (water or electric).

poçta *n.* mail; post office.

pomidor (R) *n.* tomato.

Privyet (R) *interj.* Hello (informal); Hi.

pyçak *n.* knife; scalpel.

R

restoran (R) *n.* restaurant.

Ruhnama *n. The Book of the Soul* was written by former president Niyazov. It is part-autobiography, part-revisionist history, and part-moral and spiritual guide. During Niyazov's presidency, the book was compulsory reading in schools, universities, and government institutions.

S

saç *n.* hair.

sadaka *n.* an act of love, compassion, or friendship; a religious sacrifice.

sag *adj.* sane; healthy.

Sag aman bar *excl.* Go safely and in good health.

Salam *interj.* Regards; Hello.

samsyk *adj.* stupid; foolish; idiotic; fool (*n.*).

shashlik *n.* a dish of meat cubes which are seasoned, skewered, and grilled.

sik *n.* dick; cock.

Sikdir *excl.* Fuck you; Get fucked.

sikmek *v.* to fuck.

siýdik *n.* piss.

siýmek *v.* to piss.

smetana (R) *n.* sour cream.

somsa *n.* fried dough triangles filled with meat.

sormak *v.* to suck; to pump; to vacuum.

sowadyjy *n.* refrigerator.

stakan (R) *n.* glass (for drinking).

suw *n.* water; pool.

sygyr *n.* cow.

Ş

şakäse *n.* bowl.

şaryk *n.* fork.

Şu gün aýyň näçesi? *interr.* What's today's date?

şu taýda *adv.* here.

T

tahýa *n.* Turkmen national cap.

taksi (R) *n.* taxi.

tamdyr *n.* traditional Turkmen clay oven.

tans etmek *v.* to dance.

Tapawdy ýok. *excl.* Big deal; It doesn't matter, I don't care.

tapçan *n.* porch; a raised porch usually made of wood.

telefon etmek *v.* to call; to phone.

telpek *n.* men's woolen hat.

täze *adj.* new; fresh.

Täze ýylyňyz gutly bolsun. *excl.* Happy New Year.

towuk *n.* chicken; hen.

toý *n.* party; celebration; wedding.

turmak *v.* to stand up; to wake up; to be awake.

tuwalet (R) *n.* toilet.

tuwalet kagyzy *n.* toilet paper.

Türkmen dili *n.* Turkmen language.

Türkmenbaşy *n.* Leader of Turkmen.

Türkmenistana hoş geldiňiz *excl.* Welcome to Turkmenistan.

Tüweleme *excl.* Great; Fantastic; Well done.

U
uçurym *n.* graduate.
uly *adj.* big; large; vast.
uly çaýhana *n.* the big teahouse (in Gurbagahowda).
um *n.* pussy.

Ü
Üç *num.* three.
Üç Aýak *pr. n.* was the Monument of Neutrality in Ashgabat. Also known as the 'three-legged arch' or simply the 'tripod.' In 2010 it was dismantled by President Gurbanguly Berdimuhamedow.

W
Wah-heý *excl.* How tragic; Oh no.
Wah-heý däl. *excl.* Oh that's not tragic (In response to 'Wah-heý.').
waratan (R) *n.* a large solid metal gate which opens in the middle, and often has a small door on one of its halves through which people can walk.
welaýat *n.* province; region.
wilka (R) *n.* fork.

Y
ykbal *n.* fate; destiny.

Ý
ýag *n.* oil; grease; fat.
ýaglyk *n.* handkerchief; headscarf (worn by women).
ýagsyz *adj.* without oil.
ýalançy *n.* liar.
ýaşamak *v.* to reside; to live.
ýazmak *v.* to write.
Ýetigen *n.* a Turkmen brand of bottled soda.

ýok *adj.* no; there are no; absent.

ýol *n.* path; pathway; route; road; way.

ýorgan *n.* blanket; quilt.

ýumurtga *n.* egg; testicle (ball).

ýuwaş *adj.* still; calm; quiet; slowly (*adv.*).

ýylan *n.* snake.

Z

zorlama *n.* rape.

zorlamak *v.* to force (someone to do something); to rape.